Dear Christine,

Love & blessings

Mark Steinberg

LIVING INTACT:

CHALLENGE AND CHOICE
IN TOUGH TIMES

Mark Steinberg, Ph.D.

ISBN: 1453804056
ISBN-13: 9781453804056

Living Intact is dedicated to my darling wife, Giulia, and precious children, Neal, Jeremy, and Nadia, as well as to my late parents, Daniel and Pearl Steinberg, without whom my life and this book would not be.

ENDORSEMENTS

"There are many books that offer strategies and tactics for sorting out one's life, but I firmly believe that Living Intact is special because of its breadth of perspective and the functionality and applicability of its insights and methods. Most books of this genre have a far more narrow focus.

Dr. Mark Steinberg sheds light on our efforts to better ourselves from a variety of perspectives, and he integrates the new insights gained from dramatic advances in brain science. For most of us, life is a matter of coming to terms with our limitations, perceived or actual. Often we are inclined toward resignation in the face of obstacles that seem to be deeply entrenched and chronically problematic. Living Intact furnishes a powerful holistic plan for knocking down the barriers that prevent us from functioning optimally. The prospects for attaining an optimal state of being are significantly enhanced because of exciting recent breakthroughs in mobilizing our brain plasticity. Dr. Steinberg goes far beyond simply describing the problems and issues. He recognizes the vital importance of the essential spirituality that makes us human and that underpins our complex psychological make-up and our reactions to life challenges.

Dr. Steinberg has had decades of experience as a licensed psychologist and neuropsychologist. He describes his personal struggles with a keen honesty, and he writes with a true love of language. This book is such a delight to read that our defenses are disarmed, and the messages are so relentlessly positive that they invite an affirmative response."

—Dr. Siegfried Othmer, Chief Scientist, EEG Institute

"My friend, Mark Steinberg, has distilled 30 years experience as a therapist, father, and a Christian into a remarkable book. This is not your typical self help amalgam of personal hubris and psychology, but rather a study of actual life experience with both its joys and sorrows framed within a Christian worldview and informed by a lifetime of professional therapy. Whatever your background, your understanding of how your own past choices have shaped your life for good or ill will be illuminated, and you will learn amazing practical techniques for reshaping your future in harmony with God."

—Dr. Peter Wilkes, former pastor, Santa Cruz Bible Church; former pastor, South Hills Community Church; former Professor, Dept. of Material Science, Univ. of Wisconsin at Madison

"A Grand Slam! Dr. Steinberg does a masterful job of putting in play and integrating all of the essential elements—psychological, physiological, neurological, and spiritual—that readers need to hit the ball out of the park and live a more intact life. A towering achievement."

—Lawrence Greene, best-selling author of Getting Smarter and twenty-three books dealing with education and parenting

CONTENTS

PREFACE. xi

INTRODUCTION xv

I CHOICES

CHAPTER 1 3
The Greatest Challenge You Will Ever Face

CHAPTER 2 25
Secrets and Elements of Living Intact

CHAPTER 3 31
Bridges between Self and the World

II PRACTICAL SECRETS (KEYS) FOR LIVING INTACT

CHAPTER 4 43
The First Secret: Developing Self-Control and Compassion

CHAPTER 5 69
The Second Secret: Breaking Free from Counterproductive Habits

CHAPTER 6 83
The Third Secret: Modifying the Outcomes of Your Behaviors

CHAPTER 7 109
The Fourth Secret: Eliminating Negative Emotions

CHAPTER 8 121
The Fifth Secret: Embracing the Challenges of Life

III POWER TOOLS FOR LIVING INTACT

CHAPTER 9 153
EEG Neurofeedback

CHAPTER 10 181
Thought Field Therapy

IV REALITY FEEDBACK

CHAPTER 11 217
Expectations: Where Reality Meets Desire

CHAPTER 12 245
Wisdom: Understanding and Making Life Work

V EVERYDAY PROBLEMS, ELEGANT SOLUTIONS

CHAPTER 13 275
Dealing with Desire

CHAPTER 14 287
Dealing with Conflict

CHAPTER 15 303
Anger and Hurt

CHAPTER 16 319
Guilt and Forgiveness

CHAPTER 17 337
Rejection and Loneliness

CHAPTER 18 353
Entitlement and Humility

VI AN ULTIMATE QUESTION

CHAPTER 19 379
Must You Suffer?

APPENDIX A 407
Schedules of Reinforcement

APPENDIX B 411
Behavior Reduction and Probabilities

APPENDIX C 413
Thought Field Therapy (TFT) Algorithms for Self-Healing

APPENDIX D 423
Self Habits, World Habits, and Integral Habits

PREFACE

This book was conceived in the aftermath of the 9/11 tragedy. It was a bleak time for our country, and virtually every American experienced stress, sadness, and feelings of loss, frustration, and powerlessness. As a psychologist, my visceral reaction was to reach out and help those who had been shattered by this brutal attack on our nation. However, I was in California with a clinical practice and family responsibilities, and I realized that it would be impossible for me to head off to New York.

The tragedy elicited powerful emotions in the American people and made me acutely conscious of the agonizing sense of brokenness and suffering that can overwhelm the human spirit. During a clinical career that has spanned more than thirty years, I had obviously wrestled with these issues, and I had learned lessons about repairing shattered lives and helping people become more intact.

The 9/11 tragedy may have been the catalyst for this book, but at a deeper spiritual level, I believe it was inevitable that I would write it. My own life's journey and the experiences I held in common with many of my clients had yielded insights about the human condition and the impact of life's victories and defeats on the human spirit. Yet there was another dimension at work that transcended the therapeutic interplay between client and psychologist. I was acutely aware of the spiritual forces that infuse life's schemata. As I struggled over the years to make sense of this design, I sought to understand God's wisdom and be responsive to his desire to teach me. I could not have crafted this book if I had spent my life on sidelines observing others. I needed to experience the suffering as an opportunity to soften my heart, sharpen my mind, expand my spiritual being, and acquire a respect for God's will as a means for recognizing and accepting how things unfold. I needed to struggle with my own suffering and brokenness. I needed to comprehend spiritually that life's challenges and suffering are quintessential elements of existence, elements with which we must nevertheless contend and transcend.

My clinical practice and life experience has revealed a core truth about the human condition: *challenge and suffering offer opportunities for man to create a functional plan for living intact*. This book is, then, really about *you*. It is a guide for discovering and refining your nature, your God-given gifts and vulnerabilities, your behavior patterns, and the qualities and beliefs upon which you run your life. It is not about you in the self-serving, ego-aggrandizing sense but, rather, in the spirit of enlightening and empowering you so that you can answer the important question, "Who am I?"

There are many self-help guides claiming that everything you need is within you, that you are the source and the cause of your own being. This is not one of them. Other books defrock the self, seeking to strip away the pomp and hubris of self-importance. One very popular book begins with the abrupt and confrontational sentence, "It's not about you."*

Living Intact assumes that worthy living is grounded in reality—the way life and the world are, rather than what we might like them to be. No matter how much we try to be rational, unselfish, and objective, we naturally revert to thinking about ourselves, what we believe is in our best interests, and the perspective on reality that best suits our purposes. This is only human nature, a reflection of the fragile, prideful, vain, desperate, vulnerable, suffering, insufferable, paradoxical, deity-simulating nature with which God in his infinite wisdom has endowed us. So *Living Intact is* about *you*, but not the selfish, sovereign being that you can be or the false or partial identity that you fool yourself into accepting.

Living Intact has been written for and about the person who seeks relief and a deeper knowledge and understanding, one who realizes that life involves intangible mysteries that are as real as the need for food. This book is meant for the reader who wants to get more out of life and who accepts that living reasonably and satisfactorily entails expanding the process of contributing and sacrificing while, in return, seeking to derive greater satisfaction from life. The fabric of the physical universe and of humanity substantiates that hard work, sacrifice, learning, maturation and development, and spiritual and emotional effort are more than virtues. They are central elements of surviving and living in the world as God intended.

In desiring and striving to live a worthy and satisfying life, there is a difference between making it on your own and making it on your own terms. That difference may well be the measure of living intact.

* Warren, R., (2003) *Purpose Driven Life*, Zondervan Publishing.

INTRODUCTION

I have seen the burden that God has laid on men. He has made everything beautiful in its time. He has also set eternity in the hearts of men; yet they cannot fathom what God has done from beginning to end. I know that there is nothing better for men than to be happy and do good while they live. That everyone may eat and drink, and find satisfaction in all his toil—this is the gift of God. (Ecclesiastes 3:10–13)

Once upon a time, life was better. It was easier, simpler, more rewarding. Or so we imagine. Human history clearly belies our fantasies about humankind's more idyllic past. Life, in fact, has always been challenging. From man's traumatic expulsion from the Garden of Eden to the painful daily encounters with our own traumas, we are reminded of the challenges. On some level of consciousness, we are aware of our falls from the grace of wholeness, when life seemed workable and when we felt together and intact.

Life provides us with scars, and its conditions affect our health, well-being, and attitudes. As we proceed along the path, we become both stronger and weaker, fortified and shaken by patterns and sequences of events that often distort our notions of certainty, predictability, "okayness," and self. What is inevitable is that each of us will face brokenness—insult, injury, transgression, deterioration, separation, insufficiency, insecurity, and loss—that detracts from the experiences of intactness and satisfaction.

Our culture is suffused with strictures, conventions, instructions, objects, and lifestyles that buttress us against the debilitating processes and conditions that test us. To provide for our spiritual and biological needs and to help us deal with choices and temptations, a curative industry of sorts has emerged. Religion, self-improvement gurus, must-have commercial products, healing innovations, and seemingly magical means for transformation of every conceivable stripe offer the promise of wholeness. We want to feel better, outperform, and be more complete. The world screams at us to *covet, buy, believe, indulge, do.*-

The compulsion to deal somehow with life's potential for brokenness underpins the economic forces, social fabrics, and cultural values that propel civilization. From slickly marketed morality, neatly packaged spirituality, and soothing religious teachings to antidepressant commercials and magical weight loss cures, those who seek to influence us prey upon our desires for intactness and affirm our intuitive sense that life was—and can be—better, happier, and more fulfilling.

This book doesn't claim a patent on enlightenment. Rather, it offers observations, opinions, guidance, and points of view. It is the distillate of what I have learned from more than thirty years of clinical practice as a psychologist and countless hours of study, rumination, and trial-and-error experiments in dealing with real-life challenges. I hope to persuade you that your life can be more intact. I want you to gain insight from the brokenness that I myself have suffered. I want to share the knowledge I have acquired, and I want to teach you how to use the powerful tools that have allowed me to make some sense of it all and put the pieces together. If properly used, these accessible tools can solve life's puzzles, handle life's challenges, and consistently yield tangible, comprehensible, and functional solutions that energize and soothe the human spirit and allow us to transcend the debilitating feelings of brokenness that can derail and paralyze us.

Before we begin the journey, I must advise you that this book has spiritual substrata. I was raised as an Orthodox Jew. Some thirty years ago, I accepted Christianity as my true path, and I have adopted both the Old and New Testaments to guide me. So in a very real sense, *Living Intact* is ecumenical. My wish is that the content will prove illuminating for Jews, Christians, Hindus, Buddhists, Muslims, and those of different (or no) spiritual persuasions. Rest assured that I am sensitive to the problem of spiritual stridency—announcing that one proclaimed way is THE way—and the potential for alienating those with different beliefs. Nonetheless, I do draw upon my faith and spirituality, and I do make reference to scriptural passages found in both the Old and New Testaments. God understands intactness, and he also understands brokenness. In his wisdom, he has provided us with a roadmap for taking the essential elements that comprise wholeness and fitting them together.

Long ago—but later than I would care to admit—I learned that telling the truth is instrumental in making hardship go away, that pretense isn't worth the company it keeps, and that language and prayer can take me wherever I need to go. We are about to travel together—and on this journey to get more out of life, I relish your company.

I

CHOICES

CHAPTER 1
THE GREATEST CHALLENGE
YOU WILL EVER FACE

When you have to make a choice and don't make it, that is in itself a choice.
The greatest weapon against stress is our ability to choose one thought over another.
My first act of free will shall be to believe in free will.

—William James

You make choices every day. In matters large and small, conscious and subconscious, you make choices that influence your happiness, your outlook, your functionality, and your contributions. It is through the process of making decisions that you experience yourself, others, and the nature of life. Your patterns of choice determine what you do and how you respond to what others do. In large measure, choice is what defines you and your character.

The greatest challenge you will ever face is that of exercising choice. Choice is the steering mechanism for navigating the challenges that make life difficult, complex, frustrating, rewarding, and interesting. When you make choice your ally, you will greet life's opportunities and obstacles with eagerness, confidence, faith, hope, and empowerment.

WHAT IS CHOICE?

In a nutshell, choice is the continuing act of being you. Though we can only live in the present, one moment at a time, each of us is connected with what happened in the past and what will happen in the future. Choice is the engine that makes us who we are and who we will become. As the exercise of free will, choice manifests in a myriad of active and passive decisions every day. Moreover, your choices are the mechanism by which you develop and establish your character, the set of qualities that identify and distinguish you.

It is easy to acknowledge that you make routine choices, such as whether to change lanes on the road or stop at a changing light. Choosing to watch a particular TV show or choosing to read a book or make dinner are acts of independence that will hardly seem life changing. Yet becoming aware of choices that you are making constantly and that strengthen habits or confirm attitudes and beliefs can have monumental effects on the quality of your life.

Choices are instrumental in determining your shape. Just as your choices about eating and lifestyle habits will greatly influence your physical shape and well-being, your attitudes and behavioral choices will, over time, form your character, the person you truly are.

Periodically taking stock provides a vital compass on your life's trajectory. Are you healthy, happy, generous, thrifty, positive, hopeful, genuine, confident, dependable, and trustworthy? Or are you resentful, angry, negative, anxious, depressed, uneasy, and insecure? What do you believe has made you the way you are? Did you make that happen, or are you the product of forces beyond your control? You must realize that even your beliefs reflect the choices that you are continually making.

Yes, you are the product of your genes, unforeseeable events, and the many combinations of possible interactions between you and the world. However, when it comes right down to it, *you* (the *real* you) are the result of the accumulation of choices you have made, and continue to make, throughout your life. Choice is the ultimate self-control and expression of free will.

Your choices register your "living" history in that they result in consequences for you, other people, and the course of unfolding circumstances. They determine the difference you make, and they shape your character. To a large extent, choices influence what happens in your life. To a greater extent, they determine your *experiential awareness* of what happens within you and around you. Other people and circumstances may limit your options, but the choices are up to you. Life is replete with the challenges that arise in the process of making choices. Even abstention is a choice. When you ignore a snide comment instead of getting into an argument, you are making a choice.

When you take a stand, voice an opinion (or keep it to yourself), you are exercising choice. When you decide on your child's bedtime, set limits on video time, insist that homework or chores be done, you are choosing. Spending money is choosing, and all the things you pass without buying are choices, too.

You choose your friends and your clothes. You also choose your values and your opinions about your friends and their clothes. You choose whether to exert yourself in your work and do a superior job, and you make decisions about whether you are appreciated or treated fairly. You decide when to wake up, whether you are tired, and what to do about being tired. You deal with competition, disappointments, and possibly betrayals, and your reactions reflect your choices. You choose what to put in your coffee and whether to have any at all. You decide how to use the gifts and talents God gave you and how much to brood over what you wish you had. All of these choices are interrelated and echo past choices and influence future ones.

Choice is the continuing opportunity to individuate and form an identity, to exercise being you, to make a difference, and to make your mark on historical events.

STRIVING FOR CONTROL

Each of us wants to make a difference. It is human nature to want to be recognized and appreciated, to matter, and to strive to exert control over what happens in our lives. You may feel, at times, that you are in charge and that you are steering and directing your course. At other times, you may feel that events are well beyond your control, even beyond your presence in time and place. When things are clicking and going right, you may be aware of your being "in the zone." At other times, you may experience a state of hopelessness and powerlessness about what's happening in your life.

By experiencing the good times and the bad, people develop an outlook, a perspective about what is manageable, who is responsible, and how to go about the business of coping. Over time, some people acquire a sense that they own their life, and others become more fatalistic. Some proactively choose what happens in areas that they can control, whereas others develop the sense of being victimized. If this is a difficult time for you, it may actually be a valuable opportunity to apply the principle of making choices so that you can create better outcomes in areas that you can control.

How you view choice involves much more than being active or passive. It entails having a genuine can-do attitude. Choice encompasses a larger dynamic that entails the willingness to choose and be chosen, the wisdom to discern cause-and-effect, and the acceptance of responsibility for the decisions you make.

In practical terms, this means that you can determine and change how you interpret (think and feel about) things, how you respond to what happens in your world, and how people respond to you. When you take ownership of choice, you are the *cause* of your experience. When you interpret your experiences and reactions as having happened *because* of events, circumstances, beliefs, positions, logic, feelings, etc., you are denying the role of choice. This is not to imply that you can choose any outcome and necessarily have it turn out that way. Rather, it suggests that you have an important say in the way things appear *after they happen.* Though you cannot change the past or the events that transpired, you can, in a sense, rewrite the record of your history—not the actual facts and events, but how they help mold you into what you become. You may have had a difficult childhood or problems in school. Perhaps you never had the things you wanted, or you are struggling with injustices that occurred in the past. By changing your future (beginning with right now), you can also change the spin on the past. The cancer survivor looks at life differently than she did before her illness; the post-heart attack athlete regards events in his past with different and perhaps more appreciative perspective; the overweight person whose diet succeeds takes pleasure in being thinner and maintaining the weight loss. The college graduate revels in pride and confidence that results from having established and accomplished a significant goal, and the pride and self-confidence supplant her previous doubts and anxieties about the future.

There is a key principle at work here, and you must grasp this principle if you want to live intact. You must learn to see yourself as being more the potential of tomorrow rather than the product of yesterday. Through understanding and exercising your responsibility and power of choice, you can shape a life more satisfying, more contributing, and more worth living. You can come to terms with a universe that doesn't always give you what you want or when you want it. Facing the challenge of choice will enable you to operate more competently in turning obstacles into opportunities and transforming brokenness into wholeness and living intact. Though you cannot control everything that happens to you, you can choose between living broken and living intact.

MAKING CHOICES IN TOUGH TIMES

These are tough times. The ripples of the current economic meltdown that emerged in 2008 and is extending beyond have touched virtually everyone. Economic hardships cannot help but influence mindsets, decisions, behaviors, and relationships. So many people are affected by these tough times, and this includes even those who had been making the "right" financial decisions for years. Compounding the damage of lost income, assets, and opportunities are the shaken beliefs, confidence, and faith in the world and its leaders. When things fall apart on such a grand scale, the trust and wisdom we took for granted come into question. We become more vulnerable, more broken, more disillusioned, and more fearful. Having your home go into foreclosure, losing your job, or being hounded by collection agencies can cause major upheavals in your life. Desperation can catch up with each of us at some point, and we may conclude that we are not good enough, strong enough, or sufficient, despite our efforts and intentions. We must carry on, of course, but we may be overwhelmed by feelings of emptiness and disillusionment.

Those who are stronger, more resourceful, more successful, or who have more assets may be able to weather the storm better and bounce back sooner. Those who are more exposed and vulnerable are distinctly at risk and could face crises of mounting proportion and impact. Yet despite the palpable hardships, we still have choices to make that will affect our actions and reactions.

As an individual, you cannot control the cascading effects of world events. You read about them, watch the news, hear the buzz, and feel the anxiety and pain. You form opinions, make decisions, develop attitudes, and acquire fortitude to defend yourself while you implement a personal recovery plan. All of your reactions involve choices. And these choices are intrinsically linked to feelings, beliefs, and attitudes that can determine the outcome. Though you may not be a major player on the world stage, you have a starring role in your own life, a life with purpose, determination, meaning, and impact. Be assured that your choices will profoundly influence not only the quality of your life but also the lives of others.

You can, if you so choose, develop a character of integrity and resilience that will permit you to prevail over tough times. While there may not be a sure-fire economic bailout plan that you can immediately latch onto, there are ways to turn the brokenness that results from negative circumstances into positive outcomes for living intact. You can choose to live in a manner that reflects grace, satisfaction, integrity, godliness, and wholeness and, by so doing, flourish in a world that repeatedly tests your spirit, resolve, and character.

Yes, you may feel at certain junctures cheated and disillusioned. Things may not always work out the way you expected. When this happens, it's normal to want to take time to lick your wounds. As is the case with someone who puts money in the vending machine but does not get the desired product, you feel as if you've been deprived of your due reward. What then?

When the outcome is not what you anticipated, you must decide what your responses will be. You could crumble, feel sorry for yourself, and bemoan your setback, or you could choose to push forward with resolve. It's vital that you realize that your decisions and actions will profoundly influence what happens internally and externally. Tough times are a paradigm for the procedure of confronting and prevailing over life's challenges. They make us choose how we will play the hand we've been dealt. Certainly, no one chooses to live through a serious recession, have a child who is addicted to drugs, be beset by health problems, or lose a home in a fire or foreclosure; but everyone has the capacity to make conscious and deliberate choices about how to react when life's misfortunes occur. This decision-making process is an element that God has deliberately infused in his master plan.

This may be an unpleasant time economically, but the current meltdown presents an opportunity to learn how to exercise the range of choices you can make in order to live a more intact life. You can thrive as a person, regardless of the conditions you are facing. You can exert a powerful and positive impact on others and upon circumstances, whatever these circumstances may be. And during stressful times, you can learn to take better control of external situations and internal reactions by exercising your power of choice in wise and informed ways.

It is true that money, possessions, and security are important. However, if you let these occupy front and center stage, you will be dependent upon exterior circumstances for your fulfillment, and you will diminish the power, control, and flexibility of choice.

> *I am not saying this because I am in need, for I have learned to be content whatever the circumstances. I know what it is to be in need, and I know what it is to have plenty. I have learned the secret of being content in any and every situation, whether well-fed or hungry, whether living in plenty or in want. I can do everything through him who gives me strength.*
> (Philippians 4:12–13)

THESE TIMES VERSUS THOSE TIMES

In light of today's challenges, you may ask how things got this way and how the good times have deteriorated and become so difficult. You may wonder why things are so much more challenging than they used to be. You may fondly recall when housing used to be more affordable, neighborhoods were safer, people were more respectful, and customer service was actually helpful and polite. It is only natural to reminisce about the good times and contemplate the challenges today and those down road that our children may face.

When they were adolescents, both my sons asked me whether I thought it was better or more difficult to grow up at present or when I was a child. The question prompted me to think about my own evolution and the current state of the world. I felt compelled to respond to my sons in a way that would answer the query honestly, but with reassurance. After all, they sought my wisdom, put me on the spot, and would probably use my opinion to help form their attitudes about their own places in the world. This is the essence of what I told them:

"Looking back in time, especially at your own life, and making comparisons is a vexing thing. You have the facts, but somehow they become selective and distorted. You remember things with emotional exaggeration, both the good and the bad. If you are pleased with the way things turned out, you tend to color your memories differently than if you have resentment and misgivings. The saying, 'The older I get, the better I was' is offset by the traumatic recollections of past hardships and adverse conditions.

"There is a strange paradox in growing older: you view with nostalgia and perhaps some embarrassment the fads, styles, beliefs, experiments, and innovations of the past, and sometimes you yearn for the pleasures and simplicity of the good old days. Yet you often forget that the old days were full of daunting challenges. Perhaps collectively, the world has grown more complex and threatening. But individually, the challenges of growing to maturity, finding a place in the world, resolving the paradoxes and inconsistencies in life, and developing meaning and character in the context of one's circumstances aren't all that different from one generation to the next. Human nature hasn't fundamentally changed, and God's nature hasn't either. Bridging the two natures is the main challenge, and it is played out on the stage with varying scripts in each person's life.

"That said, there are some major differences between then and now. I can tell you the things that were better when I grew up and the things that are better and easier now. In my day, we didn't have voicemail or microwaves and certainly not personal computers, video games, or electronic gadgets. There was no Internet or instant communication or mobile devices. Music was played on vinyl with phonograph needles, and electric guitars and tape cassettes were the newest rage in technology. Birth control pills had just become chic, as had LSD. Air-conditioning was not that common, and rolling up car windows by hand was the norm. There were no Starbucks, and most people had never tasted lattes or espresso. I grew up in a walk-up apartment building without an elevator. We had a black and white television and a rotary phone. There was no halogen lighting, cable TV, GPS devices, mobile phones, wireless networks, or satellite programming. You had to go to the library to do research and use the card catalogue. There were no reality shows, cooking shows, ESPN, VCRs, or TiVo. The war in Vietnam had a lot of people upset and caused a lot of controversy. There was a great deal of racism and mistrust. There was no special education. If you were depressed, fearful, or addicted, you kept it to yourself and most definitely from your employer. You took immobilizing tranquilizers and/or had electroshock. Lobotomies were being phased out as state-of-the-art medical treatment.

"On the other hand, there was no HIV, no Al-Qaeda, and no jihad. The World Trade Center had not been built. It cost $11.00 (yes, eleven dollars) to fly the four hundred miles home from my university. There were no metal detectors or security booths at airports or other public buildings. Gasoline cost less than thirty cents/gallon. Mail was delivered twice a day. Hitchhiking was common and not considered particularly dangerous. A membership at the local "night center" (a high school gym open for basketball in the evenings) cost $4.00 per year. Pizza was twenty cents a slice. A top professional athlete earned about $50,000/year and didn't sport tattoos or earrings. A ticket to a Yankees baseball game cost about $2.00. Wearing seatbelts and helmets was optional. Most people who worked had health insurance—good health insurance, paid for by their employer. There were no HMOs. College admissions were less competitive, and it was relatively easier to get a job. As a child, when I left the house, my mother couldn't keep tabs on me unless she looked out the window and yelled, or called a friend's house and happened to find me there.

"So which is better, growing up then or growing up now? I have to say that, on balance, today is a better day. Comparing conveniences, creature comforts, risks, and economies is a tricky and subjective endeavor. There are good arguments in favor of each era. However, what tips the scales for me are the technologies now available that help us meet the challenges that seem always to accompany life's ups and downs. When I grew up, we didn't have computers, and so we weren't able to train our brains and nervous systems with the expediency and efficiency that we can today. We didn't have the magnificent hi-tech therapies that today relieve so much pain, distress, and suffering. We lacked the information-gathering techniques, rapid communications, and global interdependence that now flood us with awareness of the needs and resources that exist. Today, there are much more data that can cause stress and confusion or cause confusion. Managing information and paying selective attention to sift through the bombardment of information has become an increasing responsibility for just about everyone.

"However, the comparison between then and now is, in my opinion, tilted in favor of today because the capacity for informed intelligent choice is greatly strengthened by technologies that provide us more information and greater power. This is true in the healing arts and professions where the skill of self-observation, data collection, monitoring, and modification are greatly buttressed by technologies. There are always and have always been challenges, and meeting those challenges successfully is necessary for a worthy and fulfilling life. The linchpin in the process is to exercise choice wisely."

ADVANTAGES IN TODAY'S TOUGH TIMES

In many ways, history and human nature recapitulate themselves. Biblical history recounts the reign of good kings and bad kings, benevolent leaders and despots. Yet you don't have to look far back in time to see cycles repeat themselves. In my youth, we struggled with the Cuban missile crisis, the cold war with the Soviets, and the war in Vietnam. In their place today, we have Iraq, Afghanistan, and nuclear threats by Iran and North Korea. The mortgage meltdown has recapitulated the savings and loan scandals of the 1980s, and global warming concerns have replaced the frenzy over the Three Mile Island and Chernobyl disasters. The Middle East seems perennially in discord and conflict. There is still much racism, discrimination, and mistrust. And there is also still genocide, repression, oppression, poverty, and hunger.

There are still drugs, alcoholism, depression, anxiety, financial woes, family dysfunction and breakups, and personal woes of all kinds. It can appear—as the old saying goes—that the more things change, the more they stay the same. Have children's imaginations been stifled by the onslaught of video games? Have their minds been deadened by the plethora of violence, sensuality, and rapid multimedia images? Or, perhaps, have Photoshop, Wii, and Guitar Hero taken creativity to a new level? Have YouTube, cell phones, and the Internet catapulted the emerging generation to greater challenges of sensitivity, responsibility, and management of information of resources? I would argue that they have.[1]

Today's world is more complex and arguably more overwhelming. However, the changes in technology, information, and communication give advantages for meeting challenges as never before. And how fortunate this is, since many of us need all the help we can get!

YOU, OTHERS, AND THE WORLD

Our universe is very creative when it comes to displaying human beings' many permutations, qualities, and attributes. The diverse resources people use to handle life's struggles and the multiple methods they employ in try-

---

1. Updated norms on intelligence tests reveal that people have become smarter over the last generation.

ing to solve problems, obtain satisfaction, and basically cope with life are ingenious. And yet, despite this ingenuity, the challenges often prove confusing and overwhelming, and the devised solutions often prove ineffectual.

To make the complexity of the challenges and choices more manageable, it would be helpful to sort the challenges and choices into three basic categories:

Self habits—the ways in which you maintain and run your body and mind.

World habits—the practical skills that help you operate effectively within an environment. These habits include how you deal with other people and how you get what you want and need.

Integral habits—the crossover between your personal inner world and the world you share with others. These habits are your resources for adapting to, accepting, interpreting, harmonizing, accommodating, and integrating with *what is* and *what happens* during the course of your life.

Self habits, world habits, and *integral habits* comprise the tools you use to manage the business of living and to make sense out of your experiences. These habits include many routine and automatic skills, such as regulation of body functions, ways to calm yourself, and applied reasoning skills that you develop naturally, as well as those other skills you may require to become more productive and fulfilled.

TURNING BROKENNESS INTO LIVING INTACT

Whether you are battling depression or anxiety, trying to build your career, attempting to control your kids, or lose weight, or if you are suffering from the overwhelming stresses and pressures of daily life, your effectiveness in being able to confront and prevail over your personal challenges will depend on how astutely you apply the life habits described above. (Please note that self habits, world habits, and integral habits are discussed more extensively in chapter 2, and more details are provided in appendix D.)

At this juncture, it would be helpful to provide you with a preview of what follows so that you can see how the pieces will fit together. Chapters 4–8 show you five key secrets of living intact and becoming more skilled and more accountable in your exercise of choices. In chapters 9 and 10, you will learn about two revolutionary techniques (EEG neurofeedback and Thought Field Therapy) that have helped many thousands of people live more empowered and transformed lives. Chapters 11 and 12 discuss the relevance of expectations and wisdom in living intact. Chapters 13–19 apply these secrets, skills, knowledge, and techniques to common problems and frustrations that beset us all (conflict, desire, anger, hurt, rejection, loneliness, guilt, suffering).

Before getting into the nitty-gritty of the living intact skills, I want to share with you some personal applications in my own life of the principles I have uncovered that have helped me turn defeat into victory and brokenness into living intact. It is my tale of desperation in attempting to accommodate life's intrinsic "unfairness" and refusal to bend to my will and expectations. This is the "stuff" that has compelled me to write this book.

WHEN BAD THINGS HAPPEN TO GOOD PEOPLE

In the days of my youth, slang pervaded the hip culture vernacular. The expressions "bummer," "downer," and "what a drag" were common terms to describe various experiences of dismay brought about by unpleasant situations, circumstances, or people. Another word used to describe an adverse circumstance was "bust." A "bust" was an intrusion (sometimes even an arrest), a grave disappointment, a break in smooth working, an exposure of vulnerability, and dashed expectations. To be busted was to be caught doing something not accepted or to be broken or impoverished.

You could use one of the expressions described above to indicate displeasure when things didn't go your way. You could also use the aforementioned expressions to express outrage against those who had the temerity to intrude on your lifestyle, get in your face, or create circumstances that upset you.

The hipster jargon of the time resonated with me, as I was frequently offended by life's indignities, what I believed were undeserved reprisals from other people, and the maddening indifference of life. My narcissistic mind divided conditions and people into two groups: those welcomed as "cool," "groovy," or "right on," and those eschewed as "bummer," "downer," and "what a drag." The positive group consisted of people, things, and happenings that pleased my senses, flattered my ego, or gave me what I wanted. The negative group—which, as you might imagine, was considerably larger—comprised whatever and whoever reflected unflattering information, failed to appreciate me, or stood in my way.

Because I was the center of my own world with my need to outshine others, I encountered many *bummers, busts, downers, drags*, and people whom I considered ignorant, envious, unappreciative, clueless, insignificant, or a combination thereof. My private interpretation of the unpleasant responses I received from the world was that these responses were either *bad news* or *bait-mail*. *Bad news (bummers, busts, adversity, antagonism, downers, drags)* comprised those happenings in which life wasn't giving me what I wanted. *Bait-mail* included personalized provocations and criticisms directed at me. Both bad news and bait-mail were everywhere, and strangely, they seemed to come at me from inside as well as from around me. Internally, I was constantly battling self-criticism, doubt, self-consciousness, and negative thinking, and I superimposed this jaded template onto my external interactions with the world around me. I could forecast the many ways things could go wrong and then use the resulting circumstances to confirm my suspicions. In brighter moments when I had optimistic ideas and sanguine expectations, these were often subsequently undermined by the stark reality of things not working out the way I had hoped.

I reasoned that a person as important and entitled as I perceived myself was bound to receive his share of bad news and bait-mail, but it seemed that the events and people lining up against me were, if not conspiratorial, nevertheless ungracious and deserving of my righteous indignation. Funny thing is that, as grandiose and weird as this may sound, I could associate this indignation with anything or anyone ranging from a teacher or family member to a traffic light or poorly tasting food. I was not often a happy camper, and I chose to externalize and blame fortune, circumstances, and other people for my woes. Under the guise of my own justifications and rationalizations, I could also dish it out rather ungraciously in return. That I was not living intact (or, indeed, in *tact*) is self-evident.

The key question is: do you also get bad news and bait-mail? Of course you do! It may not arrive with a stamp on it, but your share entails all that stymies and frustrates you, blocks your agenda, makes you uncomfortable, gets you in trouble, and exposes you for being wrong, insecure, prideful, self-important, and less than the captain of your circumstances and destiny. What do you do about bad news and bait-mail? What do you choose when life does not go your way?

Let me share with you what I've learned.

CHOICE WORDS

People do things for their own reasons, not yours. Though I recognized this truth long ago, it is still instinctive for me to look at life through my own lens and my own perspective and to think that I'm right and my way is best. Naturally, I expect others to assent to the value of my opinions and desires. Of course, this doesn't occur as often as I'd like, and this can sometimes cause conflict or frustration, especially if something is really important to me.

Like most people, I value attention, recognition, and appreciation. I am fortunate to get my share of it and even more blessed when I can focus on what I have, rather than what I don't have. It is natural for me to expect that others will want what I have to offer, benefit from it, and express appreciation. However, when the world doesn't beat a path to my door, I can dwell on my perceptions of others' complaints, criticisms, impositions, rejections, and demands, as verification of and justification for my observations.

The truth is that efforts often go unnoticed and unacknowledged. Though I understand the obstacles in getting people to change their ways (even with their seeming collaboration), it can feel lonely and frustrating when people don't do what I think they should. Whether it involves accepting advice, complying with suggestions, obeying explicit directions, following through on commitments and obligations, or simply showing consideration and sensitivity, I am frequently let down by others, disappointed by lost opportunities, or taken aback by criticism.

Though I know from experience to expect it, the bad news and bait-mail come—like a sudden car repair—without warning. At least it seems that way when expenses materialize, rejection abounds, criticism stings, or pain arrives. The bills mount, someone complains, my advice and recommendations are rejected, and my body betrays me.

You get the idea; these misfortunes don't just happen to me—they probably also happen to you. Certain common denominators may be shared while other elements may be distinct, but the theme that life often hurts is all too familiar.

So what do I do when the bad news and bait-mail come? I use the self, world, and integral skills and habits to convert brokenness and adversity into living intact. I depend upon discipline and self-control to manage my body and mind. I draw upon experience, skills, compassion, and sensitivity to connect with other people in satisfying exchanges of wants and needs. I connect my inner world with the outer realities that happen, even if these are not what I'd prefer. I defer to God's timing and his will, and I adjust my expectations. I have learned to discern and follow the wisdom that is divine, time-tested, and infallible. I have learned to use the techniques and technologies that make these adjustments more achievable with less distress and frustration. I have also learned to develop a transformative outlook on the role that suffering plays in my life and the attitudes and reactions with which I confront and endure adversity.

In effect, I respond to the obstacles and opportunities in life by exercising choice. The methods and principles I've learned to use facilitate flexibility, responsibility, and the ability to make wise choices. You, too, can learn how to apply the same methods in your own life.

CLOSER TO HOME

The exercise of choice and the shaping of character have not come naturally or easily for me. For many years, I looked for magic bullets, ignored my own shortcomings, and defended my choices as the only reasonable reactions to my circumstances. Even as I became more "responsible" in terms of worldly maturity, I avoided taking ownership of my experience. Without realizing it, I often chose to live at *effect*, rather than at *cause*.

Let me give you some examples. I didn't choose to be short in stature, but I did choose to be very sensitive about it until many years into adulthood. Eventually, I came to accept my height and even to joke about it sometimes.

I didn't choose to be heavyset and to struggle with weight problems. However, I formerly chose a lifestyle and a diet that made these issues more difficult. I chose to be sedentary for a decade in my adulthood. Later, I chose to change my diet and get back into exercise. I didn't choose to have spinal problems or arthritis, but I do choose to do yoga, stretching, and other exercises, and to make lifestyle adjustments in order to live relatively pain free.

I didn't choose to be depressed and anxious as a young person. I eventually chose to use the methods outlined in this book to break free of these shackles. Early in my life, I did choose to use tobacco, drugs, and alcohol; later, I chose to give them up completely. I choose regularly to do the things I have learned will make me sleep soundly, think clearly, digest well, carry hope and faith with me, and look for the good in people. On a daily basis, I choose to look my best, feel my best, and be my best. I also chose to convert to Christianity and to accept Jesus Christ as my guide, mentor, and my savior.

As a young man, I found a beautiful wife and intended to live with her the rest of my days. The marriage grew sour. Although I played an active part in this, I didn't choose to have a bad marriage—in fact, I did everything advisable to save it. Eventually, after almost thirty years, I chose to accept divorce with all its adverse ramifications. Clearly, I made choices that led down that path, too.

Later on, I chose to risk love and commitment and get remarried. My new wife and I chose to make God central in our marriage. Half my lifetime ago, I chose to give God control of my life; since then, I have been struggling and choosing with more success to put God and other people ahead of my own selfishness. It truly works!

IN MY HOME AND MY MIND

It is a mixed blessing to have psychological insight. Describing a problem is certainly not the same as fixing it. *Understanding* my motivations, personality, and vulnerabilities, on the other hand, provided me with a key tool for developing self-control and compassion. Still, it takes more than understanding to counteract selfish, maladaptive habits and to act lovingly and effectively. The combination of stress, temptation, beliefs and attitudes, and the provocations from others can often overwhelm better judgment and intentions. Meeting challenges and prevailing over vulnerabilities in tough times requires the exercise of wise choice, and wise choice grows through blending God's biblical wisdom, applying technological and scientific methods, and learning efficiently from experience.

Here is an example—a lot closer to home—of how this works for me. It is a rebuke from my wife, whom I dearly love, and who can also try my patience and challenge me with bait-mail, delivered personally. This is what she has said:

"You are so stubborn. You act like you are the only one who counts. You hurt my feelings and don't even realize it. Sometimes you are harsh, even when you mean well. It bothers me that you always think you are right. I wish you would be more sensitive to my feelings and listen to what I have to say."

Here is my wife's rebuke the way I heard it in my old selfish, vulnerable, have-to-be-right nature (*my unexpressed reactions are in italics*):

"You are so stubborn (*And you're not?*) You act like you are the only one who counts (*Look who's talking!*). You hurt my feelings and don't even realize it (*I do get that your feelings are hurt—whoa—I didn't mean to hurt you—it's not a crime, okay*). Sometimes you are harsh, even when you mean well (*I've heard this before!*). It bothers me that you always think you are right (*Maybe what bothers you is that I have common sense and experience, and I am right a lot of the time. You should be thankful for what I know and what I do*). I wish you would be more sensitive to my feelings and listen to what I have to say (*Here we go again; it's like a broken record. I do listen to you—a lot —something you don't seem to recognize or appreciate. And by the way, what about my feelings?*)."

Now, I know how my mind works. When things don't go my way, my mind leaps in two directions: self-pity and blame. It is as if I am programmed to feel sorry for myself for having to endure indignities, and then I reactively find fault with whoever or whatever is linked to my dismay. (*"I don't deserve to be treated this way." "What's the matter with her?"*) If I let my inner programming—with its seductive narrative[2]—have its way, things will surely go from bad to worse. Unless I recognize and adjust for this, I will not respond in the gracious and compassionate manner that I choose so that I'm able to live intact, develop character, and foster my own well-being and the well-being of those around me. I need to counteract those baser instincts that were previously masquerading as the "real" me by putting myself in my wife's shoes, looking at life as she sees it, considering possibilities that explain why she acts in certain ways, and consulting and consoling her with empathy and compassion.

With that objective in mind, here is my response to the rebuke I didn't deserve:

"I'm really sorry your feelings are hurt. It certainly was not my intent to hurt you. You're right that perhaps I am not always aware of all your sensitivities. I believe I do listen to what you say, and I take you seriously. That doesn't mean I always agree with you. Perhaps you can be specific

---

2. The *narrative* is your inner voice that perpetually chatters and comments, often editorializing judgmentally, criticizing mercilessly, and providing self-justification. This phenomenon is explained in chapter 4.

about what I did that offended you. First, let's heal the rift between us. I'd like us to do some TFT tapping,[3] and then let's pray together."

When I respond this way, I feel better about myself, and I am empowered and in touch with compassion for the other person. This type of response, in turn, usually elicits a softening in others. Even when that softening does not occur, my empathic and nonthreatened response allows others to witness their own defensiveness and reactivity. Whether or not I get the reply I want, I become more satisfied with my response to a challenge. Over time, I become more accustomed to meeting challenges with confident responses and successful outcomes. I can detach from the outcome I want or expect and focus on choosing the course of action and inner attitude that will lead to the character I want to manifest and a person whose choices God will approve.

It also turns out that my wife appreciates this attitude, returns it in kind, and we grow closer together and more intimate because we respond this way.

So I say, live by the Spirit, and you will not gratify the desires of the sinful nature. For the sinful nature desires what is contrary to the Spirit, and the Spirit what is contrary to the sinful nature. They are in conflict with each other so that you do not do what you want. But, if you are led by the Spirit, you are not under law. (Galatians 5:16–18)

HOW WILL YOU CHOOSE?

Does your mind work a bit the way mine does? Do you react aggressively or sarcastically to indignities and injustices and then automatically justify your responses with "reasonableness" or peer validation? Do you feel sorry for yourself or withdraw? Do you feel guilty? Do you continually profess your innocence? Are you defensive?

Life supplies enough bad news and bait-mail to keep all of us busy, defensive, and trapped in private worlds of reactivity, self-justification, hurt, and retribution for a good part of our days. It is the nature of things that these

---

3. TFT (Thought Field Therapy) is one of the power tools for getting rid of any negative emotion in minutes (see chapter 10). In this instance, we used it to eliminate feelings of defensiveness, resentment, hurt, and anger.

challenges will get the better of us unless we take a stand with the power of God and the tools he has supplied to counteract defeat, self-sabotage, and sin.

The power of choice is your gift in this life. It will never be removed, but you must use it appropriately and wisely to live an intact life. Remember: others may limit your options, but the choices for how you respond are up to you. This is not a platitude or abstract theory; it is a reality and working platform for taking control of the person you become and the quality of exchange and satisfaction between you and the world around you.

You always have a choice. Moment by moment, day by day, you have so many choices, whatever may be your circumstances. Your choices have consequences, and those consequences will influence future choices. This cycle is not completely knowable, but neither is it mechanistic or deterministic. At any point, you can intervene and change the program. *Living Intact* will show you how. This book explains profound secrets and gives you powerful tools to activate those secrets productively. You can, of course, choose to dismiss them or perhaps interpret them as different versions of what you've come across before.

You can also choose to internalize these truths and tools to expand what you already know and what works for you and, in the process, turn your life around to receive more meaning and joy and to increasingly bring blessing to others.

Choice is your vehicle for meeting challenges and for turning them into opportunities for achieving success. Ironically, you were given the power of choice *after* the choice that wasn't yours to make: you did not choose to be born in the place, time, and person that you were. These choices were made for you. In this regard, you were chosen.

YOUR CALL

You were chosen and you were called. Before the world began, you were slated to appear. You were, and are, given a role to play, but only you can perform your part and determine how you will interpret the script. Perhaps you wanted a bigger or different role in life, or perhaps you don't even want to act out the part you were given. Your particular role is not the critical matter. What does matter is that the world and God are your audience. They are watching and listening for how you will perform. You may not even be sure of your role. However, consider the following:

1. You are called to love other people and treat them decently (as you would like to be treated), regardless of how they treat you and whether they are lovable.

2. You are called to experience forgiveness, mercy, and grace. From such experience, you are called to forgive and bless others.

3. You are called to live in the world on its own terms, not as you would want it to be. This doesn't mean that you should be satisfied with or accept everything, nor should it discourage you from trying to change things. This means that you understand, accept, and live by the reality that life and the world will not always comply with your desires or expectations.

4. A major part of your role in life is to develop your character and prevail over the obstacles that life creates. The only true "bad guys" are the ones who continue to make bad choices and to develop an evil character.

5. You are called to serve others and chosen to help them develop their characters and to live more satisfying, productive, and worthy lives. You are called to make other people feel good about themselves, and God endowed you with specific gifts to execute this mission. Living intact requires you to discover and implement the realities that govern behavior, according to God's principles, so that you may better serve others.

6. You are called to live beyond circumstances, to treasure individual differences and gifts, and to appreciate reality as including spiritual truths unseen as well as material things seen. You are called to abide by the laws of nature, to figure things out as best you can, and to live with humility, awe, and respect for human limitations. You are called to enjoy the gifts of life and to know and live with the awareness that you will meet eternal judgment. In the face of uncertainty, here's what is certain: in the end, you really only have two things—your word and God's Word. You are called and chosen to treasure and abide by both of them.

Living Intact is a roadmap to guide you in following your calling. The practical principles, key strategies, and solutions described in the following chapters will help you make the right calls in exercising choice as your ally in meeting the challenges of life.

You did not choose me, but I chose you and appointed you to go and bear fruit—fruit that will last. Then the Father will give you whatever you ask in my name. This is my command: Love each other. (John 15:16–17)

CHAPTER 2
SECRETS AND ELEMENTS
OF LIVING INTACT

WHAT IS LIVING INTACT?

Most of us are consumed with life's daily concerns and challenges. We are preoccupied with getting the kids to school, shopping for dinner, cooking meals, cleaning the house, handling our jobs, managing the family budget, dealing with an occasionally cranky husband or wife, or ministering to a sick child. We plod along, trying to make a buck, maintain satisfying relationships, raise functional, well-behaved, and achievement-oriented children, find career satisfaction, attain financial security, stay healthy, and perhaps take an occasional vacation. These mundane challenges are predictable, maybe too predictable. A mix of biological, psychological, and sociological forces seem to be constantly pulling at us. On one level, we are simply trying to survive and improve our lot in life. On another more profound level, we are cognizant of our underlying yearnings, frustrations, and aspirations that cry out for recognition, resolution, and fulfillment.

Whether we consciously realize it or not, many of us are searching for miracles—miracles that have the power to uplift our spirit beyond the mundane, enhance our spirituality, and connect us with deeper meaning and contentment. Miracles are a less common manifestation of God's presence in the universe and the means by which he affirms his astounding powers, arouses people's awe and wonder, and bears witness to himself. Some seek these miracles actively and openly with an air of expectancy and faith. Others are more passive. They wait and hope with prayers, fantasies, wishful thinking, or a combination of effort and anticipation. We want life to be better, to flow in ways that are pleasing and that work for us. Though we may differ in our approaches for achieving these goals, we share in common the desire to uncover life's secrets and to acquire the resources that will help us function better and make living more satisfying.

There are many ways to describe a "life worth living" that aspires to happiness, satisfaction, worthiness, service, achievement, security, and sacrifice, to name just a few of the most commonly used constituents. Some people value material evidence of the good life, and others cherish the realm of inner spiritual being. Divergent individual preferences and agendas for attaining contentment have always existed and, throughout history, have profoundly influenced politics, art, science, literature, religion, philosophy, and commerce. One factor is shared in common: we live out our days balancing on the fulcrum that separates survival on one side from meaning on the other, facing challenges and seeking to secure, reinforce, refine, and enhance those aspects of life we hold dear. I call this dynamic process the drive for *Living Intact*.

Living Intact is an active and systematic engagement with life's challenges, using the potential of the challenge process to resolve the inherent breakdowns, dissatisfactions, and discrepancies that result from our desires for what life should be and our actual experiences living life.

This book integrates issues that span neurobiology, social and interpersonal dynamics, psychology, life skills, and spiritual development. It advocates the proactive process of confronting and prevailing over challenges and the utilization of these deliberate encounters to acquire the precious emotional and spiritual fuel that energizes, repairs, regulates, and inspires us. Though challenges can be defeating if improperly handled, the manner in which we respond to the dynamic of challenge has the potential to transform brokenness into wholeness, physical power, and spiritual strength, and to make our lives worthy, rewarding, and satisfying.

As has been previously indicated, living intact requires not only an acceptance of challenges as an integral part of the human condition, but also an actual welcoming of challenges as opportunities to develop and assert our character and potency. Challenges are not our enemy, but rather our ally. In this context, challenges are part and parcel of the embedded developmental process that is programmed by nature to stimulate our growth. They punctuate our experiences from conception and pervade the very nature of our interactions with ourselves and the world.

Here is the main challenge up front: are you willing to consider, study, and implement the principles of living intact? If so, this book will provide you with structure, insights, tips, how-tos, and, perhaps, some validation and humor that can make your life more fruitful and enjoyable.

STRUGGLING WITH THE UNIVERSE HERE ON EARTH

In an imperfect universe, light dust settles on dark surfaces, dark dust settles on light surfaces, and the realities upon which we rely often don't seem to care about our wants. Forces such as gravity, fire, and friction operate independently of our desires and can hurt or impede us just as easily as help us. So it is, too, with the rest of the world, which can often seem to be opposing us, overreacting, or appearing neglectful. Things break or don't work, people fall short of our hopes and expectations, the past sometimes haunts and hurts, the present sometimes frustrates and disappoints, and the future may loom ominously or recede from tangible reassurance. Time progresses relentlessly, age never waits, and most of us are impatient to move onto something that we envision might be better. Is it therefore surprising that life frequently brims with struggles and complaints, that we are often in a fix and feel broken, and that living intact can seem a fantasy?

In this world of broken dreams and impaired realities, how then is it possible to live intact and share, exchange, interact, and participate to our utmost? What and where are the secrets mysteriously hiding from us that will yield the joys and satisfactions of getting the most out of life while life gets the most out of us? Life indeed *uses* us and, in the process, requires energy, expense, commitment, and sacrifice. It hurts and rewards, taunts and reassures, confuses and explains, afflicts and heals, surprises and justifies. Shouldn't we try to squeeze the most out of the experience of life and get the best bargain while doing so?

This book does not offer simplistic solutions, nor does it offer an explanation of the intricate complexities of social, psychological, or physical sciences. Rather, it is a distillation of observations, concepts, and perceptions—a synthesis with a fresh and useful perspective. It is a tool forged by acquired insight and wisdom that, in turn, fashions other tools. The Bible says that wisdom is a shelter that prolongs the life of its possessor (Ecclesiastes 7:12). Clearly, each of us needs shelter from the elements, from the forces of life that seem intent, at times, upon breaking us down and obstructing what we want. The universe that will not bend to our will is indeed a formidable foe.

CODES TO LIVE BY

Nature overflows with secrets and mysteries contained in codes. From DNA to language, symbols, and relationships, the world is embedded with information about how life unfolds. Managing life requires the detection, translation, and enactment of the codes that encapsulate this information. We use codes for analyzing and synthesizing data, formulating concepts and logic, testing hypotheses, evaluating options, and generalizing from our individual and collective experiences the characteristics, resources, and courses of action that help us survive and live better. Codes sum up the rules and messages about these processes. For example, when driving, we respond to traffic lights at an intersection. We use social codes to indicate our receptivity and availability, and we react to the green/red light messages that tell whether it is okay to proceed on a course. We are attuned to people's facial expressions that convey whether to advance, back off, or wait. Codes communicate when the airplane bathroom is vacant, the degree to which a social gesture is welcome, when a boundary has been violated, and even when a partner might be interested in sex. Formally or informally taught cognitive codes that are reflected in expressive language, grammatical conventions, spelling rules, mathematics, and economic principles allow us to communicate our ideas and exchange goods and services.

Nature imparts information by means of environmental and biological codes. Examples include barometric pressure that indicates when it is likely to rain, cramping or bloating that indicate when a menstrual period is coming, and fatigue and stress that signal the need to rest, retreat, and recover.

Living intact also involves codes that help us repair brokenness, grow and thrive, and become functional, healthy, and connected. We are about to explore some powerful codes that I call the "secrets" and "elements" for living intact. They form the infrastructure for helping us achieve a more intact existence. The secrets are the instructions for solving the puzzles and problems that life presents. The elements are the infrastructure you need to follow the instructions. If we draw a sports analogy, you might think of the elements as the skills and talents and training needed to play a sport and the secrets as the distillate of practice, playing experience, effective coaching, and acquired savvy about how to play well and win.

LEARNING THE SECRETS

There are five secrets for living intact.

SECRETS OF LIVING INTACT

Secret #1: Become a person who exercises self-control and compassion.

Secret #2: Take charge of habits. By understanding and influencing the way habits form, strengthen, and weaken and by taking advantage of the natural forces that govern them, you can change behaviors that run you, and you can greatly influence the habits of others. The goal is to break free from counterproductive habits so that you can make your life work better.

Secret #3: Modify the outcomes of your behaviors. Nature uses a method called reinforcement to ensure that mammals learn efficiently enough to survive and thrive. This process is the source and bedrock of your habits. Becoming familiar with the dynamics of reinforcement will put you in the driver's seat for modifying the outcomes of your counterproductive behaviors and those of others.

Secret #4: Eliminate your unwanted negative emotions. Negative emotions keep you stuck in bad habits, drive the mind narratives (i.e., the internal monologues) that justify failure, and derail attempts to change what you are doing that is not working. These negative emotions control and sustain bad habits and can be eliminated by changing the codes that link emotions to thoughts.

Secret #5: Embrace challenge as the way to turn obstacles and frustrations into opportunities and successes.

Yes, mastering and applying these "secrets" is easier said than done, but with guidance and practice, it's eminently doable. (More about applying "secrets" can be found in chapters 4–8.)

CHAPTER 3
BRIDGES BETWEEN SELF AND THE WORLD

Whereas expectations represent your pictures, records, and desires of how life is and should be, the bridges between yourself and your world represent the concrete connections you have established with your surroundings. These connections include your ability to manage yourself, handle frustration, control impulses and moods, put things into proper perspective, and interact appropriately and effectively in social, economic, and behavioral contexts.

These are the essential tools, skills, and operating instructions for living an intact life. The amalgam of distinctive interconnectedness, characteristics, and behaviors represents your strengths and weaknesses and provides the means for functioning within yourself and with others. For example, in order to confront and prevail over the challenges that are associated with a tendency to procrastinate when you're faced with doing chores around the house, completing paperwork, or preparing your tax return, you could deliberately choose to discipline yourself and do tasks that you find unpleasant. You could also carefully assess the potential risks of not replacing worn tires or not meeting an IRS deadline. This would entail recognizing and accepting your obligation to act responsibly and maturely and model positive behavior for your family.

HABITS

Most of us recognize the habits that have become entrenched in our life, and we also recognize the habits of those with whom we have an interpersonal relationship, such as our spouse, our children, our co-workers, and our friends. Habits make it easier to do things automatically, but they can be hard to change, even when you apply conscious effort. Habits may facilitate self-control and harmony, or they may induce conflict or dysfunction.

We may be typically even-keeled, or we may tend to be moody, stoic, passive, or easily frustrated. We may become unsettled by clutter, or we may be predisposed to creating clutter. We may procrastinate and be chronically late, or we may make it a habit to arrive on time or complete a project on or before a deadline. Our habits express our persona, personality, and relationship with the world, and they sum up how we present to the world and expect from it.

To understand habits, we can categorize them according to their function.

SELF HABITS

Our *self habits* reflect predispositions and learned skills to control and regulate our bodies and minds. Self habits allow us to adjust to changing conditions within ourselves and to challenges the world thrusts upon us.

Self habits allow us to function and maintain ourselves as independent beings. These capacities do not refer to biological or social functions *per se* (such as the ability to feed, dress, get around, or carry out responsibilities); rather, they refer to regulatory capacities that enable us to adjust to changing conditions and events both within and beyond our initiation or control. For example, your ability to remain composed in the face of an insult or threat requires the application of self habits, as does the ability to handle delays, or accept that the sale item you wanted to purchase is no longer on sale or no longer available. Were you to go ballistic or become dysfunctional when confronted with these situations, your self habits would become barriers to living intact. It is relatively easy to understand the biological necessity of maintaining body temperature and respiration. It may be more difficult to conceptualize self habits as representing the capability to maintain emotional temperature and not be devastated whenever life's events surprise, confront, scare, or disappoint.

In addition to the automatic biological adjustments of physiology, self habits furnish the rational analytical skills that permit us to observe the effects of how we act and to make context appropriate adaptations. Living intact requires that you develop and practice the skill of adjusting your perspective and reactions so that setbacks, frustrations, and disappointments do not become excessively disruptive. This capacity not to "sweat the small stuff," but instead to react objectively and detach from taking things too personally is essential; it is a self habit that constitutes a critically important category of responses called *permeability*. When you have permeability, you are able to let things that detract from intactness "pass though" your filters of overreactions and ego sensitivity.

Self habits include:

- Self-regulation
- Self-soothing
- Self-control
- Frustration tolerance
- Permeability

WORLD HABITS

World habits are the pragmatic common sense skills that help us operate effectively within ourselves and within our environment. They are the pool of resources upon which we draw to get things done, meet our needs, and apply effective behaviors and resources when interacting with the world around us. We rely on world habits when we make sensible decisions, make things happen, interface successfully with other people, express ideas, anticipate and evaluate outcomes, and create plans that involve others. Living intact requires productive contact with the world and entails the strategic application of judgment, reasoning, understanding, accurate predictions, awareness of the phenomenon of cause-and-effect, and goal-directed behaviors.

World habits include:

- Reasoning

- Reality testing
- Behavior exchange
- Communication of experience
- Commitment

INTEGRAL HABITS

Integral habits form the crossover between one's personal inner world and the world shared communally with those around us. Integral habits are about adjusting to, accepting, harmonizing, integrating, or accommodating ourselves to what is and what happens.

Integral habits enable us to sympathize or empathize with another's viewpoint, defer to the needs of others, and reaffirm our commitments, obligations, and promises. These habits prepare and reinforce our understanding of our own importance in the context of the world and the scheme of things.

Integral habits help us align more harmoniously with a universe that often operates against our wishes. They allow us to grow and make the most of our experiences so that we may live more fully intact.

Integral habits include:

- Spiritual perspective
- Integrity
- Connection with others at an emotional level
- Humility
- Developing purpose beyond oneself

WISDOM

Wisdom is a bridge between self and God. It allows us to understand the nature of life and the world, as God has created.

Wisdom is fundamental to living intact and to preserving life (Ecclesiastes 7:11–12). *Wisdom is more profitable than silver and gold. It is incomparable and blessed. It prolongs life and brings riches and honor* (Proverbs 3:13–18).

Consider wisdom your invitation to appreciate and participate in the orderliness of the universe, to be parented by knowledge and blessing, and to connect with human experience and godliness.

By seeking to live intact, you are intentionally choosing to identify and resolve the breakdowns, dissatisfactions, and discrepancies that often result from your desires for what life should be and your actual experiences of living life. This necessarily involves bridging a gap between the way you look at life and the way God does. Fortunately, God has given supernatural and natural means to bridge this gap. Wisdom embodies these means. (The topic of wisdom is examined more comprehensively in chapter 12.)

As you gain wisdom, you align yourself with God. You merge and transform your ideas and habits with those of God. You defer to him, revere him, and allow him to supply you with those things you cannot attain for yourself. You accept and delight in being his child, even as you grow toward greater maturity.

CHOICES

Choices are the engine that pushes us across the bridges. Choices are exercises in determining your shape. Just as eating choices and habits will greatly influence your physical shape, your attitudinal and proactive choices will, over time, form your character, the person you truly are. Life is replete with the challenge of making choices. Even abstention is a choice.

Choice is the continuing opportunity to individuate and form an identity, to exercise being you, to make a difference, and to make your mark on historical events.

You are the product of your genes, unforeseeable events, and the many combinations of possible interactions between you and the world. However, when it comes right down to it, *you* (the *real* you) are the result of the accumulation of choices you have made and continue to make throughout your life. Choice is the ultimate expression of self-control and free will.

Your choices determine the contributions you make and shape your character. To a large extent, choices influence what happens in your life. To an even greater extent, they determine your experience. People and circumstances may limit your options, but the choices are up to you.

CHALLENGES

Challenges are the fuel that propels us from here to there. They are the energy of life that must be harnessed and directed toward purpose.

Challenge is the mechanism God uses in nature to select and effectuate survival. It also fuels development and growth and stimulates human achievement.

An oyster is a good example of how the challenge process works in biological nature. It is the sand in the oyster—the irritant—that catalyzes the process of growth and refinement from which develops the stunning pearl. The challenges you face continually stimulate you to readjust, sidestep, and overcome obstacles as you progress through life. This is the challenge process. It is natural, to be expected (though not necessarily predictable), and embraceable. It is the mechanism for getting more out of life as life gets more out of you.

ADDING DEFINITIONS AND CATEGORIES

The relationship between the living intact secrets, elements, and habits (*self habits, world habits, and integral habits*) may seem complicated and confusing at first. The seeming complexity reflects the fact that the components are interconnected and holistic. Don't be discouraged by the introduction of new terms and concepts. They are like formulas in math that help you solve new problems by applying rules that consistently work. Each of these categories is discussed later in the book.

ISLANDS AND BRIDGES

It has been said that no man is an island. However, most of us, at times, have felt like an island and have experienced a sense of aloneness and isolation. At other times, we delight in being connected with others as we respond to life and explore how the world works. But even this "connectedness" can have a downside. We may feel crowded, imposed upon, or controlled by the very people who provide us companionship and, ironically, by the very circumstances that meet our needs and produce dependencies. We crave the security of family or community, but sometimes we want to escape the obligations, interactions, and expectations of those with whom we are intertwined. We hunger after a career and achievement, and yet sometimes we feel like running from the pressures, stress, anxieties, and responsibilities that are requisites to success.

Some theories of psychological development claim that we are driven by conflicting desires. We long to be independent and self-governed, but we also yearn for security and to be understood by others and connected to our family and peers by shared interests, goals, perceptions, and intimacies.

Clearly, each of us is distinct and unique, but not separate. We are isles connected to surrounding atolls—to ourselves, to the world and universe, and to God—by pathways and bridges. These emotional and spiritual highways have clearly marked lanes that allow us to proceed to a state of living intact. As we journey from brokenness to intactness, we must identify the destination, follow the map, pay attention to roads, read the signs, obey the traffic rules, and be alert to obstacles and roadblocks. And we must cross the bridges.

For some people, the bridges of interest traverse the gulf between self and others. This gulf can be a chasm of loneliness and external interpersonal problems, conflicts, and dissatisfactions. For others, the gulf reflects internal discord—a life filled with a shopping list of displeasures and ailments that emanate from within a self that is out of sync. Even when the self is ostensibly functioning and relationships with the external and internal world seem positive, there are still bridges to be crossed. These traverse the uncharted waters of spiritual development, the ongoing need for connection with the infinite, and the transition from who we are now into the person who encompasses all that we are meant to be.

In addition to the obvious pitfalls that imperil our physical and emotional well-being and threaten our security, the human condition comprises a range of ambiguities, ambivalences, and paradoxes that may prevent us from living intact. The metaphor of islands and bridges is a functional representation of an ongoing discovery process. By visualizing the islands and the bridges that cross a sea of challenges, we can simplify this process and more effectively learn how to apply the navigational principles and tactics that can allow us to live a more intact life.

In the following chapters, you will learn about each of the secrets and the elements that will permit you to use these secrets to your advantage. These secrets and elements are revealed in a top-down approach, much like showing you a working model and then giving you the parts and instructions for putting together your own working model.

Living intact is not exclusively about preventing all bad things from happening, though it does involve minimizing the effects of vulnerabilities, taking a proactive role in preventing bad things from happening by making astute choices, reconciling your inner narrative, understanding your habits, and accepting the reality of challenges. Nor is living intact preoccupied with the elimination of suffering, though it transforms it—as you will understand when you read the last chapter of this book. Living intact goes significantly beyond any convenient "reframing" of difficult circumstances to make them more palatable. Rather, it is a proactive and systematic engagement with life's challenges, using the challenge process to address and resolve the inherent breakdowns, dissatisfactions, and discrepancies that result from our desires for what life should be and our actual experiences living.

The phenomenon of challenge is integral for living intact. Challenge is what gets you to recognize the bridges and to cross them. Recognizing and using challenge to your advantage is the most all encompassing of the secrets described in this book. (Please note: challenge is examined more fully in chapter 8.)

LIVING INTACT ASSESSMENT

You may want to take the *Living Intact Assessment* that is designed to be an integral part of this book. To do so, visit www.livingintact. com. This online assessment will reveal your strengths and weaknesses in the areas of challenges, expectations, and self, world, and integral habits. The assessment will help you derive greater benefits from the living intact program and will provide you with baseline information about your intactness. You can take the assessment periodically as you apply the principles of *Living Intact* to gauge your progress along the journey.

II
PRACTICAL SECRETS (KEYS) FOR LIVING INTACT

CHAPTER 4
THE FIRST SECRET: DEVELOPING SELF-CONTROL AND COMPASSION

<u>Secret #1</u>: *To avail yourself of this secret you must be willing to make a conscious choice to rewrite your life's story line so that you become someone who exercises self-control and compassion. Learn how to relieve stress and discomfort in healthful ways and to tolerate discomfort when you must. In the process, you will change the negative narrative in your mind that comments nonconstructively, editorializes judgmentally, and criticizes continuously, and you will become more productive, loving, satisfied, and realistic.*

Many people spend their lives trying to gain control of themselves or of others. For some, this process functions as an obsessive quest to get a handle on fears, insecurities, mood swings, overreactions, hypersensitivity, or undesirable habits.

Certainly, the need for control plays an instrumental role in human survival and development. Having power over your own body, thoughts, emotions, and desires, and being self-regulated are essential to generating and maintaining purposeful activity and establishing productive interactions between you and the world. Paradoxically, in the desire to gain self-control and exert dominance, you may be lured into trying to micromanage your environment and the people with whom you interact. For example, you may want your children to comply automatically with all of your wishes, share unquestioningly your perceptions, and acquiesce to a set of lofty, comprehensive, and perhaps inflexible standards that you have established. Convinced that these standards are beneficial for them, for you, and for your family, you may feel justified in imposing your will and your control. But in your need to control, you may be "throwing out the baby with the bath water." Your children may ultimately revolt against your efforts to regulate and dictate every aspect of their lives. This example clearly underscores that the desire for control is a double-edged sword that can produce positive or negative outcomes depending on your motives, objectives, and methods of implementation.

As a general rule, seeking control to enhance self-esteem, confidence, or performance is constructive, especially when boundaries are established that respect the needs and sensitivities of others. Common examples include: negotiating to get a better deal, encouraging or even prodding others to better performance, or setting limits when others pressure you or try to impose values that conflict with your own. Achieving positive control, as opposed to obsessive, insecurity-driven control, requires insight, deliberate self-management, self-discipline, and a willingness to accept responsibility for one's behavior. In the previously cited example about raising children, one must realize that children do require rules, externally imposed discipline, and clearly defined standards of conduct. This basic tenet of child rearing necessitates imposing legitimate and justifiable parental control. But children must also be allowed opportunities to expand incrementally age-appropriate independence so that they can learn from their positive and negative experiences, acquire resiliency, develop judgment, and practice making choices that reflect an understanding of fundamental cause-and-effect principles. Exerting excessive or inappropriate control that is driven by a parent's own emotional needs interferes with this critically important developmental process.

The absence of control, however, can be equally disastrous. It is the other side of the double-edged sword that was previously mentioned. The person lacking self-control is at the mercy of his impulses and unregulated appetites and is easy prey for becoming consumed by a range of destructive emotions that may include hostility, self-pity, blaming, helplessness, and narcissistic feelings of unbridled privileges, prerogatives, and entitlement. The key in handling the "good" versus "bad" control conundrum is learning which edge of the sword to use and when to use it.

Scripture clearly highlights the critically important function of self-control in the process of living an intact and spiritually evolved life:

A person without self-control is as defenseless as a city with broken-down walls. (Proverbs 25:28)

He will die for lack of self-control; he will be lost because of his incredible folly. (Proverbs 5:23)

Knowing God leads to self-control. Self-control leads to patient endurance, and patient endurance leads to godliness. (2 Peter 1:6)

SELF-CONTROL, COMPASSION, AND VULNERABILITY

In much the same way that a swimmer would struggle against drowning and would instinctively grasp at anything or anyone within reach, a person struggling with his own self-control would instinctively attempt to compensate for his vulnerabilities. Clutching at anything or anyone within reach and desperately trying to regulate what is happening in and around him, he is likely to become fixated on finding something that can pacify his fears and insecurities and lessen the threat to his psychological stability. Preoccupied with escaping discomfort, establishing equilibrium, and seeking relief, the person's life could become consumed by obsessions, addictions, rituals, excuses, self-justifications, and an overpowering sense of entitlement. This emotional treadmill makes satisfaction impossible because the impulse to establish absolute control over one's world is not only unhealthy, but it is also unattainable.

Our earthly struggle with the interplay between establishing positive versus negative control is an integral part of the human condition and is a compelling enduring phenomenon; however, in the final analysis, only God possesses absolute control. Acceptance of this immutable reality provides a context for comfort and contentment, a state of being that is derived from restraint, realistic and functional limit setting, and the trustful yielding of control to the transcendental wisdom that emanates from the one true authority.

There is an antidote for the extreme and obsessive need for control. God provides us with a powerful tool to help us deal with the dilemma of wanting to be in control, but not always being able or fit to control. This tool is called *compassion*, and it is a quality that God amply demonstrates as an integral component of his teaching and love. Like the helpless swimmer who needs rescue, we may find ourselves at the mercy of circumstances, desperately trying to escape danger, but needing to reach for assistance. The best we can do is to recognize our own limitations and needs, accept the help that God offers, and do whatever we can to affect the outcome positively. Toward this end, the swimmer can swim parallel to the shore to escape a riptide, and the soldier in battle can duck for cover. Survival, be it physical or psychological, clearly is a shared burden. We exert what control we can to affect our fate; but in the end, God determines the outcome, and his compassion ultimately shows us the path and saves us. Using God's compassion as a model, are we not obligated, in turn, to extend our own compassion to others? In trusting God, we acknowledge his absolute authority, and by emulating his compassion, we acknowledge his righteousness. The help that we offer to others is not only physical, but it is also emotional and spiritual.

Compassion is forged from an awareness and sensitivity to our own vulnerabilities and tempered by those human qualities and conditions that expose us to hurt, damage, and brokenness. Compassion allows us to identify, accept, and connect with brokenness and to respond to it in ways that heal and lead to intactness. Much more than a substitute for control, our compassion is an essential element in the process of recognizing and affirming God's omniscient control and compassion in a world that can subject us periodically to insults and obstacles that would otherwise be overwhelming.

Compassion involves feelings of sympathy for the suffering of others, often including a desire to help. These feelings translate into choices and behaviors that you can deliberately invoke to alter the probability of a particular outcome. The Bible repeatedly refers to the vital role that compassion plays in attaining physical, psychological, and spiritual comfort and intactness.

The Lord is gracious and compassionate, slow to anger and rich in love. The Lord is good to all; he has compassion on all he has made. (Psalm 145:8–9)

I will betroth you to me forever; I will betroth you in righteousness and justice, in love and compassion. I will betroth you in faithfulness, and you will acknowledge the Lord. (Hosea 2:19–20)

Who is a God like you, who pardons sin and forgives the transgression of the remnant of his inheritance? You do not stay angry, but delight to show mercy. You will again have compassion on us; you will tread our sins underfoot and hurl all our iniquities into the depths of the sea. (Micah 18:19)

Because of the Lord's great love, we are not consumed, for his compassions never fail. (Lamentations 3:22)

Though he brings grief, he will show compassion, so great is his unfailing love. (Lamentations 3:32)

Finally, all of you, live in harmony with one another, be sympathetic, love as brothers, be compassionate and humble. Do not repay evil with evil or insult with insult, but with blessing, because to this you were called so that you may inherit a blessing. (1 Peter 3:8–9)

Therefore, as God's chosen people, holy and dearly loved. Clothe yourselves with compassion, kindness, humility, gentleness and patience. Bear with each other and forgive whatever grievances you may have against one another. Forgive as the Lord forgave you. (Colossians 3:12–13)

But you, O Lord, are a compassionate and gracious God, slow to anger, abounding in love and faithfulness. (Psalm 86:15)

The interplay of the key elements of compassion can be represented graphically:

Feeling of sympathy for suffering of others

|

Modeling on God's example — Compassion — Making behavioral choices

|

The desire to provide help

THE SIGNIFICANCE OF COMPASSION

Without sympathy and empathy, we are little more than predators and prey, spinning around on the roulette table of natural selection. Compassion fulfills our humanity and propels us to become something more: a greater likeness to the magnificent Creator whose compassion abounds in creation and in his dealings with us.

You may question the compassion of a God who allows a young soldier to be killed, leaving a family behind, or a child to be burned and disfigured in a fire. You may taste the bitterness of suffering and wonder at the apparent absence of God's compassion. I don't claim to have an explanation or solution for the missing pieces in a universe that stubbornly or indifferently ignores desperate pleas. I do know that God's compassion is demonstrable, if not circumstantially predictable, and that he allows both suffering and compassion to thread through our lives, weaving patterns that reveal the character of brokenness and the healing stitches that make us again intact and, perhaps, better and stronger for the despair and mending. (See chapter 19 "Must You Suffer?" for an expanded discussion.)

Compassion is God's gift to us. He wants us to accept it, to bathe in its cleansing qualities, and to offer it to others. Compassion washes away the grime of life's hardship; it makes over ugliness and softens harshness; it reduces the friction caused by unlovable people; it builds bridges to reach the untouchable and manage the unthinkable. Imagine the miraculous power that transforms hatred into understanding, acceptance, and connection—such as in the transformation made by some crime victims when, for example, they forgive and relate to the killer of a family member—and you will marvel at the power of compassion to transform your struggles.

Only a rare few would suffer the trauma and achieve the compassion of forgiveness for a person who kills a family member. The brutality and proximity of this most extreme and despicable act would certainly test the limits of human compassion. Less horrific, but certainly compelling, examples of situations that can severely challenge our capacity for compassion abound. A far more common case in point is dealing with the heartbreak that results when a child has gone seriously astray. This situation necessitates having to confront the dilemma of needing to set limits and maintain standards while also meeting the challenge of experiencing and extending compassion. For example, the parent whose child is using drugs or is stealing knows all too well the agony of having to confront such a heartrending predicament. God understands this, and he provides a model for compassion and reconciliation. In the Gospel of Luke, Jesus tells the story of the prodigal son of a wealthy man who left home and squandered his father's wealthy gift in wild living (Luke 15:13). Soon thereafter, the son found himself starving. He returned home, ashamed and not knowing how he would be received.

> *"When he came to his senses, he said, 'How many of my father's hired men have food to spare, and here I am starving to death! I will set out and go back to my father and say to him: Father, I have sinned against heaven and against you. I am no longer worthy to be called your son; make me like one of your hired men.' So he got up and went to his father."*
> (Luke 15:17–19)

By the standards of the man's other son, the older brother who had been obedient, the father should have become indignant, angry, and non-accepting of the wayward son, as was the obedient brother who was envious, resentful, and angry (Luke 15:25–31). We can find modern parallels in today's attitudes of indignation, self-righteousness, and entitlement. However, Jesus recounts the father's compassionate response:

> *"But while he was a long way off, his father saw him and was filled with compassion for him; he ran to his son, threw his arms around him and kissed him."* (Luke 15:20)

A STORY ABOUT REVISING MY OWN LIFE

Let me give you an example of how compassion developed in my own life. For about forty years, intense conflict and mutual feelings of resentment and neglect characterized my relationship with my father. My dad was harsh, critical, insensitive, and indifferent to my interests. I was unwilling to relinquish the evidence that he belittled my achievements and that his need to dominate, his marginal social skills, and limited expression of compassion deprived me of the emotional support and role modeling I deserved.

My father had enjoyed an extremely close relationship with his own father (they even shared a dental practice), and my dad was obedient in taking instruction and guidance from his father, seldom veering from the prescribed course. My dad longed for a similar relationship with me— one in which I would accept, assimilate, and employ his wisdom and do things his way with little question. He was disappointed when I showed no interest in dentistry, and my independence and risk taking further vexed him. As a teenager, I moved away from home, only to return for short contentious visits over the decades.

Though he was a good provider and I was a high achiever, my father and I deprived each other of what we needed. I, at least, remained hurt and angered by his stubborn refusal to cease his constant needling and manipulation.

As I assumed a parental role in my own family, I began to see my dad's behavior from a different perspective. The work of raising my sons showed me the daunting complexities of being a good parent. I had enormous advantages in understanding behavior and human development, garnered through years of professional training and dedicated interest. Yet applying this knowledge to building good relationships with my children was very challenging. Gradually, I came to appreciate how overwhelming fatherhood was for my dad since he had precious few resources or good models for parenting successfully. Additionally, my dad had personal problems that went untreated and made him the subject of ridicule. He was a sufferer of lifelong depression (undiagnosed medically until he was seventy-five years old) and a victim of dozens of serious allergies and phobias. His intractable eczema and reactions to numerous common foods caused continual anguish, and he avoided unfamiliar things by resorting to fearful withdrawal.

While growing up, I had blamed my father for his spoilsport idiosyncrasies. Even as a young adult, I joined in the family pastime of joking about his quirks and irritable ways. I just assumed the role of defending myself against the insulting and intrusive mannerisms my father offered in his bids for relationship. If he was going to persist in being that hurtful, I simply wasn't interested. Yet despite his own eccentricities and selfish habits, he was paradoxically a keen observer of others' foibles—a characteristic I learned to value increasingly over the years.

When I was about forty years old, the stresses between my mother and father increased to the point where she planned to leave him. Instead, they lived together for fifty-two years until his death. She confided in me that the man she had really wanted to marry (and to whom she had been engaged) was killed in World War II. My father stepped in as second best, a role that must have haunted him throughout their marriage. Through these insights and realizations, I learned to have compassion for my father, a good but troubled man, torn and frustrated throughout his life by things he couldn't understand, control, or overcome. Even though he continued to harangue me throughout his days, my attitude and behavior toward him changed long before he passed away. Instead of avoiding him, I reserved more energy for buffeting his tirades. I did this out of love and especially the recognition that no one else would put up with him and that he needed contact and interaction. Compassion allowed me to see myself as strong and useful in our relationship, rather than as a punching bag. When I set limits for my dad (in practically every conversation), I did so by focusing on the present interaction, rather than a replay of old complaints and arguments. Instead of permitting him to harangue me by repeating past assaults on my character and reputation ("I've told you over and over again: you don't know the value of a dollar!") and defending myself by airing my own grievances ("Dad, you always criticize me without understanding my point of view."), I began to constrain the conversation to the here and now ("Dad, we're talking about whether to eat out and where everybody would feel comfortable. This is about enjoying dinner together, not my spending habits."). I became more constructive than critical (e.g., "Dad, I have to go now because I don't want our conversation to cause me to focus on my resentments rather than on my concern for you. Watch that video I recorded for you, and we'll talk again next time when you are in a better mood.").

Compassion changed my feelings, too, about both my father and myself. I eventually understood that the years I spent proving myself and fending off Dad's control were actually choices that allowed me to become independent rather than remain in a state of constant rebellion against his authority. He was simply a smart but unhappy man, trying to steer his son and protect me from life's dangers, intrusions, and brokenness. My belated realization that, ironically, his responses reflected his own profound brokenness ultimately tempered my knee-jerk reactions to his chronic criticism and intolerance. Besides forgiving him and laughing at his mistakes (and not at him), my heart cried out in compassion for the limited successes he had in dealing with challenges in his own life. By exercising compassion, I could, during the last decade of his life, relate to my father within the limits of which he was capable, and I could engage with and detach from his caustic manner with an acceptable sense of my own volition and flexibility.

APPLYING COMPASSION TO ATTAIN ENHANCED SELF-CONTROL

A vital element in establishing healthy and reasonable self-control involves intentionally embracing and developing compassion. Whereas the common meaning of compassion is that of feeling sympathy for the suffering of others, often including a desire to help, living intact invites an expansion of the traditional meaning. This expansion underscores the relevance of compassion in establishing healthy self-control by intentionally identifying with other people who affect your life and influence your choices and responses. Compassion is a behavior that you can deliberately invoke to alter the probability of a particular outcome. A concrete example of compassion might involve a deliberate tolerant response to a rude sales clerk or an aggressive driver on the freeway. Other examples might involve deliberately choosing to maintain your equanimity while having to deal with seemingly mindless bureaucrats, having to navigate telephone systems with their endless menus, or being kept endlessly on hold while trying to speak with a live person about a problem. As everyone knows, these incidents can test your mettle and forbearance. Compassion can be a powerful resource in these trying situations and can be used to mitigate the frustration and exasperation and defuse the anger that may be welling up inside of you.

Compassion is not only a feeling that wells from within you, but it can also reflect a conscious decision to respond in a particular way. Compassion involves deliberately discerning and sympathizing with the possible *vulnerabilities* of others, even if they are victimizing you and your natural reaction is to protect yourself and perhaps even strike back. The rude sales clerk may have had an argument with her husband that morning; the aggressive driver may be late for an important meeting because of unanticipated traffic. Of course, when you are on the receiving end of discourtesy, insensitivity, or aggressiveness, the last thing that comes to mind is your antagonist's possible suffering and vulnerability. However, compassion can actually rescue you from being controlled by the transgressions of others and your own tendencies to react negatively to them. It can allow you to transcend automatic reactions of explosive or slow-burning anger when you are mistreated. This is what turning the other cheek is all about.

The driver who cuts you off or who won't let you into a lane can quickly spark a flame of hostility and an internal dialogue that continue well beyond the traffic incident. How easy is it for you to respond to his behavior by considering that he has his own issues that may be driving his behavior?

What about the person who impudently steps in front of you in line and then becomes snide when you say, "Excuse me..." In an even more extreme scenario, what of those who rob, mock, belittle, or cheat you or the ones you love? Do these people deserve your compassion? An interesting dynamic often presents itself: people who mistreat you and trigger resentment within you may be able to justify or push their misbehavior from their consciousness while you must struggle mightily to overlook and forgive the injustice. Forgiveness is not the only issue that's involved. Your ability to weather life's petty or even major abuses by choosing to take charge of your responses is a core element in opening the door leading to an intact life. Compassion is the key to the door. What may seem at first counterintuitive and contradictory to the reflexive "don't mess with me or else" values that our culture models and extols on TV and in "action movies" will, over time and with practice and repetition, become an accessible and powerful countervailing force. This force neutralizes negativity and vehemence, soothes the spirit, and prevents spiritually debilitating intrusions that subvert graceful, intact living.

Compassion is an elevated and eminently attainable—and even God-like—state of mind and set of responses that are within the grasp of any person who seeks to live a more intact life. In effect, compassion is the brass ring that beckons us as we turn on life's carousel. All we need do is stretch, reach out, maintain our balance and resolve, and seize the ring.

On a practical level, self-directed compassion and other-directed compassion are all-purpose tools that soften the harshness and stings of life. Self-directed compassion gives us the flexibility to accept and adjust to the things we cannot change, the parts of life that do not go our way. It gives you the strength to tolerate adversity, rejection, and all manner of hardship. Other-directed compassion creates a context for tolerance and forbearance.

The practice of being compassionate can be confusing because our society gives mixed messages about it. On the one hand, the message is that we should be caring and considerate of others (especially the less fortunate) and that it is noble to respect and emulate the sacrifice and compassion of spiritual leaders such as Mother Theresa. On the other hand, the street-savvy, practical, grab-what-you-can mentality that suffuses our modern age admonishes us to live in the "real world" where compassion could be construed as weakness that diminishes us and deters us from asserting ourselves, setting legitimate limits and boundaries, and imposing justifiable consequences for real or perceived transgressions. We are told, "You shouldn't let them play on your sympathy." "Put your foot down." "Be tough." "Report her to her supervisor." "Get him fired." Despite these worldly messages, don't be misled by the simplistic comparison of compassion with weakness or naiveté. Compassion has nothing to do with gullibility, powerlessness, self-pity, stoicism, or people pleasing. Rather than expose an Achilles' heel, compassion actually reveals your power. It profoundly connects you with your humanity and godliness, and it allows you to respond gracefully to the weaknesses and vulnerabilities of others. Compassion prevents you from being ruled by fear, driven into self-protecting isolation, consumed by anger or rage, or from becoming overly reactive to illusory or imagined threats. It is a both a palliative and an antidote for potentially destructive fervor that distances you from God.

You need not be apprehensive about safety or security when you feel compassion. You have natural defenses that kick in when true dangers threaten you or when compelling negative issues thwart you that you must address decisively and proactively. As you react or prepare to respond, your mind will automatically supply a narrative that explains and justifies your response. For example, when someone at the restaurant pushes ahead of you, though you actually arrived first and have been waiting patiently, it is natural for your mind to justify the indignation, resentment, and anger you may experience by focusing on the offender's bad character and behavior. Or when someone is rude to you, the behavior might trigger your defense mechanisms. No one enjoys feeling disrespected or belittled, and the common response is to protect oneself from the behavior. At issue is how can you transition from the immediate anger/upset response to a more enlightened compassionate response? Compassion serves not only to reduce aggression and to salve social friction, but also to fashion a reality check on whether your tendencies to magnify, distort, or misperceive are causing you to overreact.

NARRATIVES TELL THE STORY

Your mind has the ability to adapt its "story" flexibly to your passions, beliefs, momentary emotions, and internal state of arousal. This story or narrative is the interpretive sum of what is perceived, evoked, and imprinted as you respond to life's machinations. The ability to construct this story is basic to survival and allows you to interpret events and integrate them into your world. Your mind uses an internal language that narrates your thoughts, opinions, perceptions, and feelings. We all have this internal dialogue, this running commentary that operates continuously; it is part of being conscious. I call this internal dialogue "the narrative," but it can also be referred to by different names, such as the editor, the voice-over, or the announcer.

The narrative is always switched on, and it can keep you quite busy. Often, it operates in the background, speaking about what's happening, interpreting events, giving opinions, cracking jokes, making sarcastic comments, discussing feelings, passing evaluations, and announcing upcoming intentions and anticipations. Examples include: "He's an idiot." "He's going to cheat me and charge me a fortune for this repair." "I'll turn on the charm." "She'll accept my proposal." "How can he not give me the raise I requested?" The narrative is like a familiar sportscaster, although sometimes its presence is uninvited and unappreciated, even by the mind that hosts it. Occasionally, it can get pretty noisy inside your head when the narrative argues with countervailing opinions that somehow show up. Sometimes, it even gets into a brawl with intrusive thoughts shouting to be heard and competing for your attention. And when the conscience presents its case, you can feel like you're caught in a traffic jam at rush hour, bound to be late again, and you can become preoccupied with the stress of making it through the next traffic light before it turns red. When this internal dialogue and incessant chatter become loud and conflicting, it is very difficult to feel intact.

Even if it's noisy or uncomfortable, the narrative serves a useful purpose in that it helps you maintain a cohesive and sequential story about what's going on. The narrative is the descriptive embodiment of the characteristics you identify with as your "self." When this self—you— becomes threatened or *perceives* a threat, you experience a reaction that combines visceral physiological response (usually heightened arousal) with emotional sensation. If a threat is perceived, the attached emotions are always negative. This is an instinctive response, and sometimes it can save you. Most often, however, negative emotions are an overreaction and, unfortunately, an adverse response to a challenge. Defenses are mounted, and the mind begins to concoct its story that is designed to protect itself and justify the nervous system's reaction.

When someone cuts you off in traffic, causing your heart to pound involuntarily in what appears to be a malicious discourtesy, you are apt to react with aggressive thoughts, emotions, and impulses to what your mind assures you is a deliberate offense by that *jerk...!* Your narrative is typically immediate, supportive, creative, and *credible* as it attempts to assist you with responding to this assault on your nervous system. It rushes to assist you in time of need, extracting evidence and arguments from your library of beliefs, attitudes, experiences, and logic—all the while subsuming the fact that it is your state of heightened arousal and programmed response to the nervous system assault that is actually eliciting the narrative. Your narrative might then rationalize and justify your response to the situation.

Though self-protective and self-justifying reactions are instinctive, they are likely to spark additional discourtesy and aggression and to feed negative thinking, vengefulness, and self-pity, and could lead to potential injury. Your mind's ability to adapt flexibly and lithely its "story" and the associated passions and beliefs carries with it a downside. Inconsiderate and insensitive behavior breeds reciprocal inconsiderate and insensitive behavior. The acceleration of this reactive, self-justifying, and counterproductive cycle can become *addictive*. The intertwining of your emotional defensiveness, your narrative self-justification, and the social reinforcement that encourages "getting even" tends to promote a subconscious[4] chain reaction. This combination response is "delicious" in the way that adrenalin feels pleasurable when it pumps you up. A sad truth is that anger, indignation, sarcasm, and scorn can feel good and can feign temporary control when aimed outward with sufficient skill and intensity. You can appear "in charge" by responding with aggression or bluster, as you watch an opponent retreat or hesitate. Your narrative will pat you on the back for being assertive. However, problems arise when the reaction continues, particularly in response to imagined or exaggerated perceptions of threat or supposed disrespect.

The temptation to follow this self-justifying narrative that rationalizes hostile behavior leads to a habitual increase in aggression. Following this path will produce more justifications, rationalizations, and selective perceptions to confirm what you already believe about the other person's character and motives. It will also incur heightened fight-or-flight arousal—which not only is deleterious to your mental and physical health, but also increases isolation and defensiveness. The provocations that spawn self-justifying narratives apply to a range of negative emotions besides anger. Fear, inhibition, jealousy, insecurity, etc., can all trigger reactions that result in a cascade of aggression, defensiveness, or withdrawal.

This loop of experiencing affront, reacting emotionally, and justifying noncompassionate responses is a common phenomenon. But its continuation is not inevitable. The reactive process can be interrupted and defused at any point along the way. However, the more each reaction accelerates and the more habitual the process becomes, the more natural it seems and the harder it is to break the cycle. The solution is to change the likelihood of the acceleration by introducing a response that is incompatible with the tempting and seemingly automatic process. Certain deliberate responses to negative stimuli can slow down and can often interrupt and defuse the automatic nature of habit patterns and deescalate mounting aggression. Asking yourself certain questions may be useful: *What is the*

---

4. Although the terms *subconscious* and *unconscious* are similar, there are slightly different connotations to each. *Subconscious* refers to mental activity that is present in your mind without your being aware of it. These memories, feelings, and thoughts can influence your behavior without you realizing it. Subconscious activity can be brought to consciousness through deliberate intention, practice, and meditative or therapeutic techniques. *Unconscious* material is mental activity that is inaccessible to you directly, but that may represent itself in dreams or dissociations and may influence your perceptions, decisions, and experiences.

threat posed by this person's behavior? What would really happen if I didn't respond? What risks are there in not responding for a period of time? What would it take/cost for me to respond uncharacteristically by being nice or accommodating? If I could respond in a Godlike manner, what would that look like? If I respond in a compassionate, rather than defensive or self-justifying manner, what will be my reward?

Alternatively, if you are in the habit of self-deprecation or are overly timid, you might question your automatic responses to a challenge that makes you feel downgraded and spurs you to withdraw. *What if I spoke up and offered my feelings? What would happen if I simply asked about the subjective intent of the person who has offended me?*

The very act of introducing questions into your internal routine involves choice (more about this in later chapters), and it may not fit, at first, with your emotions. If you are not given to introspection, stopping to question yourself may be quite a departure from your normal repertoire. The process will, however, give you more options, a broader range of responses, and more eventual choices about how you react to threat or challenge. And it will serve the purpose of slowing and disrupting the primitive, ingrained, fearful, fight-or-flight, circle-the-wagons, defensive reactions that can quickly escalate and lead to highly dysfunctional emotional scenarios.

You can deliberately disrupt maladaptive reactions by choosing to change your negative overt behaviors or, alternatively, by engaging directly with the supervising narrative. Acting graciously when you are feeling angry is not hypocritical or disingenuous. Rather, it is a willful decision to alter positively the narrative that is driving the anger by willfully transforming its tone into one that is incompatible with anger or aggression. It is also possible to interrupt the internal narrative and soothe it or reason with it. Minds are amazingly impressionable, and changing your mind can be a sign of bravery and independence, rather than one of seeming cowardice, fear, anxiety, and indecision. Consider the saying: *The longest distance between two points is that between the mind and the heart.* This, indeed, is the journey of compassion. Many people spend the better part of a lifetime trying to bridge this distance—some by choosing a path that joins the mind and heart (as in developing feelings, awareness, and empathy), and some by choosing a path that maintains a connection with proper boundaries and separation (as in exercising compassion without letting rampant emotions overrule reason and judgment). Both paths work either alone or in tandem. Yes, it is difficult to resist temptation and deliberately counteract natural tendencies. A frequently uncooperative world triggers self-defeating, countercompassionate behavior by dangling temptation and exploiting our all-too-human vulnerabilities.

Willful compassion is the antidote for the emotionally harmful reactions that cause brokenness and dissociation with our humanity and our spirituality. In tandem with focused interventions to modify internal arousal responses, purposeful compassion allows us to alter our feelings and behaviors and, by so doing, actually change many of the unpleasant behaviors and responses of others, even those of our adversaries whose behaviors, feelings, and attitudes formerly may have appeared to be chiseled in stone. It may take time, but others will find it difficult to continue to treat you ungraciously or unkindly in the face of your compassion. Regardless of what others do—even the ones who give you a hard time— you will feel much better about yourself and conduct yourself with greater intactness when you convey grace, forgiveness, and compassion, without letting the circumstance dictate your attitude.

If you are like the vast majority of people in the world, you have, on occasion, undoubtedly been wounded by situations in your life. You may have suffered an injustice, rejection, and lack of caring or appreciation. You may have been mistreated in spite of your good intentions. Many of your grievances may have gone unrequited. You may have been snubbed or disrespected by people who matter and by people who really don't matter at all. Yet you are called by God to love all people, even the ones who act like jerks and who treat you abominably. Despite the affronts and mistreatment, compassion summons us to find forgiveness, and this forgiveness permits us to transcend the injuries we suffer.

DEVELOPING COMPASSION

How do you develop compassion? Amazingly, compassion develops from your own experience of receiving it from others. Compassion is the original "gift that keeps on giving." When you experience mercy, forgiveness, and compassion, you become humbled because you understand that these gifts do not depend on your efforts or merit. Rather, compassion is extended to you based on the intuitive sense that others have about your essential needs and vulnerabilities. This response is modeled on the compassion that God has for all he has created (Psalm 145:8–9).

These gifts and mercies impel you to want to give to others the joy and blessing that you yourself have experienced. The only catch is that you have to be willing and able to receive and experience compassion. This capacity can be impeded because of deficiencies during early development, traumatic experiences, or a freewill decision to remain emotionally insulated. The phenomenon is often attributable to being deprived of nurturing parental compassion during childhood or later in life from one's significant relationships. Though this is tragic, it need not irrevocably stymie the capacity to receive and provide compassion throughout life. Highly effective spiritual and secular therapeutic paths can heal the obstructions (see also chapters 8 and 15). The secular therapeutic remedies are powerful, but they are not substitutes for a personal relationship with God. These remedies, however, can greatly assist in hearing and being receptive to God's communication. In tandem, focused therapy and spiritual enlightenment furnish potent, accessible instruments for enhancing compassion and achieving alignment with God's plan for intactness.

God gives the best living examples of his extraordinary capacity to express and model all-embracing compassion through his Word (the Bible), the person of Jesus Christ, and through his Holy Spirit. These mark the way for you to experience compassion in your everyday circumstances. God wants to relieve your discomfort, and he gives you spiritual and secular tools to do so. He wants to strengthen you through trials and tests so that you may attain endurance and tolerance. He wants you to proactively rewrite your life story and to allow you to be filled with compassion in carrying on and flourishing despite hardships. This is called transformation.

Consider 2 Corinthians 4:7–9:
But we have this treasure in jars of clay to show that this all-surpassing power is from God and not from us. We are hard pressed on every side, but not crushed; perplexed, but not in despair; persecuted but not abandoned; struck down, but not destroyed.

And Romans 5:2–5:

And we rejoice in the hope of the glory of God. Not only so, but we also rejoice in our sufferings, because we know that suffering produces perseverance; perseverance, character; and character, hope. And hope does not disappoint us, because God has poured out his love into our hearts by the Holy Spirit, whom he has given us.

In sum, you develop compassion by receiving it and experiencing it. A relationship with God is the best model, and God works through people. Compassion is God given, and when you experience it, you are receiving the gift of God through others. The natural response to this is to become grateful and eager to share it with others. As a practical guide for the ways you can open yourself up to compassion, consider the following:

1. Acknowledge your own vulnerabilities, thereby facilitating your identification with the foibles, mistakes, and intrusions of others. Encourage empathy in yourself and others by tolerating weakness and imperfection, recognizing similarities in the human struggle and downplaying defensiveness and aggression.

2. Pray for others and for your own ability and willingness to forgive them for their trespasses. Ask God to intervene and do what you find it hard to do. Humble yourself before God's power, justice, mercy, and love.

3. Practice revising the narrative in your mind so that it allows for the vulnerabilities of others and gives them the benefit of the doubt regarding their own selfishness. Embrace the context of forgiveness and God's sufficiency for you to forbear insult, trespass, even injury. Strengthen the connection and shorten the distance between your mind and your heart.

4. Recognize that you have an important role in modeling compassion for others. People identify with those close to them, and many behaviors are learned and copied from others. You are more influential than you may have realized. If you are a parent, think of the examples you want to set for your child.

Responding compassionately, interrupting the cycle of escalating self-justification and aggression, and revising the narrative in your mind are all facilitated by the context that God has given in his Word. When you need a substitute response to reprogram the maladaptive habit, why not use the narrative that God has already supplied? This approach works magnificently. Consider, for example, Paul's words in I Corinthians 13:4–7:

> *Love is patient, love is kind. It does not envy, it does not boast, it is not proud. It is not rude, it is not self-seeking, it is not easily angered, it keeps no record of wrongs. Love does not delight in evil but rejoices with the truth. It always protects, always trusts, always hopes, always perseveres.*

MAKING REVISIONS IN YOUR LIFE

You may not be able to overwrite the actual events in your personal history, but you can rewrite and interpret how these events affect your perception, behavior, and attitudes. Though you may have already been exposed to various behavioral methods of "reframing" or reinterpreting experiences, reliance on these techniques exclusively may fall short of rendering you to be a person who possesses self-control and compassion.

The technique of cognitive reframing is a case in point. This is an accepted psychotherapeutic technique in which the client substitutes thoughts or evaluations that have a more positive spin than the client's habitual inner dialogue. For example, instead of complaining about how hopeless life seems or how poorly one performed, through cognitive reframing the person posits self-statements such as: "I will do better next time—this wasn't such a disaster." "I have three things to look forward to in the next week..." "My parents weren't so bad—after all, I am functioning very well on my own..." "I shouldn't take it personally—he's probably having a hard day."

Cognitive reframing can be useful in redirecting embedded negative thought loops, changing expectations, and developing greater flexibility, but it requires the power and sensitivity of compassion to engage and reconstitute thoughts that have become part of the fabric of your identity and sense of self. Mere self-directed statements that attempt to override the subconscious cannot empower you in the way that connecting and empathizing with the needs of others can. Certainly, the cognitive activity that forms your narrative is important and can be directly altered. However, in order to revise your interpretation of how the past fits with your current and future choices, you must integrate the emotional "language" that tells your mind and body where you really stand. For example, you may experience the frustration of thinking/feeling/believing that nothing you do will be "good enough" for a particular person in your life—someone you have tried hard to please or satisfy. Emotionally, you are motivated to deliver the goods, do the right thing, and receive appreciation. However, rational evaluation of your experience leads you to conclude that, no matter what you do (and you have tried many approaches), it won't be quite good enough for the other person. So you are stuck in conflict, ambivalence, frustration, and resentment. A good and flexible solution to this dilemma involves the combined approach of changing your self-statements and evaluations of events and the emotional impact they have upon you. This is the language that integrates and mediates your mind/body split and resolves the power struggle between your visceral instincts and your self-protective defenses. Imagine, for instance, that this is your internal narrative:

> *"I have tried for so long to make my partner sensitive to my needs. I have been patient, responsive, constant, and loving. I have explained things and shown him the effects of his behavior. He has promised many times to change his ways, but has not fulfilled his pledges. I, on the other hand, have bent over backward to do what he asks. Yet he doesn't show appreciation or even recognition for my efforts. He always has some complaint or new hoop for me to jump through. I'm resentful and tired of it. This is typical. Why do I put up with it? Does he think I don't matter? Why aren't I good enough? Is this what I deserve? I'm sick of trying!"*

Now, consider substituting the following inner dialogue for the preceding negatively charged narrative that currently governs your thoughts and feelings:

> *"I have a problem because my expectations aren't being met. They seem reasonable to me, yet it's clear that my efforts are not working. I have a great deal of resentment about this, which I need to acknowledge. I'm not going to stuff away my feelings. Continuing to nurse my grievances will not be productive, nor will it make me feel better over time. I may not be able to change my partner (though I really want to!). But I can change several things, and I have choices. My partner's stubbornness devastates my motivation, so I find it hard to keep trying. One choice is whether I keep trying, knowing that he probably won't reward me. So is there any other*

reward I can find that doesn't depend on his appreciation—say, my own satisfaction in the fact that I've been considerate and graceful? I suppose I would have to change my outlook and wounded feelings in order to have that reward. How can I do that? How long would it take? How would my partner react if I didn't get offended and respond in the way that has been scripted? My partner probably has feelings and opinions that he won't share easily with me because he knows I don't want to hear them or agree with them. I bet that's a problem for him. I can sympathize with that problem (even though I think he's mistaken and willful). I know what it's like to be willful. I hate it when people are willful and contrary. Just to be flexible, generous, avoid unnecessary conflict, and improve myself, I'm going to be less willful toward him. Maybe he'll get it. I'm not going to depend upon his reaction to determine my motivation, although I recognize that I'm human and, therefore, am affected by his responses or lack of them. God doesn't always respond immediately when I want, but I know that he observes me and sees and hears my needs, motivations, and my heart."

Compassion makes this more rational and more functional inner dialogue possible. It provides greater emotional equanimity, releases you from inflamed reactive emotions, and allows you to exert the self-control, restraint, and more deliberately measured and regulated responses. This is the essence of intentionally applied self-discipline. If you think of cognitive reframing and the narrative as the steering mechanism, then compassion would be the command mechanism that allows you to brake, accelerate, and regulate your thoughts, feelings, and behavior.

The intertwining of compassion and self-control creates a context for choice. In order to have free choice about your beliefs and to base your actions and your values on wise judgment and rationality along with empathy and sensitivity, you must integrate compassion and self-control. As you seek to live intact, you are faced with a constant challenge: you must accommodate the events in your life as they pass through the filter of emotional arousal. Compassion is instrumental in meeting this challenge because it helps you mediate emotional over-arousal and the reflex of self-justifying narratives. Revising your life becomes possible when you learn and practice the skills and behaviors that regulate your internal arousal and reduce or eliminate negative emotions and distress. This self-regulation will allow you to transcend discomfort, pain, fixations, compulsions, fears, insecurities, negative thoughts, catastrophic expectations, and suffering.

Easily said, but perhaps you are skeptical. You may have tried medications (prescribed or otherwise), pursued therapy, and applied self-discipline, and you may still find that being able to control yourself, circumstances, and habits remains elusive and seemingly hopeless. Your reservations about being able to achieve self-regulation may be understandable, but consider the following information with an open mind.

There are two vital elements in the process of establishing reasonable and healthy self-control that will help you immensely, regardless of your past attempts to successfully manage yourself and your responses to negative stimuli emanating from within you (for example, specific job-related insecurities) and from the world outside of you (for example, a tyrannical boss). One element entails the easy-to-master regimen of deliberately practicing *self-regulation* and *self-soothing*. These are broad terms for self-management modifications that allow your body and mind to achieve or rebound to normal, functional states of dealing with your internal and external challenges (for example, demands, responses, rest and work rhythms, disruptions—in other words, the phenomenon of challenges). *Continuous* self-management modification occurs at a neurophysiological level (such as when a muscle relaxant loosens up general tension or tightness, or when supplements help your body replenish lost nutrients). You probably already practice self-management that involves active conscious physical interventions, such as massaging a cramp or intentionally breathing deeply to calm yourself. The second vital element in establishing healthy and reasonable self-control involves intentionally embracing and developing compassion.

For now, suffice it to say that although there are numerous ways to fortify your tolerance or relieve yourself from discomfort and pain, my experience with thousands of patients shows that two unique methodologies—EEG neurofeedback and Thought Field Therapy—have proven remarkably effective. During the last twenty years of my clinical practice, these procedures have helped literally thousands of individuals achieve and maintain higher states of mental, emotional, physical, and spiritual functioning and satisfaction than they've ever had and have repeatedly demonstrated their efficacy in eliminating emotional and physiological discomforts and, in the end, providing greater self-control and freedom from negative symptoms. (See chapters 9 and 10 for more information about these highly effective therapeutic interventions.)

DISCOMFORT AND COMPASSION: THE DANCE OF BODY AND MIND

Living intact does not mean that you smother discomfort or sweep it under the rug. Nor does it mean that you blithely and blindly resign your malaise to the "will of God." Living intact involves an active interaction between you, your environment, your circumstances, and the Creator. This regular contact will eliminate and relieve discomfort and displeasure, provide tolerance and acceptance of adversity and discomfort, and spur the development and use of compassion to bridge the abyss between your own survival and pain-avoiding self-interests.

My father used to say, "Life looks different and opinions sound different on a full stomach." This axiom aptly describes a hidden aspect of living intact: the mind follows the internal state of physiology, yet the mind proudly flaunts itself as the leader. It is so tempting and easy to think that opinions are based on high moral principles when, in actuality, life looks rosier or ideas seem more realistic because your body and nervous system are feeling good. In describing the allocation and balance of spiritual gifts and social harmony, the apostle Paul uses a striking analogy that can well be applied to the balance of mind narratives and physiological self-regulation. Consider 1 Corinthians 12:14–26, where Paul argues:

> Now the body is not made up of one part but of many. If the foot should say, "Because I am not a hand, I do not belong to the body," it would not for that reason cease to be a part of the body. And if the ear should say, "Because I am not an eye, I do not belong to the body," it would not for that reason cease to be a part of the body. If the whole body were an eye, where would the sense of hearing be? If the whole body were and ear, where would the sense of smell be? But in fact God has arranged the parts of the body, every one of them, just as he wanted them to be. If they were all one part, where would the body be? As it is, there are many parts, but one body.
>
> The eye cannot say to the hand, "I don't need you." And the head cannot say to the feet, "I don't need you!" On the contrary, those parts of the body that seem to be weaker are indispensable, and the parts that we think are less honorable we treat with special honor. And the parts that are unpresentable are treated with special modesty, while our presentable parts need no special treatment. But God has combined the members of the

body and has given greater honor to the parts that lacked it, so that there should be no division in the body, but that its parts should have equal concern for each other. If one part suffers, every part suffers with it; if one part is honored, every part rejoices with it.

When the mind and body argue or engage in competition for control, you are bound to suffer. When you are duped by the tendency to rationalize or somaticize (i.e., become preoccupied with physical complaints and discomfort that substitute for facing or resolving other issues), you are in conflict with yourself and are attempting to resolve the conflict by the arbitrary delegation of authority or supremacy to one part of yourself. But God's design is one of integration, reconciliation, and self-regulation. Compassion is often the mediator.

In broad terms, when you are balanced, compassionate, and able to tolerate, empathize, connect with others, negotiate, compromise, share, and accept limitations, life and its possibilities will seem much more promising. Setbacks and obstacles, for example, are taken more easily in stride when your "stomach is full"—that is, when you are not feeling deprived or needy, either emotionally or physiologically. In a nondeprived and nonoppressed state, you are better able to look at the big picture, see opportunities, strategies, and solutions, and put challenges into perspective, knowing that you have, can, and will meet these challenges. When you are in pain, feeling wronged, undervalued, or rejected, your mind will paint a bleak and resentful picture of "reality." Your mind will perennially construct and redirect a narrative stream to explain what your "being" (in large part, your neurophysiological, emotional, and spiritual being) experiences. Thus, when you are run-down, fatigued, beset with trauma, neurologically imbalanced, or spiritually bereft, you are much more likely to hear an inner narrative describing a gloomy, unrewarding life and outlook. Your ability to form a narrative to match how you "feel" carries within it the embedded tendency to think the narrative is the leader when, so much of the time, it is merely reflecting the lead set by other parts of you that are having great difficulty meeting challenges. The narrative-driving identity you commonly associate with your "self"— the one that, at times, contains that chattering, jabbering, critical, noisy, dissatisfied internal dialogue—may be smart, but it still has enormous blind spots. That persistent chattering narrative can fool you into thinking this is really you, thereby usurping your control and your access to compassion.

Understanding and taking charge of this self-protective (and frequently self-deceptive) process—the dance of the mind's narrative and the body's arousal—is one of the secrets of living intact. This is the essence of Secret #1 that was briefly described at the beginning of this chapter.

Developing compassion and using it to reroute your perceptions, feelings, and behaviors is a significant and valuable tool in rewriting your life story line and in exercising self-control. This might translate into realizing that it isn't necessary to get angry or harshly admonish your child to make the point that he is unequivocally obligated to comply with the family rules. Compassion and self-control may not guarantee that another person will refrain from displeasing behaviors, but they will go a long way toward reducing the resistance and resentment. As you read through the subsequent material on regulating body and mind arousal, you will better understand how specific thoughts and actions will foster the development of compassion and let you hear God more fully.

The next step is to review the ways that nature has programmed the rules for forming, changing, and eliminating behaviors and habits. Secret #2 explains the scientific and practical mechanisms for modifying the conditions, causes, and consequences that result in unwanted habits and undesirable outcomes.

CHAPTER 5
THE SECOND SECRET: BREAKING FREE FROM COUNTERPRODUCTIVE HABITS

<u>Secret #2</u>: *To avail yourself of this secret you must be willing to take charge of habits. By understanding and influencing the way habits form, strengthen, and weaken and by taking advantage of the natural forces that govern them, you can change behaviors that run you and you can greatly influence the habits of others. Break free from counterproductive habits. These principles and techniques can also play an instrumental role in helping you achieve your goals.*

PUSHING AND PULLING AT OLD HABITS

There is a story about a woman who was famous for her cooking. The author of cookbooks and a familiar figure on television food shows, she was beloved in the public eye, and her recipes were favorites. One day, she received an inquiry about her recipe for a roast, which called for "slicing off two inches at both ends of the roast before further preparation." The question was: "Why cut off the ends of the meat?" She had prepared her delicious roast this way for so many years that she had forgotten why the recipe called for cutting away four inches of seemingly good meat; she just remembered that this was her mother's recipe and the way she had learned from childhood. So she called her mother and asked why it was necessary to cut away the ends of the meat.

The mother answered, "My beloved daughter, the big-shot celebrity, do you remember that small apartment we had when you were a child?

The only way I could fit the roast into a pan in that tiny oven was to cut off the ends!"

I have a personal story that reiterates the power of habits and the way they can condition us and block our ability to meet challenges as we work around life's obstacles. Gym shorts and sweatpants are among my usual attire when I'm at home. On occasion, I've found myself dealing with a particularly pesky problem: the waistband string from the pants has an annoying tendency to recede into the recess of the waistband. Typically, I try to pluck the tip out with my fingers or by using an implement, such as a tweezers, to pull the recalcitrant string. More often than not, I am unsuccessful and am left muttering in frustration at the fugitive waistband, the manufacturer, and at the world in general.

One day, I decided to deal with the problem once and for all, and I visited my dry cleaner. Sheepishness notwithstanding, it had come time to confront and conquer this obstacle in my uncooperative world. I presented the shorts and explained the problem, suggesting strongly that perhaps the seamstress could bend the waistband and reach further than I had been able to do. The lady turned to her assistant and mumbled something in a language I did not understand. However, as they giggled, I knew they were talking about me. Since I had a good relationship with these proprietors, I asked the younger one to please translate.

"Oh, she just said, 'No wonder—it is because you are a man that you don't know these things.'"

"What things?" I questioned, my consternation and embarrassment growing.

"The trick for fixing the waistband," she replied, whereupon she demonstrated the technique of pulling the string out entirely (as I watched in horror) and affixing one end with a safety pin. She then guided the string and pin quickly through the elastic tunnel, deftly pushing the pin that was attached to the head of the string with her fingers until it emerged around the waistband through the other hole. The whole procedure took about forty-five seconds. Though my manly ego received a thrashing, within minutes, my fixed shorts were back in my hands, along with a valuable lesson about overcoming obstacles and a reflection of my own tendencies to pull at life when pushing is needed.

This story lays the groundwork for understanding how behaviors strengthen and weaken, increase or diminish, and for learning how to use the processes that govern them so you can live in a more intact way. The key point is that when conditions arise that impede your progress, you must find an alternate way to achieve your goals. Such ways are accessible when you understand the "secrets" of how nature has organized the mysteries and necessities of everyday life, including the characteristics, dynamics, and interactions of behaviors and their consequences.

Later in this chapter, as we look at getting rid of bad habits, the "push-pull" episode with my waistband will help you figure out how to solve many seemingly unsolvable problems.

THE NATURE OF HABITS

You may have heard the saying that we are all creatures of habit. Understanding and influencing habits is a key secret of living intact.

We tend to be acutely aware of the habits that undermine us, the ones that are hard to change, despite our desires to do so. For instance, you may find it difficult to resist the temptation to order something in Starbucks that contradicts your "best-interests" diet. Or perhaps you react improperly to your child or your spouse when he or she pushes your buttons. Maybe you are determined to get up earlier and accomplish more or stick to that regimen, but you have been thwarted by old habits. In many ways, habits form the infrastructure of our behaviors, attitudes, and outlook on life.

A habit is a behavior chain, a stringing together of bits of behavior (with varying degrees of complexity) related by contingencies (i.e., the "if-then" phenomenon—first this and then that.) As mammals, we manifest many behaviors that are instinctual and biologically programmed for our survival. Though these natural behaviors share characteristics with learned habits in that they are regular, repetitive, and often unconscious or automatic, it is the learned habits that concern us here. Some learned habits are what we call "functional" in that they promote our welfare. They are based on the verifiable reality of repeated, predictable goal achievement. On the other hand, some habits do not reliably lead to success and, therefore, cannot rationally and logically be justified. Despite ample evidence of their counterproductive effects, these habits tend to be maintained (see chapter 6).

Just as atoms and elements have particular properties that react to and combine with each other in predictable ways, behaviors and their relationships also operate according to observable and predictable patterns. The formation and deconstruction of these patterns that we know as habits operate within a set of rules that are described by terms such as reinforcement, contingencies, and schedules. By acquiring a basic understanding about how these phenomena operate and interact, you can exert remarkable influence over yourself and others, and you can change both your own habits and those of others that may have been problematic for a long time.

This is not to say that you will routinely and completely alter or eliminate the ways that others behave or act toward you. Rather, by understanding, accommodating, and manipulating the control mechanisms of behavior, you can significantly influence the outcomes of your interactions with others and the ways that they affect you.

As an illustration, consider the story of a patient I treated whose mother had an irritating habit of screaming constantly. This young adult lived at home with two parents whose dysfunctional relationship had created disharmony and tension in the household. While Mom persisted in her intermittent tirades, Dad secluded himself in his bedroom. This resulted in an escalating pattern of Mom yelling louder so he might hear her and in her resuming the diatribes whenever Dad emerged from his room. It was clear to my patient that his mother derived satisfaction (and, in this case, reinforcement) from the knowledge that her husband was hearing but was deliberately avoiding her complaints. However, the plaintive outbursts from his mother also greatly irritated him even though he wasn't the intended target of the tirades. When the young man attempted to reason with his mother and persuade her to stop yelling, she continued to shout, while explaining and rationalizing why Dad justly deserved to be on the receiving end of her ire. She would then direct her tirade at her son and refer to his hapless father in the third person.

The son could not eliminate his mother's yelling, probably because there was too much reinforcement for it in the context of the parents' relationship and in the home environment that supported the dysfunctional behavior. However, the son was able to confine his mother's yelling to those times when he was not around to hear it. He accomplished this by means of a gradual process of setting limits for his mother and by leaving whenever she would raise her voice, thus causing her to imprint the association between her yelling, his leaving, and the conditions under which he would do favors for her or keep her company. Although he couldn't eliminate his mother's tirades or change the dynamic of her relationship with his father, he was able to calm himself, evaluate the situation, set limits for his mother, put her hot-tempered behavior on a different schedule, and change the consequences of her screaming in his presence. The net result was that she was less apt to "go ballistic," and he was more satisfied with his responses to her.

REINFORCEMENT RULES

Unless you are a scientist or science-minded person, you are probably more interested in the benefits of technology than how technology operates. However, comprehending the workings of a particular gadget or scientific discipline can help you harness it for your purposes, fix or adjust it when necessary, and use it more skillfully and for broader applications. Knowing how to fix or reconfigure your computer, for example, may not be your bailiwick, but becoming familiar with loading software or virus protection or figuring out how to deal with memory or DSL problems can save frustration and time, make you more independent, and lead to more confidence and self-sufficiency. The benefits of grasping the basic underlying principles and interactions are not limited to technology and science. You don't necessarily have to be a veterinarian to profit from learning about the needs of your pet and how to keep it healthy, provide basic first aid, and recognize signs that signal the need to seek professional help.

The same is true of understanding the basic technology, principles, and dynamics of modifying behaviors. If the results you want are to get a promotion, receive better grades, communicate more skillfully, or stop being driven by debilitating forces or bad habits, knowing something about the way habits form and relinquish can prove an invaluable resource.

BEHAVIORAL PSYCHOLOGY AND LEARNING THEORY

The underlying science of changing behaviors is known as *learning theory*, and the applied principles fall under the heading of *behavioral psychology*. The field of behavioral psychology deals with empirical (i.e., experiential) observations and measurable events. It is *reductionist* in the sense that it deals only with what can be observed, recorded, and quantified. In this way, the number of variables are reduced or restricted to those that are more objective and concrete. Phenomena beyond this range of empirical data are either disregarded or translated into the language of behaviorism (for example, speculation about the source of a behavior such as overeating is deferred to identification and measurement of episodes of overeating and their association with specific triggers). Behavioral psychology has produced a technology that is useful for understanding and modifying behaviors and habits—including behaviors that cannot be "seen" in the strictest sense, such as thoughts and feelings. Even learning—a concept we all take for granted—cannot actually be seen; however, we can reliably infer its occurrence through the observation and measurement of performance. For example, a child's aversion to and negative associations with mathematics may be influenced by negative feedback from a teacher in second grade. We cannot necessarily be certain of the source of the aversion and negative associations, but we can measure the effects quantitatively and develop creative, pragmatic, and effective strategies for changing the behavior and improving mathematical performance.

ELEVATOR BEHAVIORS

In the reductionist, empirical view of behaviors, we observe properties of the behaviors without regard to subjective opinions or feelings about the value of those behaviors. The elevator is a good analogy. Elevators go up and down. What makes them go up and down is an electromechanical arrangement operating by physics and controlled by signals given to the elevator by its passengers. When the elevator circuitry receives a call from a certain floor, it goes to that floor. It queues the calls in sequence and executes that sequence without preference or concern for the whims or desires of passengers. If you press the wrong button, or if someone presses a different button ahead of you, the elevator will take you to the location dictated by the call. Undoubtedly, you have occasionally expected an elevator to go down, only to feel the surprising compression as the lift pulls you to an ascending floor. A working elevator is always correct, even though it may take you in an undesired direction. It operates according to principles and instructions, even the ones you didn't think were given.

Behaviors are much like elevators in that they go up and down, and they operate faithfully according to rules and principles—in this case, those described by learning theory. If the behaviors you don't like (the bad habits) are persisting or increasing, then someone or something is pressing the call button that keeps them in the up direction. In psychology, this principle is known as *reinforcement,* which was initially defined at the beginning of this chapter.

Behavioral psychology relies upon certain demonstrable principles, the bedrock of which is *reinforcement.* This principle of reinforcement denotes the strengthening or encouragement of behaviors contingent upon consequences that raise their likelihood of occurrence. For example, you may conclude that you perform considerably better at work when you get enough sleep, and the demonstrable and predictable improvement in your performance will reinforce your habit of getting sufficient sleep before making an important presentation at a staff meeting. We say that a behavior (noticeable or otherwise) has been reinforced when it *maintains or increases* in *frequency, intensity, or duration.*

Reinforcement has some very interesting characteristics and properties. For one thing, it is, as in the case of gravity, an equal-opportunity force. (Reinforcement and gravity don't care!) Reinforcement will exert influence upon behaviors you like and behaviors you don't like. It is a scientific control mechanism, an operating principle in our universe. For another matter, reinforcement is ubiquitous; it occurs when you plan it, and it also operates behind your back. The good news is that if you take charge of reinforcement and harness it, you can exert a great deal of control. The not-so-good news is that reinforcement occurs in your life quite routinely, whether or not you recognize or understand it. Thus, behaviors and habits that persist can do so *only* because they are being reinforced. The really bad news is that this reinforcement often occurs without your knowledge or ability to stop it. Thus, that bad habit you can't seem to break, that irresistible temptation, the habitual appearance of that annoying "person" who darkens your doorstep are all being reinforced, despite your will to have it otherwise and your best efforts to cease rewarding or feeding the nemesis. Don't despair. There's also good news about entrenched habits, but you will have to read further to understand how to make the habit-breaking procedure work.

CONTROLLING BEHAVIORS

Now that you realize that reinforcement strengthens behaviors or, to return once again to the elevator analogy, makes them "go up," let's examine the next logical questions: What makes behaviors go down? How can you press the elevator button to send those destructive habits and the unwanted behaviors of others down to the basement?

The answer is twofold. Behaviors go down through the processes of *punishment* and/or *extinction*. You probably understand punishment. It doesn't feel good, and it discourages behavior, acting as a deterrent. For the record, punishment is defined as the application of an aversive consequence that, when associated with a given behavior, *decreases* that behavior in frequency, intensity, or duration.

Punishment is an invaluable tool in the arsenal of survival. Punishment was designed by God to correct us and keep us from harm. It is sprinkled throughout history and throughout the natural world. When you touch a hot stove or fire, you instinctively withdraw your hand, and this is a good thing. It is also a quintessential example of how punishment decreases a behavior. Traffic tickets and jail sentences tend to deter certain behaviors. So, too, does punishment operate in the repertoire of effective discipline when, for example, a parent punishes a toddler for running out into the street or a child for playing with matches. Punishment is useful in situations where learning over time (multitrial learning) could be dangerous. However, punishment has distinct disadvantages and side effects, including the following:

1. Punishment is aversive. It creates distance, wariness, resentment, fear, and even paranoia in the person being punished. This is inimical to loving relationships. You don't want to hurt or drive away someone you care about.
2. Punishment can leave scars. It can be overdone or induce trauma.
3. Punishment can have unintended consequences for the punisher. Many forms of punishment that are meted out by parents can have dire repercussions and can be divisive and undermine family cohesion.
4. Punishment induces tolerance—the medical kind, not the social justice kind. Like drugs, medications, and chemical substances, repetitive punishment can lead to a resistance or to the person on the receiving end becoming increasingly inured, thus requiring higher and higher doses to achieve the desired effect.

5. Punishment teaches people to become sneaky. It can also encourage people to avoid the punisher rather than to curtail the unacceptable behavior. Punishment may reduce or inhibit the behavior because of the fear of aversive consequence, but if the fear factor is absent, people are more likely to devote more purposeful effort to avoid getting caught, rather than to curtail the behavior. Punishment can backfire. If the attempt to diminish or eliminate the undesired behavior fails, the punishment can actually (and ironically) reinforce and further perpetuate the behavior.

6. Punishment as a deterrent doesn't work well when people have an unconscious psychological need to be punished that may turn a punishment into a reinforcement. A case in point can be found in the recidivism rate of convicted felons who have been sentenced to prison. People who have been warped by their negative life experiences and who are often self-destructive may chronically make flawed choices and may seem intent on sabotaging themselves. In extreme cases, they will commit crimes that are guaranteed to land them in prison.

The process that causes a particular behavior to strengthen or increase is called reinforcement. The processes that cause behaviors to weaken or diminish are called punishment and extinction. You can think of extinction as *nonreinforcement* or, more commonly, ignoring a behavior. When we extinguish a behavior, we make it go away because we take away what it needs to continue and thrive. In the case of extinguishing a fire, we remove fuel, oxygen, or heat, or we douse it with water or retardant. In the case of behaviors, we extinguish them by taking away reinforcement.

In an ideal world, we would positively reward the behaviors we want to encourage, and we would ignore the behaviors we want to discourage. And of course, we would punish—severely, but rationally—those appalling behaviors, such as rape or homicide, for which societal needs compel quick and decisive deterrence and incarceration. Unfortunately, the world is not ideal, so it's just not that simple. There are several important factors to consider about the way reinforcement, extinction, and punishment work and for behavioral basics to be successfully applied to the complexities of our daily lives and the welfare of those about whom we care.

DISTINGUISHING REWARDS FROM REINFORCEMENTS

A reward is something desirable in the mind of the recipient. Rewards *feel* good, and we often look forward to them and will work for them. However, rewards do not always act as reinforcements, because they do not always make desirable behaviors increase. A personal example illustrates this point. I happen to like pizza, and for me, pizza is a reward. However, pizza is not usually something that will get me to finish my work (probably because I can get pizza without having to finish work). Although pizza is a reward for me, it does not function as a reinforcement because there is no contingency (an *if-then* arrangement) linking the delivery of pizza with productive work.

It is a common mistake to assume that people will work for things that you (or they) believe are rewards. For example, many parents set up a reward system whereby they offer something the child likes in return for the performance of a task (e.g., homework or chores). Though the child may indeed want or value the rewards, they are reinforcements *only* if they serve to strengthen the intended behavior. Parents often become frustrated when the inducements they offer don't initiate lasting positive changes in performance and attitude. Parents will often blame the child further and complain that nothing works to motivate their child. Unfortunately, this reaction belies a proper understanding of the way reinforcement works, especially with regard to *schedules* and *incremental shaping*, which we will discuss shortly.

Now, let's look at how reinforcement operates in contrast to rewards. Though rewards often do serve as reinforcements, in many cases they do not. The rewards are still rewards—desirable commodities that may be offered as consequences—it's just that they do not strengthen the behaviors they are intended to strengthen. What about situations in which behaviors are strengthened by consequences that seem quite *un*rewarding? For instance, the parent who offers treats or privileges in return for task performance may become frustrated when the child opts not to perform, despite the generous reward. All too often, the parent then yells at the child because "it's the only way to get him to do what I've repeatedly told him to do." The child may perform because of the yelling, but in this case, the parent and child would be setting up an unwitting trap: the yelling becomes the reinforcement that conditions the child to perform. Nobody likes being yelled at, so we would certainly not consider yelling a reward. However, if the yelling (or anything else) strengthens the behavior (or raises the probability that it will occur again), then that is the definition of reinforcement. Most people would consider yelling or hitting or any undesirable consequence to be a punishment. Remember, however, that punishment makes behaviors go *down*. The elevator never goes up when you press the punishment button. So if the behavior goes up, something is reinforcing it, even if you don't intend for it to work that way.

Indeed, for certain types of people—particularly the oppositional ones or the street-smart ones who manipulate and don't deal in open communication—punitive consequences usually make their behavior worse. The unacceptable behavior draws attention and elicits a strong unpleasant response. What seems like a punishment intended to reduce or eliminate the behavior actually makes the behavior stronger by reinforcing it. How can you tell whether a "punishment" is really a reinforcement? You must observe and ask: What happens to the behavior? Does it go away briefly, only to resurface with consistency? If so, then it is being reinforced.

PARADOXICAL OUTCOMES

To make matters more complicated, people who don't seem to respond to material or social rewards or freedoms often gain reinforcement surreptitiously through the satisfaction of frustrating (and thereby controlling) the people trying to reward them to change their behavior. They (often misbehaving children) are able to withstand surprising levels of aversive consequences because the satisfaction of resisting and not altering their behavior outweighs the temporary discomfort of the yelling, being grounded, takeaways, etc. Mom may yell and threaten, and Dad my take away things and privileges, but in the end, Junior simply endures it. The behavior doesn't change, and Mom and Dad become visibly frustrated. Junior continues the negative behavior (despite the cost). And Junior wins by staying the same. For many people, the reward/reinforcement represents a sweet, though usually subconscious, victory.

IN CASE YOU ARE CONFUSED

This discussion may leave some readers confused. After all, the concepts and described actions seem contrary to common sense. The concepts and rules governing reinforcement paradigms are sensible and consistent, but they may be different from the way you instinctively think, especially when emotions are involved. Remember when you learned that if your car starts to skid, you are supposed to steer *into* the direction of the skid, not away from it? This feels counterintuitive, but the laws of physics show that it works. Behavioral programming also has some counterintuitive features. However, once you learn the general principles and practice correctly until you get great results, the confusion will go away (or, at least it won't bother you).

So in this sometimes upside-down world of reward/reinforcement, punishment/extinction, cause/effect, and elevator behaviors gone haywire—how can you figure out what to do to make the desirable behaviors stronger and the undesirable behaviors weaker?

Before I show you the answers, I want to prepare you for the worst by emphasizing how really bleak the situation is. This is much gloomier than light dust settling on dark surfaces and dark dust settling on light surfaces. The realities of bad habits and behavioral resistance epitomize the difficulty of living in a frequently uncooperative universe.

Remembering that behaviors only go up or stay up through reinforcement and they only go down via extinction or punishment, we now confront the practical reality that *it is exceedingly difficult to ignore bad behaviors*. The screaming or whining child, the craving for foods, drink, cigarettes, or the pull of compulsive temptations such as chronic gambling, overeating, or nail biting do not quiet down or go away when we turn aside and temporarily resist them. As a matter of fact, they get louder or stronger or more insistent until, sooner or later, we offer some response that acknowledges them. Try as we might to do otherwise, it is virtually impossible not to pay attention to annoyances. The moment we notice them—even slightly—we reinforce them. It seems like a curse.

To make behaviors diminish or attenuate, the alternative to non-reinforcement is punishment. However, remembering all the significant disadvantages of punishment, you may (and should) be reluctant to dispense it for all but the direst behaviors. So it seems we are stuck. Punishment is often overkill, yet nonreinforcement is impractical and often backfires into reinforcing the behaviors you want to reduce.

THE SAVING GRACE

Like a sneaky joke that sets you up before delivering the punch line, life has set you up at the mercy of reinforcement tendencies that are hard to fathom and even more difficult to control. Rather than set you up, I have tried to clarify the dismal picture of unwanted habits in order to give you tools to change the probabilities of reinforcement—for that, indeed, is the secret of taking control and the saving grace for manipulating desirable and undesirable behaviors.

Remember the story about my gym shorts waistband and drawstring? Here we can apply the push-pull principle to the more complex issues involving reinforcement. With my shorts, the more I tried to seize the withdrawn string, the further it receded. In effect, my activity was driving the string away or strengthening its retraction. A different approach was needed. The string had to be moved through a process that could be "inched" along. Rather than see the string as so many inches short of the hole, the safety pin approach methodically pushed or "shaped" the head of the string in a controlled manner toward the goal. The progress of the pin and string through the waistband could be guided and its probability predicted and strengthened.

SECRET #2 IN A NUTSHELL

In summary, it is usually easier to make behaviors go up than go down because the mechanism for strengthening behaviors—reinforcement—occurs so prevalently and naturally, even when we don't intend to reinforce certain behaviors. It is simply in the nature of things that whenever we *notice* something, we increase the probability that it will become more noticeable in the future.

This is an advantage when we want to introduce or strengthen a desirable behavior. However, it is a distinct disadvantage when we confront a behavior that is undesirable and whose level we want to diminish. This is because *any* kind of attention to it (even thinking about it) will tend to reinforce and thus augment it. This is a big part of the reason bad habits are so difficult to break.

The workaround, so to speak, is to avoid reinforcing the undesirable behavior by diverting reinforcement to other (sometimes new) behaviors that are incompatible with the undesirable behavior. This diversion is not a distraction, but rather a planned behavioral programming that has a double influence. It builds and strengthens behaviors that are at odds with the undesirable behavior while simultaneously providing a channel for diverting reinforcement from the undesirable behavior, thereby reducing its probability. A real-life example would be the development of exercise habits and hobbies that supplement gratification, provide outlets for anxiety, and substitute an object focus of attention and thought in place of the constant rumination about food that tends to reinforce overeating.

Manipulating the strength of behaviors—that is, the probabilities that they will recur—is a key secret of living intact. It is instrumental in choosing and augmenting the behaviors that work (such as compassion, meeting challenges productively, etc.) and in diminishing problem behaviors, both in yourself and in others. These include thoughts, attitudes, beliefs, desires, and feelings, which are actually behaviors because they are events with antecedents and consequences whose outcomes can vary and change.

In order to manipulate these probabilities effectively, you need to master a few salient aspects of *schedules of reinforcement*—i.e., the properties and predictive patterns of reinforcement that I dub "breeding patterns." These principles are explained in the next chapter, along with an example of a common problem—nagging a child who won't perform—and how you can use these principles and techniques to fix the problem.

CHAPTER 6
THE THIRD SECRET: MODIFYING THE OUTCOMES OF YOUR BEHAVIORS

<u>Secret #3</u>: *To avail yourself of this secret you must be willing to modify the outcomes of your behaviors. Nature uses a method called reinforcement to ensure that mammals learn efficiently enough to survive and thrive. This process is the source and bedrock of your habits. Becoming familiar with the dynamics of reinforcement will put you in the driver's seat for modifying the outcomes of your counterproductive behaviors and those of others.*

Many are the plans in a man's heart, but it is the Lord's purpose that prevails. (Proverbs 19:21)

The sun rises and the sun sets, and hurries back to where it rises. The wind blows to the south and turns to the north; round and round it goes, ever returning on its course. All streams flow into the sea, yet the sea is never full. (Ecclesiastes 1:5–7)

There is a time for everything, and a season for every activity under heaven. (Ecclesiastes 3:1)

If you keep doing more of what you are doing, you will get more of what you already have. (Papa Daniel Steinberg)

"GOOD" MORNING

You may not have a child named Josh, but you can probably recognize his behaviors. Perhaps, Josh's circumstances and antics are similar to those in your household. Josh is a nice kid, but he is slow as molasses. He's not slow in the dumb sense—in fact, he's quite bright—but slow to get in gear, get organized, and get out of the house on time. From the moment he gets up in the morning, typically late and after several insistent reminders, through the various activities involved in getting ready, Josh is constantly running behind schedule. His pattern of getting through his day is understandably exasperating for his parents, who prompt and cajole him. As a last resort, they often end up yelling, "JOSH! IT'S TIME TO GO! GET MOVING NOW!"

Josh takes forever to get dressed. Since he is almost always behind schedule, there is little time for breakfast, a critically important meal for a child in school. Josh's pokiness invariably makes everyone late. Every morning his parents must nag him through the steps of brushing teeth, getting dressed, and getting to the table. Even then, he takes his sweet time eating. They then have to rush him through breakfast and literally push him out the door. Despite having first-rate academic skills, the fourth grader's lackadaisical *modus operandi* has begun to have a negative effect on his schoolwork. He chronically puts off doing his homework until the last minute, which predictably results in homework that is incomplete, full of errors, and illegible. He's rarely prepared for school. At the last minute, he typically has to run upstairs and find something he neglected to put in his backpack. Precious time ticks away, and tempers flare. The frustration is as inexorable as heat in the summer. His despairing parents are at their shared wit's end. They are calm at first, but their tempers invariably flare, and they end up yelling, threatening, being punitive, and taking away privileges. Procrastination, prodding, resistance, and exasperation have clearly become entrenched elements in the daily morning routine. The ten-year-old is obviously running the show and has become masterful at pressing his parents' buttons.

DÉJÀ VU ALL OVER AGAIN

Life has repetitive cycles. There may be comfort in routine and familiarity, but there is also frustration in the sameness and intransigence of repetitive behaviors that we wish to change, but seemingly cannot.

Struggling with renewed determination all too often only reverts to the same maddening patterns and the same undesirable outcomes. You have probably heard the cute maxim that "the definition of insanity is doing the same thing over and over again and expecting a different result."

We all repeat ineffective strategies and become enmeshed in a pattern of maladaptive behavioral forces. The programmed responses occur because we are unaware and/or not in charge of the patterns of reinforcement that either strengthen behaviors or keep them the same. If we are to interrupt the patterns of stimulus-consequence and cause-and-effect dynamics that relentlessly drive undesirable habits, we must have practical understanding of how to change the "timing relationships" that link *antecedents* (or precursors) and the *consequences* of behavior that determine how entrenched they become. These interactions and timing relationships, which I call "breeding patterns," involve the predictable effects that reinforcement will have on the occurrence and endurance of behaviors, based on when and how the reinforcement is applied. The more common—and scientific—name for this phenomenon is *reinforcement schedules*.

REINFORCEMENT SCHEDULES

Behavioral psychology has discovered that reinforcement organizes around patterns of occurrence and effects known as schedules. For example, airplane departures, salaried paychecks, and football games are reinforcements for many people; that is, they encourage and strengthen certain behaviors. They also occur on schedules (e.g., the Giants' home games begin at 1:00 p.m., and the snacks need to be on the coffee table in the den by twelve forty-five. Your stomach begins the growl at twelve forty). By observing, understanding, and implementing reinforcement schedules, we can, to quite a large extent, determine the influences on behaviors (called *operants*) and predict and control outcomes. We can help solve the mystery and frustration of counterproductive behavior by reducing the undesired schedules that result from inattentiveness or inconsistency. Many parents fault themselves for being inconsistent, but this self-criticism shifts the focus from the real issue: first, lack of knowing the critical details of behavior management and then, in a few cases, failure to apply the appropriate reinforcement schedules to form and strengthen desired behaviors. Everybody has lapses, distractions, and multiple demands competing for attention. Though some inconsistency is inevitable, it is rarely the culprit for faulty behavior. Rather, the schedules that reinforce faulty behavior are the major culprits.

The whining or noncompliant child, the screaming parent, and the spouse or companion who complains or doesn't follow through have each developed their habits through conditioning on reinforcement schedules. The people who interact with them may not like these behaviors, but they have likely (and unwittingly) helped to strengthen them by paying attention to them intermittently.

In reinforcement and learning theory, different schedules exert differing effects on the occurrence, strength, and longevity of behaviors. A schedule is a pattern of reinforcement, whether it occurs naturally or by planned intent. (For a more in-depth discussion of reinforcement schedules and their effects, see appendix A.)

Simply stated, many interventions aimed at changing behaviors are doomed to failure from the outset because they unwittingly and paradoxically develop schedules that *reinforce the behaviors that are targeted for reduction or elimination.*

You may, for instance, want to modify the way someone talks to you. Perhaps your partner reacts disdainfully when you mention a sensitive issue, or your child is disrespectful or complaining. You prudently plan your response, noting that when this happens, you will react unemotionally by presenting an unpleasant consequence if the behavior continues. Furthermore, you are careful to offer differential consequences for desirable and undesirable behaviors.

For example, you might say to your spouse:

"Honey, if you react that way when I bring up the subject of our family visiting my parents, I will simply not include you in my decision making about social plans or shopping habits. And maybe I will just forget to buy those special items you like when I go to the store. On the other hand, if you discuss the pluses and minuses of visiting my parents in a manner that respects my feelings while expressing yours, I will make extra efforts to check with you before I make plans, purchases, or shopping trips."

Or you might say to your child:

"Justin, when you complain or raise your voice to me, I will turn my back on you and raise my hands. That's a signal that you have crossed the line and, therefore, must earn back privileges. However, if you talk to me in a soft and respectful voice, I will extend your TV time, let your friend come over, and provide an extra treat."

So far, so good. You rehearse your response and deliver it flawlessly the next time your family member treats you rudely. The first time you respond this way, your spouse or child will most likely look at you oddly because this is a new reaction and he's testing you. On the second occasion, he complies, and you get cooperation. Hallelujah! You're on the road to reforming the behavior. Eventually, though, real life intrudes: you're tired and impatient with your mate's lack of understanding, or you are out in public and your child embarrasses you with mortifying disrespect. You snap in reply (because he deserves it, and besides, you have to set limits). Your feelings and responses are understandable. Indeed, they would be validated by peers, relationship gurus, and parenting pundits alike. However, your justifiable response has a behaviorally fatal flaw: you have (again) paid attention to an undesirable behavior, thus reinforcing it. How? By noticing it and reacting to it (especially with charged emotion). On top of this, your prior "good" responses (the planned ones) have established a different reinforcement schedule by spacing out the "bad" attention (your visceral habitual reactions) so that the person subconsciously learns that eventually his rude behavior will draw the familiar (and ultimately reinforcing) response from you. This is known as transitioning from a *continuous* to an *intermittent reinforcement schedule*, and it has the predictable effect of strengthening almost any behavior—even the ones you don't like. In other words, you're applying the reinforcement schedule intermittently or inconsistently. (Again, refer to appendix A for a better understanding of these behavioral principles.)

If this is hard to fathom, think of yo-yo dieting, a vicious cycle in which the alternating schedules of dieting and binging teach the body's metabolism to retain weight because the cycle simulates a biological crisis of expected food shortage. Following the same principle, the mind learns that reinforcement (any consequence that strengthens behavior) may be withheld for varying and protracted periods of time, but that the familiar and expected response will eventually present itself. When it does, the behavior derives a new life that sustains it through periods of nonreinforcement. The practical application of this principle is that both inconsistency and unawareness of factors that reinforce undesirable behaviors result in reinforcement schedules that accomplish the opposite of what is intended.

Your best intentions and resolve to teach your partner or child the new rules about interacting with you may be thwarted by the inadvertent reinforcement of their old behaviors. In order to avoid this trap, *you must observe the results you are getting rather than your opinions about what you are doing*. Do you recognize the familiar refrain: *"I tried this technique and it didn't work,"* or *"It worked for awhile, but then it stopped working, and he doesn't seem to care about the consequences"*?

When I hear these reports, I look for the pattern of reinforcement that is keeping the undesirable behavior in place. To paraphrase a previous metaphor: I look for what is pressing the up button on the elevator when it is supposed to go down.

STRIKING OUT AND LASHING OUT

Here is another example to illustrate the difference between offering your opinion and observing the result: when a baseball umpire calls a strike, the batter may react in disbelief. *"Hey, Blue, that was way outside—that was a ball!"* The next pitch comes, and it bounces in the dirt, a ball for sure. The batter steps away confidently. *"Strike two!"* *"What? Are you blind?"* Looking around for support, the batter hears the validating jeers of his teammates and fans. But the umpire rules, and he has called another strike. If the batter is savvy and wants to get on base, he had better adjust to the umpire's reality.

The baseball example emerged in my office one day as I counseled a couple whose daughter was manipulative and resistant. The girl had an ingrained habit of blaming others for her own shortcomings. She blamed her lack of concentration on distraction from classmates and her parents' yelling. When she followed her own agenda, it was "because the teacher was boring or didn't give her enough time to finish an assignment." Altercations arose from the meanness and selfishness of others, and so on and so forth. She was full of excuses, and the pattern of them was exasperating her parents.

A KEY LEARNING PARADIGM METAPHOR

On one occasion, the parents of the child described above recounted to me a particularly stressful day in which the delays and excuses had simmered to a boiling point. Mother had been trying to hurry her daughter through a procession of daily activities and had met with resistance and blaming for hours. When her daughter dawdled doing a task, the mother gave her a choice, neatly outlining two courses of actions and their consequences: *"Either you stop doing what you are doing now and we will have time to go to the ice cream place, or you continue with what you are doing and we will not have time to go."* The girl, of course, continued with her own agenda. Later that day, when the mom discovered that the girl had left her materials at school and offered this as an excuse for not doing her homework, the mother marched her back to school and found the janitor who opened the classroom so the girl could retrieve her materials. Mother was wise to her daughter's habits and had learned about the principles of reinforcement. She had made many inroads in curtailing the daughter's manipulations. However, she fell prey to the lure of puerile complaints and accusations. As so often happens when reinforcement is withheld, the person will accelerate the behavior in order to obtain the expected reinforcement. In this case, the daughter blamed the mother for not having time to take her for ice cream because the mother insisted on going back to the school. Caught unawares by the audacity of her daughter's allegation, the mother responded by engaging her in a corrective discussion.

"Strike one!"

In reviewing this situation with the parents, I explained how, despite mom's understanding of reinforcement, she was reinforcing her daughter's excuse making by engaging with her in conflict over them.

The mother continued, "Then, she told me that she wouldn't have time to finish her homework because I made her go back to school, and that wasted time. I couldn't believe this reasoning, so I explained things again to her."

"Strike two!"

The mother looked at me with such wariness that I momentarily felt like an umpire. She thought she was doing the right thing and was expecting my approval. Instead, I called "Strike two!"—my way of emphasizing to her that she was missing something. Despite her meticulous explanations (or perhaps because of them), she was inadvertently reinforcing and strengthening her daughter's outrageous and manipulative ploys. The solution for this parent was to see that the result of her actions was unfavorable, despite her conviction that she was doing the right thing. In her case, the productive course of action was to enforce the consequences without justifying, explaining, or otherwise verbally react-ing to her daughter's provocations.

In order to avoid "Strike three!" this mother had to accept the umpire's call and approach the batter's box in a different way. The daugh-ter's pitches had been reinforced, even though the mother didn't like the call.

GAMES THAT REINFORCEMENT PLAYS

Although the breeding patterns of the various reinforcement sched-ules are well documented, in real life they become intertwined and more complicated. Typically, behaviors start on a continuous reinforcement schedule (where each occurrence is reinforced) and gradually transition to an intermittent schedule (where only some occurrences are reinforced), even without conscious awareness on the part of the participants. In dog training, for instance, the deliberate process involves pairing a reward (food) with an increasingly approximate response from the dog. If you want Fido to give you his paw upon command, you give him a treat at first when he lifts his paw slightly. Then, you gradually withhold the treat until he comes closer and closer (approximates) to giving you a rapid handshake. This process is known as *shaping* the desired behavior. Even-tually, Fido will give you the paw without getting any treats—and he will do this regularly and automatically. So where's the reinforcement? Two things have usually happened. First, the trainer has "thinned" the reinforcement by offering Fido a treat only *sometimes* after his giving the paw. Thus, Fido has been transferred from a continuous reinforcement schedule to an intermittent one. Second, praise has gradually been intro-duced as a food substitute, first continuously and eventually only some-times (intermittently). The longer Fido has been trained on a schedule that varies (once the paw giving has been reliably established), the longer he will deliver the paw, even in the absence of extended periods of non-reinforcement. Fido has learned the habit of giving the paw, and he may continue to do so for the remainder of his life, even without a specific reward for that performance.

Whereas Fido's paw training exemplifies deliberate and desirable conditioning, the same patterns frequently occur in the formation and continuation of bad habits.

When a behavior (including actions, thoughts, feelings, expectations, beliefs, attitudes) has a relatively high probability of occurrence even in the apparent absence of reinforcement, we say that it is *resistant to extinction*. The reinforcement schedule that produces the strongest resistance to extinction is known as a *variable ratio intermittent reinforcement schedule*. Such schedules are formed through the introduction of varying and unpredictable episodes of reinforcement and nonreinforcement for the same behavior over time. (Two common examples of such schedules are: schedules that reinforce gambling and schedules that reinforce repeating instructions or yelling at people to get them to do things.)

The technical terms used in learning theory (such as *variable ratio intermittent reinforcement schedule*) may be daunting to the uninitiated reader. You may want to read through this chapter more than once and also refer to appendix A for more detail. A word of encouragement: if you acquire a basic grasp of the principles presented in this and the preceding chapter, you will be more knowledgeable about the practical applications of behavior modification than most of the graduate students I have taught.

In the anecdote at the beginning of this chapter, Josh's dawdling behavior was *resistant to extinction*—that is, it continued even when his parents didn't raise their voices or nag him. Although unpleasant, the parents' loud voices and reminders served as reinforcers for Josh's dawdling. The parents alternated between refraining from nagging Josh and intervening to get him moving. This created the *variable ratio intermittent reinforcement schedule*.

TWO IMPORTANT CAUTIONS ABOUT REINFORCEMENT

In order to better understand how bad habits form and why they are so persistent and difficult to break, it is important to remember two important truths about reinforcement in the natural world. These caveats were mentioned in the previous chapter, but it would be opportune to review them here, so you will find it easier to apply them in your efforts to make changes.

Reinforcement exerts influence upon behaviors you like and behaviors you don't like. It is nondiscriminating; it is, as is the physical phenomenon of gravity, an equal- opportunity force. It is simply a scientific control mechanism, an operating principle in our universe. Additionally, reinforcement is ubiquitous and inadvertent; it occurs when you plan it, and it also operates behind your back.

Let's apply this to some of Fido's other learned behaviors that are not as favorable as giving the paw. Suppose that Fido's owner decides that the dog's habit of begging food from the table needs to be terminated. So the new rule is that no one in the family may give Fido any scraps from the table. Common sense would dictate that Fido (smart dog that he is) would soon get the message and adjust to the new order. Since Fido has been a longstanding fixture at the dinner table, we can assume that he has been conditioned on a continuous reinforcement schedule (one in which he is given food on every occasion). Theoretically, if the reinforcement is cut off, Fido will soon "extinguish" his begging response. So nobody gives Fido food from the table, and, despite his heart-wrenching pleadings, inching toward the table, and soft muzzle on the various laps, members of the family are resolute. Relatively quickly, Fido will back off and stop begging— true to the response decrease predicted by the continuous reinforcement schedule. But now let's add in some real-life scenarios. After a week of nonreinforcement, Fido has stopped begging. Fabulous! Then, in clearing off the table, Mother inadvertently drops some meat scraps onto the floor. Boom! Fido is there! Unintentional? Yes, but reinforcement all the same. The family redoubles its efforts to consistently deny Fido food from the table. Two weeks later, Father is sitting at the table reading the paper, munching on a sandwich. No one is home, and he has had a rough day. He is a bit lonely and trying to distract himself from self-pity. Along to the rescue comes Fido, a loving and all-accepting confidant. Father strokes Fido's head in reciprocation of the dog's affection. Fido inches forward, and before he realizes what he is doing, father offers a nibble to his friend. Bam! More reinforcement for the clever (or unwitting) dog. Gradually, without intending it, Fido is being shifted to a variable ratio intermittent reinforcement schedule. That is, he never knows when his overtures will be rewarded by food, so his persistence increases as a function of the occasional, but unpredictable, reinforcement. It won't take many instances of such intermittent reinforcement for Fido to maintain his "bad" begging habit indefinitely. Such is the nature of how these schedules form and perpetuate. I call them "breeding" patterns: like the breeding patterns of mammals, their yield is a function of nature, rather than a product of convenience or desirability. (For a review of terminology and meanings, see the following glossary.)

GLOSSARY OF BEHAVIORAL PSYCHOLOGY

Antecedent—Something that occurs *prior* to a behavior that becomes connected in sequence to that behavior and associated with it.

Consequence—Something that occurs *after* a behavior that becomes connected in sequence to that behavior and associated with it.

Contingency—An "if-then" relationship (e.g., if you complete your homework, then you can watch TV. Watching TV is *contingent* upon completing homework).

Continuous reinforcement—Each and every occurrence of the behavior is reinforced. Continuous reinforcement is useful for establishing or strengthening a behavior because it produces high rates of response early in the conditioning process.

Extinction—The process of nonreinforcement that reduces a behavior to zero occurrences. By withholding reinforcement you can *extinguish* a behavior to the point of extinction.

Fixed schedule of reinforcement—A schedule in which the amount or number of responses or the interval necessary to gain reinforcement is set (such as the response from putting money into a vending machine to get a bottle of soda, or a pitcher throwing three strikes to strike out a baseball batter, or the rent or mortgage payment due date).

Incremental shaping—The process of forming habits or complex behaviors by gradually reinforcing small parts of those behaviors and *chaining* or connecting them.

Intermittent reinforcement—A pattern of reinforcing some, but not all occurrences of a behavior. Intermittent reinforcement is effective for keeping behaviors intact once they are shaped and for maintaining them over time. Because the amounts and times of reinforcement can be reduced, intermittent schedules are economical and favored by nature.

Interval reinforcement—A pattern of reinforcement that depends on a time schedule that is either established (e.g., receiving your paycheck) or changeable (e.g., playing musical chairs). Interval schedules tend to produce spike-type response levels in which there are low response levels and prolonged periods between responses in accord with the expected interval.

Nonreinforcement—Instance in which a behavior occurs without a consequence that reinforces it.

Operant—An action or response that does not appear to have a stimulus; a behavior that influences or determines a consequence.

Operant conditioning—A form of learning that takes place when an instance of spontaneous behavior is either reinforced by a reward or discouraged by non-reinforcement or punishment.

Probability—The likelihood that an event or behavior will occur. Mathematically, it is the ratio of occurrences divided by the number of opportunities of possible occurrences. Reinforcement schedules influence probabilities of behaviors in predictable ways.

Punishment—The application of an aversive consequence, that, when associated with a given behavior, *decreases* that behavior in *frequency, intensity, or duration.*

Ratio reinforcement—Reinforcement that occurs after a certain number of responses. This may be one response, such as ordering a meal, or a multiple of responses, such as making numerous sales calls. Ratio schedules tend to produce high levels of consistent response.

Reductionist—Dealing only with what can be observed, recorded, and quantified; the analysis of something into simpler elements or organized systems, especially with a view to explaining or understanding it; reducing or restricting the number of variables to those that are more objective and concrete.

Reinforcement—The strengthening or encouragement of behaviors contingent upon consequences that raise their likelihood of occurrence. A behavior (noticeable or otherwise) has been reinforced when it *maintains or increases* in *frequency, intensity, or duration*.

Resistance to extinction—Characteristic of being difficult to eliminate or extinguish. (Behaviors that are resistant to extinction are usually maintained on a *variable intermittent reinforcement schedule*.)

Reward—Something desirable in the mind of the recipient. A reward may be a reinforcer or it may not. It is a reinforcer only if it results in the maintenance, strengthening, or increase in a behavior.

Schedule of reinforcement—The pattern of reinforcement and the "timing relationship" between the delivery of the reinforcing consequence and the behavior that it encourages. Types of reinforcement schedules are associated with predictive effects on the occurrence and endurance of behaviors.

Variable schedule of reinforcement—A schedule in which the amount or number of responses or the interval necessary to gain reinforcement varies (e.g., sales calls, gambling, asking for a date).

YOUR OWN BREEDING HABITS

Though you don't bark, you have been trained (and have conditioned others) on multiple variable reinforcement schedules. Thus, you have response patterns that are quite ingrained. Many of these patterns work to your advantage, helping you to function efficiently and automatically. But some of them may cause you and those around you great distress.

What are the habits you would like to change? Are you prone to irritable outbursts, yelling, or other kinds of blaming? Do you react unfavorably in the face of provocations? Do you brood, worry, or dwell on the small stuff? Are you touchy about being treated unfairly or being taken advantage of? Are you a slave to your appetites or cravings?

Though the preceding examples may or may not represent your own hot buttons, it is important to recognize that they are all examples of behavior in which the elevator is up and the desire is to make it go down. Behavior stays up through reinforcement. (You can never make a behavior go down by reinforcing that behavior; this would be as nonsensical as trying to use gravity to make things go up.) So undesirable behaviors are persistent and recalcitrant because they have been formed on schedules that are resistant to extinction—that is, they can go for long periods of time without any reinforcement and still remain intact. To the extent these undesirable behaviors are intact, your life is less intact.

APPLYING SECRET #3

When you're trying to make a behavior go down, the temptation (and the trap) is to pay it some sort of attention. Whether lavish or begrudging, loving or angry, patient or demanding, any acknowledgment or attention will further strengthen the behavior. How do you make a behavior go down? Either punish it or ignore it. And ignoring it is almost always eventually impractical. People fall off the wagon after years of abstinence. More commonly, people violate their diets, raise their voices, stay up later than is healthy, or they respond to a child's defiance, lack of performance, or evasion of challenges and responsibilities by engaging with this counterproductive conduct "reasonably," thereby unintentionally reinforcing them. Behaviors bred on intermittent variable ratio reinforcement schedules (and almost all of the obstinate ones are) need very little nourishing to keep on flourishing.

Diverting reinforcement to other (often new) behaviors that are incompatible with the undesirable behavior can counteract this discouraging situation. For instance, you can divert your own attention from noticing (and thus reinforcing) complaining to offering praise or support whenever the complainer makes a positive or even neutral statement. Thus, when your child complains about homework, refrain from engaging with the complaint, even in seemingly reasonable and responsible ways. Saying, "Now think of the fun you'll have with your free time once you finish your homework" may *sound* logical and positive; however, it will likely reinforce complaining. Better to completely ignore such a comment. Instead, wait for a comment like "I can't wait to play that video game," to which you can respond, "I admire how you really get into computers. You sure are an expert game player! I bet homework will go smoothly when you apply your enthusiasm to it. Make it like a video game, and just get to the next level."

Such planned behavior programming builds and strengthens behaviors that are at odds with the undesirable behavior while simultaneously providing a channel for diverting reinforcement from the undesirable behavior and thereby reducing its probability. Manipulating the strength of behaviors—that is, the probabilities that they will recur—is your ticket to modifying your habits and restoring your intactness.

In practical terms, how does this work?

Let's return first to Fido. Dogs happen to be fine students and great teachers. The problem with Fido's table manners is that it may be impractical to deprive him totally of scraps, even if he obtains scraps by mistake. Intention is not always rewarded by desired result. (Consider the saying: "The little boy throws the rock in jest, but the dog dies in earnest.") We can minimize the impact of Fido's intermittent variable ratio reinforcement schedule by planning and shaping him on a schedule that we can control, one that is incompatible with table begging. For instance, we could teach Fido the behavior of lying down in a corner during family mealtimes. Even better, have his corner be in a different room. We could train him to a schedule whereby he eats a certain interval of time *after* the family leaves the dinner table. And we could build and strengthen a new behavior in Fido, such as the announcement of "Dinner time" to become a cue for Fido to go to his corner and lie down until he is told, "Get up, Fido." Such new connections and schedules would go a long way toward keeping Fido away from opportunities to rekindle his old begging habit. They certainly are more strategic and effective than simply reacting to his encroachments by shouting at him, "Go away!" when he is inches from food on the table.

WHAT ABOUT JOSH?

Remember slowpoke Josh? Let's apply the secret to Josh's bad habits.

Step 1: Identify the behaviors you want to change.

Josh has several behaviors his parents want to go "down." These are staying in bed, dawdling, taking too much time for routine activities, being late, and making excuses for these behaviors. Keeping in mind the "elevator" metaphor, think in terms of targeting behaviors by determining whether the desired outcome is for the behavior to go up or go down. This will determine your strategy and implementation of the tools of behavior change.

Step 2: Plan a reinforcement strategy.

Consider the strategic problem: behaviors only go down through punishment or extinction (consistent nonreinforcement). For reasons already explained, punishment is problematic, and extinction is impractical. (It's impractical to ignore Josh being and making everyone late; however, attending to these behaviors only reinforces them.) It is much easier to make behaviors go up because reinforcement is something you can generate and invoke, and it is easy to do this with small-step behaviors you introduce and associate with reinforcing outcomes. *The secret is to formulate behaviors that you can reinforce and schedule.* This is done in two ways:

1. Transform the desired "down" behaviors into "up" behaviors.
2. Introduce new behaviors that are incompatible with the problem behaviors.

To do this with Josh, establish behaviors that are essentially the opposite of his problematic ones. For example, behaviors identified as targets could include: getting (and staying) out of bed by a specified time, having his teeth brushed within two minutes, being dressed by a specified time, finishing breakfast by the next specified time. The key is to be specific and to break down and sequence the behaviors so that the likelihood of succeeding with each step increases and, in turn, influences the likelihood of mastering the next step. Thus, rather than monitoring Josh from the other room through nagging ("Josh, have you finished brushing your teeth?"), address the specific behavior in such a way that Josh gets a small "reward" for showing you that he has finished brushing his teeth by a specific targeted time (e.g., 7:20 a.m.). It's *much* easier to get a distractible child to come to you and flash a smile than it is to remind him four times with increasing irritation to perform a neglected task. If you remind Josh to brush his teeth, you are training him to respond to the cues of your reminders. More reminders and heightened sternness will condition Josh to attend and respond to the escalated cues. Josh has learned that he really has to brush his teeth only when you raise your voice and breathe down his neck. Eventually, he will brush. The cost, however, is the extension of a variable intermittent reinforcement schedule that cements a pattern of nagging parent, dawdling and dependent child, and much irritation. Better to sidestep this hamstrung schedule by building a different schedule, a continuous one in which you can set the behavior and influence the probability of success. If you hand Josh the toothbrush and dangle the reward in front of him, he will likely brush and come running to you, flashing his teeth and seeking his reward. Soon thereafter, you can fade your prompt of handing him the brush, and you can transition the immediate reward to something that is reinforced at later and less frequent times.

Rather than tackle the dawdling directly, sidestep the tendency to reinforce bad behaviors by redefining and compartmentalizing the behaviors into desirable versions. Since any way you address them is going to reinforce something, you might as well get Josh to respond to the schedule you set up.

Here are some examples of reinforcement schedules you could use that are incompatible with Josh's problem behaviors:

a) Instead of focusing on Josh's staying in bed, find something he likes and lure him out of bed by promising him he can have it only if he gets up by a certain time. One example: *"Your bacon is almost cooked. It will burn unless you come and eat it now."* Or another: renting or purchasing a video game to reinforce small steps toward good habits that counteract the bad ones. This may seem extravagant, but several consider that video games are far less expensive than therapy sessions. Moreover, the new habits form quickly, and you can "rent" him the game on a daily basis, thereby stretching the economic value and extending your control.

b) Since Josh comes up with interfering behaviors such as running upstairs to get something or making excuses in response to reminders, institute a heavily rewarded "new" behavior that is incompatible with the maladaptive ones. You could reward him for each morning that he gets out of the house without going back to get something and without making excuses. You can invent things for which to reward him—on your terms.

By working in this manner, you will not only avoid reinforcing bad behaviors and strengthening their schedules, but you will also form the habit of engaging with Josh in a positive manner. Gradually, both of you will develop the expectation that interacting with each other will be rewarding.

A note on the universal problem of inconsistency leading to inadvertent reinforcement: this undesired outcome can be diminished by planning a time to deliver the rewards that are reinforcing. It follows the principle of planning a schedule over which you exert control. You may be caught unawares reacting to some bad behavior. It may happen before you can avoid it. However, you can focus on specific times to interact positively and to evaluate and administer the rewards earned. For a young child, being "good" to get a reward on the weekend is not a realistically motivating reinforcement schedule. Yet even young children can collect coupons or tokens or some representative symbol that can be redeemed for a tangible item within a few hours.

Step 3: Use incentives that work.

It is reasonable and observable that people will work for a payoff. The tricky part is that what you think or someone else thinks is worth performing for may not, in reality, serve as a reinforcement—that is, it actually strengthens or increases behaviors (cf., the difference between reward and reinforcement, as explained earlier in chapter 5). Rewards are simply desirable and pleasurable commodities. Although they often serve as reinforcements, don't assume that they will reinforce until they are tested.

Make a list of items and privileges that you think Josh wants. These can edibles, clothing, toys, books, accessories, activities shared with friends or parents, access to hobbies or friends, trips, special perks, relief from duties, etc. Show Josh the list and get his reaction. Perhaps he has other ideas about what he wants. Chances are that if you listen to his ideas, he will be more motivated and more willing to make and abide by a deal.

The bottom line is that you have to see if the behaviors you target do strengthen in order to determine whether the "reinforcers" are actually working.

This approach is very much driven by results.

Step 4: Evaluate the results.

Keep track of Josh's behavioral progress. At the beginning, take a baseline measurement of the behaviors you want to change. In Josh's case, the baseline behaviors that Josh would get out of bed on his own, brush his teeth, and get ready without any reminders may well be at or close to zero. This is not surprising since he has been trained to wait for his parents' cues. Chart or graph each of the behaviors and share the results each day with Josh. This should occur in tandem with distributing the reinforcements. Remember that the reinforcements need to be given in close time proximity to the performance of the desired behavior; this is so that the connection of behavior and consequence is secured. The younger the child, the more true this is.

Step 5: Anticipate the effects of reinforcement schedules and make adjustments.

When you generate or transform behaviors that you want to reinforce, you are creating a connection that you want Josh to learn and repeat: *do what I want and you get what you want*. Talking yourself blue in the face won't accomplish nearly the desirable results that you will get by structuring behavior and consequence in small steps with a high probability of success (shaping). Nature has facilitated this process by the way that continuous reinforcement schedules work. That is why you should consciously and strategically use them. However, continuous reinforcement schedules have limitations in that they can become tedious, costly, labor-intensive, and prone to extinction. Josh's parents are weary veterans of token point or coupon systems that seemed to work for a short time, only to dissipate in Josh's reversion back to his maladaptive ways.

The problem that Josh's parents didn't anticipate or handle is the need to accommodate the way schedules work and the need to transition them. Continuous reinforcement schedules are great for building behaviors, but to continue them into an enduring repertoire that fosters good habits and independence, transitioning to a variable intermittent schedule is necessary.

The objective for Josh is to prepare and take care of himself on his own. Whereas the novel continuous reinforcement schedule can start him on a new path, his parents must gradually space apart and vary the levels of reinforcement so that Josh can continue these behaviors on his own.

There is another factor regarding reinforcement schedules that comes into play with Josh's morning scenario: the target behaviors are on both ratio and interval schedules. The ratio schedules involve the behaviors Josh must perform (brushing teeth, eating, breakfast, getting ready) and the number of times the stimulus must be presented (i.e., parents' cues). Ratio means the number of times something must be done in order to get reinforcement. You might think that Josh only has to brush his teeth once and eat breakfast once each day; although this is true, it that would not be the correct way to look at it. If Josh's parents remind him four times to brush his teeth, then Josh's *parents* are on a ratio schedule whereby *they* have to perform four times in order to get reinforcement (which, for them, is Josh's brushing). Obviously, this ratio needs to be adjusted.

Interval schedules involve time determinations of when reinforcement will occur. Remember the predictive attribute of interval schedules: behavior accelerates around the time of anticipated reinforcement. There is a critical reason why choosing and managing intervals is important and useful, and the example of Josh's control of the daily rhythms of his family demonstrates this below.

Josh has to take certain steps and get ready at particular times in the morning, culminating in leaving the house prepared and on time. Therefore, we would expect his behaviors to increase as each time of reinforcement nears. This is indeed what happens. Notice, however, the behaviors that are being reinforced: dawdling and delaying! As each deadline for punctual performance approaches, Josh avoids and delays. The more he delays, the more nagging his parents provide (that's one reinforcement). Here's the kicker: sometimes, Josh delays and avoids long enough to be successful at not performing the task. As the clock ticks, the need to leave the house becomes more pressing, so on some days, Josh skips breakfast and leaves unprepared. This is interval reinforcement, subversive style. (By the way, the same paradigm applies to many behaviors. For example, if you avoid studying before a test, your avoidance of studying is eventually reinforced by the test occurring at a specific time—after which, the need to study ends. Sure, there are consequences, but your avoidance of studying gets reinforced on an interval schedule—once the test is over, you don't have to avoid studying until the next test.)

The solution to interval reinforcement of undesirable behaviors like delay and avoidance is twofold:

1. Intercede with incompatible, small-step ratio and interval reinforcements before the probability of the stronger avoidance behavior becomes higher. That means: *introduce baby-step, non-avoidance tasks before the deadline approaches.* In Josh's case, providing significant payoffs for showing his brushed teeth early in the morning, instituting reinforcement for going downstairs before he normally would (incremental step toward breakfast), taking away his food at a certain time, and rewarding him based on how much he finished eating would all counter the established maladaptive schedules.

2. Where possible, substitute ratio schedules for unproductive interval schedules, thereby removing the interval reinforcement. For example, *arrange the family schedule (temporarily, while you are reforming Josh's behavior) so that he must perform each assigned task, no matter how long it takes.* His reinforcements would be proportional to his timeliness and completeness (with costs and deductions for each delay). However, he would have to complete each step before leaving for school. Tardiness, of course, would be factored into the administration of reinforcements. Another type of reinforcement that could be used is a "ride to school." The rule: if he's not ready by the specified time, he walks to school. (This may not especially bother him unless detention is required for being late.) Once Josh learns this cause-and-effect sequence, he will adjust his behavior. In order to teach him that "the buck stops here," you will have to *plan* on being late for work a few times. Planning, however, is on your schedule, not on Josh's.

WHAT ABOUT YOU?

What about your behaviors?

Are you yelling at your spouse or kids? Do you find it unbearably hard not to indulge your love for chocolate or, perhaps, for another craving? Do you have uncomfortable or destructive thought patterns?

Maybe you are more concerned with the intransigent behavior of others. Your children won't listen? People cross your boundaries? Others try to control you or offer unsolicited advice or gratuitous criticism?

Whether the behavior is yours or someone else's, the first step in changing it is to check out the elevator direction. Observe and ask: is this a behavior I want to go up or to go down? Your answer will dictate the manner in which you plan and use reinforcement. If the behavior should go up, then you can apply reinforcement directly to that behavior. (Remember, this is called shaping—reinforcing successive approximations toward the goal.) For example, if you want to exercise, start perhaps by reinforcing the behavior of simply changing into workout clothes. Drive by the gym, park and enter, get a locker. Next time, exercise moderately for ten minutes. Though these may seem like tangential baby steps, they build chains of behavior that endure (with proper reinforcement schedules). Moreover, you are more likely to be successful with small steps, and this is crucial. What should you use as a reinforcement? There are many possibilities. Bear in mind that whatever you use is a reinforcement only if it strengthens or encourages the occurrence of the behavior. Again, remember: *changing the probabilities of behavioral recurrence is a key secret to taking control and living intact.* Incidentally, once you get the hang of it, manipulating probabilities to your advantage becomes a habit, too.

If you want the behavior to go down, you will still use reinforcement (but on behaviors *other* than the one you want to go down). Why? Because reinforcement, like gravity, is everywhere. It is a potent force for you to harness to your advantage. However, you *must* be careful only to reinforce behaviors other than the ones you want to diminish, preferably behaviors that are incompatible with the ones you are targeting for reduction. Think again of my gym shorts example, where the backdoor approach of pushing reinforced the progress of the string, whereas the pulling action was ineffective and had to be extinguished (through a substitute behavior that was more reinforcing).

Having trouble resisting that Starbucks snack or that drink after work? Since this is a behavior you want to go down, search for something you can reinforce that will get in the way of the indulgent reinforcement schedule. (Yes, sports fans, this is a version of disrupting the offense!) Prior to the moments that temptation overrules, do something! Drink a *lot* of water; make a timely phone call; force yourself to walk a quarter mile. Find something that works—it doesn't have to make any sense—to introduce a different reinforcement schedule, one that you can control from the beginning.

Here's another key point: you must plan your alternate reinforcement tactic at the proper time. What is the proper time? Just prior to the acceleration of the probability that you will indulge (remember that your indulgence is the reinforcement). Craving behaviors typically have interval reinforcement schedules. On such schedules, behavior remains low until the interval of reinforcement approaches (just like walking toward the airline gate before the plane takes off). Your intervals of temptation may be predictable (fixed interval) or random (variable interval). The way to take charge of these intervals is to observe (and, at first, to keep a written log of) the patterns of temptation. This is known as taking a baseline. Once you can estimate when the temptation is likely to accelerate, you can plan and implement your alternate reinforcement intervention. To give you an idea, plan your intervention when the probability of indulgence is less than 50 percent. This will give you a running head start on successfully diverting the indulgence before it becomes overpowering. The key is observation and planning. Note how long you can go without a drink or smoke or snack before the craving starts to build. Plan your alternate reinforcement so it gets under the radar of your internal compulsion alarm. You can plan and attain beachheads against adverse probabilities. The nice thing about numbers is that they are tangible and reliable. This lends more predictability and confidence to your efforts.

Let's say you are trying to modify someone else's behavior in a downward direction. Suppose your child shows behavior problems. Record a baseline of how long he usually goes without whining, acting out, etc. Then, plan an alternate reinforcement under the time radar. You will be surprised at how easy and effective this is, even for very unruly behaviors. If you estimate that your child can go fifteen minutes before becoming unpleasant, target the reinforcement intervention at eight to ten minutes. In this scenario, the probability that your child will misbehave rises from about 10 percent in the first two minutes to about 50 percent after ten minutes to over 80 percent by about thirteen minutes. So after about eight to ten minutes of good behavior, you might comment on how much you enjoy being with him and then offer him a coupon (depending upon his age) for a treat. According to the previous math, you would be more than 50 percent likely to shape his good behavior successfully if you intervened after eight to ten minutes of good behavior, but only 20 percent likely to succeed (actually, to have your child succeed) if you intervened after thirteen minutes. You could intervene after two minutes with a 90 percent probability of success; however, this may be too small of a baby step and not enough of a challenge for your child at that stage. Reinforcement is a game in which you can play the odds and win. Of course, it takes practice.

There are many practical applications of these strategies for shaping behaviors up and discouraging them down. Before concluding this section on controlling habits, we should note two additional very important aspects that are critical to success. One is the issue of reinforcement logic or reasonableness. The other is the negative emotional component of bad habits (see chapters 5, 7, and 10).

INCREDIBLE AND UNREASONABLE REINFORCEMENT LOGIC

Many years ago, I had an extremely difficult patient, a ten-year-old boy who was violent. He often hit his mother, and neither of his parents could control him. Adding to the difficulties were the boy's learning disabilities that significantly hampered his reading and his language communications. The situation had reached critical proportions when the boy refused to sit in the backseat of the family car. The ritual was that the parents and the child would argue, and the father would sit in the backseat while the mother drove and the boy acted out in the passenger seat, occasionally swatting his mother. None of the incentives they tried were sufficient to induce the boy into the backseat. He had control. I made a suggestion that quickly solved the problem. I suggested that the parents tell their son that the car owner's manual said that all children under the age of twelve must sit in the backseat. I further suggested that they embellish their story with details, such as referring to supposed sections in the manual where the children's seating was discussed along with dangers and consequences for noncompliance. Incredibly, this strategy worked the first time, and it continued to work. The parents were amazed, as were many people to whom I have recounted this story over the years (including patients who faulted me for recommending fibbing). Now, I have some idea of why this worked. For one thing, the boy could not read well at all. Thus, he was unlikely to challenge the absurdity, given his reading difficulties and his self-consciousness about them. For another, although he was extremely aggressive and noncompliant with familiar people, he was fearful of outside authority and not confident about his ability to engage strangers in verbal arguments. These particulars notwithstanding, the intervention worked, and the achieved result explains and attests to the viability of the treatment procedure better than any adult logic. (Incidentally, I have recommended many similar illogical and absurd interventions and directives to patients over the years. Usually, they worked beautifully, once the patients were able to focus on the treatment interaction and results, rather than on their own parochial notions of what makes sense.)

The principle to extract and generalize from this story is twofold. First, people do things for their own reasons, which may or may not be the same as your reasons. Second, getting the desired result is sweeter and more productive than being "right." Former President Ronald Reagan said, "You can accomplish amazing things if you don't care who gets the credit." Whether you are reassuring your fearful child at bedtime about the boogeyman or watching that boring movie for the tenth time with your son as a reward for cleaning up his room—*what counts is whether the incentive or consequence produces the desired result.* Reagan's sage observation extends beyond people; it implies that you have to be willing to detach from *your* ideas of what works in order to notice and apply the principles by which the world works and other people respond. Logic and reasonableness may satisfy you, but sometimes you have to barter your own fixations to make better behavioral bargains with others.

Keep in mind that I am not suggesting you sacrifice your moral or ethical principles to make a deal or force a result—rather, that you observe the reality that your ideas about what's so and what *should* work may blind you to the true effects (beneficial or otherwise) of reinforcement. This myopia may keep you frustratingly stuck in bad habits.

Learning how to modify behaviors and understanding how reinforcement works leads you on a path of spiritual development, too. This is embedded in the acceptance of evidence that things don't necessarily work the way you would want them to work. Is there evidence more stark or humbling than years of frustration with bad habits or behaviors that you think you should be able to change? Knowing and accepting that reinforcement operates independently of your will and desires leads to the wisdom that God has designed our world according to *his* purposes. By observing and tracking behavior outcomes and assessing that reality does not always conform to what you want, you are better able to align yourself with God's will and his methods for productive behavior change. It's ironic how science and spirit can work together, especially when the data are collected according to God's design.

> *Many are the plans in a man's heart, but it is the Lord's purpose that prevails.* (Proverbs 19:21)

CHAPTER 7
THE FOURTH SECRET:
ELIMINATING NEGATIVE EMOTIONS

<u>Secret #4</u>: *To avail yourself of this secret you must be willing to elimi-nate the negative emotions that keep you stuck in bad habits, drive the mind narratives that justify failure, and derail attempts to change what you do. These negative emotions control and sustain bad habits and can be eliminated by changing the codes that link emotions to thoughts.*

Jennifer had lots of negative emotions. She wouldn't deny her ten-dency to become irritable and angry and to yell at her children. Although she didn't like this about herself, she justified her actions and moods on the uncooperative and often outlandish behavior of her children. She had tried numerous times, using several different methods, to control her moods and outbursts. However, she soon resorted to her familiar and unproductive habits.

Jennifer was trapped by her negative emotions. Her attempts to change things failed, largely because her emotions overwhelmed her and surreptitiously sabotaged her efforts to consistently implement the behaviors and conditions that would result in the improved outcomes she sought. It was difficult for Jennifer—bright and responsible as she was—to see the cause-and-effect connections between her feelings, her children's behaviors, and the effect these had on her mind and her actions.

By discovering a rapid method of ridding herself of negative emotions, Jennifer was able to identify and separate the negative emotions that thwarted her efforts from the planned and logical steps that soon resulted in the outcomes she wanted: her own composure and self-control and the respectful cooperation and follow-through by her children. Her newfound ability to eliminate negative emotions allowed her to strategically implement the behavioral tools that would adaptively change her own and other people's behavior.

NEGATIVE EMOTIONS AND BAD HABITS

The previous two chapters focused on the scientific mechanics of how reinforcement works for and against our wishes. By understanding and taking advantage of some practical principles about how behaviors and consequences are connected, you can considerably influence and change the outcomes of behavior patterns.

Another vital element plays a pivotal role in changing habit patterns: negative emotions can cause us to remain stuck in recycling counterproductivity and can cause the same discordant music to play over and over in our lives. Most people are run to a great extent by their negative emotions. It requires insight to realize this linkage, and it requires powerful tools to counteract it.

Being able to understand, relate to, and effectively apply the concepts and principles of reinforcement in one's life is analogous to being able to understand, relate to, and effectively apply the concepts and principles of gravity, inertia, and fire. Just as you wouldn't jump from a tree limb, you wouldn't want to unwittingly reinforce your young child's proclivity to ride his bicycle without a helmet. In the final analysis, simply knowing when there is danger and how to avoid it may not be enough to make you take effective action. For many people, even knowing when there is no real danger (as in phobias) does not alleviate the anxiety that arises, despite the logical evidence that there is no actual threat. Negative emotions are powerful inhibitors, and they can immobilize or sabotage the most passionate intention to change your responses to recurring stimuli and consuming temptations. Negative emotions are often what allow counterproductive reinforcement schedules to build in the first place, and they can derail the most determined attempts to correct faulty patterns.

Consider that bad habits are maladaptive response patterns comprised of two things:

1. Undesirable behaviors that are conditioned (strengthened) on persistent reinforcement schedules.
2. Behaviors that serve to reduce or mask negative emotions (usually anxiety).

Up to this point, I have presented behavioral principles and relationships that are fundamental to changing behaviors in the desired direction. Before we proceed, make sure you are up to speed with a basic understanding of these points. If you need a review, refer back to chapters 5 and 6 and the glossary of behavioral psychology terms in chapter 6.

As you now realize, consequences that reinforce don't *necessarily* reward. They simply strengthen the probability of recurrence. When it comes to bad habits, the specific behavior that constitutes the bad habit is often a reinforcement that reduces the negative emotion leading to the bad habit. The behavior, however, is not being reduced, but rather is being strengthened. Thus, the cost of relief from the negative emotion is the perpetuation of an undesirable behavior. We don't typically think of certain behaviors as "rewarding," but they can be in the sense that they serve to reduce negative emotions (such as anxieties, withdrawals, and cravings in addictions) or they get a job done at the cost of strengthening an undesirable habit. Common examples include the following:

- ☐ Yelling gets the kids to quiet down or do something
- ☐ Biting nails reduces the anxiety of the temptation
- ☐ Eating or drinking certain foods induces a physiological state that's familiar or satisfying

Many bad habits are simply counterproductive patterns that get practiced repeatedly and become ingrained. Common examples include the following:

- ☐ Chronic lateness
- ☐ Poor eating and sleeping habits
- ☐ Overreacting to insults or provocations
- ☐ Sarcasm or criticism

To get rid of bad habits, you need to do two things:

1. Eliminate maladaptive responses
2. Shape adaptive responses

Eliminating maladaptive responses comprises the range of reactions you may have that work to your disadvantage or to the detriment of those around you. For example, overreacting, persisting in negativity or damaging actions, reinforcing self-defeating narratives or tendencies to extend your nervous system's fight-or-flight response would fall in the realm of maladaptive responses. Alternatively, shaping adaptive responses means engaging in step-by-step reinforcement of behaviors and habits that contribute to positive self-image and productive engagement with the world around you. These may include developing compassionate, empathetic responses, building better work or self-care habits, finding and accentuating the positive aspects of your efforts and the behaviors of others.

You have learned that you can shrewdly use reinforcement to build behaviors that you want to encourage and whose reinforcement schedules you can largely plan and control. You can also use workarounds to counteract maladaptive, but persistent, reinforcement schedules[5] involving the predictable effects that reinforcement has on the endurance of undesirable behaviors, such as creating and shaping a behavior that is incompatible with the behavior you want to reduce. For example, if your child constantly interrupts or badgers, you can create a reinforcement schedule that shapes quiet time periods.

For most people, the biggest problem in eliminating maladaptive responses is the negative emotions that keep those responses in place. Keep in mind that the bad habit is the result of trying to suppress the negative emotion—anxiety, fear, anger, depression, worry, etc. All too often, this negative emotion disables or paralyzes the flexibility to engage in an alternate response at those previous moments when the probability of success is most in your favor.

---

5. Reinforcement schedules are "timing relationships" or "breeding patterns" among behaviors and their consequences that predict the effects that reinforcement will have on the occurrence and endurance of behaviors, based on when and how the reinforcement is applied. (Refer to chapters 5 and 6.)

This problem requires a power tool!

Fortunately, there is one at your disposal. It goes by the name of Thought Field Therapy.[6] In chapter 10, you will learn how and why this technique works to eliminate so many problems. You will also learn how to use this technique on yourself. For now, focus on the impeding role that negative emotions play in maintaining maladaptive habits and on the marvel of using a natural and effective technique to vanquish negative emotions.

Thought Field Therapy (TFT)[7] is a method of rapidly and completely eliminating negative emotions. More specifically, it involves a finger-tapping technique that you perform on yourself to eliminate the negative emotion. (Actually, what gets eliminated is the coded information that links a negative emotion to a thought, once the thought is attuned. Hence the name, Thought Field Therapy.) This technique can be learned and self-administered. However, many people find it advisable to seek the help of a trained therapist, particularly for recalcitrant problems that require a more precise and higher level of professional intervention (such as Voice Technology).

Quite frequently, the administration of a single application of this technique can eradicate a problem that has persisted for years. This has been repeatedly demonstrated, and I have successfully used this powerful procedure in my practice thousand of times. If this sounds implausible, you would not be the first person to think so. In trying to understand results without making them fit preconceived notions, it may be helpful to remember Ronald Reagan's aphorism about credit: "You can accomplish amazing things if you don't care who gets the credit." If it works, then go for the result and adapt your explanations accordingly.

When the TFT technique eliminates the problem (as, for example, the curing of phobias, cravings, or depression, which I have done many times), it is reasonable to conclude that the "perturbed" thought field was responsible for the symptom. When a problem persists, various maladaptive reinforcement schedules and "narratives" form that serve the purpose of justifying the persisting problem. The reinforcement schedule is not responsible for maintaining the problem, only for seeming (falsely) to

---

6. Discussed in chapter 10.
7. Thought Field Therapy (TFT) and Voice Technology (VT) were discovered and developed by Dr. Roger Callahan.

explain it. In other words, there are still reinforcement schedules that condition in predictable ways; it's just that they condition *consequences* of the negative emotion, rather than *precursors* to it. This key differentiation distinguishes the causes of the problem from the effects. For example, imagine a person who is phobic or becomes extremely anxious about certain objects or activities, such as a fear of flying. Logic (and many psychologists) would suggest that the person has been conditioned through powerful associations to connect airplanes and flying with a strong negative reaction. Accordingly, the solution would then be to break those associations, either by extinguishing the fear response or by practicing new reinforcement schedules that are incompatible with fear (cognitive reframing). However, the advanced level administration of TFT (Voice Technology) can eliminate this phobia in about fifteen minutes with extremely high reliability—without invoking reinforcement schedules.

In my experience, TFT is remarkably effective for eliminating negative emotions. However, this advantage is curative when the negative emotion is itself the problem. Eliminating the negative emotion spontaneously allows the person to build new and adaptive schedules, without environmental modification. In the case of curing a flying phobia, once the person discovers the absence of paralyzing anxiety, he then flies repeatedly, practicing the exercise of his new freedom, and building a self-image that excludes the former anxiety.

For most bad habits, though, a combination of approaches works best. First, we eliminate the negative emotion that restricts the implementation of an alternative response. Then, the person is more free, flexible, and able to craft the reinforcement schedules that will be more adaptive. This is usually the way to beat compulsive behaviors or addictions. Some practical examples follow.

COMPULSIVE SELF-BEHAVIORS

Nail biting is a common and frustrating bad habit. It is hard to stop nail biting because the habit is *self-reinforcing*—that is, no one can stop you from reinforcing yourself. This dynamic is not the same as getting a reward for desirable behaviors, such as good grades. The habit consists of an undesirable pattern of providing self-reinforcement (the reduction, albeit temporary, of anxiety and temptation) at the cost of perpetuating a behavior that is contradictory to one's wishes and self-control. Furthermore, the cycle embellishes the originating anxiety with other negative emotions and self-recrimination (guilt, embarrassment, anger, etc.)

GLOSSARY OF THOUGHT FIELD THERAPY (TFT)

Cure—The elimination of all subjective experience of distress[8] and symptoms associated with a problem. In TFT, a cure is brought about by eliminating perturbations in the thought field.

Perturbation—The fundamental cause of all negative emotions, perturbations are the physiological, neurological, hormonal, chemical, and cognitive events that result in the experience of specific negative emotions.

Thought Field—A field is an invisible, nonmaterial structure in space that has an effect upon matter. A **thought field** is a connection between cognitive awareness and emotions that generates a field that may contain perturbations.

Thought Field Therapy—A treatment for psychological disturbances that provides a *code* that, when applied to a psychological problem on which the individual is focusing, will eliminate *perturbations* in the thought field, the fundamental cause of all negative emotions.

To interrupt the pattern of self-reinforcement and break an unwanted cycle, we would first treat the thought field that involves any and all negative emotions about nail biting. At minimum, this would include the temptation or compulsion to bite or pick at one's nails. It is important at the outset to recognize this compulsion as being an anxiety derivative and to note that the anxiety that leads to nail biting is reduced by the act of biting itself (even though the cycle perpetuates anxiety). By treating the thought field with tapping, the desire or compulsion to bite or pick is totally eliminated. The "charge" or the "obsessive preoccupation"

---

8. In psychological treatment and research, a measure of subjective distress that is often used is a rating scale called a SUD (Subjective Unit of Distress), whereby a person rates his distress on a scale of 1–10, where 10 is the most distress conceivable and 1 represents no distress or symptom.

vanishes. However, the "habit" is still there. The habit is the collection of reinforcement schedules that predict and evoke absent-minded nail biting, because the frequency and probability of such occurrence has been repeatedly reinforced. Conquering the temptation or anxiety is a vital first step in eliminating the habit, but the probability of continuing an absent-minded (habitual) behavior may still be high.

Once the compulsive urge is eliminated, the person who is compelled to bite his nails can plan to self-reinforce adaptive responses, such as short periods of time without biting, reporting on success to others, showing off nails, getting a manicure, opening sealed containers with ease, etc. Now that the compulsive urge is thwarted, incremental progress can be made in changing the reinforcement schedules that have perpetuated the bad habit.

WHEN OTHERS GET YOUR GOAT

In contrast to self-reinforcing behaviors such as nail biting, many bad habits involve the environmental influences of others, where negative emotions are triggered either on ratio or interval schedules. A classic example is the family member who makes you yell or makes you distressed or crazy in some way.

After mastering the principles of reinforcement, you resolve, once-and-for-all, not to yell at your child for his various misdeeds. Ideally, you have learned that your exclamations and editorials about the child's transgressions only serve to reinforce them. Let's say that you decide to change your standard approach. You plan to note and reinforce only good behavior and to ignore (as much as possible) the messiness, screams, disrespect, provocations, and defiance. You are determined to change everybody's ways and to prevail with peace and success. However, even thinking about doing this triggers doubt, worry, and annoyance.

Then, it happens. Your child does something outrageous, inconsiderate, beyond the pale. Without thinking, some primitive and well-practiced response bursts forth from the recesses of your nervous system. You yell and blame because your child's peevish conduct is uncalled for and needs to be assertively discouraged. You can't let him get away with this, again!

Guilt, mortification, embarrassment, and frustration set in as you realize that you've been had again. A mental bumper sticker flashes before you:

REINFORCEMENT HAPPENS

You've reinforced undesirable behavior again, despite your best intentions, all because an uncontrolled negative emotion triggered and tricked you.

The way out of this trap is to identify the negative emotions and their related thought fields and to treat and eliminate them *before* being provoked. We are again dealing with precursors (antecedents) of counter-productive behavior versus the consequences of this behavior. With the help of TFT, you can escape the trap. By so doing, you will experience profound relief and an exhilarating release from being maneuvered by the strings that others have repeatedly been pulling to control you.

TAMMY'S LONGEST YARD

Tammy, the mother of an eleven-year-old patient named Justin, had been arguing for years with her son. The boy was oppositional and defiant. His behavior and adjustment difficulties were compounded by learning and attention problems. Justin tended to ignore his mother and then suddenly explode. Basically patient and self-controlled, Tammy had learned and utilized many of the previously discussed behavior modification principles. However, she internalized Justin's outbursts and insolence. This drove her "crazy" and often derailed her good intentions and follow-through.

In one fifteen-minute session, Tammy and I eliminated her negative emotions about herself and her son by using Voice Technology, an advanced version of TFT. The thought fields we targeted were frustration, feeling out of control, and dreading confrontations. After the treatment, Tammy described her experience as having the problem shift from "here (pointing to her heart) to here (pointing to her head)." She commented that *Justin's behavior still seemed difficult and inappropriate, but that it no longer bothered her. She simply had a job to do that involved correcting her son's behavior, and she felt confident about persisting and succeeding.* She no longer felt threatened and was free of the negative emotions.

The longest distance between two points is that between the mind and the heart.

Tammy had taken an important step toward living intact. Her struggle with emotion, impulse, compassion, and self-control had led her across the bridge—the longest yard—between the mind and the heart.

In this case, she joined compassion and reason without letting rampant emotions overrule reason and judgment.

COMMON THOUGHT FIELDS AND NEGATIVE EMOTIONS

To liberate yourself from negative emotions that control your behavior, you must deliberately practice distinguishing between thoughts and feelings. A thought is a statement, an opinion, an observation, a narrative comment. A feeling is an emotion, not delimited by time, reason, logic, or appropriateness. Though they are not always appropriate or fitting to particular situations, feelings simply *are*.

Often, when I ask patients to express their negative feelings, they will ramble for paragraphs. In the short versions, they will say things like:

"It shouldn't happen that way. I try to avoid it, but..."

" He criticizes me so often. I don't mean to..."

"There are lots of bad things that could happen..."

"She does this just to annoy me..."

"That no-good, son-of-a..."

These statements are thoughts (or cognitions), not feelings. Most of us have become so accustomed to sublimating and rationalizing our feelings that we have trouble articulating them. Perhaps this is the logical result from years of frustration about not being able to relieve negative emotions effectively and from having smarted from the aversive reactions of others when we express them.

If you are to disband the negative feeling, become unshackled, and implement new behaviors and reinforcement schedules, you must identify the feeling that occurs when the thought is attuned. You need a target at which to aim the incredibly powerful healing effect of Thought Field Therapy.

Here are some examples of thought fields (represented as statements) and the range of negative emotions they subsume:

- "I can't do it." (Hopelessness, sadness, frustration)
- "I forgot again." (Embarrassment, frustration, guilt)
- "Now, I'm really gonna pay." (Fear, anxiety)
- "I hate having this problem." (Anger, frustration, anxiety)

- **"I've never been good at this."** (Hopelessness, sadness, frustration, embarrassment)
- **"I just don't know where to start."** (Feelings of being overwhelmed, anxiety, frustration)
- **"There's too much to do. I'm so far behind. I can't say no to people."** (Defeat, anxiety, depression, feelings of being overwhelmed)
- **"I've been severely criticized or put down."** (Hurt)
- **"He's a jerk. Who needs him anyway!"** (Rejection, anger)

These thought fields, emotions, and examples of reinforcement are by no means an exhaustive list. They are simply representative of common maladies and frustrations. They can serve as catalysts for deliberately identifying your own thought fields and negative emotions and for trying your hand at applying the described strategies and techniques to change counterproductive behaviors. These tools can be applied successfully to internal behaviors as well as to the ones that others can easily observe.

Living intact is about recognizing and embracing the give-and-take between you and your circumstances. In a preceding chapter, we talked about compassion and the role it plays in this give-and-take relationship, your options for setting limits on what statements and actions by others are tolerable to you, your options for response, and the possibility of rewriting the narrative (personal internal dialogue) that assumes such an important part in determining who you think you are and how you express this personal image in your actions and attitudes. The self-control principles and strategies that have been described will provide you with tools to increase your awareness so that you can be more effective in listening to your narrative, in modifying the interactions between you and the world, and in monitoring your conduct.

Living intact is also about something larger, more abstract and spiritual, the confluence between intention and acceptance, and the union of determination, purpose, skills, awareness, and wisdom. Living intact involves choice, and the more informed these choices are, the better. It is also preparation for the deeper and more pervasive aspects of living intact—the embracing and engagement of challenge to get more out of life while life gets more out of you.

CHAPTER 8
THE FIFTH SECRET: EMBRACING THE CHALLENGES OF LIFE

<u>Secret #5</u>: *To avail yourself of this secret you must be willing to embrace challenge as the way to turn obstacles and frustrations into opportunities and successes.*

JANIS AND THE THREE LEVELS

Janis was incredibly bright and sensitive. She was also moody and given to self-pity. At twenty-six, she was still trying to earn her bachelor's degree. Though her intelligence measured at the ninety-eighth percentile, she had dropped out of college several times and was, at the time she sought my treatment, recovering from a kind of "nervous breakdown." Her previous psychologist had diagnosed her with bipolar disorder and attention deficit. Though she began to make significant progress rather quickly, Janis was dubious about how far she could go and how long any positive changes would last. To provide a perspective on growth, I described three levels of living that were realistically attainable.

In discussing the first two levels, I gave credit to a man named Charles Jones, a.k.a., Charlie "Tremendous" Jones. Mr. Jones was a very successful businessman and popular motivational speaker. He peppered his optimistic, inspirational speeches with the word "tremendous"—hence, the moniker, Charlie "Tremendous" Jones. I once heard a speech he gave entitled, "Life Is Tremendous." In this speech, he coined the term *"miserable-miserable"* to depict the despondent state of mind characteristic of those who are suffering constant angst. Jones asserted that, whereas most people are *"happy-miserable,"* some are downright *"miserable-miserable,"* a condition that cries for immediate attention and relief. Jones's description of *"happy-miserable"* struck me as similar to what Thoreau had called "lives of quiet desperation," the condition in which people resign themselves to plodding along, trying to survive as best they can, putting up pretenses, constructing defenses, mouthing platitudes, and hoping that tomorrow will somehow be a little better.

According to Charlie Jones, the idea was to go from being "miserable-miserable" to being *"happy-miserable."* When I told this to Janis, she laughed, but then she became serious again.

"Is there anything better than *happy-miserable?"* she asked.

"Yes!" I responded. "I wouldn't shoot for *happy-happy,* because it's somewhat unrealistic and overly euphoric. And not everybody is a fan of Jones's tremendous attitude. I believe that the more realistic, attainable, productive, and contented level is what I call living intact. To live intact requires that you must be willing to engage proactively with life's inherent challenges."

For Janis, one of the challenges was dealing with her defeatist and negative attitude. The disregulation and mood imbalances that had for so long colored her outlook led to a mind narrative that rationalized and reinforced the dark side of her life experiences. Her reality was based on the expectation that she would not be able to finish things, that people would reject and disappoint her, and that feeling better would only be short-lived.

It was true that Janis had a history of overwhelming struggle with a brain and nervous system disorder. She also had made many poor decisions, experienced devastating disappointments, suffered physical ailments, and had established a pattern of attracting and forming unhealthy relationships. Given her downtrodden state, one might understandably feel compassion and sympathy for her. Her counterproductive behavior patterns and mindset were reinforced and strengthened by her circumstances and conditioning. Such was the pattern that Janis had established. It was keeping her stuck. She was caught in the quicksand of her negative perspective and could not see beyond the bleakness of the landscape she had created.

Over the years, she had formed the habit of attributing inaccurate motivations and intentions to the behavior of others. This was a self-reinforcing tendency: by selectively interpreting what others did to fit her preconceived notions and expectations, Janis filtered events to confirm what she already believed.

In order for Janis to get better, she had to respond differently to the world. She needed to face the challenges in her life in a more productive and welcoming way. Unless this reorientation occurred and she was provided with concrete guidance in how to overcome her dysfunction, she would continue to feel isolated and unlovable, and she would continue to underachieve.

To provide Janis with a tangible plan of action for changing the dynamics of her relationship with life, I used the model upon which *Living Intact* is based. The impetus for *Living Intact* involves the dynamic process of balancing survival and meaning in life, facing challenges and seeking to secure, reinforce, refine, and enhance those aspects of life we most cherish.

Living Intact is an active and systematic engagement with life's challenges, using the potential of the challenge process to resolve the inherent breakdowns, dissatisfactions, and discrepancies that result from our desires for what life should be and our actual experiences living life.

To free herself from the quicksand, Janis would need to develop her capacity to counter her mood instability with better self-regulation, and she would have to form more productive habits for discipline and taking care of herself. She also clearly needed to improve her interpersonal relationship and self-management skills, determine what she wanted to accomplish, and identify what she believed stood in her way. My job was to help her accomplish these objectives.

CHALLENGES THAT OPTIMIZE OUR DEVELOPMENT

For many people, the word *challenge* connotes competition. In sports, challenge is commonly used to describe "in-your-face" battles that will yield defeat and failure or success and exhilaration. Challenges are also often associated with trials and tribulations that involve provocations, demands, and obstacles and that can potentially prevent us from fulfilling our intentions and attaining our goals. The very thought of having to face a challenge that may entail conflict or that might force us out of our comfort zone can trigger apprehension and insecurities. Dreading the possibility of becoming entangled in an *"I win"* or *"I lose"* showdown, we may be tempted to protect ourselves, choose the path of least resistance, and flee from the situation. Examples of challenges that might test our capabilities and expose us to the possibility of experiencing failure or rejection include trying out for a part in a play, returning to school for an advanced degree, competing for a promotion, seeking a partner, or deciding to write a book.

Challenges may also involve other elements. These may include confronting circumstances that test our mental capabilities, physical skills, determination, integrity, cleverness, focus, and purpose. Janis's situation was a case in point. Challenged by physiological irregularities, academic difficulty, parental disapproval, lack of faith, and a mind that often acted as her adversary, Janis needed to step forward and embrace the challenges she was facing with practical tools and a spiritual outlook that would allow her to prevail and flourish.

Whether a particular challenge involves competing to make the varsity basketball team, acing a test, winning a scholarship, or closing a business deal, the experience can sorely test us. On the downside looms the risk of failure and discouragement, and on the upside, the possibility of invigorating involvement, confidence-inspiring mastery, and pride-building triumph.

On a more benign level, challenges may also involve games, contests, tests of strength, endurance, or skill, and day-in and day-out encounters with difficult tasks. A child may find reading challenging, and an adult may find putting up the winter storm windows challenging. Physicians have their own distinctive usage of the word *challenge*. They use the term to designate a patient's response to medication dosages, calibrated treatments, and training regimens to arrest potentially harmful substances that may trigger allergic or toxic reactions.

Despite the range of definitions and applications, the *phenomenon of challenge* is an integral part of life's obligatory trials and tribulations. At the same time, challenges are endemic to life's opportunities. We may want to run a marathon or earn an MBA, and we realize that to do so will require sustained focus and effort. These challenges gauge our abilities, skills, focus, and grit. Overcoming the obstacles and attaining our objectives testify to our capacity to weather adversity, handle competition, prove merit, and prevail in a demanding world that can be harsh and unforgiving of those who lack fortitude and determination.

If we desire to live intact—that is, develop functional solutions that energize and soothe us and allow us to transcend the debilitating feelings of brokenness that can derail and paralyze us—we cannot run away from challenges. We must not only accept these tests as part and parcel of the human condition, but we must also welcome them as chances to assert our worth, character, and potency. Challenges provide the fuel for human development. They are one of the key elements that God, in his infinite wisdom, has infused into the natural order of the world. Their purpose is to condition us for endurance, protect us against outer intrusions and inner vulnerabilities, stimulate our growth, and inspire motivation and achievement.

THE ORIGINS OF CHALLENGE

Human beings encounter challenges from virtually the moment of conception. The fetus must survive and grow *in utero*. From the newborn's first breath nine months later, the infant faces the challenges of physical survival. As the child matures, he or she is confronted with the neurological, psychological, and physiological challenges inherent in the extended process of learning, developing perceptual discrimination, forming judgments and orientations, and acquiring adaptive patterns of behavior and emotional attachments. The child must identify what is food and what isn't, determine whom to trust, and figure out how to elicit the attention that will provide comfort, stimulation, pleasure, and safety. Later, the challenges translate into more variegated and complex developmental milestones. Physical growth that begins with movement, crawling, walking, and self-care progresses inexorably to higher levels of motoric proficiency, strength, and dexterity. As the child develops physically, he or she also develops mentally. His cognitive development comprises ever-expanding necessity for abstraction, mental flexibility, and intellectual agility, and these necessities pit the child against his own limitations, the skills of his peers, and the impositions and tribulations of the world and society. These demands are catalysts for the expansion of self that, when juxtaposed with a child's aptitudes and abilities, determines what can and cannot be accomplished. And concurrently, there is the core issue of emotional development that interacts with—and even predicts—the child's relationships, capacity to adjust, and success at establishing an identity. All of these elements create an individualized niche that will ideally furnish the child and the subsequently emerging adult with satisfaction, control, productivity, achievement, and self-actualization.

To this complex mix of elements we must add another that is best described as "life experiences." The impact of real-world familiarity, the distillation of knowledge, and insight gained from these occurrences in tandem with maturity, conditioning, character, attitude, spiritual outlook, and the interplay between the entire spectrum of developmental factors essentially shape who we are.

The phenomenon of challenge is embedded in the DNA of the human species and is the impetus for the on-going process of an individual's evolution. In his master plan for mankind, God has clearly ordained that we experience repeated challenges and occasional trials and tribulations. This is his way of making certain that we use the gifts he has provided us, that we develop our full range of abilities, transcend our real and imagined limitations, and soar in communion with his spirit.

We are hard pressed on every side, but not crushed; perplexed but not in despair; persecuted, but not abandoned; struck down, but not destroyed. We always carry around in our body the death of Jesus, so that the life of Jesus may also be revealed in our body. (2 Corinthians 4:8–10)

Yes, challenge has the potential to make us broken; but it also provides the momentum, nourishment, and fuel that energize, sustain, and inspire us. The manner in which we respond to challenge has the potential to transform brokenness into the wholeness, physical and emotional strength, and spiritual power that makes our lives worthy, rewarding, and satisfying.

Therefore, put on the full armor of God, so that when the day of evil comes, you may be able to stand your ground, and after you have done everything, to stand. Stand firm, then, with the belt of truth buckled around your waist, with the breastplate of righteousness in place, and with your feet filled with the readiness that comes from the gospel of peace. In addition to all this, take up the shield of faith, with which you can extinguish the flaming arrows of the evil one. Take the helmet of salvation and the sword of the spirit, which is the word of God. (Ephesians 6:13–17)

TRADITIONAL THEORIES ABOUT WHOLENESS

Traditional psychological and developmental theories attribute personality, achievement, social adjustment, and happiness to environmental conditions conducive to the successful "resolution" of conflicts that arise early in childhood. In other words, these theories assert that we are the sum of our life experiences and that children must learn to reconcile what they want with what the world allows them to have. This linking of early life experiences with later attitudes, habits, and adaptive and maladaptive accommodations is certainly logical, but such assumptions pose problems for the following reasons:

1. No hard evidence exists that *unequivocally* establishes that particular early life experiences or habits produce specific or predictable outcomes later in life. For example: *Can we assume that the child who has been abused is destined to become a psychopath? Or might the child become a famous actress, talk show host, or universally respected humanitarian?*

2. Belief in or reliance upon these assumptions about environmental influences provides no *reliable* therapeutic path to avoid character defects or psychological damage that putatively results from early experiences and provides no *reliable* therapeutic roadmap for repairing the defects or the damage. For example: *Can we assume that a person who chronically overeats was deprived of love and is trying to fill some void? Or might we look to other reasons that depart from psychodynamic inferences, such as physiological reactions combined with limited knowledge about nutrition and the gradual development of counterproductive eating and lifestyle habits?*

3. The contention that early and largely immutable character formation and coping skills development suggests a determinism that overshadows free will, intention, purpose, fortitude, miracles, and divine intervention. For example: *Can we assume that a shy, unpopular, and "nerdy" child is destined to become a social misfit? Or might he evolve one day into an inordinately rich, self-assured, popular, and respected hi-tech guru?*

4. The traditional theories of psychological development that link behavior patterns to early programming exclude those many exceptions where the apple "falls far from the tree," and children

do not turn out as expected, based upon their early childhood environment. For example: *Can we assume that the son of a chronic felon will one day himself become a felon? How do we reconcile this theory with the wayward departures of children from "good and upright" families who become felons?*

From traditional psychological perspectives, challenges are entities to be avoided, removed, or assuaged. They are viewed as threats and impediment to psychological integrity and mental health. In psychoanalytic lingo, the ego (or self) and id (instinct or desire) are in conflict, and challenges only intensify this conflict. Thus, challenges are erroneously perceived as enemies and dangers rather than as allies that stimulate in our psychological and spiritual growth.

CHALLENGES AS OPPORTUNITIES

When we perceive challenges as impediments and as something to be avoided, we deprive ourselves of invaluable opportunities to respond to life in a manner that is consonant with natural spiritual, biological, and developmental principles. Challenges are not our enemy. Rather, they are our inspiration and motivation for self-realization.

Our response to challenges at every level—within ourselves and in reaction to the world around us—allows us to grow, strengthen, recover, adapt, and discover deeper meaning in life. Learning about the nature of challenges and recognizing how individual "tests" of our bodies, minds, beliefs, integrity, and character mold us. Evolving to greater acceptance and embracing of challenges is the bedrock for the path leading toward living intact.

The act of gravitating toward challenges is an affirmation of self that reflects the confidence and emotional resiliency derived from routinely meeting challenges successfully and the expectation that future challenges will bring enhancement, pride, and verification of our abilities. In the introductory anecdote to this chapter, Janis associated challenges with a circumstantial proof of her inadequacy. She recoiled from these challenges because her negative emotions hampered her courage and follow-through and because she had built (and reinforced) her beliefs about her own insufficiency into a kind of self-fulfilling prophecy. In a palpable sense, her brain and her spirit had learned to resign whenever challenges appeared, rather than to respond adaptively. To become effective and intact, Janis needed to surrender to dependence upon God's sufficiency and also to step up to the plate. Her overriding challenge was to develop a track record of incremental successes and to reflect upon these as evidence of her own abilities to meet challenges.

I used the challenge confrontation procedure as an integral element in the therapeutic process to enable Janis to express her desires and beliefs, target her goals, test her assumptions, monitor her own progress, and evaluate the results she obtained by employing different strategies. First, I challenged her belief about the inevitability of her continued failure. The elements of the treatment methodology that I used consisted of the following:

1. Modifying cognitive behavior (thoughts, reasoning, perception, and evaluation) based upon logic and evidence.
2. Recognizing the impact and limiting effects of negative emotions and using treatment methods and strategies for eliminating those emotions.
3. Developing a spiritual faith and reliance upon God's promises, his word, his instruction, and his faithfulness.

Specifically, I encouraged Janis to use logic strategically, and I appealed to her intellect with sound counterarguments about the inevitability of failure. I also provided evidence of improvement and success attained by people who had initially shared a similar negative mind-set. At the same time, I helped Janis understand that her negative emotions were limiting her ability to achieve and were the underlying source of the problem. I highlighted the importance of belief and faith and the promises of God that assure that brokenness is the sacrifice he wants as a rudiment for living intact. Though the techniques I used with Janis would, by themselves, be effective in reducing her frustration and helping her progress toward her identified goals, I underscored that the methodology would be far more powerful when linked with faith and dependence upon God.

The sacrifices of God are a broken spirit; a broken and contrite heart, O God, you will not despise. (Psalm 51:17)

In addition to implementing the procedures described above, I disputed Janis's perceptions and interpretations of people's attitudes and interactions with her. I helped her explore alternative and competing explanations for her social contacts and the outcomes of these contacts. I invited her to consider these options and to test them covertly in actual situations. Though she was initially hesitant, the idea of using highly functional techniques to eliminate her negative emotions, in tandem with guided rehearsal and an agreement to evaluate the results together, defused her resistance. Eventually, Janis was able to add more successful and satisfying experiences to her repertoire of interactions with the world, and this expanded her portfolio of adaptive and realistic judgments and choices.

Using the challenge process to alter Janis's habits, together we actually changed her response to challenges. Once she began to perceive that answering challenges was an opportunity to grow, she made huge and rapid gains in her physiological and mental self-regulation and fitness, flexibility, and skills. She also acquired the confidence and security that she could depend upon both her own resources and upon God's sufficiency when she came to the end of her own.

Being *"miserable-miserable"* was no longer a mode in her new life. Her standards changed as she became more experienced, confident, and adept. Being *"happy-miserable"* was not an unattainable dream but, rather, a steppingstone toward fulfilling her expectation of living intact.

To become more intact, recover from brokenness, and protect herself from her vulnerabilities, Janis acquired an increasing trust and faith in God, and she realized that she could lean on him whenever she needed. She also learned about her own expectations and about how her desires influenced her view of reality and her satisfaction. She practiced and improved her reality testing and self-observation; this helped her see how her unmet needs and desires colored her interpretation of events and people and clouded a clear and relatively objective view of situations.

Janis took stock of herself through the process of assessment, and she used the concepts of self, world, and integral skills to understand her limitations, compensate for weaknesses, and fortify her skills. After having spent years battling life, she became much more able to live life on its own terms, changing herself and circumstances where she could, accepting adversity, tolerating the frustration she could not eliminate, and consciously discerning the efficacy of responding to life's curve balls with improved judgment. I'm happy to report that Janis "got it." She learned that wisdom and choice play key roles in getting more out of life while life gets more out of her.

Before we explore in more detail the methods and principles that helped Janis, let's take a look at another client. His name is Robert, and he was also saddled with burdens that challenged his ability to live intact.

LIVING ON THE RAZOR'S EDGE

"Robert, when you speak with the purchasing agent at Optical Technology, we want you to ask him if their company would be willing to make a contribution to Save the Forests Fund. We're asking all of our customers to contribute." Anticipating the salesman's negative reaction to this directive, the sales manager clenched his jaw and pursed his lips.

Robert stared at the man incredulously. He couldn't believe what he had just been asked to do. The sales manager was actually telling him to solicit a contribution from one of his best accounts. Robert realized immediately that the idea had to be the brainchild of the vice president, an engineer whose understanding of sales procedures was, at best, marginal. Robert knew that the request would not only be inappropriate and embarrassing, but that it could also jeopardize one of his most important accounts. If his customer resented the solicitation, as Robert was certain he would, it could seriously harm his relationship with the company.

"You've got to be kidding, Neil! My job is to sell memory chips, not to solicit contributions," Robert replied with barely controlled anger.

"Just do it, Robert. This is not my decision. I have to follow management's orders, and you also have to follow orders."

Robert shook his head in disbelief, turned, and walked away.

As a consummate sales pro, Robert consistently racked up impressive numbers in a world where numbers translated into income and job security. His new position with a hi-tech start-up company was generally going well, but there were wrinkles. The challenges of establishing credibility within his firm and hitting his sales targets seemed more dependent on the erratic whims of upper management than on his track record of dealing with his customers.

The challenges were compounded by the fact that the top tier of the company consisted of doctoral level scientists with questionable marketing experience, compulsively meddlesome behaviors, and inappropriate conduct when interacting with clients. Unreasonable in their expectations and embarrassingly juvenile, their intrusions not only made

Robert's job increasingly difficult, but the interference was also having a negative impact on his income and mental health.

Robert was in a constant double bind. If he couldn't produce the targeted sales figures because of management's ineptitude and interference, he risked being fired, but if he pointed out the problems and antagonized his bosses, he was equally at risk for losing his job.

Living on the razor's edge was an all too familiar story for the forty-three year-old. He straddled the same blade at home. His wife had held a secure well-paying job for two decades, and her income exceeded his. Although she had repeatedly assured him at the beginning of their marriage that money didn't matter to her, Robert learned that these assurances meant nothing when it came to dealing with the day-to-day realities. His succession of sales jobs and intermittent unemployment threatened the security she craved. Recognizing his wife's priorities, Robert had long ago abandoned his interest in pursuing a career in science and had instead gravitated to sales because he believed that this would provide more income for his family.

Robert's skills as a salesman and the confident demeanor he projected to his customers camouflaged a negative outlook on life. Depressed and lacking in self-esteem, he was certain that nothing he did was good enough to please Rebecca and blunt her criticism and disillusionment with him. His wife was equally gloomy and depressed. Because of his erratic employment track record, she expected that any job he held would be short-lived, and her catastrophic expectations were a primary source of resentment for both of them.

Dreading hearing his wife express her disenchantment with him, Robert didn't dare to share his career frustrations and dissatisfaction with her. His self-concept was already shaky, and he was sure that she would react to his discontent by painting a doomsday scenario and accusing him of undermining the family's security.

Robert had become habituated to waiting for the other shoe to drop and for his wife to find fault, and he felt powerless and insignificant. Being scolded for his inadequacies had become a constant in his life.

From Robert's perspective, the challenges that he faced seemed insurmountable. This misconception drove his insecurities. Of course, I knew something that Robert hadn't yet learned: the starting point in making his life work was to realize that most challenges are, in fact, surmountable. The process of confronting and overcoming these challenges would provide him with an opportunity to alter the dynamics of his marriage, enhance his self-concept, and live a more intact and fulfilling life. My job as his therapist was to help him alter his attitudes and furnish him with a game plan for prevailing over the challenges he was facing.

OPPORTUNITIES ABOUND—THE CHALLENGE CHAMELEON

In the preceding anecdote, Robert's associations with challenges were decidedly negative. The objective of the therapeutic process that we embarked on was to transform Robert's entrenched negative associations into positive associations by helping him better understand the issues and dynamics of these associations and by providing him with more functional alternatives to his maladaptive behaviors. I knew that this process of identifying and handling challenges differently would liberate him from the dysfunctionality that suffused his life and would provide a pillar for building his self-esteem. Robert needed to discover and take pleasure from his many talents and from those areas where he excelled. He also needed to stop beating himself up for his perceived shortcomings.

Those fortunate enough to have an early formative environment enriched with nurturing and buttressed by carefully orchestrated elements that reinforce achievement clearly have an advantage, as do those who learn how to confront and prevail over challenges early in life. These important elements set the stage for being able to meet challenges confidently later in life. But life does not proceed in a straight line, and there are frequently unforeseen curves and detours, and early programming often ends up not being that reliable or predictive. Perhaps another dynamic creates a conduciveness to positive change and regeneration that transcends any misfortunes and obstacles that might have occurred during the early formative years. The character development so necessary for living intact and being righteous in God's view tests everyone and compels them—irrespective of their particular backgrounds and natural abilities—to confront and prevail over the many challenges that they will inevitably face in life. These challenges will differ, but they share a common denominator in that they provide us with repeated opportunities to build true self-esteem and to view ourselves in a way that integrates confidence, respect, humility, and an appreciation for the needs of others.

Let us not become weary in doing good, for at the proper time we will reap a harvest if we do not give up. Therefore, as we have opportunity, let us do good to all people, especially to those who belong to the family of believers. (Galatians 6:9–10)

GUIDELINES FOR CONFRONTING GROWTH-INDUCING CHALLENGES

Throughout our lives, we periodically have to confront roadblocks that stand between us and our goals. These barriers may be visible and well-defined, such as dealing with a person or situation that blocks our path; or the obstacles may be less evident and may involve having an atypical blood cell count, irregular brainwave patterns, or other metabolic or physiological anomalies. The goals to which we aspire may vary from the concrete, such as acquiring a job, a car, or a relationship to the less tangible such as overcoming temptation or bad habits or becoming more worthy. Irrespective of the nature of the roadblocks we face and the goals we define, the ongoing dynamic of self-realization and attaining and maintaining intactness invariably require that we confront and prevail over challenges. The process comprises three elements.

STEPS INVOLVED IN DEALING WITH CHALLENGES

1. **Recognize and face, and then clarify and assimilate the challenge.**

   This step requires some form of reality check to identify and acknowledge what is so. Because life doesn't always give us what we want, we are bound to face disappointments from time to time. We might lose our job, experience a romantic rejection, miss an opportunity, or perform less than optimally in a particular situation. We might misjudge someone else or ourselves; our efforts may be unappreciated or discounted, or our intentions may be misperceived. By deliberately identifying and acknowledging the existing conditions, we reduce the likelihood of overreacting, minimizing, rationalizing, or being in denial. Instead, we are positioning ourselves to come to terms with those aspects of the challenging situation that seem alterable, those that appear immutable, and those effects that will most likely ensue from accepting, negotiating, or responding strategically to the reality of the situation. Recognizing the nature of the challenge is clearly step one, but even this recognition can in itself be challenging. We all have experienced the frustration of understanding something intellectually, yet still feeling powerless to alter our behaviors and attitudes. The real challenge is to accept that we must periodically go through a tortuous process in which we struggle to comprehend situations and sort out the underlying elements. We must be willing to develop our capacities to integrate our insights both cognitively and emotionally, and we must deliberately expand our abilities to apply functional problem-solving skills when confronting everyday challenges, problems, and crises. This may sound daunting, and it is certainly easier said than done, but you will learn that it is eminently doable. Rest easy. This book will furnish you with the requisite problem-solving skills to make this happen.

2. **Adapt to the challenge and use this mechanism to your advantage.**
This may involve changing behaviors, attitudes, and understandings. In the process, you will experience emotional growth and become more self-controlled, functional, and compassionate.

Meeting a challenge successfully often requires deliberate adjustments, focused effort, and a degree of discomfort as you marshal your resources and modify your accustomed *modus operandi*. This is why it is a challenge! You will need to step outside of the confines of your comfort—or more fittingly—your "discomfort" zone. As quoted earlier, a wise man (my father) often repeated, "If you keep doing more of what you're doing, you'll probably get more of what you've got." Sometimes, redoubling efforts will attain the desired result, but more often than not, responding effectively to a challenge involves modifying your response patterns when you recognize that such a modification is needed. To handle the challenge, you must be ready to evaluate and monitor yourself and prepared to make changes proactively. Robert, the salesman described in the preceding anecdote, learned this lesson, and the knowledge dramatically enhanced the quality of his life.

Most of us are highly attuned to our comfort levels. When we sense we're being nudged or jolted out of our secure harbor, we often react to the discomfort by short-circuiting strategic planning, analytical and critical thinking, astute observations, or an objective assessment of the effectiveness of our reactions. We tend to latch onto responses that help us regain our equilibrium, maintain our stability, and preserve our comfort zones and sanctuaries. These responses are likely to be internalized and reused, and before long, they become ingrained habits. This automatic reaction occurs irrespective of whether our response to the challenge is healthy or not. For instance, a student might respond to a poor grade on a test by concluding that he is incompetent and, in so doing, reinforce his negative self-image and diminished expectations and aspirations that are based on previous negative experiences. The student might also react defensively by becoming angry with the instructor and by lamenting the unfairness or stupidity of the test questions. He might rationalize why he didn't study enough or claim to have no idea why he did poorly. The far more productive choice is for the student to assess his performance, study his miscues objectively, and develop a strategy for improving his chances of doing better on the next test.

Regaining our equilibrium, maintaining stability, and preserving our comfort zones can also occur at physiological and subconscious levels when responding to challenges. Cravings and addictions, for example, are massive challenges that disrupt our balance and demand our attention. Yielding to these desires can result in continuing servitude to the anxiety, the compulsion, and the substances or behaviors that temporarily placate it. Yes, resisting cravings and addictions is easier said than done, but the first step is to see the condition as a challenge, to map out a plan, make behavioral adjustment, and commit to altering the emotional and physiological dynamic. Trust me. It's achievable!

Emerging from a safe, secure, and comfortable harbor that, despite its comfort, restricts our development often requires new behaviors, produces new experiences, demands a realistic evaluation of our resources, and necessitates greater functionality and flexibility in our responses. Exiting from that which is familiar, predictable, and commodious usually generates stress and anxiety at first, but these emotions are invariably growth inducing, if properly managed. I am reminded of Plato's allegory about the cave. This allegory is relevant and bears retelling.

THE CAVE

Imagine prisoners who have been chained since their childhood deep inside a cave. Not only do the chains immobilize their limbs; their heads are chained as well, so that their gaze is fixed on a wall.

Behind the prisoners is an enormous fire, and between the fire and the prisoners is a raised walkway, along which people carry statues of various animals, plants, and other things. The statues cast shadows on the wall, and the prisoners watch these shadows. When one of the statue-carriers speaks, an echo against the wall causes the prisoners to believe that the words come from the shadows.

The prisoners engage in what appears to be a game, naming the shapes as they pass by. This, however, is the only reality that they know, even though they are seeing merely shadows of images. They are thus conditioned to judge the quality of one another by their skill in quickly naming the shapes and dislike those who begin to play poorly.

Were a prisoner to be released and compelled to stand up and turn around, at that moment, his eyes will be blinded by the sunlight coming into the cave from its entrance, and the shapes passing will appear less real than their shadows.

The last object he would be able to see is the sun. In time, he would learn to see this object as the source that provides the seasons, presides over all things in the visible region, and is in some way the cause of all these things that he has seen.

For those of faith, the sun is symbolic of God, the source of all within man's worldly and spiritual life. The cave is symbolic of the comfort zone in which we ensconce ourselves and seek refuge. Unless man frees himself from the cave and emerges into the light, he will see, at best, only indistinct shadows dancing on a wall.

On a less allegorical and more secular level, the process of evaluating your resources and responding with greater flexibility is akin to finding yourself in a foreign environment where you encounter unfamiliar food, accoutrements, culture, and language. To function successfully in this new context, you need to be willing to step away from that which is familiar and comfortable. Although perhaps disconcerting initially, the new experiences extend your horizons, expand your worldliness, and enhance your confidence in your ability to adapt to unfamiliar situations. Flexibility and adaptation are core physiological and psychological survival capabilities that allow you to adjust to the realities of the world, prevail over its challenges, acquire emotional potency, and enhance your self-concept.

3. **Use your success at meeting challenges as a springboard for improved exchange between you and others and for giving more and getting more.**

    When you handle challenges better, you will discover more power, and you are likely to uncap the desire to extend yourself to others. This may launch you into a teaching or modeling role, or it may serve as an impetus for you to share your own personal story and relate better to the challenges that others face. Struggling with your own challenges is also likely to make you more humble and sensitive to the angst, fears, and insecurities of those around you. What begins as a quest for self-repair can evolve into a more compassionate and functional perspective about the foibles and failures of your fellow man.

    Handling challenges more effectively can also enable you to set limits more clearly and successfully. For instance, many people are afraid to offer criticism or set boundaries for fear that the other person may respond by pointing out their deficiencies reciprocally. (*"Honey, I want you to take this in a constructive way. Your lack of punctuality when we're invited to a social event is an inconvenience and a sign of disrespect." "Really! Well, look whose talking about inconvenience and disrespect. What about your forgetting to follow through on your promises?"*).

    Meeting challenges provides a blueprint for achieving self-integrity on the one hand and a simple a mechanism for survival on the other. Cleaning up your own act, not in a prideful manner, but in a way that allows you dignity, clarity, and confidence in delineating what is acceptable, cannot help but enhance your self-concept. Handling challenges creates, in effect, ever-higher standards of living.

New skills create new opportunities and responsibilities. As you become more adept at handling the demands and disappointments of life that once brought defeat, you will find joy and fulfillment in using your new self-image, capabilities, and outlook about challenges for the betterment of other people. You will also attain respect and recognition—invaluable elements in the living intact formula.

Challenge is a phenomenon that occurs at the infinitesimal levels of our cells and at the colossal levels of the larger environment and universe. Thus, regulating your moods or being able to get a better night's sleep are significant conquests at a personal level. Finding a cure for AIDS, caring for the environment, feeding the world's hungry people, or settling international disputes are examples of meeting challenges at more expansive levels. Despite the larger scale of these desires, actualization involves the same process of confronting and prevailing over challenges.

The process integrally involves people. It is about you in relation to others. The primary function of a nervous system in those biological species having one is to mediate interactions between the self and other organisms in the environment. When you interact with others, you are doing something far beyond socializing casually. You are obtaining feedback that helps you reinforce adaptive behaviors and modify maladaptive ones. As you become better at meeting challenges, these social interactions will provide emotional sustenance, feelings of connectedness, and pleasure. The successful social interactions will also guard against a wide range of vulnerabilities that are often associated with brokenness, isolation, or ill health. Everybody has areas of vulnerability and weakness that are essentially unmet challenges and that can threaten survival. These may be genetic predispositions, life habits, or the chance impingements thrust upon you by life that break down and scar you.

To be socially competent, you don't have to be a social butterfly or meeting planner. Perhaps the social arena in which you are being challenged and tested involves handling embarrassment or physical rigor in a fitness class, handling the expression of intense emotion in a cancer support event, or conducting a worship service. Whatever the circumstance, bringing your struggle and successes with challenges to the forum represents a big step in forming habits of living intact.

4. Regard challenges as a communication and planning vehicle between you and God.

Facing challenges does not mean that you will always prevail or get what you want. However, the ongoing challenge process makes you stronger in strength and faith. Note James 1:2–3:

Consider it pure joy, my brothers, whenever you face trials of many kinds, because you know that the testing of your faith develops perseverance. Perseverance must finish its work so that you may be mature and complete, not lacking in anything.

The Bible speaks of challenge in a number of ways. One aspect of challenge is that of *trials and tests*. This is the instructional and guidance role that God extends to us through his word. Trials and tests are a natural part of life. God tells us this, and he reminds us that he is there to help and guide us and that if we listen and obey, the outcome will be filled with sufficiency and grace.

Dear friends, do not be surprised at the painful trial you are suffering, as though something strange were happening to you. But rejoice that you participate in the sufferings of Christ, so that you may be overjoyed when his glory is revealed. (1 Peter 4:12–13)

Our fathers disciplined us for a little while as they thought best; but God disciplines us for our good, that we may share in his holiness. No discipline seems pleasant at the time, but painful. Later on, however, it produces a harvest of righteousness and peace for those who have been trained by it. (Hebrews 12:10–11)

Life's tests are challenges God has made to shape us, and he clearly uses the process of reinforcement. When we pay attention and gravitate toward what he wants for us, we get reinforced. We get rewarded, encouraged, and find doors opening that had seemed closed or nonexistent previously. God wants us to welcome challenges as a sign of openness toward him.

Search me, O God, and know my heart; test me and know my anxious thoughts. See if there is any offensive way in me, and lead me in the way everlasting. (Psalm 139:23–24)

Test me, O Lord, and try me, examine my heart and my mind; (Psalm 26:2)

For you, O God, tested us; you refined us like silver. (Psalm 66:10)

But, O Lord Almighty, you who judge righteously and test the heart and mind, let me see your vengeance upon them, for to you I have committed my cause. (Jeremiah 11:20)

Blessed is the man who perseveres under trial, because when he has stood the test, he will receive the crown of life that God has promised to those who love him. (James 1:12)

Do not conform any longer to the pattern of this world, but be transformed by the renewing of your mind. Then you will be able to test and approve what God's will is—his good, pleasing and perfect will. (Romans 12:2)

Test everything. Hold on to the good. (1 Thessalonians 5:21)

Another biblical aspect of challenge is that of **trouble**. When we're confronted with this aspect, God invites us to come to him, to lean and depend on him for protection in the face of adversity. He is not endorsing an avoidance of consequences, but rather a faith in his knowledge, his care, and his ability to guard us and to make things right. In times of adversity, overwhelm, enmity, and challenge, we are to reach out for God's protection. God warns us that we will have trouble, but he also tells of the good news:

"I have told you these things, so that in me you may have peace. In this world you will have trouble. But take heart! I have overcome the world." (John 16:33)

For in the day of trouble he will keep me safe in his dwelling; he will hide me in the shelter of his tabernacle and set me high upon a rock. (Psalm 27:5)

You are my hiding place; you will protect me from trouble. (Psalm 32:7)

God is our refuge and our strength, an ever-present help in trouble. (Psalm 46:1)

And call upon me in the day of trouble; I will deliver you and you will honor me. (Psalm 50:15)

He will call upon me, and I will answer him; I will be with him in trouble, I will deliver him and honor him. (Psalm 91:15)

Though I walk in the midst of trouble, you preserve my life; you stretch out your hand against the anger of my foes, with your right hand you save me. (Psalm 138:7)

Yet another biblical meaning of challenge is the message of burden and frustration. God reminds us not only that the nature of the world includes difficulty, problems, adversity, and frustration, but also that his challenges and protection are meant to teach us that we should identify with and carry the burdens of others. When challenges are burdensome, we should not shirk or complain. Instead, we should reach out to God and to others, sometimes to get help, and sometimes to give help. This is the essence of getting more from life while life gets more from you.

For the creation was subjected to frustration, not by its own choice, but by the one who subjected it, in hope that the creation itself will be liberated from its bondage to decay and brought into the glorious freedom of the children of God. We know that the whole creation has been groaning as in the pains of childbirth right up to the present time. (Romans 8:20–22)

Praise be to the God and Father of our Lord Jesus Christ, the Father of compassion and the God of all comfort, who comforts us in all our troubles so that we can comfort those in any trouble with the comfort we ourselves have received from God. (2 Corinthians 1:3)

Praise be to the Lord, to God our Savior, who daily bears our burdens. (Psalm 68:19)

Carry each other's burdens, and in this way you will fulfill the law of Christ. (Galatians 6:2)

"Come to me, all you who are weary and burdened, and I will give you rest. Take my yoke upon you and learn from me, for I am gentle and humble in heart, and you will find rest for your souls. For my yoke is easy and my burden is light." (Matthew 11:28–30)

God tells us that we should carry each other's burdens. Sometimes this is the challenge to be compassionate, and sometimes it is the challenge to bear on our own shoulders the problems of our fellow man. This can be both an active and passive process. If you carefully and earnestly seek and observe, you will often find spiritual and practical correlates to your own challenges.

HOW ROBERT AND JANIS FACED CHALLENGES

Let's take another look at the stories that appeared earlier in the chapter. In Robert's case, the challenges he faced spiritually dovetailed with his day-to-day worldly obstacles. Robert's negativity had been habitually reinforced, and he could find all kinds of selective confirmation to justify his feelings of being overwhelmed and frustrated at every turn. When he began to understand that his negative and avoidant attitude really masked self-pity, resentment toward God (with whom he did espouse a believing relationship), and a sense of prideful entitlement, Robert opened his spiritual receptiveness and capacity for change. He accepted that his wife's skepticism, mood regulation problems, and self-absorption were also *his* burdens. This allowed him to recognize the opportunity to become a resource for her, and it also made his own issues seem less overwhelming. In this way, he was able to relieve his own depression and indecision. He was also able to draw on his newfound willingness to identify with his wife's vulnerabilities and to comfort her while still setting limits and trusting God to direct him and restore him when he was faced with opposition and lack of environmental support for his efforts. Though burdened by the possibility of losing his job as he navigated through the double binds in his life, Robert became comforted and clear minded in the knowledge that God had set this challenge before him. His job was to find ways to answer the seemingly opposite demands while remaining true to himself and God's principles. Those principles included God's oversight, direction, and, ultimately, his protection. When Robert added this dimension to his coping abilities, he could strategize a plan for dealing with his job stressors, and he could evaluate its effectiveness and make adaptations. As it turned out, Robert was able to sidestep the solicitation he was ordered to make just long enough for his senior management to come to their senses, and they ultimately scrapped the directive. In the meantime, Robert had devised new ways of communicating more effectively with his immediate manager, and their working relationship became more harmonious and productive.

The spiritual dimension for Janis, the protagonist in the first story, evolved into her coming to grips with God's tests. Janis clearly needed more self-discipline. Her mood disorder and attention problems made this a difficult challenge for her. Yet even when treatment interventions alleviated these problems, her mind's narrative told her that life was "harder" for her, which indeed it was, partly because of her ineffective work habits and negative forecasting regarding success in school and in relationships. Because she was so smart, Janis was quickly able to apply the principles of reinforcement to alter conditions and change her habits. However, she still faced real challenges of putting into practice the principles she intellectually had grasped. She knew how to correct her study habits, and she realized that her mother's reactions to her provocations were justifiable. Janis also realized that she needed to be willing to decisively face the challenges to her assumed expectations and integrity (in large part, her practice of inconsistently keeping her word). Rather than resent her lot in life, Janis needed to see her personal challenges and circumstances as God's way of testing, instructing, and leading her. As she confronted these issues, she experienced God's comfort and guidance, and she was able to glimpse regularly the future that he held for her—a life that was more disciplined, functional, and full of achievements, satisfaction, and reality-based confidence. Once she accepted and embraced God's tests and developed her skills, character, and habits of proper self- and God-reliance, Janis could envision and enact this new life.

WHAT DO YOU BELIEVE?

If you are not a believing Christian, you may wonder what applications the principles in this book have for you. You may ask whether the tenets and techniques will work without your espoused spiritual devotion or acceptance of God and his supremacy.

Rest assured that the principles, tips, techniques, and how-tos offered here will benefit you—if properly applied—regardless of your spiritual persuasion or lack thereof. Antibiotics, anesthesia, and corrective lenses, for example, will have their intended effects, regardless of your beliefs. They are part of a scientifically organized universe that is, in large measure, understandable and predictable. However, there is a bigger picture. In my view (which is shared by millions of others), the knowable and reliable—as well as the inscrutable, mysterious, and confounding—were created by a magnificent creator who established the orderliness of principles, science, natural forces, and all that we take for granted. You can use these things without giving credit to their founder. They will still work, for that is the glory of how they were made. God does not demand copyrights or patents. But he is a jealous God, and he longs for your allegiance and the acknowledgment that he created you in his image. He abhors the worship of other gods, warning against idolatry. In God's view, anything that humans value above God amounts to displaced values, if not idolatry. Using his gifts and principles without acknowledging him and crediting him is a form of plagiarism and forgery. Though you may get away with it temporarily, you will bear the knowledge of deception that detracts from the fullness of intact living. If you truly believe you are not cheating by relying exclusively on the "natural world" because you are not convinced there is a Creator, then I pray you will discover spiritually the lesson I learned as a young child (before I knew God) when I first confronted my need for glasses.

At about the age of nine, it became apparent that I was nearsighted. When my mother took me to an eye doctor, the experience was frightening and traumatizing. The doctor was a large and imposing woman with a determined manner and a high-pitched voice like that of Julia Child, the revered TV chef. I was terrified by the idea that I would have to wear glasses. In my defense, I blabbered to the doctor about the sufficiency and intactness of my eyesight. In my nine-year-old language, I tried to assure her that I could see just fine. She countered with a line I'll never forget:

"You're like the little fly in a bottle who thinks it's a huge park, because he's never been outside the bottle," she said. "Like the fly, you don't know what you're missing."

Regarding logic and senses, the doctor literally opened my eyes. This experience has served me many times over as a metaphor for freeing my closed mind and steeled heart. The comfort zone of habit and the defense of fear are poor substitutes for an enriched and liberated life.

You need not credit or acknowledge God in order to use and benefit from his tools. However, not to credit him is not to see fully nor to wholly experience the dimension of living intact that is supplied only by his grace. If you are fortunate, you will run into someone like my old eye doctor. Or perhaps you will fly into the jarring wall of the glass bottle, and so awaken.

Shall what is formed say to him who formed it, "He did not make me? Can the pot say of the potter, He knows nothing?" (Isaiah 29:16)

But who are you, O man, to talk back to God? Shall what is formed say to him who formed it, "Why did you make me like this?" Does not the potter have the right to make out of the same lump of clay some pottery for noble purposes and some for common use? (Romans 9:20–21)

THE CHALLENGE THEME

Without challenges in our life, we would vegetate and dissipate. This phenomenon of physical, emotional, and spiritual dissipation has been extensively described in many famous nineteenth century English and Russian novels. A central character in these books inherits a comfortable yearly stipend and, unfettered by financial concerns, proceeds to meander through life without focus or impetus. Unchallenged by life's typical demands, existence devolves into a self-indulgent, stagnant, dissolute, and incontrovertibly broken routine.

Absent challenges, we do little more than mark time from the beginning of our earthy existence to our end. Our lives are incomplete and flawed; opportunities for self-actualization are missed, and the potential for psychological and spiritual intactness is diminished. Unless we deliberately change course, we are destined to live marginalized lives of silent desperation.

LIVING INTACT

We live in an imperfect world. When it comes right down to it, most of us find it hard to accept on a visceral level that life may fail to work the way we want and may not give us all that we want. Though we may understand this intellectually (and even spiritually accept our limitations), there is something in human nature that wants to have its own way. So we fight, cry, resent, complain, rebel, regroup, plan, scheme, and redouble our efforts to prevail and control our circumstances and proactively direct the course of our lives and our destiny. Though this component of human nature helps us survive and has healthy aspects, it also gets us into trouble. As necessity mothers invention, so, too, do obstacles and brokenness conceive and impel the meeting of challenges. We desire to be whole. That is part of our nature.

Nonetheless, we have each experienced what it is to be broken, and we have each—wittingly or unwittingly—caused brokenness. Each of us has broken our word. Each of us has disillusioned others. Each of us has acted self-centeredly. Each of us at some point has acted dishonorably. Certainly, there are exceptions to self-centeredness—extraordinary people such as Mother Teresa, Billy Graham, Mahatma Gandhi, Florence Nightingale, Joan of Arc—but I would wager that even these highly evolved and spiritual human beings would admit to acts of omission or commission, however trivial they may appear to us, acts that they themselves would consider dishonorable.

When we experience brokenness, life becomes labored, disjointed, and dissatisfying, and unfortunately for many, this condition occurs all too regularly. The dilemma is how to get back on track and how to become once again intact. Let me reassert that meeting challenges effectively is key. To repair the brokenness, we must be prepared to respond proactively to challenges with increased flexibility, skill, and astuteness, and with a clear leaning toward what is right and appropriate under the existing conditions. (Yes, we know in our heart, if not our mind, what is right and appropriate, though we may be sorely tempted to disregard these truths.) Though brokenness is not a desirable state, the experience of brokenness is both inevitable and constructive in dealing with a universe that doesn't always give us our way.

Most of us—those of us who are not masochists—want to avoid brokenness, heal ourselves, and remove the conditions that are having negative impact on our life, diminishing our happiness, and undermining our productivity and efficacy. Thus, the notion of achieving "intactness" is alluring. Intactness is the antithesis of brokenness. At issue is how we can use life's realities, conundrums, and problems to recover from, include, accept, and even embrace the broken parts of our existence to achieve intactness.

In the next chapter, we will examine in greater depth the phenomenon of achieving intactness and its implications and permutations. We will also explore how living intact can be made concrete and accessible to you. Yes, it's doable.

III

POWER TOOLS FOR
LIVING INTACT

CHAPTER 9
EEG NEUROFEEDBACK

What if you had a "device" that could control how you feel, how alert or tired you are, and whether other people, disappointments, frustrations, and setbacks perturb you? What if this device allowed you to turn up pleasure and turn down pain? Further, what if you could use this device to recall the past, plan into the future, and record and edit in five sensory modalities? Even better, imagine that this device could communicate with other such devices and could run on its own energy, recharging itself by simply going to sleep.

Well, you actually have access to this remarkable piece of equipment. I am referring to your marvelous brain! This extraordinary tool has amazing capabilities. It is the power-packed onboard computer that manages and regulates all the systems in your body, and it is the portal through which you experience and respond to life. Your brain is a delicately balanced, multifaceted instrument that interprets and reacts to challenges, and the manner in which it accomplishes this directly determines the extent to which you are able to live intact.

It is vital that you nurture, protect, and nourish your brain. It's also vital that you take a deliberate and proactive role in developing its full range of capabilities. There are many ways to achieve this objective that include intentionally keeping your brain vibrant through learning, analyzing and solving problems, and performing mental exercises that "stretch" your brain's capabilities. Even such mundane pursuits as doing crossword puzzle, reading a book, playing chess or Scrabble, or doing research on the Internet qualify as deliberate "brain-feeding" pursuits.

The term "mental exercises" can be somewhat misleading, as it could imply something other than physical or physiological. We are talking here about actual deliberate or automatic physiological responses to stimuli. Throughout the day (and night), our brain becomes activated and deactivated as we interact with our environment and our own internal circuitry. The activity in our brain encompasses a series of physical processes that affect our thoughts, emotions, hormonal secretions, and vascular and muscle activity. Our brain determines whether we like something and how we will react to it. This dynamic of stimulus/reaction even includes how our digestive system reacts to specific foods.

Of course, your brain is not an autocrat, but rather acts in response to those areas within the body or the environment that send it signals. If you stub your toe or eat something that your body doesn't tolerate well, your brain will be notified by the particular stimulus, and you will experience pain and discomfort. These physical sensations are nervous system responses, and they will influence the brain's narrative. From earlier chapters, you will recall that your arousal state greatly affects how you perceive things and what your mind says about them and your relationship with them. Mental attitudes, awareness, and physical states are inextricably intertwined. However, these elements are not preordained, nor are they immutable, and you can take charge of your experiences and choices in a number of ways.

What if you could train your brain to take charge in the ways that you want? What would you choose? To alleviate physical or emotional pain? To focus and organize more productively? To get more restful sleep? To reduce anger, irritation, fear, or procrastination? To banish addictions and compulsions? To become more compassionate?

Here is some great news: in a short period of time, you can train your brain to accomplish these things and much more. You can achieve improved levels of self-regulation, self-control, performance enhancement, cognitive focus, and emotional well-being. You can even recover from many of the injuries that impair functioning and detract from living intact.

The method for doing so is called EEG neurofeedback (also called EEG biofeedback). This is a procedure for training your brain by using computers that teach your mind and body how to function better. The method works relatively quickly—in days for some people and in months for others—and it uses the same principles by which nature allows you to grow and heal: the principles that permeate the physical world and universe. These are the principles of *timing*.

Timing mechanisms form the basis of physics and also of biology. Our DNA contains timing information that controls growth and development (and possibly the onset of disease and breakdown). The timing of our brain and nervous system determines whether we are impulsive, impatient, sleepy, and even whether we understand something.

By training (or tuning) the timing mechanisms in our brain and nervous system, you can use nature's principles to influence states of being and to correct minor and major ailments and impairments that derail the ability to live intact. EEG neurofeedback can effectively initiate and enable a healing process and allow you to harness your brain's capabilities and potential.

WHAT IS EEG NEUROFEEDBACK?

EEG neurofeedback (also called EEG biofeedback or simply neurofeedback or biofeedback[9]) is a procedure that directly trains your brainwaves through the use of computers and specific, carefully calibrated software. The program is based on electrical brain activity that is measured by the electroencephalogram, or EEG.

Neurofeedback permits the brain to function more efficiently and proficiently by taking advantage of the brain's *plasticity*, or ability to adapt and utilize different aspects of itself when this flexibility is advantageous. During neurofeedback training, the practitioner[10] observes your brain in action from moment to moment. We show you this information on a computer screen and simultaneously reward your brain for changing its activity to more appropriate patterns. This is a gradual learning process. It affects and conditions any measurable aspect of brain function.

---

9. EEG biofeedback is the training of brainwaves. There is another type of biofeedback, called EMG biofeedback (electromyelogram) that is used to train specific muscles; it is much more localized and limited than EEG biofeedback (neurofeedback).

10. People beginning neurofeedback should work with a trained professional. Eventually, many people take charge of their own training by obtaining their own equipment and learning how to train themselves. It is analogous to someone practicing at a gym with a trainer and then getting home equipment. The first person "we" also refers to the collaborative process of client and therapist observing the client's brain patterns during the training session.

Neurofeedback is training in self-regulation. This self-regulation is a necessary part of good brain function. Self-regulation training makes your brain and central nervous system function more capably.

Neurofeedback works by monitoring your brainwaves and converting the electrical signals (EEG) from your head into filtered digital information that is then used to modulate a video game on a computer screen. To do this, we attach electrode sensors to your scalp. Nothing goes into your head via these wires—neither electric current nor information. The sensors simply monitor and conduct the signal from your head and brain to an amplifier and from there to one or more computers. The computer equipment digitally transforms your brain signals into audiovisual information, usually presented in the form of a variety of entertaining and engaging games. While your brain is being trained, you "play" the game for about thirty minutes at a time and make the game proceed by actually controlling it with your brainwaves. The marvel of electronics makes this possible, but the key to its efficacy lies in the technology of filtering your brainwaves and in the science of selecting the range of signals that your brain should alter in order for you to feel and function better.

The feedback you get happens when the game goes better, seemingly on its own. Actually, you control the game by producing more of the brainwave signal that the therapist selects to allow through the filter (the reward) and less of the brainwaves selected for inhibition. Thus, your brain is subtly influenced and coached to make more of certain brainwaves and less of others. This is a form of *operant conditioning* (the behavioral term for the strategic use of reinforcement schedules) that conditions your brain and nervous system in a safe, subtle, and persistent way. (Refer back to chapter 6 for a review of reinforcement.)

While playing the game, you are being reinforced neurologically at the rate of approximately three thousand "rewards" per hour. Your brain is shown persistently how to adjust its timing mechanisms to more functional and "feel-good" levels. All you have to do is sit in a comfortable chair and observe the computer screen. Your job in the training process is to bear witness to your own brain activity. It is fascinating! But how can this exercise possibly work to help you overcome challenges, symptoms, illnesses, setbacks, and the conflict that results from living in a difficult world?

HOW DOES NEUROFEEDBACK WORK?

In neurofeedback training, you are actually observing your brain in action from moment to moment. Specialized computer equipment reflects your brain's performance as this is happening. Electrode sensors conduct signals from your scalp to sensitive equipment that digitally filters and transforms those signals into entertaining video games that you control, just by observing the game on the screen. Unlike typical video games, you don't use your hands to control the game.[11] As you play the game, your brain is rewarded for changing its own activity to more appropriate patterns. This is a gradual learning process. It applies to any measurable aspect of brain function. Neurofeedback is essentially biofeedback applied directly to the brain.

Many conditions that detract from living intact are caused by a brain and nervous system that is *disregulated*. This disregulation causes the brain to be inconsistent in its "housekeeping" functions and to wander into activity that does not suit the demands of the situation. Neurofeedback uses the brain's natural bioelectrical rhythms to self-correct.

You can think of the process as teaching your brain and nervous system to stay consistently within a lane while driving on a road and navigating different speeds, terrains, and conditions. It is not verbal instruction or logical thinking that induces these capacities. Rather, you develop these capacities by training your brain to monitor and focus its attention on the relevant events, both inside your mind and outside in the environment. In so doing, your brain makes necessary adjustments—automatically, continuously, and without strain—in the same way as you would in steering a car. The process becomes a natural interplay of subconscious and conscious influences.

In the EEG neurofeedback training procedure, the process of learning "how to make different brainwaves" occurs as your brain adjusts and interprets the cause-and-effect relationship between its own activity and the resultant video game responses.

The beauty of neurofeedback is that it makes this cause-and-effect relationship so observable and accessible. It is as simple as noticing when a variety of elements on the screen appear and disappear, go faster or slower, or when sounds become more frequent, rhythmic, or melodic. Games can

---

11. Some people prefer to augment their involvement by using steering or gamepad devices to control parts of the games. However, the essential game activity and progress is controlled by brainwaves.

range from fast moving, stimulating, and sleek (such as car or spaceship games) to quiet and calming games (such as those with flowers, bubbles, and music). Many of the games appeal easily to children's natural abilities. For example, in some games, geometric shapes on the screen become bigger or smaller, objects are positioned higher or lower, and sounds go on or off. Following such cues is easy and natural, since we develop the basic perceptual skills that are required by the age of two. Because the games are nonverbal, even very young and severely impaired children can engage with them successfully. A key feature to the efficacy of neurofeedback is that the games are interactive with your nervous system, not with logic, achievement, language, or other higher cognitive skills.

The brain characteristics of critical importance involve the various brainwave frequencies (electrical cycles per second). These "carry" information from one part of the brain to another, much like radio signals carry information from the transmitter towers to your personal radio. There is a natural ebb and flow in this activity, detected by sensitive computer instrumentation. The information about the preferred brainwaves is represented within the game itself. For instance, larger brainwaves may appear as a larger box or a wider bar on the screen. Or they may advance the spaceship or slow it down. Remarkably, your brain can figure out what's required to make the game go as easily as you can determine that steering a wheel to the left will make the car turn in that direction. You make the game advance just by watching the screen; the brain likes continuity and will alter its brainwaves in order to keep the game "going." Eventually, your brain learns and continues the key elements and subtleties. The neurofeedback software has inhibit thresholds that simultaneously show your brain when it is engaging in "out-of-control" activity. Eventually, you achieve control of your brainwaves through making these changes happen on the computer screen. This improved control translates into more appropriate and functional behaviors in everyday living.

This process of training the brain experientially is called operant conditioning. The brain assimilates, processes, and reacts to feedback. A child, for example, quickly learns in kindergarten that he is expected to raise his hand before he speaks. He also learns that he will be chastised or punished if he doesn't conform to this rule. In effect, he is conditioned to form behaviors that rapidly become automatic and continue through the internal process of self-regulation. This is the same process by which we learn just about everything that is not evoked by pain or instinct (such as not touching fire, by contrast). We use operant conditioning to learn all kinds of habits, such as automatically brushing teeth before going to bed, stopping at red lights, waiting for the walk signal at intersections, and to develop skills, such as spelling, cooking, fixing things, arguing, and avoiding arguments.

The distinguishing features of neurofeedback are that it:

- Initiates learning at a neurological level. We are training brain behavior, to which people may not feel strongly connected, and for which they may not feel particular responsibility. But when brain behavior is normalized, outward behavior follows. Eventually, life becomes more manageable, often with little additional conscious effort.
- Makes you a witness to your own brain in action. You watch it meander from success to struggle and back again. The neurofeedback process teaches you about your visible behavior while, simultaneously, your brain is learning about itself in a unique and replicable way.
- Accelerates learning and modifies behavior rapidly and efficiently (producing up to three thousand reinforcements per hour).
- Develops brain abilities that translate to other situations in life. This is because these abilities are fundamental, allowing your brain to remain calm, organized, and focused, whereas otherwise it might escalate into too much excitability or lapse into disorganization.

HOW EEG NEUROFEEDBACK CAN HELP YOU

Your brain is the master control for all the systems in your body. It is also the vehicle through which you perceive and experience "being"—cerebral, emotional, and spiritual. Because neurofeedback trains and fine-tunes your brain capacities, it is an effective intervention for a broad array of problems and conditions.

Here is a partial list of challenges that respond well to neurofeedback:

- Attention problems, including ADD and ADHD
- Moodiness and serious mood disorders (such as bipolar disorder)
- Behavior problems and disorders
- Sleep problems

- Learning problems
- Autistic spectrum and pervasive developmental delay
- Head injury and brain injury
- Seizures and subclinical seizure activity
- Birth trauma
- Headaches and migraines
- Teeth grinding
- Asperger's syndrome (a type of mild autism)
- Anxiety and depression
- Addictions
- Bedwetting and soiling
- Nightmares and night terrors
- Sleepwalking and sleep talking
- Sleep apnea
- Obsessiveness and compulsions
- Tics and Tourette's syndrome
- PMS and menopause
- Antisocial behavior
- Stroke
- Tremors and restless leg
- Fears and worries
- Eating disorders
- Weight and appetite control
- Study habits
- Recovery from surgery and anesthesia
- Chronic pain
- Anger
- Language disorders
- Indifference and motivation problems
- Oversensitivity and lack of sensitivity
- Muscular coordination
- Memory

EEG NEUROFEEDBACK AND THE SECRETS OF LIVING INTACT

In earlier chapters, you learned about the secrets of living intact. Self-control, proper sensitivity, flexibility, awareness, and the functional use of challenges are endemic to implementing these secrets. Neurofeedback is a highly effective method of developing and refining these qualities in people of *all ages and functional levels*. Though the brains of senior citizens and toddlers may be quite different, both young brains and older brains respond well to the learning and healing that neurofeedback facilitates. Older people can benefit in a variety of ways, from improved sleep and memory to relief from pain, irritability, and depression. Children of all ages benefit because neurofeedback catalyzes the developmental processes, helping children to learn more quickly and efficiently and helping to normalize and mature neurological functioning. Because neurofeedback is so effective at improving concentration, focus, and response to challenge, it is an ideal adjunct to achieving peak performance levels in many areas of life: athletics, academics, business, art and music, research, and relationships.

By training your brain, you become more self-regulated, and this leads to better self-control. You can concentrate better and focus on outcomes and goals more effectively. Because neurofeedback develops brain and nervous system response, you will become more flexible and less prone to unwanted excitability and overreactions. As you progress, your mind and body will recover more easily and fully from stress, and you'll be less likely to depart into "excursions" of brain activity that promote and sustain negative emotions. This process builds upon itself, and as you become less likely to fall victim to brainwave excursions and overreactions, you are likely to become more compassionate and empathetic.

As discussed in chapter 4, developing and exercising compassion is key to living intact. This ability is vital in establishing healthy and reasonable self-control. Fluency in compassion helps you deliberately alter the probability of a particular outcome. Compassion serves not only to reduce aggression and to salve social friction, but also to fashion a reality check on whether your tendencies to magnify, distort, or misperceive are causing you to overreact.

On a practical level, self-directed and other-directed compassion are all-purpose tools that soften the harshness and stings of life. Self-directed compassion gives us the flexibility to accept and adjust to the things we cannot change, the parts of life that do not go our way. It gives you the strength to tolerate adversity, rejection, and all manner of hardship. Other-directed compassion creates a context for tolerance and forbearance.

HOW EEG NEUROFEEDBACK DEVELOPS COMPASSION

To understand how brainwave training can possibly make you more compassionate, you need some basic information on how the brain processes emotion and thought.[12] The substructures of the human brain are housed in left and right hemispheres that function distinctly and interactively. Many people have one hemisphere that is underdeveloped or functioning in a compromised manner. Factors such as genetics, deprivation, faulty learning, and injury can stunt or alter the development of empathy and compassion, as well as other important functions.

The brain's right hemisphere does most of the processing of emotional information and primitive subbrain perception and response. When this hemisphere is functioning with limited capacity, the results can include anger, impulsivity, insensitivity, aggression, overt selfishness, irritability, and the inhibition of empathy and compassion.

Neurofeedback training calms the brain and sensitizes the right hemisphere appropriately. With this training, people become more amicable and socially appropriate, more understanding, and more empathetic. Emotional sensitivity and compassion go hand in hand with perceptual awareness and a reduction in the fight-or-flight response that so often keeps the right hemisphere vigilant, distant, and defensive.

When a person does neurofeedback training, the people in his or her life often report that the person becomes far less argumentative and much more cooperative. The neurofeedback trainee frequently is reported to "lose interest" in arguing, resulting in less frequent and less intense opposition and quarrels. This turnabout is sometimes described as "having the wind go out of the sails" in the middle of a dispute, wherein the trainee gives up trying to dominate and prevail. By contrast, motivation and persistence toward productive and cooperative endeavors simultaneously increases.

---

12. The vast and amazing field of brain complexity is, of course, too broad for a short discussion to do justice. However, this basic simplification may help to illuminate the points about how compassion can develop in response to direct brain training.

Remember the "narrative" discussed in chapter 4? This narrative reflects your mind's ability and its habit of creating a constantly adapting "story" to accommodate your passions, beliefs, momentary emotions, and internal state of arousal. The story or narrative is the interpretive sum of what is perceived, evoked, and imprinted as you respond to life's machinations. Your mind uses an internal language that narrates your thoughts, opinions, perceptions, and feelings. This narrative is always switched on, interpreting events, giving opinions, cracking jokes, making sarcastic comments, discussing feelings, passing evaluations, and announcing upcoming intentions and anticipations. When this internal dialogue and incessant chatter become loud and dissonant, it is difficult to feel intact.

Even if dialogue and chatter are noisy or uncomfortable, the narrative serves a useful purpose in that it helps you maintain a cohesive and sequential story about what is going on. The narrative is the descriptive embodiment of the characteristics you identify with as your "self." When this self—you—becomes threatened or *perceives* a threat, you experience a reaction that combines visceral physiological response (usually heightened arousal) with emotional sensation. If a threat is perceived, the attached emotions are always negative. This is an instinctive response, and sometimes it can save you. Most often, however, negative emotions are an overreaction and, unfortunately, an adverse response to a challenge. Defenses are mounted, and the mind begins to concoct its story that is designed to protect itself and justify the nervous system's reaction.

One of my patients aptly described her narrative as the "hamster wheel" that keeps spinning and going nowhere. She was delighted when neurofeedback calmed her mind and let the hamster rest.

A metaphor to describe the neuropsychological aspects of hemispheric coordination might be the juxtaposition of "text" and "context." The left hemisphere deals more with text, and the right hemisphere deals more with context. That is, the left hemisphere controls language, logic, linear cause-and-effect reasoning, symbology, and sequence, whereas the right hemisphere controls nonverbal processing, body image and perception, spatial reasoning, emotional tone, and the background setting and relative importance of individual bits of information streaming into the filters of the brain.

This is a very simplified model. Brain functioning is complex, and therefore, neurofeedback operates on the complexities of the brain by using biological and physical principles that take advantage of the brain's inherent plasticity. However, for the purpose of communicating how it is possible (and routine) to develop compassion, interest and ability for intimacy, and more mature sensitivity, be assured that when the left hemisphere improves focus and sequential processing and the right hemisphere calms down and self-regulates, that hamster stops running and gnawing, and the needs and interests of other people become more apparent and attractive.

NEUROFEEDBACK AND CHALLENGE

It may seem astonishing that playing video games with your brainwaves can change your life. However, neurofeedback is so powerful and effective because it utilizes the *challenge principle* in asking and guiding your brain to step up. Actually, it is neurofeedback that taught me this principle, and I have been integrating and expanding it ever since my first encounter with this magnificent technique.

The essence of neurofeedback is that it challenges your brain continuously. Professionals in the field of neurotherapy often refer to this challenge process as "appealing" to the brain to engage in slightly different activity. The mechanism of neurofeedback is that it filters brainwave signals and selects only portions of them to reinforce. In other words, as the computers filter the signals produced by your brain, the video game "asks" you to make more of certain brainwave activity and less of other activity simultaneously. The "asking" or "appealing" takes the form of rewarding your brain when you do so and ignoring it when you do not. The process is gentle, subtle, relentless, compelling, and efficacious. Neurofeedback uses only reward and no punishment. It works both consciously and subconsciously. It is easy and yet challenging, enticing and yet boring emotionless and yet evoking emotion. In a nonadversarial, nonthreatening way, neurofeedback "nudges" your brain to less familiar angles and levels, and your brain—less accustomed to these new impingements—pushes back. It is this "push-back" response that elicits and strengthens adaptive responses to challenge and increased flexibility.

You might think of physical training as an analogy. When you tax your muscles and cardiovascular system, they "push back" with greater strength and endurance. Indeed, I call neurofeedback the core of *mental fitness training* (Steinberg and Othmer, 2004). Unlike physical training, however, most people experience lasting change after a sufficient amount of neurofeedback training without the need for constant upkeep. This is because neurofeedback takes advantage of your brain's ability to change its *timing mechanisms*—these are the various frequencies at which nerve cells fire.

Timing mechanisms are fundamental to the scientific underpinnings of the natural universe. Planets move, seasons change, babies are born, genetic patterns unfold, aging occurs, food grows, and people communicate and problem solve all according to timing mechanisms. The key role of the brain lies in communication. Communication is all about timing. The brain's internal timing mechanisms have to work faster than anything else that the brain is asked to do. And when the brain operates at "brain speed," it is also subject to failure. These failures can be of two kinds. There can be a hard failure, such as a lapse into coma. Or there can be soft failures, where we just don't function as well as we might. The "soft" failures are the domain of neurofeedback. When you change your brain via neurofeedback, you are utilizing the mechanism nature gave you to modify and adapt, the same mechanism by which your brain learned how to behave in the first place.

Isn't that incredible?

FIGURING THINGS OUT WITHOUT REASON

There are many ways to problem solve. Some problems require conscious thought and planning, and others tend to be more automatic. When you know how to ride a bicycle, you don't have to calculate the degrees of leaning or turning in order to keep your balance in real time. Amazingly, but not surprisingly, you are monitoring internal gyroscopic body sensations while simultaneously reacting and adjusting to terrain changes, all the while steering and controlling the bicycle. The conditions are constantly changing, yet you are almost effortlessly adapting in real time—and the process is usually fun!

Your brain problem solves continuously at many levels, whether you are sleeping, waking, or somewhere in between. Responding to internal and external challenges continuously and modulating and integrating what's going on inside and outside, your brain is a 24/7 challenge-and-change detector.

Your brain responds to body signals that indicate what you need very soon (such as water or temperature change or relief from pain) and sooner or later (such as desires for certain foods that your body knows will supply needed nutrients). Your brain also tells you in subtle ways that you need contact with certain individuals or perhaps to pay attention to particular issues. Additionally, your brain is the filtering device for spiritual and creative stirrings. Many of these signals result from something other than logical reason or cause-and-effect analysis.

Neurofeedback takes advantage of your brain's ability to problem solve, figure things out, and strengthen itself, even when you are not consciously dictating what to do. Neurofeedback facilitates this process by using electrical signals and the biophysics of nature to challenge your brain in ways that almost always produce highly desirable results.

BIOPHYSICS AND BLESSINGS

Some readers find their understanding enhanced by more details or a more technical discussion of topics. If you are so inclined, this section on how neurofeedback works on your brain may interest you.

There are three principal mechanisms by which neurofeedback modifies brain activity:

1. Encouraging (or reinforcing) your brain to produce brainwaves helpful and relevant to desired outcome states
2. Discouraging (or extinguishing) those brainwaves interfering with desired outcome states
3. Presenting your brain with specific challenges designed to train particular brain areas to strengthen, problem solve, and communicate better with each other

Encouraging (or reinforcing) your brain to produce brainwaves helpful and relevant to desired outcome states

The nuts and bolts of neurofeedback training comprise how the procedure encourages your brain to make greater *amplitudes* (strength of the signal) at particular frequencies (electrical cycles per second). The computers processing the signals emanating from your brain extracts information about certain key brainwave frequencies. The video game continuously shows you the ebb and flow of this activity. As you play the game, you are changing the activity levels of different brainwave frequencies. Eventually, your brainwave activity is "shaped" toward more desirable, more regulated performance. The frequencies we target and the specific locations on the scalp where we "listen in" on the brain are specific to the conditions we are trying to address and specific to the individual.

By promoting greater production of amplitudes at certain frequencies, we are teaching your brain (actually, *you* are teaching your brain) to gravitate toward more functional states and to maintain these states as is useful and appropriate to varying situations. People prefer different names for these states—such as "being in the zone," "putting on your game face," "chilling out," and so forth—but the basic idea is that you learn to *activate* and *deactivate* your brainwave activity as suits the situation. The training on the computer generalizes to varying real-life circumstances, much as weight training or running would generalize to heightened fitness that would allow you to meet the physical demands and challenges of daily activities.

Discouraging (or extinguishing) those brainwaves interfering with desired outcome states

In tandem with teaching your brain to make more of the brainwaves associated with desirable outcomes, neurofeedback discourages the brain's excursion into dysfunctional states. These excursions may be so brief that they are unobservable in overt behavior. Rather, we infer them from the existence of certain patterns in the EEG. Such excursions, however, are rare. The coupling of overt behavior and EEG "behavior" is so intimate that we may assume that the production of anomalous brainwave patterns interferes with desired outcome states. The neurofeedback procedure accomplishes control over excursions by inhibiting the reward (forward motion, points, sounds, etc.) on the video game when you are generating amplitudes on the less desirable frequencies above thresholds set by the therapist on the computer. In particular, this modality teaches your brain to avoid significant *departures* from the functional flow of activity that suits a particular brain state. This may sound abstract or complicated, but it is really a simple principle, ingenuously applied to neurobiology via the miracle blending of digital technology, learning theory, and the brilliance of devoted engineering.

Think of the process as though you are driving on the freeway with sensors attached that allow you to drift slightly within a lane, to change lanes gradually, and to slow down and speed up within a range of allowable speeds. However, should you suddenly veer way out beyond the freeway lanes or slow down or accelerate in a manner that posed danger, the system would notify you and diminish fuel supply to the engine until you regained control.

Or here's another analogy: in baseball, a runner is allowed a lenient margin of sideways drift when running from one base to another. However, he is not allowed to veer too far outside of rule-based limits, and he must touch each base as he makes progress.

The significant feature of this *inhibition of rewards* (inhibition of continuous movement) process is that there is no punishment involved. The reward is simply cut off until you regain control and resume progress within the allowable margins. This process is supportive and efficient, since people generally do not learn as well under conditions of punishment or stress. Remember, neurofeedback is attempting to teach brains that are already stressed. You don't learn to drive well by having multiple accidents. Rather, you master the process of adapting to changing conditions via the gentle persistent nudges in the right direction provided by correct practice and subtly noticeable reminders of when you exceed limits (such as the bumps in the lane stripes).

The inhibit features of neurofeedback training are especially helpful to those individuals who struggle with an unstable brain that routinely deregulates into overreactive electrical activity. For example, people with seizures, intractable anxiety, migraines, cerebral irritability, and other conditions are prone to this disruptive brain activity without being aware of it. By bringing it into subliminal awareness without the penalty of symptoms or censure, neurofeedback allows the brain to self-correct its own aberrations in a manner that is natural, comfortable, and enduring.[13]

---

13. One might argue that psychotropic medications do this by force, acting as a kind of neurochemical "cruise-control" guided by time release and the approximate judgment of the prescribing physician. The problem with the medication approach is that, in the interests of short-term economy and collision prevention, it adds unpleasant side effects and sacrifices the autonomy and flexibility of "driver-guided" control.

Presenting your brain with specific challenges designed to train particular brain areas to strengthen, problem solve, and communicate better with each other

Basic models of neurofeedback training have used the first two principles for decades with cumulative and far-reaching efficacy; many practitioners continue to succeed with these models. Again, these basic principles are:

1. Encouraging (or reinforcing) your brain to produce brainwaves helpful and relevant to desired outcome states
2. Discouraging (or extinguishing) those brainwaves interfering with desired outcome states

However, in recent years, neurofeedback scientists have increased its success with the challenge model significantly. The emphasis on two aspects of neurofeedback interaction with brain function has quickened and deepened the effects when the brain is challenged by a task and then learns to "push back" and become more capable.

One remarkable advance is the neurofeedback training of *phase relationships* between brain sites. Another extraordinary innovation is the introduction of *infralow frequency* (ILF) reward-based training.

IT'S NOT JUST A PHASE

To appreciate these innovations, it is helpful to understand some mathematical principles of physics and electrical signals. *Phase* refers to the timing relationship of two electrical cycles operating independently. As a practical matter, the parameter of phase is useful only when the two cycles are operating at the same or nearly the same frequency. But this happens to be precisely the situation when the brain is organizing communication between two locations on the scalp. These two regions have to be attuned to each other, much like the radio station and the receiver.

When an electrode is placed on the scalp, it samples the signal coming from that area (site) and displays the information as a cycle ranging from a peak of +1 to -1. The height or depth of the wave is measured in *microvolts* (millionths of a volt) and displayed in an undulating line a certain number of times per second. For example, a brainwave pattern of 12 Hz at 75 microvolts would mean that there are twelve up-and-down complete wave patterns each second. Each cycle would include a peak of +1 and a nadir of -1 at its particular amplitude (see Description of sine wave figure). The point at which the waveform crosses from plus to minus in each cycle can be assigned the phase value of zero. Phase values for each waveform vary continuously and smoothly until the wave undergoes a complete cycle, and then it repeats.

Description of sine wave

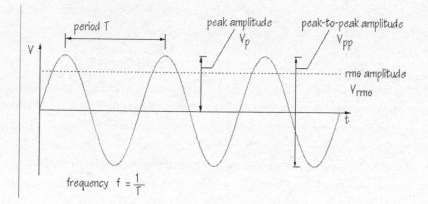

The first two principal mechanisms described above explain how neurofeedback operates by focusing on individual brain sites. This mechanism measures and feeds back information about a single (monopolar) signal. Neurofeedback training that uses a monopolar amplitude-based approach is appealing to the brain to generate greater and more consistent amplitudes at selected frequencies. This approach generally disregards phase because it addresses brain activity at selected sites.

Phase training, however, involves training the phase relationship between two sites in order to promote *phase differences*. This procedure trains the brain's ability to meet challenges, become more flexible, and problem solve automatically and without conscious reasoning. This is because the timing relationship between different brain sites is the most critical variable when it comes to the brain's internal communication in connection with state management.

Here's how it works:

Electrodes are placed at two scalp sites during each training period, and the rewards (moments when the video game progresses) are set to occur when the *two sites show phase differences in activity*. Let's explain this mathematically and then relate it to improvements in brain activity and daily life.

Signals from two sites are said to be *in phase* when their amplitudes reach peak (+1) and nadir (-1) simultaneously. They are *out of phase* when one signal approaches +1 and the other approaches -1 simultaneously. (When two signals are perfectly in phase, they are said to be *synchronous*.) As you train by playing the video game, your brain is intermittently rewarded for "figuring out" how to make the frequency cycles from each site occur at slightly different times. ("You" think you are piloting a spaceship on the screen, while your brain is in the control room, working furiously to figure out the timing codes to keep things moving.) In phase-based training, the reward is not based on the amplitude, but rather on the timing differences between when each of the two signals reaches that amplitude. Mathematically, the rewards occur when the differences become greater (i.e., move away from zero toward an absolute value of one, either positive or negative).

You can think of this as similar to teaching instrumentalists in an orchestra to play different notes at the same time (or teaching your hands to play different notes on the piano at staggered time intervals). The effects of this kind of flexibility are staggering and infinite. When you can master playing different notes in varying combinations of time synchrony, you are becoming a master, perhaps eventually a virtuoso.

Taking the musical analogy a step further, phase training is like teaching your brain to sing in harmony, in choral rounds, and in synchrony, as needed.

Phase training tunes and trains your brain modules to coordinate among themselves and to communicate with the outside world like a practiced and well-timed group of musicians. Perhaps you are familiar with singing in staggered choral rounds. Remember the song, "Row, Row, Row Your Boat"? When two groups sing it together, they are in phase, and the timing code looks like this:

Group 1

Row, row, row your boat	Gently down the stream	Merrily, merrily, merrily, merrily,	Life is but a dream.

Group 2

Row, row, row your boat	Gently down the stream	Merrily, merrily, merrily, merrily,	Life is but a dream.

However, when they sing in choral rounds, they are out of phase, and it looks like this:

Group 1

Row, row, row your boat	Gently down the stream	Merrily, merrily, merrily, merrily,	Life is but a dream.

Group 2

Merrily, merrily, merrily, merrily,	Life is but a dream.	Row, row, row your boat	Gently down the stream

Notice that singing in rounds and transitioning back to unison requires careful attention, as well as the ability to focus narrowly and then expand that focus to incorporate the context and its sequence and timing. In order to do this properly, you must be able to shift as necessary. This is a complex task, yet most elementary school students are able to do it (provided that their brains are functioning well). When your brain can shift time codes and integrate and adapt different timing mechanisms, you can pay attention, screen out distractions, maintain continuity, sift and shift to accommodate salient details, and follow a task through to its conclusion.

Does this sound like something you want to be able to do better and more consistently? Neurofeedback—and phase training in particular—will help you far along that path.

When your brain learns to differentiate its timing mechanisms (which is what phase training conditions it to do), you progressively achieve the following:

- Freedom from symptoms

- Improved performance and efficiency
- Better, quicker accessibility to appropriate responses
- Faster recovery from fatigue and stress
- More endurance
- Greatly enhanced flexibility
- Less vulnerability to overreactions
- Better self-regulation and self-control
- Enhanced creativity
- Better concentration
- Improved perception and coordination
- Better sensitivity to people
- Reduced carelessness
- Less defensiveness, hypervigilance, or fight/flight mode
- Increased empathy, compassion, contentment
- Reduced tendency to become overwhelmed or absorbed by pain
- Improved ability to filter distractions, focus sharply, and multitask

The general consensus in the field of neurofeedback is that these results are achieved with most populations using any of the methodologies described. The collective success rates reported by neurotherapists worldwide (who, at the time of this publication, have collectively administered several million sessions) are approximately (and conservatively) 80 percent. Such success notwithstanding, the advent of *infralow frequency* (ILF) reward-based training has sped up the progress for most people and has advanced the success level and quality of life impact upon especially difficult populations and conditions: autism, bipolar disorder, seizures and migraines, and addictions.

HOW LOW CAN YOU GO?

For decades, EEG neurofeedback utilized the training of brainwaves in the frequency ranges (bandwidths) recognized to incorporate common waking and sleeping neurophysiology. Technically, this refers to the frequency range between 1 Hz and approximately 60 Hz (cycles per second). Actually, the functional range for training has been more stringently between 1–30 Hz, and the focus of reward and inhibition has typically been between 3–22 Hz.

In recent years, researchers and clinicians at the Brian Othmer Foundation (www.EEGinfo.com) have pioneered and developed new software and treatment training protocols that utilize *infralow frequencies* (ILF). These are brainwave frequencies below 0.5 Hz. Training with these protocols may concern itself with brain activity as low as .0001 Hz, training phase relationships in the same manner described above. The effects of these ILF training protocols are powerful and rather rapid. The results for many people—including people with previously intractable conditions—have often been amazing.

From a neurobiological and electrophysiological perspective, brainwave signals below 1 Hz represent biological phenomena that are fundamental to self-regulation, but which occur well beneath any radar of consciousness. Whereas frequency bandwidths in the 5–20 Hz range are associated with mental activities ranging from creative imagining to debating, studying, planning, and calculation, frequencies below 0.1 Hz are associated with longer-term biological encoding. At the extremely low frequencies, we are most likely paying selective attention to those brain mechanisms involved in organizing our persistent states. These ILFs relate to cycles of mood and of physiology correlated with mood, such as the state of the autonomic nervous system. They also relate to issues of maturation and aging and the recording and encoding of primitive memories by brain substructures. These encodings often carry information about traumatic events the brain has experienced throughout a person's lifetime.

From a metaphorical standpoint, one might compare the relationships and continuum of traditional brainwave frequencies and infralow brainwave frequencies with the life-forms on land and beneath the surface of the sea. Yes, there is a vast and only partially explored world down there, teeming with life energy and the potential to teach and nourish us. We concern ourselves for the most part with the visible and tangible phenomena that we can access and to which we can relate. In perspective, however, that which is above sea level is, quite literally, the tip of the iceberg. So it is with the new frontier of infralow brainwave frequencies.

By training at these ILFs, the brain can nonverbally and subconsciously "figure out" how to meet self-regulation challenges that affect conscious perceptions, experiences, and behavior. ILF neurofeedback training has opened a new world of healing and growth possibilities for populations ranging from the severely impaired to high-functioning individuals in all walks of life who want to break through barriers and perform at the top of their capacities.[14]

Not surprisingly, the empirical findings with regard to ILF training find support in the latest research in the neurosciences, where brain-imaging studies are revealing the existence of distinct, well-organized "resting states," to which the brain returns after mastering a challenge. It is the quality of organization of our resting state networks that determines how well we function. Neurofeedback applied in the ILF ranges seems to most effectively challenge the brain to organize its resting state networks.

RECAPITULATING CHALLENGE AND TRANSFORMATION

I have described the benefits, efficacy, and some of the mechanisms of how neurofeedback works to relieve symptoms, promote self-regulation and self-control, and develop brain function and capacities. By explaining some technical aspects of how neurofeedback engages the brain, I've attempted to shed light on how neurofeedback is really a vehicle for teaching the brain to meet challenges. Indeed, neurofeedback is a very expedient and efficient means of doing this, since it reinforces the brain about three thousand times per hour; it is an operant conditioning method that exercises and conditions the brain and nervous system safely, subtly, and continually.

In the manifestation of God's wisdom, nature recapitulates itself in so many ways. The essential organizing principles and patterns that pervade the natural world, art, science, and mathematics generate countless variations that express fundamental themes in familiar yet diverse iterations. This is also true in the matter of timing mechanisms. The themes of the universe are writ large and small, from the vastness of astronomy, the wonder of the speed of light, to the smallest microorganisms and the infinitesimal wavelengths and speed of evolutionary change.

As humans, we are wired into this natural fabric. Neurofeedback helps us to modify and align our timing mechanisms in adaptive ways. Using the same principles that govern the universe, we can influence

---

14. I am indebted to Siegfried Othmer, Sue Othmer, and Kurt Othmer for their continuing brilliance, dedication, and perseverance in bringing neurofeedback innovations to the world.

patterns that have shaped us neurobiologically and neuropsychologically, even historical and genetic contributions, by using technology to teach our brains to function better.

Just as exercising on a treadmill or Stairmaster can recapitulate its specific challenges and result in better fitness for your everyday activities, so, too, can neurofeedback exercise and train your brain timing mechanisms for better responses to the challenges you face, the ways you handle them, and the narrative in your mind that interprets what's going on and how you fit into it.

As you train timing relationships of brain cellular assemblies at milliHertz frequencies, you are also training preparedness and power to accommodate challenges you have faced in the past and those you will face in the future.

In the limited picture of the present, you may yearn for relief from pressures, symptoms, angst, and the burdens of daily life. In the bigger picture of developing your character as you strive to live intact, recapitulating your brain functioning to the outward manifestations of how you handle yourself and life is a transformative approach to meeting challenges and living intact.

HOW TO MAKE EEG NEUROFEEDBACK WORK FOR YOU

Assuming you are interested in exploring what neurofeedback can do for you, how can you go about involving yourself in neurofeedback training?

There are hundreds of qualified neurofeedback providers in the United States and around the world. In my opinion, those providers who have trained with the Othmers (www.EEGinfo.com) have access to the cutting edge in theory, practice, and technology in this exciting field.[15] There are a number of books on neurofeedback. Many of these, as well as research references, are listed on the www.EEGinfo.com website.

As a guide for venturing into neurofeedback, the following is excerpted from the book I wrote with Dr. Siegfried Othmer, entitled *ADD: The 20-Hour Solution* (2004, Robert Reed Publishers):

---

15. Dr. Siegfried Othmer, Sue Othmer, and Kurt Othmer offer training courses in neurofeedback around the world (visit www.EEGinfo.com).

For many people, finding the right health care professional can be a difficult endeavor, shadowed by self-doubt about making the right decision, fraught with anxiety about the unknown, or complicated by a lack of understanding and information (or, sometimes, by too much information). Some people may be determined to pursue EEG training, only to face long distances between their homes and the nearest suitable provider. Others may live in a metropolitan area with numerous providers. For many, the decision is simplified by a referral or recommendation from someone they trust—a doctor or therapist, teacher, or a parent whose child improved greatly through the treatment.

Recommendations from satisfied people are excellent and confidence-inspiring leads to successful neurotherapy. Besides the natural kinship and identification with those who have "walked in your shoes," people who have tried neurofeedback can give you tips about their journey and the beneficial decisions and mistakes they have made. Veteran clients are likely to have waded through the doubts and misgivings of those opinionated professionals who cast doubt on neurotherapy (despite their conspicuous dearth of knowledge about it!).

As the practice and benefits of neurotherapy become widely known and accepted, more and more medical professionals are considering and recommending it. Grass roots word-of-mouth, however, remains a valuable inroad to finding and selecting a neurotherapist (also visit www.EEGdirectory.com).

Once you've found one or several potential neurotherapists, you may want to consider the variables most important to you in entrusting your brain to such a professional. Let me emphasize two components that make neurotherapy so inviting and so powerful:

A. Neurofeedback is reliable and robust enough that people from many backgrounds (parents, too!) can successfully administer it to the benefit of children (and adults). Its effects have been well established and replicated many thousands of times; therefore, to a great extent, successful neurotherapy is a *likely* outcome, even with wide variation in experience and technique.

B. As you might expect—and, as happens in so many fields—technique, training, and experience *do* matter; in some cases, they make all the difference. Though the actual effects of neurofeedback grow from the natural abilities of your child's brain to learn and to regulate itself when given appropriate information, there are important variables that can influence your decisions, your confidence, follow-through, and the overall efficacy and thoroughness of the treatment. The matters of comfort, confidence, respect, and communication between you, the therapist and your family members can determine how much you and they derive from neurotherapy.

Your search and selection for a neurotherapist may depend on particular criteria important to you—perhaps credentials, experience with a particular condition, insurance coverage, etc. As you seek a provider, bear in mind the three salient factors we anticipate will determine whether the neurofeedback experience is likely to be a good one for you and your child:

1. **Training and experience in neurotherapy**—where has the therapist trained, how long has he/she practiced neurotherapy, and how does he/she keep up with developments and advances in the field?
2. **Therapist training and experience overall**—what are the credentials and training of the therapist besides the field of neurotherapy? Education, kinds and amounts of experience, and what types of clients and problems the therapist has worked with all count toward the likelihood of a good outcome. Some therapists specialize in certain disorders, while others treat a wider variety of problems. The important factor is whether the therapist has been successful *with people*, using the modes and methodologies he/she has employed.
3. **Your comfort level with the therapist**—the personality, office location, ambience, and décor, and the manner of the therapist will not determine the effectiveness of neurofeedback for your child. However, these factors may determine your willingness to openly share, confront, and continue with the therapist and the process. After all, the therapist is working with your child's brain, and your commitment will be to follow through for multiple visits.

You are likely to find a wide variation in credentials, disciplines, and experience among neurotherapists. This is fortuitous, and it is not clear that any particular specialty makes for a more effective therapist. Skilled counselors, nurses, or teachers are often great neurotherapists, even though they are lower on the professional pecking order than medical doctors (and, there are an increasing number of medical doctors including neurotherapy in their practices, too). By asserting this, I am neither patronizing particular specialties, nor minimizing the value of specialized training, schooling, and expertise. The effectiveness of neurofeedback stands on its own merits as a robust and replicable treatment. All of the other rules about professional care and competent and appropriate relationships between therapist and clients still apply.

Here are steps for finding a suitable neurotherapist for your situation.

1. Review the material in this chapter and other information you may have read or researched. Use what you deem relevant in guiding your search and decision process.
2. Locate one or more neurotherapists within driving distance from your home or office. Remember that you will be making the trek at least two times per week; that is part of your commitment, but be realistic.
3. Ask about office hours. Most neurotherapists have evening hours. Some work on weekends.
4. Decide how important credentials are to you, and factor that in with other variables ahead of time. Credentials often make a difference in third-party (insurance) reimbursement.
5. If you speak with your physician, ask what he/she *knows* about neurofeedback, not what he/she *thinks*. You can ask your physician for a recommendation or referral, but be prepared to come up empty. You might even get a lecture trying to deter you from trying EEG biofeedback. If this happens, have sympathy for your doctor's position, but stand your ground. Tell the physician that you are determined to follow through, even without his/her support, which you would prefer. Ask the physician if he/she would be willing to work with your neurofeedback provider (especially

where medication is already prescribed), and whether he/she would be interested in the results of your experience with neurotherapy. Depending upon the physician's response, you will either forge a better relationship and increase your doctor's breadth of understanding—or you may need to find another physician.

6. Get recommendations from people who have experienced neurofeedback. Ask at school, ask at parent groups, and ask at church or synagogue.

7. If you or a family member visits a psychotherapist or other specialty therapist, these may be good resources to locate a neurotherapist.

It is important to begin neurofeedback under the care of a qualified professional. For many people, it is realistic to eventually assume control of their own neurofeedback. This is done by leasing or purchasing equipment from a qualified professional who can teach and supervise you.[16]

Because neurofeedback is based upon learning and the brain's plasticity, your brain will *remember* and *adopt* what it learns; thus, the benefits of neurofeedback tend to endure. However, some people struggle with conditions that need sustained training, and others simply aspire to new heights and better levels of functioning. Training on your own—remote training—under the periodic supervision of a qualified professional can provide an economical and beneficial mode of using neurofeedback to improve the quality of your life.

In light of the established track record and mounting evidence of the broad-based efficacy of neurofeedback, dismissing the value of this intervention would signal close-mindedness and an unwillingness to recognize and accept the brain's documented ability to heal itself. On your journey toward living intact, neurofeedback is one of the most powerful tools available to you.

---

16. Beware of purchasing commercial and inexpensive equipment over the Internet or from manufacturers who are primarily in the toy or educational business. In general, these products lack the technical sophistication and flexibility that good neurofeedback requires. Of course, these products don't come with qualified professional care.

CHAPTER 10
THOUGHT FIELD THERAPY

In the previous chapter, you learned about EEG neurofeedback, a procedure for training your brain by using computers that teach your mind and body how to function better. In this chapter, you will learn about a revolutionary technique for rapidly eliminating any negative emotion in minutes!

The technique is called Thought Field Therapy (TFT), and it's something you can use to treat yourself. It does not require any equipment, and you don't need to hire a therapist, although some people may be wrestling with complex issues that do not respond as well to self-treatment. Most people, however, can self-administer TFT with quick and effective results. You'll learn in this chapter the basics of self-treatment, as well as the reasons TFT works so well.

In chapter 7, you learned that the fourth secret for living intact entails *eliminating negative emotions*. All too often, these negative emotions drive our behavior and attitudes, even without our realizing that they are so pivotal in promoting or interfering with our capacity to live intact. The negative emotions can disable or paralyze the psychological flexibility that is required to engage alternate responses, and can collude with the mind's narrative to keep us stuck.

WHAT IS TFT?

Thought Field Therapy (TFT) is a powerful treatment for dealing with psychological disturbances. TFT provides a code that, when applied to a psychological problem the individual is experiencing, eliminates perturbations in the thought field that are the fundamental cause of all negative emotions. (A *perturbation* is a disturbance in the encoding of information that connects a thought with a feeling. TFT acts upon these perturbations to collapse them and render them inactive.)

TFT was developed by Dr. Roger Callahan,[17] who has pioneered this revolutionary treatment and who conducts training courses to teach TFT. Dr. Callahan began this work in the 1970s and has continued to expand and refine the methods and applications. He has published seminal works about TFT and has trained thousands of professionals in its therapeutic utilization. (To learn more about TFT and Dr. Callahan's work, visit www.tftrx.com.)

At its inception, TFT was used primarily to eliminate anxiety-based problems (such as phobias and panic) and various types of trauma. Over the years, practitioners have expanded the range of applications and are now effectively using TFT to assist in the treatment of many ailments, including physical ills such as headaches, digestive upsets, and body pain.

Startling developments in the practical applications of TFT have included its use in Kosovo and Africa to treat war trauma and many variants of the posttraumatic stress and injury associated with violence, loss, abandonment, torture, and deprivation.

CODES

In chapter 2, you learned that nature uses codes to embed information. Codes are akin to shorthand. They are shortcut methods for abbreviating, storing, and communicating information. In a sense, they are like your Social Security number and the many PIN codes you've created that identify you and that you use to access private information. For example, when you click on a computer link, you may be asked to enter a code before entrée is granted. Though you may not realize it, information you hear or see is also in code. The English language contains twenty-six letters that can be combined to form words, sentences, and limitless ideas. When you read or listen to information, you're decoding the words in accordance with accepted rules of phonetics, pronunciation, and grammar. If you understand what the decoded words mean, you can process and assimilate the encoded information. If the information is represented in numbers (e.g.,

---

17. I am indebted to Dr. Callahan for his scientific expertise, rigorous training and mentorship, and for being a true friend.

the balance of your checking account) and you've mastered the meaning of these number codes, you would then be able to respond accordingly.

Nature also imparts information in the form of environmental and biological codes. These data can be decoded, and by breaking the codes, beneficial alterations in human response patterns can be achieved. You can essentially replace harmful or distressing codes with those that are beneficial and healing. TFT allows the replacement to occur. For many people, this is a radical concept to consider: that the body and mind store coded information that keeps emotional and physical problems in place and that by decoding and reprogramming this information, negative feelings and problems can be alleviated within minutes.

You can think of the function of the codes that your body stores as a kind of emotional alarm system. The alarm is set within you by reactions you have to traumas, upsets, and even to foods and medicines. TFT works by deactivating the internal alarm and by offsetting the signals that trigger the alarms. You accomplish this by tapping with your fingers on specific points on your body in a specific order. The tapping sends energy signals throughout your nervous system via meridian points and pathways. These signals disrupt the *perturbations* that are causing your distress, and they essentially reset your system back to normal for the particular problem that was upsetting you.

To grasp the concept of how pressing with your finger can create so much impact, think of a garage door opener. Or better yet, think of how tapping several numbers into a phone can send specific messages over a great distance with great speed and impact.

The negative emotional charge is removed, so you can think clearly about the problem, but it will no longer bother you at all. *Poof!*

It is an interesting and common phenomenon that after a rapid TFT treatment that totally eliminates the problem, the treated person often says, *"I can't think about it anymore."* What he really means is: *"When I think about it, it doesn't bother me, so why think about it?"*

In general, tapping on meridian points can have a beneficial effect. Indeed, there are several "look-alike" tapping treatments that claim efficacy, and some of them work to a certain degree. However, it's the detection of the disruptive codes and application of the functional codes that are the real secrets to TFT's astounding and consistent success.

These curative codes are elicited through TFT's causal diagnostic procedure (beyond the scope of this chapter) that permitted the development of the TFT algorithms. (Algorithms are shortcuts or general tapping recipes that have emerged over time as common tapping sequences. They can be self-administered while thinking of the problem, and they are often effective in eliminating the problem—see appendix C.) An algorithm treatment is presented in this chapter to help you get started in eliminating your own negative emotions.

The fundamental cause of emotional distress, including anxiety and cravings, is the phenomenon of "perturbation(s) in the thought field." A perturbation is a specific type of information that resides in the thought field. This information contains the instructions for triggering and thus generating the chemical and neurological events that lead to what we call negative or disturbing emotions. Many of these perturbations are inherited, and some are established during the lifetime of the individual. Regardless of the origin, TFT makes it possible to eliminate these negative emotions at their fundamental source.

It is true that there are chemical events in the human body that result ultimately in the negative emotions as well as associated cognitive thoughts and related neurological activity. The basic premise of TFT, however, is that the perturbations in the thought field precede and generate these chemical and cognitive events. The perturbation in the thought field, which is subsumed and rendered inoperative with successful TFT treatment, is the fundamental and basic cause of all disturbed or negative emotions. The successful therapeutic treatment of the perturbation eliminates the chemical and cognitive consequences. Therefore, the perturbation is the basic causal factor. The chemistry and cognition are considered secondary and tertiary.

There is actually proof of this phenomenon at both physiological and psychological levels. At the physiological level, published research shows that *heart rate variability (HRV)* improves dramatically after TFT treatment.[18] (Because of this, I would recommend that anyone who has a history of heart problems engage in TFT treatment.) At the psychological level, a person's

---

18. Heart rate variability (HRV) is a primary indicator of the body's resources to survive and adapt to internal and external challenges. Poor HRV is associated with morbidity and pre-morbid disease conditions. HRV is one of the most researched variables in medicine. However, you don't hear much about it because, although it is a significant health indicator and predictor of death, until recently, scientists did not have methods of improving HRV significantly and rapidly. My colleagues and I have shown dramatic improvements in HRV after a single TFT session (Pignotti and Steinberg, 2001).

narrative changes dramatically after treatment. Patients in distress routinely feel impelled to repeat their description of symptoms and all the negative ramifications. I ask my patients to please do the TFT treatment first, and then I promise to listen to their story for as long as they want. Almost always, after a TFT treatment of just a few minutes, the patient has no story to tell— that is because the symptoms that were driving the story (and which seemed to be very real and rooted in external circumstances) have *disappeared*.

HOW TFT DIFFERS

Using TFT to eliminate distress is different from other approaches. Conventional methods and beliefs rely upon assumptions that you must target neurochemical imbalances directly (through medication) and/or modify cognitive patterns of thinking and beliefs in order to rid yourself of negative emotions, unpleasant mood states, intrusive thinking, and their associated dysfunctional behaviors. TFT unabashedly challenges and disproves these assumptions by virtue of its tangible and consistent success.

You might imagine the consternation and dismissive attitude on the part of those who believe that this seemingly silly and innocuous treatment could not possibly work. Yet despite their skepticism,[19] TFT is scientifically based, highly researched and replicated, and continues to gain adherents who benefit from its simple, natural, and effective methods.

In chapter 8, you learned that it is reasonable to question traditional assumptions (based on their lack of evidence) that particular early life experiences or tendencies produce specific or predictable outcomes later in life. Furthermore, traditional theories of psychological development that link behavior patterns to early programming exclude the many exceptions and the huge variability in how people turn out, despite earlier life disadvantages. Most importantly, the belief in or reliance upon these assumptions about environmental influences provides no *reliable* therapeutic path to avoid character defects or psychological damage that putatively results from early experiences and provides no *reliable* thera-

---

19. I have appeared many times on television demonstrating TFT and Voice Technology. In 2001, CBS sent a news team to my office to record a Voice Technology treatment in which I cured a woman of her fear of bridges from which she had suffered for almost twenty years. After the treatment, the news team took my patient in their CBS van and drove her over some local bridges in the San Francisco Bay area to test her reaction. To their amazement, she remained calm and cured of her phobia. CBS then showed this film to a local university psychology professor, who dismissed the whole thing and said that merely the soothing sound of my voice temporarily calmed the patient.

peutic roadmap for repairing the defects or the damage. Sadly, the traditional contention that early character formation and development are immutable suggests a determinism that overshadows free will, intention, purpose, fortitude, miracles, and divine intervention.

In place of this self-fulfilling cycle of determinism and victimization, I have suggested in previous chapters that the *phenomenon of challenge* denotes the undergirding reality that can turn trials and tribulations into opportunities and successes. A primary practical way to use challenge to your advantage is to apply it to controlling and eliminating negative emotions. You must learn to differentiate the negative emotions that intermittently bring about anguish and distress from the unique, enduring, and positive qualities (including some negative emotions) that form your character, your sense of self, and the ways in which you interact with others. This distinction is vital in eliminating disturbing and incapacitating symptoms quickly. To feel better, you don't need to spend years in therapy remodeling your personality.

During my thirty-five years of psychological practice, I have treated thousands of people who had been previously (and unsuccessfully) treated. These people remained troubled after traditional treatment, and their failure to be cured reflected a fundamental paradox inherent both in the traditional talk-therapy therapeutic model and in the belief systems of most people who are experiencing emotional distress. Traditional therapy (and its influences on popular beliefs about the requirements for getting better) is predicated on the concept that those in treatment can find relief from negative symptoms only through an understanding and analysis of deep-seated conflicts, motivations, habits, and early traumas. With this model, clients are conditioned to accept a long course of introspection, treatment, and character development and an extensive analysis of the psychological determinants of behavior. Clients may sometimes believe they are getting better, but they are never cured. Frustration is inevitable.

Realistically, this frustration is unnecessary. With a highly focused and effective intervention, negative emotional problems such as anxiety, depression, anger, compulsions, cravings, stress, loneliness, and trauma can actually be eliminated in minutes.

There is a central irony in psychotherapy: the very benefits that appropriate psychotherapy[20] can achieve are blocked by the negative emotional

---

20. When a person is thinking clearly and is not dependent upon the therapist to soothe his disruptive moods, psychotherapy can be useful for issues such as exploring one's identity and

states that prompt the therapy in the first place. For example, a person may enter therapy to change dysfunctional relationship patterns in which he or she is hurtful or abusive. Ironically, such a person is often unable to appreciate or implement psychological advice or insights because of uncontrollable feelings (anger, rage, rejection, jealousy, etc.). Eliminating negative emotional control is a *prerequisite* to effective psychological change; it is not a result of it. Confusion over this principle has kept too many people suffering and powerless for too long. Fortunately, the extraordinary healing of Thought Field Therapy can change this fast—at last!

THAT FAST?

The skeptic in you may ask, "How can this possibly happen within minutes?" Good question!

Let's begin to answer the question by reviewing some realities we take for granted and compare their relevance to feeling well. Take body temperature, for example. We are warm-blooded animals who must maintain body temperature within a relatively narrow range in order to function. When body temperature fluctuates more than a few degrees, we become not only symptomatic (chills, fever), but we also become at risk for survival. Fortunately, the human system has built-in mechanisms for maintaining and regulating body temperature, as it does for many other functions (including emotional "temperature").

When body temperature is controlled, it is difficult to feel, or even imagine, a physical threat from heat or cold. However, try stepping outside in subzero temperatures or sitting in a bath that is too hot, and you will know firsthand the experience of responding rapidly to environmental changes with negative feelings. However, the reverse (experiencing rapid changes in positive feelings) is also true, and yet taken for granted. Physical examples that illustrate this principle also provide relevance to emotional healing.

When you come in from the cold or remove the source of the heat, your body quickly acclimates back to its accustomed range of comfortable operation. Unless you have been exposed to the point of actual physical injury (burns, frostbite, or hypothermia), you will recover relatively quickly, usually within a few minutes. Given the degree of threat posed

---

values, challenging belief systems, reality constructs and perceptual distortions, developing better communication skills, and practicing life skills.

by the elements, this rapid recovery might seem surprising—yet it is something we assume, since the temperature reacclimatization is within our experience and happens automatically and consistently.

Physical illness also illustrates the self-healing/self-regulating phenomenon. We have all been stricken by viruses such as the "twenty-four-hour flu," and we have all experienced the massive discomfort that accompanies a high fever as our bodily defenses mobilize to contain the offending microbes. Although such illness takes longer than a few minutes to dissipate, there is often a critical period when the fever "breaks," followed by a rapid acceleration in recovery and a noticeable subjective relief in "feeling better." This process occurs, with or without medication, independent of the sufferer's beliefs or understandings about what is happening.

We take for granted that the process of returning to normalcy will happen relatively quickly. With rare exceptions, people don't live with high fevers for very long. The body's immune system must overcome and contain the invading pathogens. Biological science explains that our white blood cells surround foreign organisms to encapsulate them and prevent them from multiplying and taking over our bodies. This happens automatically (although there are things we can do to facilitate the process), regardless of whether or not we intellectually comprehend the ever-vigilant, self-healing phenomenon operating within our body.

In a similar manner, nature has encoded within us mechanisms for absorbing, fighting, and mitigating emotional and psychological invasions. To ensure survival, nature insists that we subdue threat, lest it overpower and defeat us. Whereas the biologically programmed mechanism for conquering the onslaught of proliferating microorganisms is to cut off their life support, the psychologically programmed mechanism for reducing emotional threats is to isolate them by encoding them into specific energy and nervous system disruptions, where they are much less of a threat to the entire organism. These isolated and specific disruptions—known as perturbations—are activated by *thought fields*. That is, emotional discomfort is aroused when a person thinks about something connected to perturbations that his or her biological system has encoded (tucked away), so that it is a reduced threat to survival. "Thought contact" with the encoded threat is experienced as the symptoms of a psychological problem.

In nature's system, eliminating the threat eliminates the problem. This can happen in the time it takes to warm up, cool down, or break a fever. The integrity of this process exists independent of our belief systems about it.

Although our beliefs about reality do not alter the outcomes, having confidence in nature's operating characteristics usually leads to more realistic acceptance and more astute understanding. Science is, of course, a helpful tool in discerning what's real. So, too, are our eyes, ears, and physiologically programmed instincts. Let's use these tools to delve into the world of emotional control and healing.

When negative emotions subside, exceptional learning, progress, and positive behavior change can occur. Once freed from the pressure of fear and anxiety, people are much more receptive to guidance, feedback, new opportunities, and growth.

HOW TFT WORKS IN PRACTICE

TFT is applied by tapping on meridian points on the upper body. This tapping can be done with either hand and on either side of the body. It can also be done to oneself, or another person may administer it. Self-administration is conventional and preferable, as this is more convenient, allows for greater autonomy and self-sufficiency, and diminishes potential problems that may arise from "touching" patients.

Regardless of who administers the tapping, its effectiveness derives from energy that is put into the body. The meridian points that are used in acupuncture are also receptors to noninvasive pressure such as tapping. When applied at the appropriate junctures and in the correct sequences, the tapping *transduces* the slight physical/kinesthetic energy into signals to the brain and nervous system that change information and reprogram linkages between thoughts and feelings (thereby allowing people to eliminate negative emotions and empowering them to change behavior).

This concept may be unfamiliar to many mental health professionals; however, it is easy to recognize its application in other operations taken for granted. For example, garage door openers work on the same principle; a slight touch on a remote sends a signal that transduces radio waves into mechanical energy, causing a physical change that is disproportionate to the energy applied. Another example is the programming of an alarm, where tapping in the appropriate code will disengage the alarm.

This is how TFT works and why it is so powerful and consistent in the elimination of negative emotions like anxiety and addictive urges.

When the mind and body are in distress, the thought field is connected to a negative emotional state by a code. Appropriate tapping breaks the connection according to the code that set it.

TFT uses the body's natural wisdom to store, manipulate, and unlock codes that affect our conscious and subconscious thoughts, feelings, and behavioral motivations. The treatment itself is implemented by tapping. The locations and sequences of tapping points are determined by codes. The process of decoding the disturbance (caused by perturbations) comprises the diagnostic aspects of TFT.

STEP-BY-STEP INSTRUCTION FOR ELIMINATING NEGATIVE EMOTIONS (SELF-HELP THROUGH ALGORITHMS)

Are you ready to get rid of your negative emotions? This section gives you a hands-on experience with TFT algorithms.

The TFT method can be used with any negative emotion. For the purpose of introduction and instruction, let's use anxiety and cravings (or addictive urges) as the negative emotion you want to eliminate. (Cravings and addictive urges span a spectrum of severity and frequency, but most of us have urges and cravings we wish not to have. Anxiety is the cause of these urges, and anxiety is a fundamental negative emotion that drives much of uncomfortable narratives and problematic behaviors.)

To locate the tapping points, refer to the diagrams below. Generally, you should tap each point ten times (except for the gamut spot, as described below).

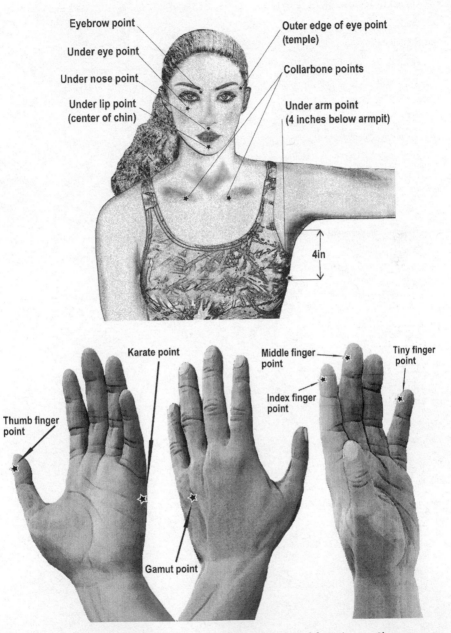

The first time you do the treatment, you should wait until your urge is quite high in order to experience fully the dramatic power of the treatment. After that, repeat the treatments any time you are aware of any urge or craving at all.

1. RATE YOUR URGE.

It is important to rate the degree of your urge on a ten-point scale in order to guide the treatments. Write down the number from one (no urge at all) to ten (the urge is as high as it can get) that best expresses the degree of your urge right now, at this moment.

2. TREAT THE URGE.

Throughout the treatment, you should think of your addictive urge and how good it would be to indulge your particular addictive craving. Take the first two fingers of either hand and tap underneath one of your eyes (see diagram). Tap solidly and firmly, but do not hurt yourself.

Now, tap (ten times) the collarbone point; next tap the underarm point that is located four inches below your armpit, and then the collarbone point again.

If your urge remains the same after these treatments, proceed to the section called "Psychological Reversal." Do the corrective procedure, and then tap under your eyes again. You should then notice a definite, not a subtle, but a definite and clear reduction in your addictive urge.

Next, do the nine-gamut treatment sequence (see below).

When the urge disappears, some people assume that they are not following the instructions since they "can't think about or focus on the problem" any longer. This is the phenomenon of the logical mind (or left-brain interpreter—see section below on the Apex Problem) trying to rationalize the new experience, which is the disappearance of the urge.

THE NINE-GAMUT TREATMENT SEQUENCE

The nine-gamut treatment will result in your urge being reduced even further. Continue to think of your urge and tap solidly (with two fingers) the gamut spot on the back of your hand (see the hand figure). It is located behind and between the little finger knuckle and the ring finger knuckle on the back of your hand. It doesn't matter which hand you use, but many prefer to tap with the dominant hand on the back of the nondominant hand. Keep your head straight with your nose pointed ahead while you do the nine-gamut treatment. Tap about five times for each one of the nine gamut positions while you continue to think of your addictive urge throughout the whole series:

While tapping gamut spot on back of hand, do the following:

a) Close your eyes
b) Open your eyes
c) Point your eyes way down and way over to the right
d) Point your eyes way down and way over to the left
e) Whirl your eyes around in a circle
f) Whirl your eyes around in the opposite direction
g) Rest your eyes, and hum any tune—more than just one note (for about five seconds)
h) Count aloud to five
i) Hum again (it is important to repeat this)

Now, repeat the tapping under the eyes, collarbone point, under arm, and collarbone point while you think of any remaining urge.

The urge or interest in your particular addiction should now be completely gone. Try to resurrect your urge. You should not be able to do so. Think of the pleasure in engaging in your urge. This, too, should have no effect on you. The reason is that you have, temporarily, eliminated your stress in the form of anxiety. You no longer need your favorite tranquilizer, and your need and interest in it should be completely gone.

After the treatment, observe how relaxed you feel. It is a natural relaxation brought on by the removal of an underlying problem. It is normal and healthy, not false and destructive, as is the so-called "relaxation" that occurs from indulging in an addiction.

Tapping correctly treats the underlying problem causing the addictive urge. Although many problems amenable to TFT require only one treatment, addictive urges tend to recur. Because of the ease and expediency of self-treatment, it is simple and practical to keep treating the anxiety/urge.

The recurrence of urges or any problem once successfully treated is usually due to an *individual energy toxin (IET)*. Toxins are a critically important issue for many people and especially for those enmeshed in addictive cycles. Toxins often induce a condition called psychological reversal (see below) that has the effect of "undoing" or reversing a previously successful treatment and also of interfering or blocking the progress of an incipient treatment. Aside from its impact upon TFT treatments, the effect of psychological reversal is also a major factor in many other treatment protocols and can undermine desired goal-oriented motivational states.

PSYCHOLOGICAL REVERSAL (PR)

A psychological reversal exists when a person claims he desires to achieve a specific goal, but his actions and major motivation, as well as his results, appear to be contrary to his professed goal. The person may appear to be striving to achieve (in the *specifically reversed* area), but he will significantly or subtly sabotage the effort.

Psychological reversal (PR) can be tested when a person is attuned to a thought field. A field is an invisible, intangible structure in space that has an effect upon matter. A *thought field* is defined as a connection between cognitive awareness and emotions that generates a field that may contain perturbations. For example, for a phobic person, the thought of getting on an airplane or confronting an insect may generate an intense negative reaction. In such situations, we say that the thought generates a field that contains perturbations (disturbances) responsible for the negative emotions. Testing for the reversal is part of the TFT diagnostic routine. It is easily determined in a matter of seconds. Suffice it to say that psychological reversals must be corrected in order for treatment to progress successfully. The corrections involve tapping either on the side of the hand or under the nose, depending upon when the reversals occur in the treatment sequence. As psychological reversals can impede any treatment or goal-oriented efforts, it is a critical element in countering self-sabotaging behavior. Because TFT treatment works so rapidly, psychological reversals are easy to detect and play a key role in determining the success of treatment outcomes.

Psychological reversal is reflected in physiology and muscle strength and weakness that people experience when stressed. Lie detection methods measure stress indicators such as heart rate, blood pressure, respiration rate, and GSR. Bates (1977) discovered that when an inaccuracy is stated, even without deceitful intent, visual acuity declines. Many have demonstrated that an indicator muscle goes weak when a person doesn't tell the truth.

From a motivational standpoint, a psychological reversal is a dysfunction in how one's system ought to work. When a person thinks about his aspirations or his positive goals he should feel strong and healthy—not weak and sick. Anyone who works with people is aware that some very intelligent and seemingly highly motivated individuals fail, no matter what program, method of treatment, coaching technique, or educational procedure is used. With such chronic failures, it seems likely that when some particular technique is successful, it may be a function of the ability of the technique, coach, or doctor to unwittingly correct the PR that is the most relevant factor in treatment success. Conversely, some teachers, coaches, or doctors may induce a reversal in some of their clients.

Many psychologists and others have stated over the years that certain patients *want* to be ill, or *want* to be disturbed, or even die, even though the patient actively seeks out help. Freud postulated a death instinct. Ellis (1962) pointed out that most neurotics are self-sabotaging and self-defeating. It is fascinating that some traditional psychoanalytic constructs find parallels with modern neurophysiological findings. The wonderful difference is that here and now we can fix these "subconscious" obstacles *in seconds* with several specific and sequential taps.

An interesting fact about psychological reversal is that it can be specialized, affecting only certain areas of one's life, or less commonly, it can be massive and affect most areas of one's life in a negative way. The incidence of massive reversal is higher in people who have struggled with severe addictions or other psychological problems for a long time.

The will, or control over oneself, is definitely limited in a reversed state. The choices available are restricted to negative choices: one's thoughts and ideas tend to have a negative slant. In a severe state of psychological reversal, there will be strong resistance very often against doing the recommended procedures, treatments, or lifestyle changes that would aid in relieving the affliction or symptoms.

The phenomenon of psychological reversal is measurable; its effects are predictable, regular, and scientifically lawful. If a person is in a state of psychological reversal, he is unable to respond favorably to an otherwise effective treatment. If the reversal is corrected, he will then respond to an effective treatment.

The incidence of psychological reversal varies from problem to problem. For example, anxiety and phobic problems have a reversal incidence of about 40 to 50 percent. That is, about one-half of all phobic problems are blocked from getting better or completely better. Some may get partially better and then not improve any further. When the treatment for psychological reversal was discovered, the success rate for treating phobias and anxiety immediately increased dramatically. Most of the phobias that were previously untreatable became treatable after the simple and fast correction for psychological reversal was administered.

The incidence of psychological reversal is higher among addicts than for any other group. In fact, virtually all addicts suffer from some psychological reversal that blocks them from getting better. This is the primary reason why addictions are the most difficult to treat and why so many addicts relapse, even after they seem to be getting better.

The TFT treatment for psychological reversal is simple. The subject must tap either on the side of the hand (karate point) or under the nose (see figure 2) when attuned to the thought in the treatment sequence. Correcting psychological reversals becomes more targeted and effective when the therapist is trained in TFT diagnostic methods.

THE APEX PROBLEM

Sometimes, the mind gets in its own way. Many people are familiar with "overthinking" a situation. Another variant of mind games is thinking the wrong way, which usually presents as dismissiveness, or what is known as the *apex problem*. The *apex problem* is an interesting aspect of TFT treatment; it probably occurs because TFT works so rapidly (and seemingly illogically) that the mind has to make things up in order to avoid dissonance with existing beliefs. Anyone who does TFT regularly with others is certain to encounter this phenomenon, and it is important to understand what is happening.

The term is borrowed from Callahan (2002) who cites Koestler (1967), wherein he refers to the operation of mind at its peak or apex. The *apex problem* refers to the absence of the mind working at its peak. Those uninformed about this prevalent phenomenon in advance will be quite surprised and puzzled by it when conducting successful TFT treatments.

Briefly, the apex problem refers to the commonly observed fact that many people who receive the TFT treatment for any particular problem will *accurately* report the expected and predicted improvement, but *will not typically credit the treatment* for the improvement. They may invoke explanations such as "placebo," "suggestion," "distraction," etc.

The identification of the apex phenomenon has basic scientific relevance in that its frequent occurrence leads to a prediction that the recipients of treatment may not credit the treatment for the dramatic change of state they report after the treatment. It is further predictable that many who are successfully treated will invent other explanations in order to avoid the obvious fact of the role of the treatment.

Why this avoidance of acknowledging the obvious efficacy of the treatment? It seems that in order to credit the surprisingly effective treatment, some people find it necessary to diminish cognitive dissonance (with logic) by considering the treatment as a "miracle." A small number of successfully treated individuals will actually say, "It was a miracle!"

Since the typical TFT recipient is not familiar with this unusual treatment, it does sometimes appear as a kind of miracle (a miracle being something amazing or extraordinary and unexpected, something seemingly contrary to the laws of nature).

However, TFT does work according to the laws of nature, including scientific laws. Despite its replicable efficacy, many people have trouble accommodating the seemingly nonlinear effects. Thus, many will, after successful treatment, *apex*—that is, they will either deny the problem they had before the treatment (or minimize it), or they will acknowledge that they feel better, but attribute the change to some explanation other than the treatment. Frequently, people will say, "Oh, you distracted me from thinking about the problem with that tapping" or "I just can't think about it right now." What they really mean, of course, is that when they think about the problem that previously had caused severe emotional reaction, they no longer feel any distress or preoccupation about it. Thus, the reaction of "I just can't think about it right now" really translates to "Since it's gone, it's no longer there for me to think about?"

Similar examples of the same phenomenon are shown in split-brain subjects and are cited by Gazzaniga, who says, "the normal human is compelled to interpret real behaviors and to construct a theory as to why they have occurred" (Gazzaniga, 1985, 74).

Gazzaniga attributes this confabulation to what he calls the "left brain interpreter." In his split-brain[21] experiments, he discovered that

---

21. One of the major notions of consciousness is its global or totality characteristic; i.e., we have (we believe) but one mind, and apart from the phenomenon of multiple personality, this important rule appears to hold. The split-brain subjects of Michael Gazzaniga have had their brains cut at the connecting commissure, and in effect, they have two minds—each separate—which Gazzaniga calls "the left brain (or language part of the brain) interpreter," where something very similar to the apex problem regularly occurs during the interesting tests administered by

the language aspect of the left brain will invent and create "explanations" for phenomena that are introduced to the nonverbal right brain and not known to the left. However, the left brain, observing the behavior, will compulsively "explain" what is taking place, even though there is no basis in fact for the "explanation." It is pure irrelevant invention. Treated patients never seem to wonder about the possible curative role of their surgery, just as the successfully treated addict ignores the role of the therapy he or she experienced, along with its implied prediction that the treatment will succeed.

Another striking example of the apex problem—for those familiar with hypnosis—is when a good hypnotic subject is given a posthypnotic suggestion with amnesia. The subject may offer irrelevant "explanations" of his behavior because the behavior seems strange to him.

It seems evident that in the addiction treatment, the mind is confronted with a phenomenon it can't comprehend, i.e., immediate successful treatment; so the logical "left brain," in Gazzaniga's terms, begins inventing (irrelevant) explanations even though, in the addiction treatment, the commissures (also referred to as the corpus callosum) connecting the brain's hemispheres are intact and there is no hypnosis nor induced amnesia.

This phenomenon probably occurs in most of us, at times, and the commonplace nature of this interesting phenomenon will become obvious to anyone using TFT regularly.

If a person were functioning at or near the apex of the mind (thus, when he does not have an apex problem), the explanations offered in an apex problem would not be acceptable to him. The compulsion to invent familiar and effortless explanation appears to override critical thinking.

The speed and stunning effectiveness of the treatment seem to generate the apex problem in those vulnerable to it. Nothing that a person has known before could account for the dramatic result. Therefore, many subjects and observers will compulsively *tell* (not ask) why the change took place. Common explanations include placebo effect, hypnosis, or

---

Gazzaniga (Gazzaniga, M. 1985. *The Social Brain*, NY: Basic Books). His subjects invent stories just like Bob, who was hypnotized, and similar to our clients and observers of our successful TFT therapy. They are compelled to make up stories to explain their strange (to them) behavior. Gazzaniga notes that it never seems to occur to them that their strange behavior might have something to do with the surgery that split their brains (and minds) into two separate parts. A more common name for the above is "cognitive dissonance."

distraction. The fact that the explainer has never witnessed similar demonstrations of the power of placebo, hypnosis, or distraction appears to carry little weight.

I have found that prior explanations before treatment appear to have little effect upon reducing the apex problem. Perhaps this issue will subside as an obstacle or objection as TFT and its results become more generally known.

It has been repeatedly shown that the apex problem is not at all an issue of intelligence; indeed, many (though not all) highly creative and brilliant people show an apex reaction rather than acknowledge the easily demonstrated power of TFT treatments.

HOW LONG WILL IT LAST?

When the addictive urge, anxiety, or other negative emotion has been significantly reduced or eliminated, a pertinent question is, "How long will the treatment effect last?" The answer is that the endurance of the treatment varies from person to person; the time it lasts will even vary for the same person at different times.

In my professional experience administering thousands of treatments (mostly using Voice Technology, the highest level of TFT[22]), about 80 percent of the people I treat require only one or two treatments to experience successful results that last indefinitely. The other 20 percent have recurrences due mostly to toxins, as described earlier. Surprisingly, the severity of the problem (according to the dismal success rates of conventional therapies) is not a good predictor of success with TFT. For example, traumas respond exceedingly well to single TFT treatments. You might think that abuse, sexual molestation, war horrors, loss of a loved one, etc., would be so deeply entrenched that little could relieve, much less eliminate these sufferings. Yet using Voice Technology TFT, I have routinely eliminated issues such as these in one treatment. Among them are the following:

1. A woman who lost her husband and son in a car accident that she survived. She had been depressed by this trauma for nine years.
2. Numerous cases of sexual molestation and childhood abuse.
3. Flashbacks from war experiences.

---

22. Voice Technology has a success rate of 97 percent.

4. Survivors of Nazi concentration camps.
5. A man traumatized by an incident that occurred a half-century ago, before my single treatment eliminated what had been plaguing him for fifty years.

This is not to suggest that TFT is magic or miraculous or that it can undo the horrible realities that people endure. Rather, it is to state unequivocally and with solid proof that the emotional sting of these traumatic experiences can be removed completely within minutes.

Returning to the topic of using TFT to help yourself with an array of problems that beset so many people: the success and endurance you experience with TFT will depend on a number of factors:

1. The degree of your psychological reversal
2. Your sensitivity to toxins
3. Your correct implementation of the procedures and persistence in repetition, when necessary
4. Your general health
5. The nature (typically not severity) of the problem you are treating

Notice that your *belief* in the efficacy of the treatment is not listed as a factor in predictive success. This is because *it does not matter*. Like an antibiotic, TFT will either work or it won't, *irrespective of your beliefs*. You simply have to administer it.

Admittedly, self-help treatment is not as effective as professional treatment for more complex cases. However, self-help treatment has the advantages of being free, convenient, and private—and they do often work splendidly. So why not try it? There are no negative side effects with TFT. The only downside to self-help treatment is that if you don't get satisfactory results quickly, you may give up, dismiss TFT, and pass up an extremely valuable tool for living intact, simply because you didn't get significant relief the first or second time.[23]

The vast majority of people will experience profound calmness and significant reduction in urges and cravings the first and every time they

---

23. This is why you should contact a professional when the self-administered procedure does not appear to be working. You should also be aware of how TFT works, how it differs in practice and theory from conventional treatments, and how the apex problem can lead you astray.

use the TFT algorithms. A small minority of people can do just one urge reduction treatment and then never have a further desire for their addictive substance. This, alas, is a rare response, but it does happen.

For most people, cravings will return at the first sign of stress, and it is imperative to repeat the treatment each time an urge arises. Frequency of treatment depends upon the degree of stress. It is important to keep in mind that repeated treatments are not wasted—rather, each administration of the procedure treats the underlying cause of the addiction problem. Since the underlying problem is addressed and treated, rather than being masked as with tranquilizers, the repeated treatments may also eventually eliminate the underlying problem.

LEVELS OF TFT TREATMENT

There are three levels of treatment in TFT: algorithms, causal diagnosis, and Voice Technology.

Algorithms are summary recipes for administering TFT that have resulted from applying the commonalities of thousands of individually diagnosed perturbation sequences. Algorithms are what nonprofessionals typically use to treat themselves. (You can use some of the algorithms listed in appendix C. Also, I teach seminars in TFT, as do some of my colleagues; visit www.marksteinberg.com.)

Causal diagnosis is the objective scientific procedure of identifying perturbations (specific to particular thought fields) and determining which tapping points and in what order will be most effective in *collapsing the perturbations*—that is, decoding or deprogramming the thought field so that the perturbations that cause the disturbance are no longer active.

Causal diagnosis involves a combination of having the person *attune* the thought field and then using variations of applied kinesiology (muscle-testing) to identify the active perturbations. The practitioner typically does this by "testing" various points on the patient's body.

Voice Technology is the practice of diagnosing the points through information provided by the person's voice. This is the most advanced level of TFT, and it offers a number of advantages including the obvious expediency of treating someone effectively by phone. Voice Technology (VT) is also quicker and often more precise in treating patients with greater complexity or long strings of perturbations. VT is also expedient in the identification of *toxins* that may cause psychological reversals and interfere with treatment.[24]

Nature encodes both the sources of distress and their solutions within our bodies and minds. Because of nature's recapitulation and signaling system, the human voice indicates with precision the causes of emotional and physical disturbance and can be used in tandem with Thought Field Therapy to eliminate the source and symptoms in minutes.

APPLICATIONS OF TFT TREATMENT

TFT is useful for eliminating a wide array of problems. Though it works on physical problems to a greater extent than you might imagine, let's restrict it conservatively to the realm of negative emotions. By eliminating negative emotions with consistency, a new world will unfold for you—a world of personal freedom in which you can set your mind to achieve some goal, identify the emotional traps that so heavily and surreptitiously disrupt your well-being and impede your purposefully desired behavior, and attain one goal after another as you progress on your journey of living intact.

Here is a partial list of negative emotions you can eliminate with TFT:

- Anxiety
- Depression
- Frustration
- Anger
- Feeling overwhelmed
- Stress
- Irritation
- Impatience
- Fear
- Embarrassment
- Guilt
- Hopelessness
- Rejection

---

24. Toxins are substances that cause a psychological reversal and may block or reverse the effects of successful treatment. Typically, many foods, toiletries, aromas, and supplements act as toxins for a percentage of people. For many people, the sustained positive effects of treatments and better health require the identification of and abstention from toxins.

- Grief
- Hurt
- Worrying
- Cravings
- Disgust
- Emotional and behavioral overreactions
- Jealousy and lovesickness

As you gain success with eliminating these unwanted negative emotions, you can devote your efforts using TFT along with other skills and techniques to meet and overcome the following challenges:

- Procrastination
- Addictions
- Bad habits
- Behavior problems
- Sleep problems
- Obsessiveness and compulsiveness
- Weight and appetite control
- Eating disorders
- Study habits
- Relationship dysfunction
- Avoidance
- Phobias and fears
- Habitual worrying
- Negative thinking
- Choking under pressure
- Self-defeating attitudes
- Fatigue
- Jet lag
- Finishing projects

Appendix C provides a number of algorithms that are useful for specific problems and negative emotional states, such as anxiety, cravings, depression, and so forth. This appendix also includes some tips and techniques I have found successful in treating many people and problems over the years.

INTEGRATING TFT WITH LIVING INTACT

TFT can be one of your power tools, tremendously effective by itself and even more powerful when you integrate it with the secrets and elements of living intact.

As indicated in chapter 7, for most people, the biggest problem in eliminating maladaptive responses is the negative emotions that keep those responses in place. Keep in mind that the responses are the result of trying to suppress the negative emotion—anxiety, fear, anger, depression, worry, etc. All too often, this negative emotion disables or paralyzes the flexibility to engage in an alternate response at those previous moments when the probability of success is most in your favor.

In my experience, TFT is remarkably effective for eliminating negative emotions. However, this technique is not only advantageous, but is curative when the negative emotion is *itself* the problem. In other words, when negative emotions are the principal force in driving or inhibiting behaviors (as in traumas or phobias, for example), the successful application of TFT obviates the need for other therapies, "processing," or follow-up routines to allow for flexibility or goal-acquiring behaviors. Eliminating the negative emotion spontaneously allows the person to build new and adaptive reinforcement schedules, without environmental modification.[25] In the case of curing a flying phobia, once the person discovers the absence of paralyzing anxiety, he then flies more frequently, experiences new freedom, and constructively modifies a self-image that averts the emergence of his former anxiety.

For most bad habits, though, a combination of approaches works best. First, we eliminate the negative emotion that restricts the implementation of an alternative response. Then, the person is more free, flexible, and able to craft the reinforcement schedules that will be more adaptive. This is usually the way to beat compulsive behaviors or addictions.

TFT, ANXIETY, AND ADDICTIONS

We live in a world where most of us become highly stressed and over-aroused, causing a habitual parasympathetic nervous system response.

---

25. For example, once TFT totally eliminates a fear, then he doesn't need to set up practice strategies to slowly reduce his avoidance of the feared object or situation, nor does he need to structure the environment to help compensate for his problem.

This heightened and continued fight-or-flight syndrome is so detrimental to health and so subjectively intolerable that many people resort to addictive behaviors or substances to relieve intense and persistent misery.

Without effective interventions and proper supportive lifestyles, the oppression of anxiety and overarousal will drive people to spiral downward, preventing them from living intact and from leading what could otherwise be lives of productivity, satisfaction, and contribution.

TFT can be so instrumental in breaking the addictive cycle because of its powerful and immediate effect on anxiety, the culprit responsible for the addictive urge. This important area that afflicts so many people deserves some further attention in this chapter.

WHAT IS ADDICTION?

Addiction is a dependency on some substance or activity that causes some degree of harm to, or interference with, a person's life. The dependency is powered by the tranquilizing (i.e., anxiety masking) effect of the substance or activity.

Addictions always originate from anxiety. All addictions are responses to relieving (or masking) anxiety. They also generate the belief that the addicted person cannot live without the necessary substance/object/behavior. In these cases, the challenge to living intact involves instituting a safe and viable way of *eliminating anxiety*. Once this is in place, habits can be changed, which may include revisiting the belief that one *must* engage or indulge in the desires that propel the addictive substance or behavior.

Anxiety is a terrible emotion to experience and is worsened when there is no apparent cause for it. The anxious person not only feels bad due to the anxiety, but he also feels stupid for feeling bad, because he knows that the emotion makes no sense. If an anxious person can take something or do something that blocks awareness of the anxiety, he feels tremendous relief.

The relieved person feels calm, serene, tranquilized, and temporarily free of the agonizing feeling of anxiety. The relief feels so good that it makes a profound impression on the anxiety victim's body and mind. Though many addicts are aware of this sequence of actions leading to addiction, not every addict is aware of the process. This sequence happens to each addict at a profound level of being, regardless of the level of conscious awareness.

The process of addiction creates a state of self-sabotage in the victim. This state makes it especially difficult to overcome the addiction because it drives the addict to engage in self-defeating activities and to become his own worst enemy, such as not doing a simple treatment that can eliminate the addictive urge. (See the previous section on psychological reversal for a fuller discussion of this problem.)

Why do certain substances or activities mask anxiety? This is an important question, and the answer is not yet fully known. Some drugs appear to physically block awareness of anxiety, via the nervous system or the brain, and certain activities such as thumb sucking or hair pulling appear to be intrinsically soothing to some individuals, and the apparent comfort of the activity appears to block awareness of anxiety.

The term "addiction" is often used rather loosely; as a result, this may lead to misunderstanding. For example, some might say that people are addicted to sports or books. But this questionable wording is not meant to indicate a problem. It is meant to indicate a strong or intense fondness for sports or books.

In a psychological or medical sense, the term "addicted" has the clear implication of indicating a problem. An addiction interferes with a person's life, functioning, health, or well-being to some degree.

It is unreasonable to call natural, wholesome, and healthy good feelings an addiction. To feel good physically and mentally naturally, without drugs, is a sign and a consequence of good general health.

HABIT AND ADDICTION

Many people confuse habits and addictions. There is a great deal of difference between the two.

A *habit* is a behavior pattern that is done regularly and is so established in our behavioral repertoire that it is usually done or carried out without conscious effort. Since a certain amount of effort went into establishing a habit, a certain effort is required for changing a habit.

A good example of a habit is how we train ourselves to automatically remove our car keys when we leave our car so that we don't lock ourselves out. When we go to a car wash, a car repair, or leave our car with a valet parking service, a special conscious effort is required in order to not walk off with the car keys when we shouldn't. When we make the conscious effort, it is not that difficult to change the habit; the difficulty is remembering to be conscious about it. People think that habits are like addictions. They are not. In addiction, no matter how conscious one is, one finds the addictive urge to be rather compelling or overwhelming, depending upon the severity of the addiction.

Addictions, unlike habits, are extremely difficult to give up. Whereas in the case of an addiction a person is driven and compulsive, in the case of habits, the person's actions represent highly learned activities that are often amenable to conscious efforts to change.

THE ANXIETY-ADDICTION CONNECTION

There are legions of people in the world who, though not in chronic physical pain or in combat, feel just as bad or worse as those who are in chronic physical pain. These people are described as having anxiety.

Anxiety is the presence of fear or overarousal when there is no objective external reason to be afraid or to maintain the overaroused state. While others may dismiss or even scoff at *perseverative*[26] anxiety, the victims know how inappropriate their anxiety is. This knowledge only complicates their plight, for they suffer not only from overbearing anxiety, but also from the embarrassment and self-deprecation that accrues from having the problem.

Addiction problems result from the anxiety-masking effects of abusing substances or counterproductive or self-defeating activities. The essence of all addictions is that they involve a powerful, often overwhelming, urge to consume an anxiety-reducing substance or participate in an anxiety-reducing activity. An addiction is a behavior pattern characterized by a strong urge to act in a way that compromises the independence of will and its influence over the determinants of behavior. Addictions are "have-to-do" behaviors that persist despite the known harm they bring.

Addictions include: drugs and chemicals that alter consciousness and state of arousal and typically involve the ingestion of tranquilizers, pain pills, alcohol, tobacco, cocaine, heroin, and foods. They also include a range of behavioral addictions, which are epitomized by the excesses found in obsessive-compulsive disorders. People can even become addicted to

---

26. Perseverative is a psychological term used to indicate continued responding on a perceptual, emotional, cognitive, or behavioral level in the absence of the original or appropriate stimulus; think of the afterimage when you look at the sun or a bright light and then look away.

behaviors that are natural and/or instinctual, such as sex or anger. In its appropriate context, sex would not be considered an addiction. However, sex, too, can become an all-consuming behavior that can be carried to excess and be harmful. The excessive conduct reflects an effort to reduce or mask overwhelming anxiety. Despite his legendary sexual "conquests," Casanova, the ultimate iconic *ladies' man*, was incapable of living intact. Rather, he was the victim of his own overpowering sexual addiction.

Though addictive syndromes contain many substrata, the common denominator that is operative in all addictions is the *addictive urge*. It is the desire for its relief that maintains the addiction. The unrelieved or temporarily assuaged urge results in a state of withdrawal, thus perpetuating the dysfunctional cycle.

FOUNDATION OF THE ADDICTIVE URGE AND ITS TREATMENT

Addressing the addictive urge (or craving) is the basis of effective treatment for any addiction. As indicated above, anxiety is the underlying source of all addictive urges. Addictive substances or behaviors serve the purpose of masking anxiety, but do not eliminate anxiety. *Withdrawal* is the formerly hidden anxiety coming back into the realm of conscious awareness and provoking crises. The anxiety-addiction connection is key to understanding and successfully treating addictions.

Addiction is a dependency on a certain substance or activity that causes some degree of harm to, or interference with, a person's life. The dependency is powered by the tranquilizing (i.e., anxiety-masking) effect of the substance or activity. Anxiety is a terrible emotion to experience, and it is worsened when there is no tangible or "reasonable" cause for it. The anxious person not only feels bad due to the anxiety, but he also feels sheepish because he knows that the emotion makes no sense. If an anxious person takes something or does something that blocks awareness of the anxiety, he feels tremendous relief.

The person feels calm, serene, tranquilized, and temporarily free of the agonizing feeling of anxiety. The relief feels so good that it makes a profound impression on the body and the mind of the anxiety victim. Though many addicts are aware of the actual underlying dynamics of the process, this sequence happens to each addict at a profound level of being, irrespective of the level of conscious awareness.

The reasons why certain substances or activities mask anxiety are not fully known, though research is progressively uncovering information about changes in brain function and structure resulting from repeated indulgence. Newer findings in the realm of "hard" drugs like methamphetamine and cocaine suggest that usage itself changes the brain's ability and response capacities with regard to satiety and satisfaction. *Reward deficiency syndrome* is now a popular hypothesis linking drug usage to the brain's failure to derive pleasure from previously satisfying experiences once it has experienced the intense highs induced by certain substances. This hypothesis notwithstanding, changes in pleasure thresholds in the brain do not mitigate the originating problem of the addictive urge and its destructive stranglehold over adaptive goal-driven behavior. We are faced with the problem of reducing or eliminating the addictive urge.

THE CAUSE OF ADDICTION

Although well documented, addiction problems invariably arise from the repetitive anxiety-masking effect of certain substances or behaviors. Most people who use drugs disregard the predictable dire consequences and continue to use drugs in order to feel good. Actually, what those prone to addiction call "feeling good" is the temporary illusive feeling of the freedom from anxiety. The anxiety may be so chronic that they might not even be aware that they are feeling bad until they actually try a drug and discover that they are capable of feeling much better than they ever imagined. The common anxiety-masking tranquilizers, such as alcohol, marijuana, or cocaine, diminish general awareness, which then results in a seeming reduction of anxiety.

An addict is one who suffers from chronic or situational anxiety that feels almost unbearable. He finds, perhaps accidentally, that a substance or an activity gives him *apparent* relief.

It is important to understand that the "relief" is actually a temporary tranquilizing, masking, or blocking effect. This masking effect carries a danger because it sets the stage for an addiction to develop. The person gains much needed but only short-lived escape from the anxiety.

If the drug or activity actually eliminated anxiety, there would be no addiction problem. The person could then refrain from indulgence once its deleterious effects were appreciated. However, most addictive behavior occurs repetitively, despite the addict's acknowledgment that it is harmful.

In fact, what happens is that the anxiety usually gets worse as the addiction progresses. The serious crisis in withdrawal from an addictive drug or activity is a crisis of revisited anxiety. Those familiar with anxiety patients or with addicts undergoing withdrawal can appreciate how difficult and excruciating a problem this anxiety of withdrawal can be.

Also, an addict who has been successful in quitting may go through a renewed crisis if something stressful happens, such as losing a job or relationship, or having a family member become ill. Any upsetting event may trigger an extreme renewed intense need for the favored tranquilizer.

All addictions, therefore, are addictions to the tranquilizing effect on the anxiety aroused and experienced as the addictive urge. Of course, the cycle of addiction subsumes many complex biological and psychosocial factors; however, the addictive problem predisposed by other life problems begins resolution with the successful focus upon and treatment of the addictive urge.

TFT is a viable and rapid treatment for the anxiety-spawned addictive urge.

JUST EXPERIMENTING

In our current age, drug use is often viewed as rite of passage. Many college students "experiment" with drugs and alcohol and with other behaviors that tempt them in their quest for pleasure and independence. One may go to a party where drugs are available and, out of curiosity, experiment with crack or methamphetamines and become "instantly" addicted. Instant addiction, however, is a misnomer. Certainly, drugs like cocaine, methamphetamines, and heroin have profound impact upon neurochemical structures, even with very limited exposure. The brain becomes "wowed" by extreme excitation or numbing after which there is a "crash"—withdrawal—and the brain desperately wants relief. It is critical, however, to discern that the withdrawal itself brings on the anxiety that, for some people, is intolerable. Nobody with an intact nervous system or adequate coping resources would repeat the agony of withdrawal unless the *intolerance for overwhelming anxiety was resident*.

The atavism that "once you try it, you're hooked" reflects the pernicious intolerance for withdrawal-based anxiety more than the "permanent" or "irresistible" allure of "addicting" drugs. This is not to diminish the incredible destructive power of such substances—only to emphasize that addiction of any sort is based upon anxiety.

MAKING WORLDWIDE IMPACT

A curious phenomenon is that changing the world begins with changing yourself. In a world of paradoxes and meanings that are often hidden or coded, many events and truths can have related meaning or compounded meaning. In science, we make progress by intertwining theory with experimentation, hypothesis testing, data collection, and, in turn, more newly developed theories. When you are able to change yourself, the world looks different and listens differently to you.

Philosophy is wonderful, but so is practicality. As Kierkegaard said, "The society that exalts philosophy and looks down upon plumbing will have both bad philosophy and bad plumbing." TFT is a practical method of ridding yourself of negative emotions, curtailing the overarousal that chips away at your health and contaminates your narrative, and freeing yourself from the impediments and attitudes that make you a slave and a victim.

Imagine what could happen worldwide if people practiced these techniques and habits. *One could easily imagine the earthshaking effects that the techniques described above could have on reducing hatred, prejudice, and aggression. It can start with you literally tapping into this powerful and accessible resource that is at your fingertips. Flowing from within you are the powers to heal yourself and change the world!*

A number of my colleagues and dear friends have taken and still do take TFT around the world, even to third world countries. They help trauma victims in Africa, South America, Asia, and Europe. They teach seminars to lay people and to clergy, showing them how to use the tapping techniques in villages where people have very few resources. They go into countries where genocide, malaria, and natural disasters have left populations devastated and bereft. These are millions of human beings who have hunger and hurt feelings and grief and agonies and—meridian tapping points. And they get better and heal from their hurts, thanks to brilliant innovations of Dr. Roger Callahan and those who have taken up his work with TFT.

You now have a powerful tool to integrate into your arsenal of improving life for yourself and others around you. How will you use it?

But I will restore you to health and heal your wounds, declares the Lord, because you are an outcast, Zion for whom no one cares. (Jeremiah 30:17)

Nevertheless, I will bring health and healing to it; I will heal my people and will let them enjoy abundant peace and security. (Jeremiah 33:6)

Jesus said to them, "Surely you will quote this proverb to me: 'Physician, heal yourself! Do here in your hometown what we have heard that you did in Capernaum.'" (Luke 4:23)

IV
REALITY FEEDBACK

CHAPTER 11
EXPECTATIONS: WHERE REALITY MEETS DESIRE

"I'm an old man who has seen many troubles. However, most of them never happened."

—Mark Twain

We all have expectations. They are a product of the conscious mind, the conglomeration of previous learning, the images of things to come, the desires for what we want, and the beliefs about what should happen. Without expectations, we could hardly plan or build models and concepts of the way the world operates. Expectations help us predict, categorize, and simplify. They form a cornerstone of what we know as reality. At a biological level, expectations propel our survival by guiding behavior toward physical needs and functions. Animals in the wild go where they expect to find food and water. People act in ways that they think will bring rewards. At a physiological level, expectations gear our nervous systems to states of arousal necessary or appropriate for anticipated events. At a psychological level, expectations drive the mind's narrative to support evaluations of experience and predictions of what will happen next.

There is, however, a downside to expectations: desire, need, or faulty evaluation can drive expectations to the point where hopes are dashed, beliefs are unrealistic, and disappointments prevail over satisfaction and fulfillment. Examples abound. A student is rejected by his first choice university. A loyal employee is passed over for a promotion. A house doesn't sell for the asking price during a real estate market downturn. Becoming aware of how expectations influence you and shape the opinions and assumptions you take for granted can empower you to confront challenges with greater effectiveness. You'll discover that by understanding the impact of expectations upon your motivation and happiness, you can significantly expand your capacity to live a more intact life.

Expectations are mediators between reality and desire: they help us navigate through the world as it is toward the world we wish to create.

Your expectations are your assessments, your plans and schematics, aspirations and maps of the world and yourself within the world.

GREATER AND LESSER EXPECTATIONS

Expectation connotes a general meaning with subtle nuances and variations. An expectation is a confident belief or strong hope that a particular event will happen. It can serve as a standard of conduct or performance demanded or anticipated by or of somebody. An expectation may also be a mental image of something awaited that can often be incongruent with how one's desires play out.

The term *greater expectations* indicates results hoped for or desired. Whereas *greater expectations* involve aspirations, ambitions, imagination, wishes, and dreams, *lesser expectations* refer to the results realistically anticipated based upon previous experiences and conditioning. *Lesser expectations* involve predictive validity, accuracy, boundaries, practicality, and directions.

Expectations reflect your conscious and unconscious assessments, plans and schematics, and maps of the world and of yourself within the world. Expectations unfold at different levels, and these levels mediate the ways that you want things to be (great expectations) with the ways you have learned through experience that they are likely to play out (lesser expectations).

*The difference between your greater expectations and your lesser expecta-
tions approximates your satisfaction and disappointment in life. It is an
indicator of the extent to which you reconcile the outcomes you get with
the way you would like life to work. It is also a reflection of the way you
balance reality testing with desire.*

Let me provide an example that differentiates greater from lesser
expectations and illustrates how expectations operate in the real
world. The story involves a fifteen-year-old patient. Certain alterations
have been made to protect the teenager's identity, but these identity-
protecting modifications do not affect the underlying dynamics of the
story.

During the second semester of her high school freshman year, Brittany was adjusting to the academic challenges she faced much better than
might have been predicted, based on her abysmal eighth grade performance in middle school. She raised her grades and, of particular note, was
that she had eliminated the two Ds she had received the first semester.
Although she still struggled in math and science, her lowest grade was
a C-, and she had an A- in history. She had made new friends, wasn't
getting into any trouble, and she actually liked and looked forward to
school. Given her history of ADD and bipolar disorder, this was encouraging and even remarkable. Brittany's regular outbursts, disruptions at
home and school, and poor academic achievement and attendance had
marred the last few years. This had resulted in an accelerating downward
spiral, and this was despite the intensive regimen of medications that had
been prescribed by her psychiatrist to control her condition.

Given this downward spiral, I had recommended a treatment protocol
of EEG neurofeedback training that had, over several months, stabilized
Brittany's moods. (See chapter 9 for an in depth discussion of neurofeedback.) She had become more focused and contained, and she was able to
eliminate totally the toxic medications she had trouble tolerating. Her
outlook was brighter, her empathy more palpable, and her forays into the
role of "drama queen" had diminished significantly.

As Brittany and I talked about her schoolwork, it became apparent that her expectations were skewed. She estimated that she did about
75 percent of her homework, and she volunteered with pride that she
felt this was pretty good. According to Brittany, this was because most

students in her classes only did about 50 percent of their homework. Thus, she stated she was exceeding her teachers' expectations.

When I asked why she didn't do the remaining 25 percent of her homework, Brittany claimed that it was because she didn't understand the work. Our discussion touched upon other aspects of her school and home life, including her anxiety and trauma over teachers criticizing and embarrassing her when she did ask questions and her resentment and conflict regarding her father's pressure to do better in school.

Clearly, Brittany had unresolved issues regarding her skills and interactions with others, but a salient feature of her predicament was the mismatch between her expectations of herself and others and the realities surrounding *their expectations of her*.

I asked Brittany how she knew that teachers expected only 50 percent of the homework turned in and if she had any evidence that the estimate she quoted was close to accurate. Her answer reflected her expectations and her projections of a reality that would fit those expectations. In other words, Brittany held low expectations of herself and low expectations of others. She neither knew how nor felt any particular need to overcome the understanding gap that accounted for the 25 percent of her missing work, and she rationalized that her teachers didn't expect much anyway. She was less able to avoid the glaring discrepancies in expectations between herself and her father regarding her school performance.

Brittany's case highlights the common problems that arise when expectations about one's own performance and the response of others don't mesh with each other and with actual circumstances.

It might seem characteristically juvenile that Brittany offered rationalizations and justifications about completing only 75 percent of her homework based on her own needs, defenses, and comparisons with her peers. Getting her in touch with the reality of her teachers' expectations and motivations would require more than shocking her with truths she didn't want to acknowledge. The far better alternative was to provide her with a concrete example that would help clarify the difference between *greater expectations* and *lesser expectations*.

Sharing with Brittany about my experiences parenting my own teenagers, I said that I expected my children to tell me the truth. I asked Brittany if she thought I expected them to tell me the truth *some* of the time.

"Of course not," she said, "you want the truth all the time."

"Yes," I responded, "but do you think my children have told me the truth 100 percent of the time?"

Brittany blushed. "No," she murmured.

"That's right," I acknowledged. "The standard is 100 percent, but we all know from experience that people sometimes lie—yes, even you and I lie.

"So the expectation—the standard and structure for the desired outcome—I call a *greater expectation*, and the results anticipated (though not necessarily accepted) based upon previous experiences and conditioning I call a *lesser expectation*."

I explained to Brittany that her teachers might have multiple expectations. They assign homework with the (greater) expectation that the homework will be completed. However, they may anticipate that only part of the homework will actually be turned in. The disparity between these two expectations may cause student/teacher conflict, disappointment, and unhappiness. Or it may result in reduced expectations, involvement, and alienation on the part of students, as well as a myriad of student rationalizations for the resulting unsatisfactory grades.

Brittany began to understand the importance that expectations played in her views about her peers, her teachers, and the demands she placed upon herself. She also took note of the conflict her father was having over his own great and lesser expectations about her school performance and the role she should play in mediating the difference. She saw that the clarification of expectations and their differences could provide significant leverage in modifying her self-perception, her accuracy of interpretation, her interaction with others, and her own performance. These insights would play a pivotal role in further enhancing her schoolwork.

UNDERSTANDING YOUR OWN EXPECTATIONS

To help you understand your own expectations and the role they play in living intact, I have developed a psychometric instrument to measure expectations and specifically the difference between your *greater expectations* and *lesser expectations*. By taking the Expectations Assessment,[27] you can measure your levels of expectations and how they reflect upon your outlook and your level of functioning.

---

27. To take the Expectations Assessment, please go online to www.livingintact.com.

Let's look more closely at the role that greater and lesser expectations play in life.

Greater expectations infuse life with purpose and zest. As previously indicated, without these expectations, it's hard to imagine that new inventions, products, and relationships would ever be created. Greater expectations often anticipate what's ahead, based on reasonable projections from the present. For instance, parents don't anticipate their children staying the same age; they expect them to grow up and attain key developmental milestones, such as being able to turn over, crawl, and then begin to walk and talk.

These reasonably anticipated parental greater expectations differentiate desirable outcomes (i.e., the child's attainment of developmental milestones) from undesirable ones (i.e., the child's failure to attain developmental milestones). The difference between greater expectations and lesser expectations in children's development is poignantly underscored when, for instance, a child does not develop appropriate language and behavior and is diagnosed with autism.

Using another example, imagine looking forward to eating at a highly recommended restaurant or one where you know from experience that the food is invariably good. Then, imagine going to the restaurant and discovering to your disappointment that it has changed hands, the chef whose cuisine you like is no longer in the kitchen, and the food is mediocre. Your expectations would clearly be unfulfilled. Unfortunately, sometimes unanticipated roadblocks may jeopardize your reasonable great expectations, and you must find the emotional resources to cope with these roadblocks that may be minor inconveniences, as in the case of the restaurant, or potentially major tribulations, as in the case of the child who fails to achieve anticipated age-appropriate developmental milestones.

Greater expectations provide incentive for improvement. Without greater expectations, we could not have the impetus to confront and overcome challenges. The process of confronting challenges is one of the core elements in our lives. We face these challenges when we compete for a scholarship, a job, a raise, or a career advancement. Such challenges expose us to conditions that gauge our motivation, integrity, competency, focus, natural talents, stick-to-itiveness, and purpose. These are the by-products of life's inevitable trials and challenges that test our grit and determination and sharpen our capacity to overcome obstacles, weather adversity, compete successfully, prove merit, and prevail.

The Interplay of Expectations and Challenges

We face challenges on multiple levels from within and without. These challenges are derived from biological, social, and environmental sources. Our responses to challenges at every level—within ourselves and in reaction to the world around us—allow us to grow, strengthen, recover, adapt, and discover meaning in life. During the course of our lives, we learn about the nature of challenges and recognize how individual "tests" of our bodies, intellect, beliefs, integrity, and character mold us. Accepting and even embracing these challenges mark the path leading toward living intact. Our responses to these tests provide an unparalleled opportunity for us to triumph and for our spirits to soar. Challenges that are successfully confronted provide vital nutrients that feed our ego and enhance our self-confidence and self-image. Challenges are, thus, not threats but, rather, extraordinary opportunities for growth.

The need to confront and deliberately create challenges impels extraordinary people in all fields of endeavor to reach for the brass ring as they stretch over the edge of the carousel while the calliope plays. Just as challenges offer the opportunity to develop ourselves, so do mistakes, errors, setbacks offer the opportunity to fine-tune our reality check and gauge our modus operandi. This process is typically called *learning from one's experience* or *learning from one's mistakes*.

Relationships are basic to life activities and satisfaction, and they are a key area in which challenges present themselves and offer opportunities for dealing with expectations. Most people desire to find a good friend or partner with whom to share and experience life. The process of dating, for example, stimulates the imagination to conjure qualities that one hopes for (or thinks one sees) in a potential mate. As the nascent relationship develops, subtle (or even glaring) signs appear that the other person is far from the ideal that had spawned excitement. Perhaps he is self-absorbed, stingy, or lacking in manners. Perhaps she turns out to be an inveterate gossip or extremely moody. One or the other may reveal, over time, prejudice, intolerance, inflexibility, or chronic jealousy. These observations of unhealthy characteristics are warning signs that must be heeded if they represent a fundamental incompatibility.

Expectations are dashed as you discover and acknowledge that she or he is *not* "the one." The insights acquired about oneself and others, albeit sometimes painful and disillusioning, represent one's personal learning curve. When distilled and integrated, the insights coalesce into intuition and good judgment, attributes that can be used to assess compatibility, protect against false hope, and deal realistically with expectations. In this way, desire and need are prevented from leading to unnecessary trials, tribulations, failures, frustration, and demoralization.

Were the dynamics of actively pursuing and welcoming challenges in tandem with greater expectations and reality-tested lesser expectations not operative in the human conditions, dazzling innovators and entrepreneurs such as Bill Gates and Steve Jobs, extraordinary movie directors such as Steven Spielberg and Ron Howard, towering writers such as Steinbeck, Hemingway, and Faulkner, astounding inventors such as Edison and Graham Bell, dominant industrialists such as Andrew Carnegie, and brilliant scientists such as Einstein, Curie, Pasteur, and Salk would have never produced their outstanding contributions. These accomplishments testify to human talent, ingenuity, resourcefulness, and perseverance in response to challenges. To live intact, you must not only be prepared to accept challenges, but you must also take delight in the opportunities they create to assert your character and potency. (Please refer back to chapter 3 and 8 for more about challenges.) Although your greater expectations provide an incentive, a roadmap, and a navigation system for the fulfillment of your desires, these greater expectations must be reconciled with your lesser expectations. Your ability to achieve this resolution is one of the most important tasks of living intact. Lesser expectations detail a terrain already mapped out and previously traveled. You might want to think of this interplay as pressing on the brakes when your navigation system indicates a sharp curve ahead. You anticipate the risk factors because you've already had previous experience with handling sharp turns. Thus, we depend upon lesser expectations for predictability, directions, timing, and the accuracy of planning.

Without lesser expectations, we could not function in the world of realistic probability. We would become untethered from practicality, detached from the needs of others, unaware of boundaries, and oblivious to the safety offered by the process of learning from experience.

Were it not for lesser expectations, we might repeatedly succumb to Internet scams, base our financial security upon the remote chance of winning the lottery, limit our options by submitting only one resume when looking for work, neglect to study for a test, or fail to stop for gas when the gauge is hovering on empty. These lesser expectations do not diminish the value of and the need for having greater expectations. Without them, how could we fall in love, take chances, invest in the future, or imagine and conceptualize goals?

Both greater expectations and lesser expectations have significant and complementary roles in our psyches. Greater expectations keep us motivated, sustain faith and hope, promote optimism, ambition, and self-worth, palliate fantasies, and allay unfulfilled needs. Lesser expectations keep us grounded and help us recognize factual realities and adjust to life the way it plays out, rather than as a product of our desires.

RECONCILING EXPECTATIONS AND CHALLENGES

You've undoubtedly observed that life does not always give us all that we want when we want it and that the world does not always conform to our standards and expectations. This is a reality that we may acknowledge, yet at some basic instinctual level that is cognitive, emotional, and spiritual, we may attempt to circumvent the reality by entertaining thoughts and desires that anticipate greater possibilities that lie just around the corner. These comprise our expectations, both realistic and otherwise. Sorting through these expectations, reconciling what we desire with what is possible and likely, adjusting our standards, anticipations, and evaluations in light of circumstances—these are the practical applications of using the challenge process to our advantage.

President Obama stated recently that he expects us to land people on Mars during his lifetime. There are, of course, many challenges and lesser expectations that stand in the way of attaining this "lofty" aspiration. Is Obama's aspiration realistic? Time will tell. Was President Kennedy's targeting the goal of sending American astronauts to the moon in the late 60s realistic? Kennedy was not deterred by the enormous challenges or the lesser expectations, although he and NASA undoubtedly considered them.

Expectations create a quintessential context for challenge in that they provide the yardstick by which we can measure our capacity to perform and by which we can cause the rest of the world to behave as we predict and desire. They are, in effect, the proverbial carrot dangling enticingly on a string at the end of the stick. Formulating expectations, assessing and interpreting their potential for fulfillment, and managing and reconciling discrepancies are among the core challenges that determine and shape the nature of our existence and our survival.

THE ROLES PLAYED BY COMPLEXITY, AND ERROR

Life is full of complexity. In order to survive, to wend our way through circumstances, and to manage in the world, we must constantly simplify complexity. Indeed, one of the best definitions of intelligence is the ability to manipulate complexity efficiently and effectively.

As we simplify complexity, we build models—internal mental maps—of how things work. Such models are required to make complexity manageable, but the simplification process carries a cost. That cost is error. The goal of simplification is the paring down of details and the distillation of essential information and rules into organizing principles that make possible order, control, and productive communication and problem solving. However, the natural result of simplification is the introduction of error.

For example, a person may decide that a particular make of car is unreliable. This conclusion might be based on his owning such a car and having more problems and expense than expected. The conclusion is reinforced by selective opinions of others who have been dissatisfied with similar cars. So the attitude and decision not to purchase that particular car prevails, thus simplifying the selection process and potentially avoiding expensive and on-going problems. However, this simplification process—though efficient—may fail to take into account that the car problem was limited to certain years and models, that such problems have been satisfactorily fixed, and that the car manufacturer has greatly improved its products and earned a stellar reputation. Conversely, instead of extending or extrapolating assumptions, the simplification process can lead to errors of overlooking problems through a false sense of security— as exemplified by Toyota's 2010 massive recall of cars because of a malfunction in acceleration mechanism.

In science and mathematics, error is estimated and accounted for by formulas that anticipate unexplained deviations from the rules and probabilities that govern expectations. Though we may not know exactly where or when the errors occur, we know from experience that errors do intrude, and we can minimize their impact by controlling the probabilities of certain types of errors. This is the nature of good science, and careful application aids in the prediction and reliability of outcomes.

In daily life, there are also errors that accrue from the simplification processes we all use to build models relating ourselves to the world and the events surrounding us. When such errors occur, they often lead to misguided and unrealistic expectations and can produce disappointment, frustration, and despondency. When we take information and build models, visions, and ideas about what *should* happen, how people *should* act, and outcomes we anticipate, we are creating expectations. Unrealized, unfulfilled expectations are essentially *errors* in our model-building, simplification processes.

For example, you may have an idea about a project you are working on. As you plan the project and envision its completion, you are consciously and subconsciously building expectations about how long it will take, what it will cost in time and effort, how it will turn out, and how it will be received. As you can imagine, there are many opportunities for errors and unanticipated events that may overshadow your initial mental pictures, plans, and expected outcomes.

Let's take a look at another example. You may have experienced a relationship in which your partner did not have expectations that matched yours regarding the nature or progress of the relationship. Your vision and expectations for the relationship were built upon your needs, past experiences, and fantasies about how the relationship should develop. Your expectations were constructed from a model that may have not accommodated factors about the other person that led to dashed hopes.

Just as science improves accuracy, predictability, reliability, and productivity by controlling for errors, we can attain a more intact life by detecting and addressing errors in the simplification processes that result in misaligned expectations.

EXPECTATIONS AND LEARNING

You have probably heard the saying that it is unwise to keep doing the same thing and expect different results.[28] With regard to expectations and behavior, then, how might you respond to frustrations and disappointments when your greater expectations are repeatedly unfulfilled?

The adaptive answers to this question depend to a large extent upon your ambitions and your reality testing skills. For instance, if your greater expectations include becoming an actor, politician, professional athlete, or novelist, then you must be prepared psychologically for potential disappointment. You must also be prepared psychologically to persevere and work hard, as these are two of the key elements that are requisites to attaining your ambitious goals. At the same time, you must possess the self-confidence and faith in your own abilities that you will need to sustain you if you encounter the possible disappointments that are often part and parcel of aspiring to exceptional achievements. In order to avoid succumbing to disappointment and negativity in their quest for their goals, many successful people have had to insulate themselves emotionally from rejection, miscues, setbacks, and failures as they single-mindedly pursued their objectives. This key characteristic is called determination or grit. Motivation, hard work, and grit are not the exclusive factors that that can determine whether or not you achieve your greater expectations. It is also crucial that you be able to learn from your mistakes so that you don't continue making the same errors. The learning process entails making the requisite adjustments in your modus operandi to attain different and better results. This is where keen observation, evaluation, and reality testing come into play. Understanding whether the discrepancies between your great expectations and lesser expectations arise from your perseverance and ambitions or they arise from faulty perceptions about what is reasonable to expect can make the difference between fulfillment and satisfaction on the one hand and frustration or embitterment on the other.

A prime example in which learning from experience and adjusting expectations plays out involves child rearing. You may have high expectations for your child to play a musical instrument or excel in sports or academics. If your child shows a lack of interest or talent, or if he or she

---

28. This is a so-called joking definition of insanity. If that is the case, then the Steinberg Insanity Defense is doing the same thing that got you in trouble, but expecting it to turn out differently the next time because you want it that way.

rebels, your greater expectations may be defeated. Your child may even reject your expectations about routine responsibilities such as homework or chores, and may refuse to live up to what you consider reasonable standards.

When your child insists that his homework is finished, but you are aware of his habit of minimizing, overlooking, or lying about responsibilities and obligations, you face challenges about how to manage your expectations as well as your outward behavior. As shown in chapters 5 and 6, how strategically you handle these counterproductive behaviors will have a profound impact on breaking your child's maladaptive habits.

One avenue of resolving the discrepancy between your greater expectations (that your child would step up, be responsible, comply, and meet the challenges) and your lesser expectations that are based upon your child's track record is to reconcile that he is doing the best he can, given his development, ability, and habits.[29] By making this choice, you are adjusting your expectations downward and tempering how far you can push your child while taking into consideration the potential positive and negative outcomes and side effects of your modified performance standards.

Another course of action would be to hold your child to higher standards of performance and to support him constructively with resources, discipline, and appropriate incentives and consequences in order to modify the behavioral outcomes (refer to chapters 5 and 6). By making this choice, you would maintain your greater expectations and modify your lesser expectations by positively altering your child's habits and increasing the probability of enhanced academic performance.

Whether you adjust your greater expectations downward or adjust your lesser standards upward so that your greater expectations can ideally be actualized, practicing and acquiring reality testing skills are crucial elements in setting goals that have a higher probability of realization and fulfillment.

Expectations form the fulcrum upon which our fulfillment and adjustment to reality hinge. The dynamics of this fulcrum will have a profound effect on motivation, and it is the critical point where desires confront

---

29. To help determine your child's true capabilities and to distinguish between competence and chronic avoidance, it is best to get a comprehensive neuropsychological evaluation by a trained specialist.

reality. This confrontation shapes our views of the world, our identities, and the way we fit in and explain what happens. Learning to form accurate impressions and expectations, resolving discrepancies between what we anticipate and what we get, and reducing our "errors" in modeling the way the world really works are vital aspects of the challenge process. As such, both our greater and lesser expectations play a central role in our ability to embrace and manage life's challenges.

DISCREPANCIES AND ATTITUDES

We all have dreams, hopes, fantasies, and standards. We stretch, reach, and implore and pray and plan for good things to happen. It is normal to anticipate and work toward goals, and to live, as it were, partly in the future. Expectations are intrinsically linked to survival. In nature, organisms must anticipate food in order to obtain the next meal. However, when what occurs deviates frequently or extensively from the realm of anticipation, survival becomes problematic. In human terms, life becomes unsatisfying and often confusing, overwhelming, even maddening.

When the differences between greater expectations and lesser expectations are significant and persistent, we are likely to feel distressed, alienated, cheated, let down, and probably demotivated and perhaps even hopeless. In essence, this happens when the world fails to live up to our expectations. Notice the implication of *failure*. Gaps between expectations and reality (or perceptions thereof) lead to disappointment, resentment, faulty reasoning, and alienation. These dynamics intertwine with attitudes.

An *attitude* is your set of responses to the relationship between your great expectations and lesser expectations. We think of attitudes as opinions, general feelings, or viewpoints in regard to something or someone. We may refer to someone's "attitude" as conveying arrogance, disdain, or negativity; conversely, we may say that a person has a positive attitude, meaning that his response to circumstances is likely to highlight the bright side.

Attitude is quite powerful and interactive. It affects how we filter experiences and, in turn, is shaped by outcomes. Glaring discrepancies between great expectations and lesser expectations tend to erode confident attitudes about facing and meeting challenges and tend to reinforce negative and self-defeating attitudes.

For instance, when we are disappointed that people don't do what we want or disagree with our ideas, we may adjust expectations downward to be congruent with the observed results and to reduce *dissonance*, which is the psychological lack of consistency or compatibility between actions and beliefs. This dissonance is an unpleasant experience. Although it may be a realistic reaction, it could become a habit that not only serves to minimize future disappointments, but also sets the stage for self-imposed restraints and altered perceptions that limit potential rewards.

Our culture places great value on attitude. When someone is grouchy, uncooperative, rebellious, defiant, or even depressed, we often say that person has a bad attitude. In evaluating a person's potential for growth and success, we often look to his attitude as a gauge for expectation and prediction about how well he will do. No one wants to hire an employee, teach a student, or parent a child with a faulty attitude. As you may already realize, attitude is very much a matter of choice. You always have choices. Pessimism and negativity and optimism and hope are among them, regardless of circumstances. How, then, can you make wise and productive choices in negotiating the discrepancies between your great expectations and your lesser expectations? That is, how can you effectively reconcile the *differences between life as it is and life as you want it to be* while maintaining a balance between realistic assessment and interpretation and the determination and ambition to tough it out and get what you want?

WHAT MANAGING EXPECTATIONS INVOLVES

Previous chapters in *Living Intact* have acquainted you with concepts and tools that can help with recognizing and managing expectations. These include the following:

- The role of your internal narrative in presenting your world and explaining and justifying your experiences
- The importance of choice as constant mechanism to assess your situation, navigate effectively, control your attitude, and respond adaptively to challenges
- The power to identify and eliminate negative emotions

- The use of self-control to modify outcomes so that they become more predictable and favorable
- The recognition of natural forces that govern the strengthening and weakening of behavior patterns which can assist in predicting and interpreting events, independent of how we feel about them

Let's now look at how you can become better at dealing with expectations so that they don't blindside you and derail your adaptive efforts. Here are some steps to include as you manage expectations:

- Recognize the role and characteristics of expectations in determining outlook, satisfaction, motivation, and effectiveness (e.g., providing a good life for my family demands commitment, focus, diligence, and perseverance).
- Adjust and reconcile expectations through monitoring, evaluating, and consciously assessing, adjusting, and modifying expectations (e.g., perhaps my unique intellectual and spiritual gifts would be more advantageously actualized if I changed my career path).
- Eliminate the negative effects of discrepancies and disappointments arising from unfulfilled expectations and mitigate the deleterious impact by reframing failures and miscues (e.g., the rejection of my novel is just a bump in the road, and I need to evaluate objectively the book's strengths and weaknesses and fix any deficiencies).
- Incorporate experience into the transformational process and incorporate biblical wisdom and instruction (e.g., in reacting to this terrible disappointment, I need to ask God what he might want to show or teach me about my desires, my responses when things don't go my way, and my faith in his wisdom for what is best).
- Identify areas and blind spots where personal preferences are perceived as entitlements (e.g., realizing that sustaining a marriage requires more than the romantic fantasies of marital bliss portrayed in sixty-second TV commercials. Marriage requires dedication, work, and empathy).

- Develop skills for predicting outcomes and assessing accuracy (e.g., I need to add the pluses and minuses and crunch the numbers to verify that my strategy and tactics are appropriate and effective).

- Improve judgment and acceptance and adopt the practice of living life on its own terms (e.g., in expecting him to keep his word, be responsible, pay me back, or be on time, am I expecting things that are out of character for this person? Am I setting up expectations based upon my needs or wishes, rather than on what this person is capable of based on history?).

TECHNIQUES FOR MANAGING EXPECTATIONS

Because expectations include both cognitive and emotional components, you can use cognitive and emotional techniques to help you adjust expectations and keep them in check and in line with reality.

Expectations form a bridge that spans the distance between perception and reality. When subjective perspective and objective results don't match, there is dissonance and disappointment—cognitive misunderstanding and emotional distress. You can employ the secrets you learned in earlier chapters to resolve these misalignments and to adjust your inner narrative to comply with what happens and also to support your feelings and views.

In chapter 4, you learned about the narrative, that private voice that interprets and justifies your experiences with your needs and inner constitution. You learned also how self-control and compassion can interface with the narrative to mitigate frustration and exasperation and defuse the anger and self-justification that kick in when you encounter things that don't go your way.

When you invoke compassion as an assistant for recasting others' selfish or hurtful behavior, you are summoning a feeling. When you do this intentionally, you are also using a cognitive control method to facilitate the prominence of this feeling. You are deliberately using a thought process to change a feeling and its associated perceptions. Psychologists refer to this process as *cognitive behavior modification*. A deliberate and specific attempt to recast or reinterpret an event is called *cognitive reframing*.

As an example of reframing an expectation, consider the following:

Suppose you find out that an old friend is coming to town. He calls you and wants to see you. A get-together is planned, and you eagerly look forward to seeing him, pleased that he has contacted you and excited about the meeting. You wait for his confirmation call the day before the meeting. Nothing. You call and leave a message. Disappointingly, he later leaves a message that he will not be able to make it—no reason, no rearrangement.

You are surprised and also crestfallen. You suddenly become angry. *How could he do this?* Your mind races, your nervous system overaroused. *This wasn't supposed to happen: you made plans! What was so important that he had to cancel? Did he not want to see you? Did you slight him or do something wrong? Wait a minute—how dare he? Well, so much for* that *relationship! You are not going to be tossed aside like that again.*

Your narrative is working overtime, justifying, protecting you, wielding whatever defense will shield you from the failure of your expectations.

Then, you remember that your great expectations are extending the problem. Sure, you wanted to see your friend; you were eagerly looking forward to it. The fact that he had contacted you and chosen to include you in his schedule pleased you as well. The abrupt change didn't make sense. But you have to accept that development, and you realize that stewing about it is no good for you. So your mind begins to consider other possibilities: *maybe he really did want to see you. Something came up, and he felt let down, too. (But why didn't he explain?) Maybe he was embarrassed and felt guilty. Perhaps he was afraid you would be angry. There will be other occasions to rekindle your relationship.* Your mood switches from hurt to shame and tenderness about secretly blaming your friend, whom you adore, for something he perhaps couldn't help. You tell yourself that there is really no harm done unless you continue to nurse a grievance. You realize that you can adjust your expectations to accommodate this missed opportunity. There will be other occasions. You congratulate yourself on being flexible and understanding. You imagine how much your friend appreciates this about you. It's time to do some tapping (see chapter 10) to eradicate whatever negative feelings might remain. After the tapping, your narrative is very different; you are calm and composed and thinking good thoughts about you and your friend. You are suddenly elated about having a free evening to devote to other important matters. You think fondly and a bit wistfully of your friend, privately wishing him well and making a mental note to e-mail him to maintain communication, and then your mind contentedly moves on to other thoughts.

In the above example, cognitive reframing is instrumental in adjusting expectations to align with reality and to help adjust feelings and the narrative. It is an adaptive mechanism to accommodate an event that departs from expectations. Notice how using TFT (tapping) to eliminate negative emotions can work hand in hand with conscious efforts to invite and self-reinforce different thought patterns.

It could be argued that cognitive reframing is merely rationalization, a self-deluding technique to pacify the denial of unfulfilled desires. However, such an argument fails to account for the role of *choice* in directing one's reaction from that of hurt victim to a position of active assumption and the preservation of one's autonomy and integrity. The narrative can be your servant, not merely an array of exposed nerve endings.

Conscious choice and tools like cognitive reframing can be instrumental in maintaining self-control and resiliency in the face of unfulfilled expectations. In my experience, this technique is most effective when used in the service of reality testing to ascertain the motivations of others, avoid self-pity, keep properly motivated and flexible, and remain open and subservient to God's providential plan. However, it must be noted that cognitive techniques, when used exclusively, usually fall short in eliminating problems of entrenched or persisting anxiety, depression, and problems emanating from systemic disregulation (refer to chapters 9 and 10).

LIVING LIFE THE WAY IT IS

A core tenet of living intact is that we need to adapt to the real world with its changing circumstances in our lives. The circumstances may be favorable or unfavorable, but our like or dislike for them should not determine our abilities to meet challenges, make wise choices, and develop more godly character.

You now know that expectations are key in helping adjust to the real world. They form the navigation system that orients us and prepares us for what lies ahead. Expectations can buffer the harsh intrusions from a frequently uncaring environment, and they get us to become motivated and excited about what we can obtain, give, and achieve. Using expectations as a guide realistically necessitates the coordination of our greater expectations with our lesser expectations.

Your narrative gives voice to your expectations, and your narrative takes for granted your desires and your sense of entitlement. These feed into the formation of greater expectations that portray what you want and hope to get. However, you must temper greater expectations with the reality constructs that come from valid assessment and interpretation of your experiences. For instance, you may be excited about getting a new job, and your great expectations could embellish the prospects of getting the job and enjoying its anticipated perks. Your optimism notwithstanding, you need lesser expectations to prepare you for the event that you do not get the job. This requires that you be able to impose restraints, make adjustments, and handle disappointments if the outcome is not what you expected, even if your expectations are based upon past experiences.

Greater expectations are inherently prone to inflated impressions. Greater expectations generally envision the upside and place a positive spin on what you anticipate. The antidote is to possess a positive attitude coupled with *discernment* that can help you temper pie-in-the sky optimism and blindsided disappointments. You need lesser expectations— inherently more conservative—to modulate the inflated expectations that often (subconsciously) accompany a sense of entitlement, eagerness, and intensely focused desire to attain an objective that might be overlaid with wishful thinking.

A BALANCING ACT

We require greater expectations to energize our outlook, give us incentive, and buttress our self-image and sense of worth and potency. We require lesser expectations to dethrone us from pedestals of self-importance and entitlement.

As you will discover in the remaining chapters, you can integrate your understanding and adjustment of expectations along with the tools and concepts of living intact. By so doing, you can better manage yourself, and you can adjust gracefully to circumstances as you appreciate God's wisdom and his caring for you while you are weathering life's ups and downs.

When life appears unfair, when disappointment, rejection, loneliness, and frustration abound, seeking to understand reality through God's eyes invariably assuages the pain and tempers the disillusionment. Greater expectations represent what you want, and lesser expectations summarize an often imperfect and unsatisfying world. Focusing on God's expectations will help you resolve the inherent differences, breakdowns, dissatisfactions, and discrepancies that result from our desires for what life should be and our actual experiences living life. This is one of the key cornerstones in the ongoing process of living intact.

> *In the morning, O Lord, you hear my voice; in the morning I lay my requests before you and wait in expectation.* (Psalm 5:3)

> *Set your mind on things above, not on earthly things.* (Colossians 3:2)

> *Do not conform any longer to the pattern of this world, but be transformed by the renewing of your mind. Then you will be able to test and approve what God's will is—his good, pleasing, and perfect will.* (Romans 12:2)

SPIRITUAL ASPECTS OF EXPECTATIONS

Though we are born into different circumstances and we develop with different temperaments and genetic predispositions, every one of us commonly faces discrepancies between our greater and our lesser expectations. Resolving these discrepancies, coping with the differences between our desires and their fulfillment, using these differences and disappointments as challenges to mold character, learn how to be content, and serve the needs of others—these are the tasks and challenges of living intact.

Expectations are not only a biological necessity for survival and a psychological reality of how our minds work, they are a vehicle for spiritual development and a conduit by which God speaks to us and leads us in his ways.

Throughout history, God has given us promises and has made covenants he asks us to believe. At any given time, the fulfillment of these promises is not yet complete. The Bible recounts historical detail and spiritual examples of how people have struggled with the discrepancies between what was promised and what was attained. Indeed, we might appreciate biblical instruction at one level as the didactic story of coping with the differences between greater expectations and lesser expectations.

Symbolically, this may be seen as the differences between what we envision and what God decrees.

In one frame of view, greater expectations represent our human will and self-centered aspirations, whereas lesser expectations are the realities and truths of God's will. In another frame of view, greater expectations are those spiritual dimensions and providence that God intends for us, the growth and gifts and potential from which we are impeded because of our humanly limited lesser expectations—the world of fleshly pursuits and sin-tainted disappointments that we draw around ourselves. A diagrammatic matrix of the dynamics of this central relationship might look like this:

	God	Man
Greater Expectations	Living as God wants Christ-likeness Spiritual peace, contentment	Self-centered will Egocentric independence Power and idolatry
Lesser Expectations	Man's abilities Human limitations Sinful nature	God's will Humility and worship Wisdom

Differences between greater and lesser expectations are a context for resolving disappointment and frustration. They are also a spiritual template for God's efforts to bridge the gap between himself and us.

God provides biblical precedent and instruction for addressing gaps between expectations and actuality. In fact, he tells us *how to expect*. (See the section below on "Faith, Hope, and Expectations," and refer to Romans 5:1–5; Romans 8:19–25; Hebrews 11:1–2; Hebrews 11:39–40).

Behavioral psychology and learning theory find precedent in scripture because of the way in which God uses reinforcement, extinction, and punishment to shape or discourage our behaviors. Sometimes, God uses significant or traumatic events to capture our attention. Often, he uses continuous reinforcement to shape our awareness, obedience, and orientation toward him. The Bible is replete with references and praise for God's continuing presence and maintenance of the universe. God also uses variable intermittent reinforcement schedules (refer again to chapter 6) to promote our faith, to turn misfortune into hope and character, to train us to listen and notice him, and to discipline and transform our expectations to conform to his likeness and his will.

Throughout history, God has shown the expert and loving use of negative reinforcement to shape behaviors he deems desirable. Since we are his children, it is fitting that we can and should use this paradigm on our own children to lovingly encourage proper and functional behaviors. Negative reinforcement is the process of removing an aversive condition contingent upon the performance of some desired behavior. For example, being released from a time-out, taking medicine to relieve pain, coming inside from a brittle cold outdoors, resting after a grueling exertion—these are all negative reinforcements, where the relief from an aversive condition teaches and encourages the behavior that preceded it. Negative reinforcement is very useful in situations where people do not seem motivated to work for "desirable" rewards. Not surprisingly, this strategy is quite effective with resistant or rebellious children, and this is recounted in scripture. The Bible describes numerous times when God rejected appeals and sacrifices by Jewish peoples, only to relieve their suffering and oppressive circumstances when they offered what God really wanted: brokenness, contrition, humility, and obedience.

> *With what shall I come before the Lord and bow down before the exalted God? Shall I come before him with burnt offerings, with calves a year old? Will the Lord be pleased with a thousand rams, with ten thousand rivers of oil? Shall I offer my firstborn for my transgression, the fruit of my body for the sin of my soul? He has shown you, O man, what is good. And what does the Lord require of you? To act justly and to love mercy and to walk humbly with your God.* (Micah 6:6–8)

> *And now, O Israel, what does the Lord your God ask of you but to fear the Lord your God, to walk in all his ways, to serve the Lord your God with all your heart and with all your soul, and to observe the Lord's commands and decrees that I am giving you today for your own good.* (Deuteronomy 10:12–13)

God uses symbolism in his Word, interweaving predictions and reca-pitulations, so that every biblical precept is entirely consistent with the Bible in its entirety. He teaches us to extend this symbolism to our daily lives, applying history and wisdom to our experiences so that we may be challenged and meet challenges with his strength. By using symbolism, God encourages *mediation*, so that we may be reinforced through his *time-less* wisdom and intervention.

Believers in God are reinforced through recognition of his presence and intervention in our lives and also through the mediated variable intermittent reinforcement he provides when our hearts absorb his Word. Our ways are not his ways, and our models are not his models; and so he shapes and reinforces us. Expectations are part of the conditioning process.

FAITH, HOPE, AND EXPECTATIONS

In our model building of reality, expectations are the links between present longing and anticipation and future fulfillment. The Bible is instructive in these matters, and we may look to Romans for some clear examples of what God intends. Apostle Paul explains that:

> *It was not through law that Abraham and his offspring received the promise that he would be heir of the world, but through the righteousness that comes by faith. For if those who live by law are heirs, faith has no value and the promise is worthless, because law brings wrath. And where there is no law, there is no transgression. Therefore, the promise comes by faith, so that it may be by grace and may be guaranteed to all of Abraham's offspring—not only to those who are of the law but also to those who are of the faith of Abraham. He is the father of us all.* (Romans 4:13–16)

In other words, the grace of wholeness and intactness, of continuity and blessing derives not solely from our own structure and logic (law), but from faith—dependence on things unseen, but promised by God and, therefore, rightly anticipated. When our expectations are not realized or made manifest, we can rely for peace and hope on the care and protection and promises of God—even when the world and the course of our lives pulls in unsatisfying directions. In Romans 5, Paul is explicit about how to deal with discrepancies in our experiences and yearnings:

> *Therefore, since we have been justified through faith, we have peace with God through our Lord Jesus Christ, through whom we have gained access through faith into this grace in which we now stand. And we rejoice in the hope of the glory of God. Not only so, but we rejoice in our sufferings, because we know that suffering produces perseverance, perseverance character, and character, hope. And hope does not disappoint us, because God has poured out his love into our hearts by the Holy Spirit, whom he has given us.* (Romans 5:1–5)

Does this mean that, through our hope and faith, God will fulfill all expectations, compensate each disappointment, and grant every desire? Surely not! If you want support and validation for the insufficiencies and lack of closure, unfulfilled promises and unmet expectations you have suffered, then look to Hebrews 11, and you will find yourself in good company. This scripture spells out the meaning and examples of faith, listing its historic role in so many well-known anticipated promises.

> *Now faith is being sure of what we hope for and certain of what we do not see. This is what the ancients were commended for. By faith we understand that the universe was formed at God's command, so that what is seen was not made out of what was visible.* (Hebrews 11:1–2)

Hebrews 11 delineates the faith of Abraham, Isaac, Jacob, Joseph, Moses, the people of Israel under Egyptian oppression, Rahab, Gideon, Barak, Samson, Jephthah, David, Samuel, and the prophets in attaining some of what they expected and being deterred in other expectations. This historical summary of "such a great cloud of witnesses" (Hebrews 12:1) concludes as follows:

> *These were all commended for their faith, yet none of them received what had been promised. God had planned something better for us so that only together with us would they be made perfect.* (Hebrews 11:39–40)

The reference to "what had been promised" augurs all that is included in the actual coming of the Messiah. So God's history and his future for us leave a present incompleteness—longing, disappointment, anticipation—manifest in discrepant expectations. Yet the mandate for dealing with such frustration is clear, as described in Hebrews, Romans, and elsewhere in the Bible. Indeed, the book of Romans explicitly addresses "Expectant Living":

> *The creation waits in eager expectation for the sons of God to be revealed. For the creation was subjected to frustration, not by its own choice, but by the will of the one who subjected it, in hope that that the creation itself will be liberated from its bondage to decay and brought into the glorious freedom of the children of God. We know that the whole creation has been groaning as in the pains of childbirth right up to the present time. Not only so, but we ourselves, who have the first fruits of the Spirit, groan inwardly as we wait eagerly for our adoption as sons, the redemption of our bodies. For in this hope we were saved. But hope that is seen is no hope at all. Who hopes for what he already has? But if we hope for what we do not yet have, we wait for it patiently.* (Romans 8:19–25)

Expectation, then, is woven into creation. It involves accounting of the past, as well as future longing and orientation. In place of present unfulfillment, we are to wait eagerly with hope and faith, growing in grace and in the character that accrues from perseverance. We are to close the gaps, cover the discrepancies, and correct the errors in our actions and judgment by seeking restoration and practicing reconciliation—following the model God gave to us.

EXPECTATIONS AND RECONCILIATION

Resolving discrepancies between your greater expectations and lesser expectations is a working model for living life on its own terms. It is the practice of *reconciling* things that don't match.

When life is overwhelming, disappointing, and even injurious, the master healer prescribes the right salve and salvation: reconciliation and restoration.

So from now on we regard no one from a worldly point of view. Though we once regarded Christ in this way, we do so no longer. Therefore, if anyone is in Christ, he is a new creation; the old has gone, the new has come! All this is from God, who reconciled himself through Christ and gave us the ministry of reconciliation: that God was reconciling the world to himself in Christ, not counting men's sins against them. And he committed to us the message of reconciliation. (2 Corinthians 5:16–19)

Not only do we attain the fullest rest and "re-creation" in God's hands and plans, but also we reconcile the mistakes in our expectations. The simplification and model-building processes we use to map the world are infused with our own self-centeredness—such is human nature. The modeling errors we make are tainted with our own desires, limitations, selfish logic, and tendencies to enshrine what we believe will grant our wishes.

God gives the corrections for these errors through biblical wisdom, worldly experience, and divine intervention. The faultless model is Christ, yet the implications for correction, reconciliation, and restoration are cognitive and emotional, as well as spiritual. In 2 Corinthians, the apostle Paul declares that in Christ we are "re-created" anew and, henceforth, regard no one from a worldly point of view. This worldly point of view may be likened to the narrow, egocentric nature that predisposes us to errors, estimates, and discrepancies in our expectations. Reconciliation in the spiritual realm is the payment for our sins, so that we may be close to God and fulfill his image in a just and righteous universe. It is the fixing of errors from God's perspective. Reconciliation in the earthly realm is the compensation for our misjudgments in expectations—how we construct, fit in, and adjust to the world that we inherently try to bend to our desires.

Along with the frustrations and natural discrepancies to which we are prone, God gives us a blueprint for correction and even conquest. Throughout the stream of history and the fabric of man, life is a series of tests, of challenges to reconcile the gaps between God and man, and to resolve the discrepancies in expectations between God and man. We are made in his image, and he gives us gifts and tools for reconciliation in these expectations. Thus, the challenge process is a mission and a ministry of reconciliation

Expectations are a view from the present toward the future and based on the past. With its "concealed/revealed" interweaving of New and Old Testaments, the Bible shows how these states are integrated. The Bible uses past history, future expectations, and present orientation in revealing God's plan. However, human time is so much more limited than divine time, and therein lies the sources of discrepancies and some secrets of healing and living intact. Timing mechanisms (see chapter 9), both internal and external, tie us to the realities of the universe and provide links to spiritual transformation, practical accomplishment, personal and social integration, and the techniques and tools for healing and developing wholeness.

Because expectations necessarily involve timing discrepancies—what we envision compared with what unfolds—we can appreciate the relevance of timing issues in cognitive, developmental, and spiritual contexts, as well is in the neuroscientific context of adjusting brain timing to facilitate self-control.

The resolution of timing issues in expectations often involves a patient waiting on God's timing for reconciliation. From a cognitive analytical perspective, we can understand misaligned, unrealized, unfulfilled expectations as essentially *errors* in our model-building and simplification processes. Hence, we can build more intact living by detecting and addressing errors in the simplification processes that result in misaligned expectations.

However, understanding and managing expectations is not merely an analytical matter of reducing error. Expectations and their discrepancies formulate content for using the challenge process to grow and develop *soul* in the spiritual as well as the practical realms.

The formation, refinement, and reconciliation of expectations that lead to living intact depend also upon wisdom—the eternal wisdom of God.

CHAPTER 12
WISDOM: UNDERSTANDING AND MAKING LIFE WORK

The fear of the Lord is the beginning of wisdom, and knowledge of the Holy One is understanding.

(Proverbs 9:10)

WHY WISDOM?

If we are to live intact, we must seek out and abide by the principles that constitute and organize not only the realities of life that shape our experiences, but also those that exist beyond our self-absorption. Each of us faces a lifelong conflict that exemplifies human nature and its preoccupation with the material world. We strive for life as we would have it, but in the end, we must accept and accommodate to life on its own terms. As an example, a child may entertain dreams of becoming a violinist, winning a scholarship to Julliard, and playing in a world-renowned orchestra. She may ultimately discover that she doesn't have the requisite talent to attain her goal, or she may be afflicted with rheumatoid arthritis that cripples her fingers. Forced to adjust her career goals, she will ideally be able to establish alternative objectives that will challenge her without demoralizing her.

There are, of course, many examples of individuals who prevail magnificently over seemingly intractable challenges by virtue their grit and determination. Illustrative cases in point include Helen Keller, who was deaf, mute, and blind, the singer Stevie Wonder, who is blind, the actress Marlee Matlin, who is deaf, and the renowned astrophysicist Steven Hawking, who suffers from profoundly debilitating ALS. The challenges faced and achievements attained by these luminaries attest to our ability to adjust and to compensate successfully as we ascend the ladder toward self-actualization. Their successes also attest to our capability to come to grips with reality and to reconcile ourselves to the hand that God has dealt us.

If not handled astutely, the mechanics of reconciling life's discrepancies and dualities that involve *what we want* and *what is so* can cause profound conflict and pain. Overcoming the roadblocks and acquiring the ability to sort out and bring together incongruities are among the core challenges that God has infused into the human condition. The challenges that he asks us to overcome can spark our emotional and spiritual development and comprise an essential element in the lifelong quest for wisdom. God's plan entails welcoming and meeting challenges, making informed and aware choices, astutely appraising and effectively managing ourselves and our environment, and actively seeking and relating to an Almighty God who created the world and by whose wisdom life continues to unfold.

By wisdom the Lord laid the earth's foundations, by understanding he set the heavens in place; by his knowledge the deeps were divided, and the clouds let drop the dew. (Proverbs 3:19)

"The Lord brought me forth as the first of his works, before his deeds of old; I was appointed from eternity, from the beginning, before the world began. When there were no oceans, I was given birth, when there were no springs abounding with water; before the mountains were settled in place, before the hills I was given birth, before he made the earth or its fields or any of the dust of the world. I was there when he set the heavens in place, when he marked out the horizon on the face of the deep, when he established the clouds above and fixed securely the fountains of the deep, when he gave the sea its boundary so the waters would not overstep his

command, and when he marked out the foundations of the earth. Then I was the craftsman at his side." (Proverbs 8:22–30)

The benefits of attaining wisdom are incontrovertible. Wisdom will bring you closer to God in many ways. You'll be able to understand more fully many of life's mysteries and paradoxes, live more peacefully, bask in the security, love, and protection of God (Proverbs 4:6; 8:34–35), receive guidance (Proverbs 4:11–12) and honor (Proverbs 3:34), prolong your life (Proverbs 9:11; Ecclesiastes 7:12), avoid evil, and maximize what you get from life and what you are able to give life (Proverbs 8:18–21; Ecclesiastes 7:19; 8:1).

Wisdom will brighten your life and enhance your harmony with others and with a world that can often be stubborn and confusing. Wisdom brings clarity and provides insight into why people think the way they do and do the things they do. Wisdom reveals underlying motivations and makes tangible and comprehensible that which is otherwise difficult to see or grasp. Wisdom lays the foundation for purity and joy and satisfying relationships, and love.

Perhaps these sound like platitudes. Perhaps you're skeptical by nature or sarcastic by nature (as I am, on occasion). Perhaps you've been disillusioned and deceived, and you don't trust or have faith in anything that's not concrete and that you can't touch and feel. Perhaps you believe that you're justified in being cautious and leery of promises and enticements that purport to enrich your life. Maybe you've been repeatedly disappointed by false claims, and you've emotionally "circled the wagons" to defend yourself against further disappointments.

Rest assured that I am not selling wisdom, for wisdom is not a commodity that's for sale. Rather, I am advocating that you actively seek enlightenment. I am pleading that you follow this path because my own life experiences have convinced me that God wants us to attain wisdom, and I can attest that my own lifelong quest has unequivocally brought me to a closer and infinitely richer communion with God (Proverbs 3:14–15; 4:7; 8:10–11). What I am doing is sharing with you what I've learned so far in my life, and I am recommending that you consider the ideas and insights that are offered and that you, in turn, ask God to enlighten you. He has promised that he will, if you ask (Proverbs 2:2–6).

WHAT IS WISDOM?

Defining wisdom is akin to defining God; the problem is that we are limited by human constraints that make understanding infinite, universe-embracing concepts so challenging. We can't put God into a box or enfold him in a finite and convenient wrapping, because he exceeds our mental ability to comprehend and define him. But God tells us how to go about the process of attaining wisdom, despite our limitations.

Essentially, wisdom is revealed in the nature and manifestation of God, his ways, and his will for each of us and for the world. *Wisdom is the understanding and application of God's principles and commands. Wisdom is demonstrated by making choices characterized by the ability to see beyond appearances and complexity to discern godly knowledge and perspective.*

What does this mean in a practical sense? Just how do you go about acquiring wisdom? Does it come from people? From experience? From within? Is the Bible the only true source of wisdom? How does wisdom compare with other forms of smartness?

These are some of the vital questions and concepts that this chapter tackles as we further expand and enrich our capacities to live intact.

ACQUIRING WISDOM

Acquiring wisdom and responding adaptively to challenges are inherently intertwined processes. God has designed man to adapt to challenges, and by so doing, we can observe God's plan and wisdom unfolding. When we are frustrated or don't get what we want, when we have to wait for answers, when we understand after a period of time that what we endured prepared us to meet new challenges—then, we are afforded a glimpse into the providence of God's ways, and we are able to expand our own understanding.

God manifests wisdom throughout the world in nature, in creation, and in the activities of created beings. It is the unifying force in existence. Human wisdom, however, must be acquired incrementally and in deliberate and personal ways. We are primarily preoccupied with that which befalls us, with that which affects those we love, and with that which transpires in our little corner of the universe. God understands this preoccupation, of course, since he made us this way. This self-orientation must be tempered and combined with openness to God's principles and revelations in tandem with an attitude of humility and a quest for wisdom. When all of the elements are harnessed, we can begin to understand and integrate our experiences, and in so doing, we can better interpret God's wisdom.

The desire to meet one's own needs and make a difference in the world and in the lives of others is a basic element in human nature. Sometimes, our self-interest and being attuned to the interests of others can seem to be diametrically opposed; however, God's wisdom magnificently blends what is good for us with what is good for others. We are all his children.

Living intact aligns with God's wisdom by unifying the duality of *getting* from life while also *giving*, contributing, serving, and sacrificing. It is through wisdom that we attain what is truly worthwhile and give to others according to divine commands and inspiration.

Wisdom is acquired in different ways, and it manifests as the distillation of lessons learned from life experiences. Wisdom accrues from successes and failures, but it must be sifted and winnowed through several filters:

1. The condensation of significant events and attributes and the organization of essential unifying principles
2. The testing of conclusions and beliefs by measuring them with God's standards and principles
3. The application of God's standards and these principles to one's daily life and challenges

Let's examine these tenets and see how you can apply them as steps toward becoming wiser:

1. **The condensation of significant events and attributes and the organization of essential unifying principles**

    In order to learn effectively, we have to be able to attend, recognize, reason, compare, and draw conclusions from what transpires in our lives. Otherwise, we will make the same or similar mistakes repeatedly and fail to benefit from experience. Intellectual level notwithstanding, a functioning brain must process and practice the following:

    • Register incoming stimuli and understand verbal communications
    • Attend to relevant stimuli and screen out nonessential stimuli
    • Follow verbal and written instructions

- Utilize and integrate memory, abstraction, and reasoning
- Comprehend recurring similarities and differences among objects and events
- Discern cause-and-effect relationships
- Develop and apply organizing principles in problem solving
- Generalize and think logically
- Respond intuitively and cognitively to visual and nonverbal stimuli (necessary to picture, sequence, or construct outcomes, as well as to understand how things fit together)—necessary for appreciating the symbolic significance of "people" messages, emotions, and feedback
- Function efficiently in space and time (e.g., organize projects and responsibilities that are independent and have different deadlines, juggle multiple obligations; multitask in problem solving and task execution, transport oneself to different locations on time, correctly estimate and judge how long things will take and how complicated they will be)
- Integrate verbal and nonverbal information

In sum, if you want to do better the next time and avoid mistakes and pitfalls, you must notice the patterns and important details that determined an outcome and apply these essential rules across a wide spectrum of circumstances that may vary (but whose underlying principles are the same). Thus, you can apply your knowledge and wisdom to enhance the likelihood of obtaining a favorable outcome.

Some concrete examples of knowledge and wisdom might include:

- Preparing for a test, based upon your knowledge of what previous tests were like and what you anticipate the teacher wants you to know
- Being attuned to the warning signs of dangerous situations (e.g., driving and weather conditions, body symptoms, aggressive threats and signals from others, etc.)
- Assessing risk by using methods that have proven reliable in the past (financial planning, decision making in the face of unknowns—should I undertake this medical procedure?

Will I be successful with this course of study? What are the hidden costs of this venture?)

- Avoiding temptation by applying cause-and-effect principles (e.g., not accurately declaring your income on your tax return will produce dire consequences; eating or drinking too much will lead to discomfort, bad health, etc.)

- Seeing behavior patterns and character indications that foreshadow relationship outcomes (e.g., Will I be taken advantage of by this slick-sounding pitch? What happened when my former boyfriend acted this way? How is this person the same or different? How will I respond more effectively this time?)

- Relating present challenges to past ones (Last time the sink was clogged, I had to do such-and-such before I could unclog it. Does that apply to this situation?)

- Combining stated and inferred information to deduce unstated realities and project a likely result (e.g., If I continue to work hard and smart, my chances of getting a promotion are good. What does it mean that my boss smiles at me less frequently, yet hasn't reprimanded me recently? The department is under a lot of pressure. Is my job at risk? How can I figure out how to ensure my security while at the same time prepare strategically for the possibility of being fired?)

2. **The testing of conclusions and beliefs by measuring them with God's standards and principles**

Worldly knowledge is not equivalent to wisdom. It is our pride that blinds us to this truth. The marvels, discoveries, and ingenuities of yesteryear fade, but God is the same yesterday, today, and forever (Hebrews 13:8). Nor is wisdom the same as intelligence, common sense, or street savvy (see the section below on "Intelligence and Wisdom").

Numerous exceptional human beings have made significant contributions that have profoundly influenced our world. Unquestionably, luminaries such as Winston Churchill, Warren Buffett, Bill Gates, Steve Jobs, Albert Einstein, William Shakespeare, Virginia Woolf, Douglas MacArthur, Abraham

Lincoln, George Washington Carver, Madam Curie, and Martin Luther King were smart and able to use their abilities to bring about astounding achievements and contributions. Whether they were wise, however, is not measured by their achievements, but by their adherence to God's principles.

History is replete with cunning and ostensibly omnipotent leaders who galvanized their supporters, amassed great fortunes, and imposed their will on others, but whose power and influence ultimately crumbled because it was based primarily upon worshiping of Self and was subject to egotism, narcissism, and evil. In the end, their "accomplishments" did not pass the litmus test of representing wisdom.

The wisdom that God called forth is not manifested by man's cleverness or ingenuity. The standards that characterize true wisdom are the fear and reverence of God and the turning from evil (all that is against God) (James 3:13–17).

You may be a great problem solver. You may admire street-smart people who can get things done in shrewd and ingenious ways, bypassing or neutralizing the obstacles that seem insurmountable. Their cleverness may be impressive, but the wisdom of their actions is assessed through the right-or-wrong crucible of God's Word.

It is interesting that, while the Lord's righteous standards appear black-and-white, the interpretation and the application of these standards are indeed less clear. That is what the discernment of wisdom is all about.

3. **The application of God's standards and principles to one's daily life and challenges**

The mental abilities and spiritual adherence to God's principles are like the ingredients and recipes that a master chef uses in the preparation of outstanding and nourishing cuisine. What remains is the cooking. These ingredients must be applied with careful skill and experience.

Just as fire, heat, oxygen, and chemicals act upon the organic matter in food to produce changes that are predictable (but must be understood and orchestrated), life's challenges act upon our human vulnerabilities in accountable ways. The wise person, anticipates, understands, heeds past successes and failures, and follows a reliable plan to sidestep snares and calamities in the quest for excellence.

Circumstances, resources, needs, and desires all change. The basic principles endure, and wisdom requires that we respect their ineluctable continuity and apply them to varying situations and challenges.

TRUE WISDOM IS AVAILABLE TO EVERYONE

Hallelujah! Anyone who seeks wisdom can acquire it from God. God says so! (Psalm 51:6; Psalm 90:12; Proverbs 1:20; 2:6; 4:11; 8:1; 15:33; Luke 21:15; Ephesians 1:8; James 1:5)

Wait, you may argue: if wisdom depends upon keen and functional mental abilities, doesn't that limit or exclude people who have impaired mental functioning? What about the special needs population and those with limited intellect, talent, exposure, or opportunity? Can they, too, attain wisdom?

The answer is a resounding YES! In order to understand this seeming contradiction between wisdom and limitation, we must bear in mind that wisdom comes from God. He created it, and he makes it available to everyone (1 Corinthians 2:7; James 1:5). Put aside your analytical mind for a time and consider the parallels and implications shown by God's revelation of his new covenant.

In the Old Testament, the Israelites were the chosen people to whom God gave his covenant. This was the covenant of the Ten Commandments and of the circumcision. (Genesis 7:3–8; Exodus 34:10; Deuteronomy 7:6–8; Acts 7:8)

Yet the coming of Jesus Christ brought a new covenant, one that included Gentiles (1 Corinthians 1:11; Ephesians 2:12–13; 2:19–22; Hebrews 8:6; Romans 9:6–8; 9:23–26). Believers in Christ are also awarded spiritual circumcision with this new covenant (Romans 2:28–30; Colossian 2:9–12). God even addresses the genetics of these covenants, showing how Abraham's two women represent two covenants (Galatians 4:24–26) and how the descendants of Hagar (the slave woman) can be included in the new covenant promise along with the descendants of Sarah (the free woman).

The new covenant is based upon faith and God's reaching down to man. This is true, irrespective of one's genealogy and genetic endowment. God's new covenant includes all believers as chosen people in Christ:

> *Here there is no Greek or Jew, circumcised or uncircumcised, barbarian, Scythian, slave or free, but Christ is all, and is in all. Therefore, as God's chosen people, holy and dearly loved, clothe yourselves with compassion, kindness, humility, gentleness, and patience.* (Colossians 3:11–12)

Does this mean that all people are equal? In the realm of individual differences, gifts, and abilities, certainly people vary, exhibiting a wide range of attributes. But God's love and inclusion is available to all people, along with wisdom for those who seek it, regardless of their skills or limitations on a worldly plane.

Because wisdom is from God, it is available (as he says in scripture) to all who ask. It does not depend upon intelligence or circumstance. Though it may be easier for brighter minds to learn more quickly, being astute is no sure path to wisdom. Often, those with high intelligence become arrogant, conceited, or overly reliant on their own abilities to the exclusion of humility and dependence upon God. Smartness can surely be advantageous, but wisdom derives from what God says, not what clever human minds invent. (Proverbs 16:1; 21:30; 28:26; 1 Corinthians 2:6–7; 2:13; 3:19; James 3:13–17)

I have known many people who were short on intellect in the worldly sense, but gigantic in their spiritual prowess and wisdom. I've known autistic and retarded people who functioned with limited cognition and sensory capacities, but whose hearts and spiritual openness allowed them to make good decisions, facilitate growth in other people, and reflect the glory and truths of God's creations. These individuals flourished in an enlightened manner because they were humble, put God first, and had the sense and guidance to flee from evil. They met their challenges with God's help and avoided overreliance on their own abilities, thus evading the trap of worshiping their own self and extolling their own shrewdness.

INTELLIGENCE AND THE NATURE OF WISDOM

We live in a world where intelligence is a highly prized commodity. In much the same way that wealth, certain physical characteristics, and social or political connections are valued, intelligence is treasured and nurtured in the belief that its identification and development will entitle the bearer to a more satisfying and more noteworthy life. However, the distribution of intelligence is limited to a large extent by combinations of genetic, environmental, and temporal factors. Not everyone will be tall, sleek, healthy, or born privileged. It may seem unfair, but that is just the way things are. Certainly, people can grow in knowledge, problem-solving abilities, and performance, but there are limits to cognitive achievement, even as we expand the envelope of understanding how the brain works and augmenting its powers.

Nonetheless, intelligence is seen as a key to a better, richer life, and as with other key attributes, it does often correlate with certain measures of worldly achievement and economic earnings.

For more than thirty years, I have been measuring intelligence and tracking its relationships with how well people do in life—on many levels and by many standards, including those of compassion, healthy relationships, admirable character, contributions, flexibility, acceptance, and the graces of living intact. I must tell you candidly: intelligence has an unimpressive correlation with many of the factors that comprise what makes life worth living. It's not that intelligence isn't dear and valuable—but it is a flicker when compared with the brighter light and value of wisdom.

Discovering that intelligence wasn't the Holy Grail may have been disappointing, had not my spiritual yearning and quest for practical tools led me to inquire about the critical ingredients for successful living. Over time, I became convinced that many of my clinical patients who were not particularly intelligent statistically, were, nonetheless, pragmatic, capable, and spiritually enlightened. They lived lives of satisfaction, importance, productivity, and value, as perceived by themselves and others. (I might add, parenthetically, that the majority came to see me in my office seeking treatment that addressed issues of self-regulation, healing, or skills training rather than because they lacked wisdom or wholeness.)

Observing people who lived well and admirably despite their possessing average intelligence clearly demonstrated that wisdom—those qualities and attributes that protect, promote, enhance, and embody worthwhile living—is distinct from intelligence.

Whereas intelligence is the ability to manipulate complexity, the capacity to learn quickly, and the accumulation of knowledge, wisdom is the application of God's intelligence to practical and successful living. Wisdom involves the ability to understand and discern inner qualities and relationships. It includes common sense, good judgment, and insight.

Intelligence typically denotes cognitive skills and reflects in performance that is clever, knowledgeable, competent, creative or novel, resourceful, or that require keen and facile associations, analyses, and syntheses. Wisdom, on the other hand, reflects a more functional and practical capacity to understand, navigate, and implement the core principles that are requisites to living a successful, bountiful, and intact life. These include the ability to handle adeptly temptations, desires, conflicts, rejections, setbacks, suffering, and the fundamental inequities in life, and a sinful and selfish nature. These competencies comprise the capacity to apply self-control and discipline, compassion, and humility.

By its very nature, wisdom implies the enduring truths and principles that underlie and govern the foundations and functioning of the universe. God created the universe, and by wisdom—his wisdom—the world operates today. Naturally, then, wisdom is revealed in the recapitulation of its tenets and principles, and these tenets and principles are infused by God's intelligent design throughout the natural world. Physical events, spiritual manifestations, and the experiences of living creatures reflect this divine infusion.

We human beings have access to wisdom through natural and supernatural means. In the natural arena, our senses, reasoning, and the logic of systematic rules, such as those that govern science, help us acquire wisdom. We *observe, interpret,* and *apply.* To gain wisdom is to utilize this three-pronged process in situations where the conditions and specifics may vary, but where the essential organizing principles, similarities, and parallel attributes remain relevant. As we acquire experience and wisdom, we'll be better able to recognize underlying truths that are common denominators in relationships and events that may, on the surface, appear different, but that are, in fact, actually cut from the same bolt of fabric. These insights will help us avoid repeating mistakes and becoming discouraged and demoralized.

In the supernatural domain, we may also use the same methods of observation, interpretation, and application. However, we have an added invaluable asset: the Word of God. For, by the same principles by which God created the world, he maintains it today, and he gives us blueprints, guidance, and many opportunities to gain wisdom. Indeed, God tells us to acquire wisdom at all costs (Proverbs 4:5–7).[30]

TWENTY-ONE PRECEPTS OF BIBLICAL WISDOM

The Bible is a long and complex canon. It's both straightforward and elusive, blunt and veiled, symbolic and literal, mysterious and plain, dense and simple, novel and repetitive. Everything in the Bible is consistent with itself: concealment and revelation, foreshadowing and recapitulation. The Bible contains all we need to know to live intact, successfully, according to God's wisdom. Yet we cannot live inside a book—we must extrapolate, interpret, and apply its principles to life in the present.

A lifetime of study does not exhaust the riches and guidance provided by the Bible. I keep returning to this treasure trove for direction and sustenance, but it can be overwhelming. I need brief reminders and cue lines. For several decades, I have studied the Bible for my way of life. Here is a condensed summary of its wisdom, as I have discerned it:

1. Love the Lord with all your heart, all your soul, and all your mind.
2. Do unto others as you would have them do unto you.
3. Humble yourself and put others ahead of you.
4. Fear and revere God. Act justly, love mercy, and walk humbly with your God.
5. Turn from sin and evil (all that is against God).
6. Worship the Lord with praise and thanksgiving.
7. Know that God sees everything and will call into account all good and evil deeds.
8. Know that God desires our allegiance and contrition of heart.
9. Believe that God sacrificed his only son to save us, to propitiate our sins, and to draw us close to him.
10. Recognize that we are special and precious to God and that the good things we have are gifts from him.
11. Understand that God has given us insight and an eternal perspective, but that we cannot know all of his ways and mysteries.
12. Live a life of service and sacrifice with eternity in mind. Love and forgive others, just as you are loved and forgiven.

---

30. Reading and meditating on the book of Proverbs in the Old Testament is especially helpful in developing wisdom.

13. Seek God's will and be attuned to his direction, providence, and discipline.

14. Accept suffering as a part of life, and use it to grow in character and spirit and to model after Christ.

15. Ask God for guidance, and do pray without ceasing.

16. Cultivate awareness that the nature of Self wants sovereignty in direct opposition to God's sovereignty, and that conflict separates us from God.

17. Allow, accept, and seek God's power in living life his way.

18. The wisdom by which God formed the universe operates today and is manifest throughout modern life. We have only to look with a sincere desire to understand, and God will impart wisdom to guide us in living successfully according to his will.

19. Absolute truth and good and evil do exist; our ability to know them depends upon our right relationship with God and our submission to his authority and sovereignty.

20. God has created duality and unity. This profound mystery underlies both man's rebellion and obedience and has pervaded the recorded development of human history. Jesus Christ is the bridge that connects the duality that separates man from God. Nature recapitulates itself in so many ways: Old and New Testaments, the creation of good and the rebellion that produces evil, death and life, law and grace, heaven and hell, Jews and Gentiles, saved and unsaved, joy and suffering, God and man, flesh and spirit. Live in such a way that accepts separation, and strives for unity. Seek God.

21. God has created the universe out of his fundamental wisdom. His wisdom is discoverable through his divine Word (scripture), through forming a right relationship with him, and through the challenge process by which he reveals truth, his nature, and the wisdom of the universe. God made truth so that everything concealed will be revealed and all that is revealed has been concealed. Everything has a future and a past, according to his divine wisdom. Our present moments are to be used by living in a way that meets the challenges God sets before us to gain wisdom and live according to God's will.

These preceding precepts are not exhaustive of God's wisdom, of course. They are a summary and reference to focus your mind and spirit on your personal quest for wisdom. Ideally, these notes will encourage you to delve into the power of God's Word, the Bible.

For the word of God is living and active. Sharper than any double-edged sword, it penetrates even to dividing soul and spirit, joints and marrow; it judges the thoughts and attitudes of the heart. (Hebrews 4:12)

WISDOM AND HUMILITY

Through history, as the Bible records, God has made and revamped covenants with man to lead man out of darkness and into wisdom and relationship with God. However, man's stubbornness and inability to abide by these covenants and unwillingness to superimpose God's Word have resulted in suffering and separation from God. Eventually, God instituted the ultimate resolution to this problem in the person and sacrifice of Jesus Christ, God's incarnate Self.

Through Christ, God manifests wisdom for living on earth—the sacrificing of Self and deferring to God for ultimate answers (Luke 1:17, 2:40, 2:52; Mark 6:2; 1 Corinthians 1:30).

Throughout the Bible, God presages, reveals, and explains the process for manifesting his wisdom (Isaiah 11:1–9). It is given to us through stories about God's dealings with ancient peoples, through didactic instruction, and through the model of Christ's ministry and revelations. God intends for us to use this model to gain wisdom and live intact.

Relinquishing what we think we know in deference to a greater wisdom is a daunting challenge, one that both necessitates and teaches humility. It is human nature to want to be "right" (and your personal narrative works hard to reinforce that your beliefs are right). It takes sacrifice—the very sacrifice that God desires—to defer to his ways. The kind of "right" that truly rewards is a right relationship with God. This requires humility. To be humble is to be modest, respectful, and without pretense. Regardless of what we may think we know, this means putting God's knowledge first.

The fear of the Lord is the beginning of wisdom, and knowledge of the Holy One is understanding. (Proverbs 9:10)

Fearing God does not mean being anxious that he will harm you. Rather, to fear God is to revere him with awe and respect. Reverential trust is what God wants, and it is necessary to receive what he wants us to have. To fear God is to be in awe of his knowledge and capabilities.

Can you remember the awe and admiration you had as a child for the abilities of adults to make their way around in the world? They could take you places, feed and comfort you, wipe away your tears, procure what you needed, and help you navigate through a seemingly Byzantine and overwhelming world. Even if you didn't always like what your parents did, if they frustrated or denied you what you wanted—you had to admit; they were awesome and powerful.

The adults in your world were just flawed humans, yet they knew and could do so much more than you. Now, imagine God's perspective as he regards humans who pretend to know so much (Job 38:4–41, 39–41). Our ingenuity and inventions come by God's grace, yet we are no match for his omniscience and omnipotence.

> *How precious to me are your thoughts, O God! How vast is the sum of them! Were I to count them, they would outnumber the grains of sand.* (Psalm 139:17–18)

Dismissing pride and pretense about self-knowledge in favor of what God reveals leads to an enlightened and rewarding experience of gaining true wisdom. You are not asked to cast aside your worldly knowledge, technical abilities, skills, common sense, or streetwiseness. Rather, God wants each of us to *test* our knowledge and assumptions by his standards. For example, opportunities and temptations that may seem harmless and popular by the world's standards can diminish your capacity for and practice of self-control. Indulgence, rationalization, and commercial advertisement may reassure and lull you into a sense of false security, but God's wisdom protects by reinforcing the need for self-control.

> *A person without self-control is as defenseless as a city with broken-down walls.* (Proverbs 25:28)

> *He will die for lack of self-control; he will be lost because of his incredible folly.* (Proverbs 5:23)

Knowing God leads to self-control. Self-control leads to patient endurance, and patient endurance leads to godliness. (2 Peter 1:6)

When someone treats you rudely or unfairly in life, your worldly smarts typically alert you to assert yourself, push back, and defend yourself; then, you may attempt to put yourself ahead of others. Remember, however, that God's wisdom recommends being compassionate, sacrificing, putting others first, and relinquishing what may be rightly yours (refer to the examples given in chapter 4). The Bible repeatedly refers to the vital role that compassion plays in attaining physical, psychological, and spiritual comfort and intactness (Psalm 86:15; Psalm 145:8–9; Hosea 2:19–20; Micah 18:19; Lamentations 3:22; Lamentations 3:32; Colossians 3:12–13; 1 Peter 3:8–9).

So you will experience conflict; your expectations will be challenged; you will have to do some reality testing and make choices about what you have learned from the world and what you are learning from God. These are the challenges and concepts we are discussing in these chapters. They are the challenges and concepts that can help you grow in grace and live intact (that is, again, *in tact*).

In order to resolve these challenges, conflicts, and dilemmas and to choose behaviors and paths of true wisdom, you will want to cycle through the three steps listed at the beginning of this chapter:

1. Condense significant events and attributes and organize essential unifying principles.
2. Test conclusions and beliefs by measuring them with God's standards and principles.
3. Apply God's standards and these principles to daily life and challenges across changing circumstances.

In applying these steps, you will have to filter the thoughts and events you experience not only through your worldly knowledge, but also through God's Word. Questions that may arise include: Have I experienced situations like this before? What are the similarities and differences? What happened when I did things in my old or accustomed way? Did I get results that were worthwhile, or did I mainly feel justified and temporarily relieved? What do my choices say to God about my character? Am I depending upon God to work out all things for the good in his way (Romans 8:28), or am I only fending for myself without faith and reliance on him?

Wisdom beckons you to appeal to God, even in the smallest matters. The narrative in your mind will go astray unless held in check by God's Word and principles.

> *We demolish arguments and every pretension that sets itself up against the knowledge of God, and we take captive every thought to make it obedient to Christ.* (2 Corinthians 10:5)

We all want to be "right." In so doing, we resort to instinctive self-protective and self-justifying reactions that are likely to spark additional discourtesy and aggression and to feed negative thinking, vengefulness, and self-pity, or harm.

In seeking and attaining wisdom, in pleasing God and expediting the right thing to do, there are more gray areas, ambiguous problems, and ethical dilemmas than there are black-and-white solutions. That's why we need the compass of God's Word and wisdom, based upon his absolute truth. The embrace and exercise of humility is vital in keeping on track with wisdom.[31] (Also, see chapter 18 for an expanded discussion of humility.)

WISDOM AND EXPECTATIONS

From minor disappointments to the harsh and sometimes devastating realities that happen, it's obvious that that we cannot and do not get our way as often as we desire. In the face of contradictions between reality and desire and in the hope of mediating their differences, we have to learn from experience, change what we can, accept what we cannot, and become wiser in our anticipations and conclusions. Remember these principles governing expectations:

> *Expectations reflect your conscious and unconscious assessments, plans and schematics, and maps of the world and of yourself within the world. Expectations unfold at different levels, and these levels mediate the ways that you*

---

31. Humility helps us give up the notion that everything is relative and accept, as the Bible teaches, that there are absolute truths.

want things to be (greater expectations) with the ways you have learned through experience that they are likely to play out (lesser expectations).

The difference between your greater expectations and your lesser expectations approximates your satisfaction and disappointment in life. It is an indicator of the extent to which you reconcile the outcomes you get with the way you would like life to work. It is also a reflection of the way you balance reality testing with desire.

Greater expectations are a roadmap and a navigation system for faith, hope, ingenuity, and the fulfillment of desire.

Lesser expectations are also a roadmap and a navigation system— these expectations detail a terrain already mapped out and previously traveled. We depend upon lesser expectations for predictability, directions, timing, and the accuracy of planning.

As you evaluate and refine your expectations, seek God's counsel on interpreting differences between what you expected and wanted and the way things turned out.

Trust in the Lord with all your heart and lean not on your own understanding; in all your ways acknowledge him and he will make your paths straight. Do not be wise in your own eyes; fear the Lord and shun evil. This will bring health to your body and nourishment to your bones. (Proverbs 3:5–8)

You will grow wiser, happier, and more practical as you deliberately make this a habit.

WISDOM AND CHOICE

Remember that choice is the continuing act of being you. Moment by moment, choice connects you with what happened in the past and what will happen in the future, making you who you are and who you will become. Your choices are the mechanism by which you develop and establish your character, the set of qualities that identify and distinguish you.

By choosing, you exercise free will in countless active and passive decisions every day. You can choose to become wiser, even if such choices are not characteristic of how you previously conducted your life. Remember this principle:

You must learn to see yourself as being more the potential of tomorrow rather than the product of yesterday.

You can choose between wisdom and folly, between doing right and doing wrong. You choose to acknowledge God, put him first, and consult him through prayer in all that you do or plan. You can value wisdom above material riches and your own opinions and consequently make choices in wisdom's direction. You can choose to fear God and shun evil—this is the cornerstone of wisdom (Proverbs 9:10).

Through understanding and exercising your responsibility and power of choice, you can shape a life that is more satisfying, more contributing, and more worth living. You can come to terms with a universe that doesn't always give you what you want or when you want it. Facing the challenge of choice will enable you to operate more competently in turning obstacles into opportunities and transforming brokenness into wholeness and living intact. Though you don't get to control everything that happens to you, you can choose between living broken and living intact. Wisdom will be your companion, your guide, and your everlasting reward.

Be very careful, then, how you live—not as unwise, but as wise, making the most of every opportunity, because the days are evil. Therefore do not be foolish, but understand what the Lord's will is. (Ephesians 5:15–16)

O, the depth of the riches of the wisdom and knowledge of God! How unsearchable his judgments, and his paths beyond tracing out! Who has known the mind of the Lord? Or who has been his counselor? Who has ever given to God, that God should repay him? For from him and through him and to him are all things. To him be the Glory forever! Amen. (Romans 11:33–36)

WORDS FROM THE WISEST MAN IN THE WORLD

The Bible records King Solomon as the wisest natural man in the world (1 Kings 4:29–34). The following passage from the Old Testament illustrates Solomon's exercise of wisdom:

Now two prostitutes came to the king and stood before him. One of them said, "My lord, this woman and I live in the same house. I had a baby while she was there with me. The third day after my child was born, this woman also had a baby. We were alone; there was no one in the house but the two of us. During the night, this woman's son died because she lay on him. So she got up in the middle of the night and took my son from my side while I your servant was asleep. She put him by her breast and put her dead son by my breast. The next morning I got up to nurse my son—and he was dead! But when I looked at him closely in the morning light, I saw that it wasn't the son I had borne." The other woman said, "No! The living one is my son; the dead one is yours." By the first woman insisted, No! The dead one is yours; the living one is mine." And so they argued before the king. The king said, "This one says, 'My son is alive and your son is dead,' while that one says, 'No! Your son is dead and mine is alive.'" Then the king said, "Bring me a sword." So they brought a sword for the king. He then gave an order: "Cut the living child in two and give half to one and half to the other." The woman whose son was alive was filled with compassion for her son and said to the king, "Please, my lord, give her the living baby! Don't kill him!" But the other said, "Neither I nor you shall have him. Cut him in two!" Then the king gave his ruling: "Give the living baby to the first woman. Do not kill him. She is his mother." When all Israel heard the verdict the king had given, they held the king in awe, because they saw that he had wisdom from God to administer justice. (1 Kings 3:16–28)

Let's deconstruct Solomon's ruling in its context and see how he displayed God's wisdom:

Solomon knew that this was a test and that he didn't automatically have the answer because he wasn't present when the event occurred and didn't have firsthand evidence about what had transpired. He only had the conflicting stories told by the two women. But Solomon understood human nature, and he used the vulnerabilities in that nature to let God help him exercise wisdom. Solomon knew that raw emotions were driving both women: the grief over the death of the baby, the rage, despair, guilt, and jealousy of the mother who had lost her child, and the powerful protective maternal instincts and justifiable despair of the mother whose living baby had been stolen.

Armed with this knowledge, he applied the secrets of living intact to develop a fitting resolution to the problem. Solomon used challenge as an opportunity to judge the conflicting stories, and he challenged both women in a way that would reveal the truth. Under the guise of applying the principle of impartial equity (cutting the living child in half), Solomon uncovered the underlying emotions and motivations of each woman.

Notice that the woman who was the real mother of the living child was *filled with compassion*. The other woman was vengeful and vindictive. The negative emotions were driving her behavior while, in stark contrast, the real mother of the infant displayed compassion and sacrifice—instead of anger—in a desperate effort to protect her child. King Solomon was also able to use negative reinforcement[32] to elicit the behavior he sought in his quest for the truth. He realized that the display of care and maternal protective instincts would indicate who was the real mother of the surviving infant.

By cunningly constructing the challenge and laying bare the underlying motivations that interplay with emotions, Solomon was able to evoke revealing behavioral outcomes in the face of confusion, conflict, and adversity. He utilized the principles of discernment and application described earlier in this chapter, and his wisdom reflected the natural qualities of God's wisdom (compassion, conscience, sacrifice, putting others first, fear of the Lord) in problem solving and meeting challenges through reasoning, emotional sensitivity, and control.

As you can see, the five secrets of living intact that you examined in earlier chapters are woven into Solomon's response to the challenge he faced. Parenthetically, courts throughout the world have used this seminal biblical story about Solomon's wisdom to epitomize the quest for judicial insight, righteousness, and justice. The parable stands as a perfect example of mortal man's deliberate application of God's immortal wisdom.

PRACTICAL APPLICATION OF BIBLICAL WISDOM

How can Solomon's actions apply to you and the challenges you face? Let's use a parallel example of a conflict between people where the evidence may be camouflaged by circumstance, emotion, and self-interest.

---

32. Negative reinforcement involves the removal of an aversive condition contingent upon the performance of a specified behavior. In this case, the aversive condition was the threat of losing the living child, and the desired performance was the display of flexibility and sacrifice that would indicate to Solomon the identity of the real mother.

Suppose you are asked to mediate an argument between two children who are blaming each other or fighting over an actual or exaggerated offense. You were not present at the triggering incident, but you know the character and reputation of each child. You may have suspicions about primary culpability, but your desire to be fair and objective takes precedence over your assumptions. How would Solomon's biblical example apply here? You can use what you've learned about the secrets of living intact, and as Solomon exemplified, you can utilize negative reinforcement and discernment to resolve the conflict.

You may or may not have evidence about which child is being more truthful. In the absence of proof, however, you can impose a condition of negative reinforcement that will allow you to manage the conflict in a biblical and pragmatic way.

First, tell the children that you are going to make a decision based upon what you already know. (Privately, your decision will also include the past track record of each child, as well as the extent to which they are insisting on getting their way.) Tell them that since they cannot work the problem out by themselves, you will charge them for your services. State that they are both guilty of causing and not being able to solve the conflict.[33] Take from each child material possessions and/or privileges that he values. Explain that, in order to earn them back, he must demonstrate the following to your satisfaction:

1. He must apologize to the sibling and earnestly ask forgiveness. (This is not for what the child insists he did or didn't do, but for his role in antagonizing and causing conflict and the unpleasantness.)
2. He must acknowledge his part in creating the conflict and verbalize at least two responses he could have offered that would have been more adaptive.
3. He must display consistently (over a period of time that you determine) courteous and respectful behavior toward the other child that includes deference and sharing.

---

33. This teaches them that protesting their innocence will not get them what they want. In a way, it is a peculiar justice similar to Solomon's threat of settling the dispute by cutting the living child in half.

The negative reinforcement in this approach involves the imposition of a restrictive condition (taking away possessions or privileges) with their return specifically contingent upon performance of the desired behaviors (i.e., treating the other child nicely, acknowledging partial fault for creating a negative situation and corresponding negative behaviors that are at least as significant as the one(s) for which the child is claiming innocence, and a willingness to sacrifice pride and self-interests and to substitute respect and compassion).

As you shift the focus away from determining innocence to their culpability in displaying self-centeredness and a sense of unbridled entitlement, you are using biblical principles of discernment. Holding each child accountable for his part in generating the conflict is a powerful and accessible tool for teaching righteousness. As your children understand what you are looking for (and what it takes to get what they want), you will witness the display of their character in the way they respond to your conditions. As they resist or accept the conditions you've imposed, you will be able to discern with more certainty each child's truthfulness. It is also likely that the child who is guiltier of actually triggering the transgression will make his culpability known by either a confession or the way he responds to your guidelines.

WORLDLY AND BIBLICAL RESPONSIBILITIES—THE WISDOM OF JESUS

In this chapter, I have tried to describe wisdom and distinguish God's true wisdom from that which passes for smarts and the worldly wisdom of man. The Bible teaches that wisdom is unsurpassed in value and that those who seek it will find it.

Yet there is no explicit map for this treasure hunt—the acquisition of wisdom is dependent upon a right relationship with God and an earnest and consistent quest for wisdom through the understanding and application of biblical principles throughout one's life.

As is the case with other areas of man's fallibilities and limitations, the discernment and exercise of wisdom can frequently seem at odds with the practicalities and pressures of everyday life. It is, once again, the conflict between flesh and spirit—viewing things with our selfish, carnal nature and acting to please that nature, or letting the Holy Spirit fill us and allow us to see things from God's perspective (Galatians 5:16–18).

God wants us to make the right decisions, those that are pleasing to him. He wants to impart his wisdom. He also understands that the world he created is a sinful and tempting place and that it is difficult for man to recognize and distinguish the truly wise paths. We are reminded to keep our eyes on that which is everlasting, rather than merely on the temporary things in daily life. So the exercise of wisdom involves knowledge and choice. But God does not expect us to live as recluses and escape the practicalities of the world. Fortunately, he provides us with the abilities, counsel, and choices to exercise godly character in each of those domains.

Jesus gives an example of this wisdom in his response to the Pharisees who tried to trick him by pitting practical responsibilities against allegiance to God.

> *Then the Pharisees went out and laid plans to trap him in his words. They sent their disciples to him along with the Herodians. "Teacher," they said, "we know you are a man of integrity and that you teach the way of God in accordance with the truth. You aren't swayed by men, because you pay no attention to who they are. Tell us then, what is your opinion? Is it right to pay taxes to Caesar or not?" But Jesus, knowing their evil intent, said, "You hypocrites, why are you trying to trap me? Show me the coin used for paying the tax." They brought him a denarius, and he asked them, "Whose portrait is this? And whose inscription?" "Caesar's," they replied. Then he said to them, "Give to Caesar what is Caesar's, and to God what is God's." When they heard this, they were amazed. So they left him and went away.* (Matthew 22:15–22)

Your efforts to live intact will certainly be burdened with having to distinguish between worldly wisdom, the temptations and rewards of sensuality and material pleasures, and the seemingly disparate responsibilities to God and the practical world. Nonetheless, when you earnestly seek God's wisdom, practice the application of the principles outlined, utilize the secrets of living intact, and keep Jesus as your living example, you will surely adhere to the truer path.

> *Who is wise and understanding among you? Let him show it by his good life, by deeds done in the humility that comes from wisdom. But if you harbor bitter envy and selfish ambition in your hearts, do not boast about*

it or deny the truth. Such "wisdom" does not come down from heaven but is earthly, unspiritual, of the devil. For where you have envy and self-ish ambition, there you will find disorder and every evil practice. But the wisdom that comes from heaven is first of all pure; then peace-loving, considerate, submissive, full of mercy and good fruit, impartial and sincere. Peacemakers who sow in peace raise a harvest of righteousness. (James 3:13–17)

V
EVERYDAY PROBLEMS, ELEGANT SOLUTIONS

CHAPTER 13
DEALING WITH DESIRE

Once our physical survival needs are handled, the dominant human preoccupation is trying to get what we want from life. Internal and external conflicts are often the by-products of this pursuit of our desires. This is an integral part of God's scheme.

To all outward appearances, we may seem to be getting life "right." We may be goal directed, purpose driven, clever, considerate, and compassionate. We may have learned to delay immediate gratification, work diligently, act responsively, parent conscientiously, save with an eye toward the future, and be able to make the requisite sacrifices to attain our objectives. Nonetheless, we are entwined in a competitive, demanding, and often harsh and unforgiving world where survival of the fittest is a ruling principle. Whether you're kind, aggressive, meek, power seeking, or basically content with the bounties that God has provided, you're not exempt from desire's lure and conflict's impact.

Many have a knee jerk negative association with the forces unleashed by desire. They link desire with intemperate passions and associate conflict with knockdown battles that must somehow be won in order to prevail in life's arena. These attitudes imply that desire and conflict (which is covered comprehensively in the next chapter) are damaging and, thus, to be avoided or resisted. Yes, it's true that desire and conflict can sometimes get us into trouble, but this is part and parcel of the human condition— a ticket to ride, if you will. Just as you must understand the central role that meeting challenges plays in the process of living intact, so, too, must you understand the central role that desire and conflict play. But comprehension by itself is not enough. You must also learn how to manage the compelling forces that are woven into the fabric of your being.

To make sure we're on the same page, let's start out by defining terms. Then we'll examine how and why this force affects everything we do in life.

Desire is an attraction to something with the expectation that its attainment will bring satisfaction.

THE ENIGMA OF DESIRE

To err is human, and to desire is also human. The range of wants and needs varies from the mundane and tangible to the spiritual and ethereal. Human beings are uniquely capable of spanning the entire spectrum. Desire is so basic that, without it, you wouldn't eat, procreate, or come in from the rain.

You might desire things that you know you shouldn't (e.g., coveting someone else's spouse) or those to which you are legitimately entitled (e.g., your baggage at the airport). For most people, the list of desires is long, and differentiating those that are illicit and narcissistic from those that are innocent, wholesome, and constructive requires insight and judgment and, of course, God's guidance as enumerated and elucidated in scripture.

Certainly, desire is a vital element in the achievement dynamic as it inspires us to develop our natural abilities and strive for goals and achievements that can benefit not only ourselves but also others. When thwarted, desire can trigger frustration, hurt, and disappointment. But without desire, bridges and skyscrapers wouldn't be built, vaccines wouldn't be discovered, and symphonies wouldn't be written. The flip side of the desire phenomenon is more pernicious. Absent abhorrent Satanically derived desire, tyrants such as Hitler and Stalin would not have crawled out of woodwork; rain forests wouldn't be destroyed; and drug dealers wouldn't ply their trade. Desire is, thus, a double-edged sword. It is one of God's ways of speaking to our heart and our special identity. It can be a manifestation of free will or the sinful nature of man.

Desire is also a chameleon—at times insistent and needy, but often secretive and surreptitiously blended into our internal narrative to justify how we feel and what we want, plan, and do. Desire works in the spirit and in the flesh. It fuels expectations and purposeful activity, but it can also be the catalyst for succumbing to Satan's schemes, the foundation for wickedness, and the product of disregulation, dysfunction, and errant living.

Desire can be best understood if we divide it into four categories:

1. Desire for that which is necessary, life enhancing, or edifying (godly desire)
2. Desire for that which is unnecessary, though appealing or enticing (human desire)
3. Desire for that which relieves a distressing physiological or emotional state (anesthetizing desire)
4. Desire for that which is believed to bring or be required for happiness or satisfaction (illusory desire)

When properly harnessed, desire helps us survive, motivates achievement, and guides us to attain growth, fulfillment, and self-actualization. Many of our desires are God-given potentials designed for the unique person he created. But many others are generated by our sinful and selfish nature. These desires can lure us away from wholesome living and lead us in the pursuit of the unattainable and the unworthy.

In a world replete with illusions that spawn self-delusions, desire can be one of the most powerful and prevalent forces that impel us. The cravings emanate from within, but seek justification in the external materialistic world where objects and acquisitions are imbued with iconic and symbolic importance. The BMW, Rolex, country club membership, and even the acquisition of a trophy wife or husband may be perceived in some circles as providing unequivocal proof of status and prestige and may become surrogates for actually living intact.

Enabled by our susceptibility, the insidious psychology and manipulation of ingenious marketing gurus and creative copywriters target our vulnerabilities and insecurities, engineer our aspirations, and tout must-have products. Cunning commercials exploit and entice our appetites and trick us into believing that what we want is needed, deserved, and healing. We are shrewdly manipulated into thinking that objects and possessions will immeasurably enhance the quality of our lives and make us feel good about ourselves. Desire has a habit of taking charge of our internal narrative. When the desire is wholesome, it serves a positive function in our life, can be harnessed to spur achievement, and contributes to our intactness. If the desire is the product of our being manipulated and exploited, it undermines our intactness and will ultimately trigger disillusionment and dissatisfaction.

DESIRE AND THE NARRATIVE

Do not infer from the previous discussion that I am denigrating the role of human desire. It's normal and natural to want things. Instincts like hunger and sexual desire drive us, and advertising functions to entice us to want things. When all is said and done, the primary role of marketing is to stimulate our desires with the promise of wellness and contentment. Our economy is largely built on this paradigm. The connections between products, desires, and needs are masterfully exploited. Successful advertising agencies are in the business of increasing desire. Consummate marketers may not express it in these terms, but they intuitively grasp that repeatedly bombarding consumers with catchy slogans, clever graphics, and high-impact commercials has a cumulative effect on the nervous system and the mind's narrative that heightens receptivity, justifies a particular desire, stimulates arousal, and induces us to seek fulfillment.

The smell or sight of delicious food can make us want to eat even when we're not hungry, and the allure of creative marketing can hook us on buying an attractive clothing item, car, or must-have gadget. So, too, can social situations, cultural values, and personal beliefs influence our desires. Wanting things that are unattainable or that require extraordinary or persistent cost or effort keeps our nervous system "stuck" in a fight-or-flight mode. This mode is useful in some situations, such as when there is potential threat or danger. However, when this intense on-alert nervous system function becomes the default tab in our daily lives, we are headed for serious trouble. Even the healthy aspiration to achieve (such as driving oneself to complete graduate school or a grueling internship) or a heroic effort to sustain functioning in an emergency can bring unintended side effects that lure the nervous system into an inflexible mode. (For example, some air traffic controllers, emergency trauma workers, or medical interns and residents may have great difficulty decelerating their fight-or-flight nervous system responses when they are off duty.) Desire can be the escort that colludes with the nervous system and causes us to derail and crash.

An anecdote from my clinical practice underscores the default phenomenon. I was treating a client who was an ambitious and gifted salesman. Blessed with excellent verbal skills and plenty of energy and drive, he was always on the lookout for potential customers. He possessed the kind of charm and social skills that made people feel comfortable and want to buy what he was selling. Persuasive but not pushy, people described him as someone who could "sell ice to Eskimos."

The man recognized his own skills of persuasion. Possessing self-confidence and desiring the "good life," he planned to exploit his sales talents and make a fortune.

Conversations and social interactions were little more than prospecting opportunities. His nervous system was geared up to treat people as targets who needed what he was selling and were destined to bend to his will. He found it increasingly difficult to relax and be "off duty." As in the case of football players who are pumped up by their coach's pep talk that's designed to stimulate their competitive spirit and inner narrative, this man's inner narrative reinforced his compulsion to treat virtually everyone as a potential customer. Despite his consummate sales skills, there were, of course, rejections. After each rejection, the man's narrative rescued him from dejection by helping him rationalize that the failure was simply part of a numbers game. If he kept on pitching hard enough and long enough, he would ultimately score. This spurred him on to the next sales pitch. The man had trained himself to live in a "never enough" mode, and his nervous system was stuck in a hunting modality. But there was an obvious flaw in the modus operandi to which he had become addicted. He could never step back, and he was never at peace. There was always one more tantalizing sale looming on the horizon, and his compelling hunger could never be appeased. He had to try for more.

Living with the gas pedal floored is not what we're designed to do. If you persist in that manner, your mind and body will eventually capitulate to the stress, and mental, emotional, and spiritual damage will surely ensue.

If someone is secure, he might say, "I know my limits," and "I can take care of myself." But if times become tough, he might complain, "Look what I have to put up with, and look at the challenges I'm facing in meeting my expenses." The central paradox becomes evident. We are all tempted to let circumstances cajole us into self-pity and helplessness.

We all periodically fall victim to fatigue and disappointments. When invited by desire, we must distinguish among the attractions that feed godly ambition and confidence and those that substitute gratification for the sense of worthiness and contentment. *Confidence is the habit of expecting favor from life's ordinary opportunities and of practicing greatness in the face of seeming insignificance.* Confidence is often based upon maintaining a string of successes. Quintessential self-esteem, however, is rooted in a positive sense of self and not exclusively contingent upon achievement or material evidence of success.

Be assured that I am not proposing an ascetic or Spartan mindset when asserting and handling your needs, desires, and dreams. Rather, I am alerting you to the simple and profound truth that what you want may be:

a)   encompassing much more than you need;
b)   accelerating your nervous system, which, in turn, accelerates your self-justifying narrative in an escalating cycle;
c)   costing you more than you realize (especially for the benefit you get);
d)   skewing your character development and ability to discern God's truths;
e)   stressing you out mentally, emotionally, and physically;
f)   causing you to engage in unnecessary and harmful conflict;
g)   disabling the skills and tools for living intact, including self-regulation, self-control, and compassion.

In order for desire to light your path and serve as your ally, it must be *regulated*. Although desire may delight, tempt, excite, or titillate, you must become its master. The training ground—and often the battlefront—is that familiar, yet elusive friend, that ever-constant companion and master of disguises: your narrative.

ENGAGING THE NARRATIVE AND REGULATING DESIRE

Desire is a conscious process. Our narrative is the master of ceremonies of consciousness. It introduces the performers and acts that comprise a stage that hosts various desires and possibilities. The narrative evaluates which ones are approved. Remember also that the narrative mediates between our arousal state, the descriptive embodiment of the characteristics we identify with that comprise our "Self," namely, our beliefs, memories, values, and conscience and the flow of events and stimuli that unfold both within and around us.

Though many different stimuli can trigger desire, your narrative is not interested in distinguishing between internal and external happenings nearly as much as it is devoted to telling you that you *want* something. You want that coffee, that pizza, that sweater, and so forth. You want to correct that person's outrageous statement. It is the job of the narrative to get your attention, increase motivation, and direct your efforts. The loyal narrative does this well. Trouble is, the narrative is an indiscriminate yes-man, a press secretary dedicated to putting the best spin on whatever occurs to get you the most and to make you look the best. It is the part of you that thinks it *is* you.

A client I was treating exemplifies this dynamic. Janet was entrenched in nightly ritual of scarfing down desserts while she watched TV. As she succumbed to the seduction of her narrative, her helplessness and her waistline were growing.

Janet told herself that she deserved a small reward at the end of her grueling day. She worked, carted the kids around, and made wholesome dinners for her family. On top of that, she exercised at least four times per week. Surely, these activities merited a little dessert. It wasn't as though she was getting blitzed at a bar. Janet not only enjoyed the nightly ritual and the taste of sweets, but she felt greatly satiated by the effects of sugar. As Janet's stress and anxiety built during the day, she anticipated the release of relaxation after dinner. Looking forward to dessert was a quiet coping mechanism, and digesting the sweets relieved her tension by flooding her nervous system and altering her physiology. In satisfying her craving and her addiction, Janet colluded with her narrative, ever her companion in rationalizing and justifying her desire. Dessert was such a minor "vice," and most women her age no longer had petite figures anyway. Despite conspiring with her willing narrative, Janet was in conflict with herself as she felt that her discipline and her weight were slipping away from her control.

You may be getting the hint that you are not entirely autonomous in the self-justifying desire-narrative loop. The dynamic is compelling: your desires lead you around, and your narrative assumes the role of the chauffeur.

GETTING OFF THE MERRY-GO-ROUND

You have taken a giant first step just by reading this far and discovering that you *have* a narrative whose job it is to *make things okay*. You have eyes and you have a mouth, but they are not you—they are only parts of you. And not everything that your eyes see or that goes into or comes out of your mouth is *okay*. Your eyes and mouth have different and specific jobs, unlike the specialized job of your narrative, which is to survey and sweep everything under the umbrella that represents the self-indulgent you, the person who needs and wants whatever your narrative is negotiating.

The *real you*, however, owns the narrative, not the other way around. So the next step is for you to assume ownership of the narrative, thereby establishing the ground rules for control. You are the landlord/owner, and the narrative is your tenant. As the landlord/owner, you must take care of the property, according to your reasonable rules. If you can't do so because of the inhabitants, then you must deliberately sanction or perhaps even evict the persistent troublemakers.

Owning your narrative doesn't mean that you have to constantly supervise or censor it. Instead, you just need to know that it can get out of line, and when it does, it is likely following the dictates of something in you that is responding at *effect* when it is *pretending to be at cause*. In other words, emotion and reason can play games with your mind by switching and disguising themselves in cahoots with your physiology and the illusion that your feelings and opinions are necessitated by circumstances.

As an example, consider cravings. Generally speaking, well-regulated and well-adapted people navigate a continuum of desire for sensory gratification. This navigation ranges from selection of and indulgence in a variety of pleasures to the monitoring and inhibition of gratifications that we may determine as excessive, off-limits, or untimely. The intact individual enjoys gratifying tastes but has the wherewithal to avoid excesses, eliminate counterproductive habits and substances, respond to budgetary and time limitations, and exercise foresight in protecting against vulnerabilities. The balanced individual indulges a yen for preferred food and drink, but knows when to stop or limit and is able to do so. The person in control of his narrative understands that he is prey to the seductive lure of material things and counteracts the ubiquitous "I deserve it" narrative theme with a variety of tools from the living intact compendium.

One of the more powerful tools in managing desire is the exercise of *permeability*. As mentioned in chapter 3, permeability is the property of allowing circumstances to *pass through* your narrative so that you do not have to become attached to them. Essentially, permeability is the ability to exercise detachment, to allow the mantra of "This, too, shall pass" to comfort and replace any distress resulting from an involvement with something frustrating, painful, oppressive, or that causes suffering.

Permeability is a great antidote to the desires that can't or shouldn't be satisfied. Note that permeability is far different from willpower. Permeability involves choice, often at a conscious level, but it is not a white-knuckled battle against a strong adversary. Permeability applies the exercise of acceptance of the desire, with its attendant sense of deprivation and preoccupation, while acknowledging the conflict created by living with an unsatisfied yearning. Permeability is about becoming larger than the desires and frustrations tugging at you. It takes you into the surprisingly satisfying realm of living under conditions that are unfavorable to you, yet does not rob you of your sense of wholeness or living intact. Permeability is a state in which you remember gratification and anticipate it in the future but are able to do without it for the time being—that is, right now! (I like to think of living contentedly in the present as being able to tolerate the condition of *NO* to all the things I really want while still having a big *W* because I am winning—that's living intact in the *NOW!*)

Permeability is a powerful tool, yet it is interactive with and facilitated by other tools that can help you put desire in its rightful place. Careful reasoning and the tools of behavior modification (see chapters 5 and 6) can assist you in assuming leadership of your narrative and heading off your impulses. You can countervail the pressures exerted by your physiology and your narrative by using the principles of reinforcement to change habits that propel your unwanted desires. Steering clear of temptation is wise advice behaviorally as well as spiritually.

INFLUENCING AND CONTROLLING DESIRE

You can influence desire by choosing where and when you shop, what you read, watch, and listen to, with whom you associate, and, importantly, how you think about and evaluate your experiences and uninvited thoughts. You can set the stage, hire the cast, and write the script for what goes on in your mind, your body, your actions, and your interactions.

If you want to avail yourself of self-discipline and willpower, you will need to train. This training of your brain and nervous system is facilitated when you employ tools such as EEG neurofeedback and tapping. (See chapters 9 and 10 to review these methodologies.) You can also get in the habit of tapping, so you can defuse temptations and negative emotions at a moment's notice. (See chapter 10 to review these procedures.)

Practice also the habit—that's right, it is a habit—of dealing with unrequited desire by embracing the challenge of permeability and prayer when life isn't giving you everything that you want. Your narrative will regularly try to lure you with the adulteress of entitlement. It will tell you that your desires are okay, natural, and should be fulfilled. You cannot take the word of the narrative. That's like allowing the tenant to decide when to sell the house. The real you must decide relying on past experience and character, which reflect the habits you use to regulate your nervous system and your willingness to embrace challenges.

Permeability emerges from backstage when there is conflict. It creates a context for the self-denial or indulgence. Permeability allows conflict to endure or resolve without a vested interest in the outcome. Therein lies its value, because it allows you to back off and relax without becoming attached to the outcome. Permeability enhances enjoyment of the contest between desire and conflict, because permeability allows you to not really care who wins.

Don't construe the preceding as my condoning unjustifiable behavior, self-indulgence, or laissez-fair morals. Rather, I'm saying that *attachment to desire* derails the perspective and ability that are requisites to regulating it. Detaching yourself from the compulsive pull of desire is not the same as self-denial, though it may result in self-denial as one of the outcome paths.

THE PRAYER FACTOR

Permeability, detachment, and the larger macro view allow you to operate in the world with a better degree of control and direction. The direction should follow biblical principles with God as the guide and the source of strength and Jesus as the model and mediator.

Prayer is a tool with multifaceted applications for handling desire. It can mitigate and mediate desire, and it can also aid in tolerating the angst of unanswered want. When you are in a state of temptation or perceived or actual deprivation, you will fare better by reaching beyond your circumstances. You need to live in the state of "This, too, shall pass." From this mindset and spiritual-set will arise the confidence, identity, and sustenance that allow you to weather the pangs of unfulfilled desire.

Like other forces of nature, desire is a double-edged sword. One edge can work for you in the quest for survival, realization, and attainment, and the other can work against you with the shackles of compulsion, reckless appetite, and skittering self-control. Thus, you must use this sword adroitly.

Bringing desire under control requires understanding. Breaking down desire into types may help you comprehend what goes on inside and around you relative to your desires. One way to think about desire is to concede that desire is not solely a human entity. God has desires, too, and it is the foundation of proper character formation to align your human desires with what God desires for you. Think of studying for a test: you want to ensure that what you study and know about the subject aligns with the questions the teacher is likely to ask on your test. God is the master teacher, and any concentration and effort devoted to desires should be validated by whether it's on his tests. Your textbook for this course is the Bible.

Godly desire and human desire comprise one subcontext. Another reflects the difference between desire based on *necessity* and desire based upon *belief*. Certainly, desires based on necessity reflect physical needs and yearnings implanted in our very souls by the Creator. These inner stirrings, intuitions, muses, and cherished dreams can be the spiritual callings that are designed expressly for man.

The desires born of belief, however, respond to a different type of compass. The magnetic pull of beliefs draws powerfully upon hearts and exertions, even to the point of self-sacrifice to achieve the goal. Determining whether your intense desires are godly or human, necessary or based upon belief, can greatly assist you in harnessing useful desires and dismissing the counterfeits.

The following diagrammatic representation categorizes the different types of desire:

	Godly Desire	Human Desire
Desire based on necessity	Life-enhancement Survival Quest for Edification and Humility	Physical appetites Relief of discomfort Control & predictability Material security
Desire based on belief	Closeness to God Fulfilling relationships Purpose and worthiness Achievement & recognition	Addictions & obsessions False entitlements Temptations Luxuries, indulgence & comfort

Ultimately, the proliferation of desire and, especially, its unchecked or unfulfilled escalation can create the context for external and internal conflict. This propensity to escalate human desire in tandem with other aspects of human nature waves a red flag that we must heed.

Conflict is a thread that God has deliberately woven into the fabric of human existence. By design, he has embedded this thread in order to challenge and test us both on a temporal level and on a spiritual level. We must rise to meet the many challenges and studiously prepare to pass the many tests that we are certain to experience in life.

Being able to manage conflict is, thus, a key element in the process of living intact. We will address the dynamics of this critically important element in the next chapter.

CHAPTER 14
DEALING WITH CONFLICT

THE NATURE OF CONFLICT

We all encounter conflicts in life. Some are relatively minor (e.g., a conflict with a child over his use of his iPod) and some are major and lead to dysfunctionality (e.g., a family feud, the settlement of an estate after a death of a family member, or the division of assets or custody after a contentious divorce). Many conflicts are internal. They pit one voice inside your head against a countervailing voice (e.g., do I dare give up my well-paying corporate job and pursue a career in teaching?). How we handle these conflicts can serve to derail or enhance our capacity to live intact. One thing is certain: conflict affects the nervous system and the mind's narrative in much the same way as persistent desire. Conflict cumulatively and progressively accelerates nervous system arousal and aggression, and it solidifies the narrative by justifying one's position in the conflict.

Let's begin by defining the term *conflict*:

Conflict is the frustration of desire or a disagreement that entails opposition or competition.

Some people are temperamentally prone to avoid conflict. They conclude on the basis of experience that any conflict is a lose-lose proposition. These people tend to be more passive and less assertive and aggressive.

Other people are prone to engage in or even welcome conflict, either because the stimulation rewards them or because they see the conflict as resolvable, and thus, it becomes a goal. These people tend to be assertive and confrontational.

In managing conflict, there is something more important than whether you are passive or active, avoidant or confrontational. In fact, to get a handle on the phenomenon of conflict, we must differentiate *confrontation* from *conflict*. A confrontation is an interactive encounter between opposing forces or points of view. A confrontation may or may not be hostile, but it involves disagreement and could precipitate reaching a decisive decision point that could lead to a chain reaction that magnifies the confrontation and produces dire consequences. For example, someone taking your belongings, threatening you, or inconveniencing you may trigger a confrontation. In contrast, a conflict may exist without necessarily being confronted or exposed. As many conflicts are internal, repression or denial may cloud the underlying issues. Certainly, most of us have internal conflicts that pit opposing desires against each other (e.g., "I want to tell him what I think, but I don't want to hurt his feelings or get into an argument." "I know I should spend more quality time with my kids, but I want to get a promotion and earn more money, and this requires that I spend more time at work.")

Conflicts may or may not be adversarial, but they are always oppositional. They involve the *frustration of a desire*, and this characteristic is what is most important.

Let's examine this dynamic using a case study from my practice. The story illustrates how conflict may have a negative impact on the interactions between a married couple who are in disagreement, but who are not adversarial.

Maria was adored by her family and friends and admired for her equanimity. She was a model of stability and dependability. Though well spoken and opinionated, Maria was nonconfrontational. Sensitive, empathetic, and compassionate, she gave the other person the benefit of the doubt. She was easy to please, affable, and generally content, and she counted her blessings. Despite Maria's many positive qualities, some "sand had crept into the oyster." She had a conflict with her husband, Dave, about sex and money.

Maria and Dave had stopped having sex, and she was the holdout (or so it seemed). Actually, Maria was confused because she had not consciously decided to withhold sex. In fact, she even missed being physically intimate with her husband. She didn't understand the wedge that had surfaced between them or why the arguments and tension had increased. She knew that Dave was irritated with her for not being "in the mood" and for vetoing his plan to buy an expensive large-screen TV. From Maria's point of view, this was an excessive expense, and she was apprehensive about their growing debt. She also worried about meeting future expenses, and she had often urged Dave to put money into savings.

Dave also had his own point of view. He reminded her about how long he had restrained himself from buying the new 60" flat screen that he fancied, and he pointed out how hard he worked for his money. This triggered resentment in Maria, and she winced when Dave talked of "his" money. Though he was the breadwinner, Maria considered it "their" money. She felt her vote was unequal, and she began to brood and lose romantic interest. Vacillating in her mind and heart, Maria was inclined to give in to Dave's forcefulness and persistence. She wanted their conflict to end, and she wanted a return of their closeness. Disposed toward deference and being a person who "goes along to get along," Maria found it difficult to confront Dave and stand her ground about the money issue. She agonized over the overt conflict about spending lavishly and the internal conflict about being true to her principles, having justifiable concerns about equality, and regretting the lack of teamwork in their marriage. Her husband's conflicts reflected his frustrated desires for sex, trust, and autonomy.

The dynamics and emotional impact of the conflicts that Maria and her husband were experiencing can be better understood by studying the following templates that identify and differentiate the origins of desire and distinguish which conflicts are resolvable and which are irresolvable.

Whether in the spirit or in the flesh, conflict can arise as follows:

1. Resolvable conflict that entails individual choice, free will, natural differences, and the management of natural instincts
2. Resolvable conflict that involves human desire, intercessory mediation submission, and compromise
3. Irresolvable conflict built into God's created universe
4. Irresolvable conflict based upon rejection of God and sinful human desire

The following diagrammatic representation categorizes the different types of conflict:

	Natural Conflict	Conflict Caused By Desire
Resolvable Conflict	Conflicting choices Survival instincts Miscommunications & misperceptions Temperamental & Individual differences	Disrupted relationships Mental ambivalence Human selfishness & competition Sin & redemption
Irresolvable Conflict	Food chain position Good & evil Absolute truth & falsehood Godliness & sin	Predominance of sin Rejection of God Divisive beliefs Self as source & reference

CONFLICT RESOLUTION AND ITS LIMITS

The matrices above illustrate that conflict sometimes arises from the natural order of life and sometimes from human deviations from God's design. Conflict can be based upon need or unmodulated desire. Not all conflict is resolvable, despite good intentions and an objective of seeking peace. However, by understanding the dynamics of conflict and how conflict intertwines with desire and the narrative, it is possible to reach more satisfying outcomes as well as personal acceptance about what can be changed and what cannot.

Maria and Dave were able to come to terms with their conflicts when they were helped to identify the origins of the problem and were helped to differentiate which conflicts could be resolved and which could not be resolved. Although their disagreements centered ostensibly on money and sex, at the root of their conflicts was a common denominator: each partner felt that the other was insensitive to his or her legitimate needs. Maria's financial concerns and her conviction that she was not being consulted about a key financial decision triggered emotional isolation and a lowered desire for physical intimacy. Dave, on the other hand, experienced sexual rejection and felt that his wife doubted his ability to handle the family's finances responsibly. This was threatening to him, and he developed resentment that fueled his self-justifying narrative. His defensiveness obscured Maria's actual desire for intimacy and caused internal frustration in reaction to his wife's perceived inability to express and resolve the conflicts. Dave felt "entitled" to the TV because he wanted it and because he earned the money. He also felt legitimately entitled to having sex with his wife.

Maria actually concurred with Dave's feelings of entitlement for sexual intimacy. She did not, however, believe that his desire for a new TV was justified simply because he wanted one and because he was the one who brought home the paycheck. She reacted to her husband's forcefulness with passive resistance.

Once Dave and Maria were better able to communicate and set some rules about joint decision making and entitlements for physical intimacy and joint fiscal management, each was able to make concessions. Although neither of them was completely satisfied, both felt that they had scored a win in terms of their self-esteem and their respective material and emotional needs. Maria recognized her pattern of withholding sex because she felt robbed of power, and she became determined to communicate better with her husband about her inner conflicts and feelings and about her own struggle to separate money from sex. Dave realized that Maria's thwarted need for partnership in financial decisions affected her sexual desire. They decided that cooperation, financial responsibility, and physical intimacy superceded the immediacy of a new material possession. In response to Dave's unabated yearning for a new TV, Maria began a savings plan that would allow Dave to purchase the TV, and she showed him each week how the fund was increasing. She was amenable to supporting the purchase because she realized that Dave was ready to acknowledge her need to participate in the family's monetary decisions.

Basic differences between Maria and Dave in terms of physiology and beliefs remained irresolvable. Their sexual triggers were different, and each had a different belief about financial security. They also each retained their differing responses to conflict that reflected their respective temperaments, personalities, and life experiences. However, they were able to amend their positions, negotiate, compromise, and focus on what they wanted in common. They also learned how to identify and acknowledge their own self-interests, temptations, self-justifications, and physical and emotional wants, and they accepted the need to make appropriate and expedient sacrifices and to cooperate with each other.

REASONS FOR CONFLICT

Conflict occurs because of the natural conditions that exist in the world and because of ways the mind deals with desires. Let's review the reasons for conflict, and then we can examine what to do about it.

- **Survival hierarchy**
  Natural selection and survival of the fittest involve principles ensuring that conflict will occur. Predator and prey are endemic to God's ecology.

- **Cross purposes**
  People have different interests and different goals. Variety and viable self-interest produce conflict.

- **Context of insufficiency**
  The idea that "there is not enough to go around" induces conflict. Poverty, deprivation, or hardship can breed conflict, as can beliefs about the quantity of resources and who is entitled to them. In a context of insufficiency, conflict becomes an expected survival tool.

- **Sinful nature and breaking the rules** (Galatians 5:19–21)
  Let's face it: conflict arises when the sinful nature prevails. Satan loves to use conflict as a distraction from God's purposes and as an instrument of dissension. Breaking the God's rules and violating his boundaries will produce painful conflict.

- **Misperception, misinterpretation, misattribution**
  Conflict also occurs when people form inaccurate ideas about the motivations of others. Life is complex, and the signals from others are often ambiguous or confusing. The camouflage that protects can also send inadvertent or unintended messages. Also, misperceptions are a predictable result of imperfection and complexity. This is why reality testing is such an important skill.

- **Selfish ambition**
  God created a world that evolved into survival of the fittest. Competitive conflict became inevitable. Then, God said, "Love your neighbor as yourself" (Leviticus 19:18; Matthew 19:19; Mark 12:31; Romans 13:19; Galatians 5:14; James 2:8). How is this manageable? Again, God's Word shows how to do this—but it is not without struggle and conflict. Ungodly conflict comes from enthroning the Self.

- **Errant desire**
  Since conflict is the frustration of desire or a disagreement in the context of opposition or competition, errant desire (e.g., coveting what you are not entitled to have) will accelerate conflict. Errant desire is that which God forbids.

- **Law and spirit—flesh nature and spirit nature**
  So I say, live by the Spirit, and you will not gratify the desires of the sinful nature. For the sinful nature desires what is contrary to the Spirit, and the Spirit what is contrary to the sinful nature. They are in conflict with each other, so that you do not do what you want. (Galatians 5:16–17)

Many of the conflicts we experience are material counterparts of the spiritual conflict between good and evil (Ephesians 6:12). Conflict between good and evil is God's program for the world until the end of days. It is also the stage upon which character is built and exhibited.

ATTITUDES TOWARD CONFLICT

Though conflict can be unsettling and overwhelming, proper attitudes are critical to responding in the face of it.

- **Natural part of life**
  Reality dictates—and your own experiences confirm—that conflict is endemic to human interaction and the mind. Conflict can be helpful or destructive, but will exist as long as we have the

present earth and life as we know it. Therefore, though conflict may not be welcome or pleasant, it ought not be surprising.

- **Accept the inevitability of some continuing conflict**
Conflicts are inevitable and mostly intermittent. As previously stated, not all conflicts are resolvable. Therefore, a proper attitude about conflict includes acceptance of its existence and perseverance. This acceptance should not be construed as an endorsement for having conflict. Rather, it is a practical and spiritual acknowledgment of and response to what God has woven into the fabric of our existence.

- **Active and consuming or dormant and background**
Some conflicts *are* confrontational; these force a response and may even precipitate a crisis that requires immediate action. Other conflicts are ongoing, but they assume a background role and take time to work out. An adaptive attitude toward conflict is one that incorporates a perspective of the priority that the conflict assumes in one's life and consciousness.

- **Seek peace**
Though a certain amount of conflict will enter your life at some point, you should, wherever possible, try to minimize or resolve the conflict. This means seeking peace through peaceful means. Peace and peacefulness do not imply avoidance, passivity, or caving in. You can use peace to achieve peacefulness (most of the time) while also meeting challenges. Just because somebody or some situation challenges you does not mean that a brawl must ensue.

- **Clear conscience (no offense pending before God)**
In dealing with conflict, it is critical to act in ways that are pleasing to God, regardless of the outcome. It is not wrong to want to get your way or prevail over another person. However, you should act to resolve the conflict and/or present your position in a way that meets both your and God's approval. Doing your best and having God smile upon your efforts and position is far more important than "winning" a conflict. Additionally, recognize

that, no matter what you do or how earnestly you seek peace and reconciliation, the other party may behave in a way that thwarts your good intentions. Knowing that you've done what God wants you to do trumps any investment in or reward from a conflict that you try to coerce in your favor.

- **Spiritual battleground**
  So I say, live by the Spirit, and you will not gratify the desires of the sinful nature. For the sinful nature desires what is contrary to the Spirit, and the Spirit what is contrary to the sinful nature. They are in conflict with each other, so that you do not do what you want. (Galatians 5:16–17)

  What seems important at a given time reflects both our spiritual development and our circumstances. Satan uses both of these against us whenever he can. Satan will try to exploit both your desires and your situation to gain the upper hand in control over you. Because of who he is, Satan tries to draw you into conflict that is truly irresolvable. This is the conflict between good and evil, truth and falsehood, godliness and sin. These forces will always be opposed to each other, so you must take a stand. What appears in the circumstances to be a problem of differing opinions, ambivalent desires, or opposing competition may also be a conflict between spiritual forces using you as the battleground. Your awareness of and response to conflict should reflect this consideration.

REACTIONS IN CONFLICT

How should you react to conflict in ways that help you live intact? Here are some basics:

- **Seek forgiveness**
  Conflict tends to bring out selfishness and breeds temptation to put self ahead of God in the process of trying to get your own way. Conflict itself often undermines the golden rule since you are trying to prevail with your own interests over another. Therefore, it is important to seek forgiveness from both God and those

with whom you conflict. Seeking forgiveness may help to resolve the conflict; whether or not it does, such efforts will certainly augment your integrity and allow the Holy Spirit to fill and guide you.

- **Attempt reconciliation**
One of the noblest things you can ever do is to offer and work toward reconciliation in the fractured relationships that often accompany intense conflict. To *reconcile* means to *change*, and what you are trying to change is the condition of enmity or opposition that has arisen between you and another of God's children. To the mind geared for battle, it may seem strange to engage the mode of reconciliation; however, God directs us to reconciliation, even in the midst of opposition (Matthew 5:24; Luke 12:58; Acts 7:26; Romans 5:10; 2 Corinthians 5:20; Colossians 1:20). Orienting your efforts toward reconciliation may not result in reconciliation. But heading in that direction will bring more peace into the picture. Importantly, seeking reconciliation will restore your nervous system and interrupt the fight-or-flight acceleration that is so detrimental to health (refer to chapter 4). Seeking reconciliation is the vehicle for bringing out the compassion that you want to be prominent in your being.

I consider that my own greatest conquests have been those of reconciliation.

- **Identify and clarify your opponent's view**
From a practical standpoint, there are steps you can take to resolve conflict, or at least to determine whether it can be resolved. One of the most helpful steps is to make a practice of identifying and clarifying the position of the person opposing you. What does this person really want? Is it clear to him, and has he expressed it in a way that is clear to you? Making sense of someone else's point of view is not the same as endorsing it. Ask the person to be specific about what he wants and then restate it to him and ask if you got it right. It may seem as though you've done this so many times that it would be pointless; after all, each of you knows where you stand, and the conflict is simply a stalemate, right? Not always the case—many times, people become entrenched in

their positions, so that any interaction serves to reinforce making themselves seem right. If, however, the interaction is handled positively and strategically, you can open the door to exploring new avenues for reconciliation or compromise.

Another good tactic in restating and reflecting the other person's position is to incorporate it—or attempt to do so—into your own internal narrative conflict. For example, suppose you are in disagreement with a boss who is imposing work hours beyond your limits. You might say, "Let me see if I understand: you want me to work late on three nights this week because we have a deadline. I understand that. I, too, want to meet the deadline. However, I don't know how I could do that and get around the major problems at home it would bring. My son has a playoff game on Wednesday evening, and I promised him I'd be there. My wife has been on my case about the late hours, and I did agree to make dinner twice this week. So if I work late again several nights, I know I will have conflict at home, and that will detract from my giving you my best efforts all the way around. How can I manage these together?"[34]

Glib rephrasing will not ensure a resolution. However, by incorporating your opponent's viewpoint into your own thinking process and verbalizing it to him, you will accomplish two things that tend to be productive. You will show him that you are indeed considering his needs and point of view, and you will expose (in a nonthreatening and nonconfrontive manner) the imposition (and perhaps the unreasonableness) of his demand.

Clarifying your opponent's view completes the communication and lets him know you got the message. You still may not agree, but this step defuses the intensity and frustration that often underlies the aggressive repetition and reiteration of the conflict.

- **Question assumptions of inevitability in *this case***
  Not every conflict is resolvable. Sometimes people become so dug in, or their values and needs are so diametrically opposed, that

---

34. It's possible that the boss may be intransigent and may say, "Sorry, but you'll have to make a choice. You have to prioritize doing your job or having a temporary disruption in your family plans." Recognize that sometimes conflicts are not resolvable.

near-term resolution is highly improbable. Alternatively, however, many conflicts that seem inevitable and intractable can be
avoided or defused before they escalate. Conflicts that arise or
intensify even though there are ways around them usually result
from assumptions made by at least one party about the conflict's
inevitability. This is often borne by attitudes about the other
person's unwillingness, limitations, unreasonableness, prejudice,
etc. Though it may be true that your opponent embodies many
problematic traits, you want to question your assumptions about
whether, *in this particular case*, these attributes will prevent conflict resolution.

For example, you may have a child who balks and bickers
about routine activities. Anticipating his resistance or quarrel-
some attitude about going someplace may steel you for battle.
Your anxiety rises, your nervous system quickens, and your mind
rehearses the expected argument. This chain of events seems to
occur as if it were scripted. This time, however, you question if
it *has* to happen. Maybe your child will respond differently to a
different approach. Perhaps you could even ask him. "Son, I have
a problem I'd like you to help me with. You know how we often
argue when I ask you to go... (wherever). My problem is that I
don't know how to get you to do something that is really important without annoying you in the process of asking. Do you think
that we might figure out how to prevent this from happening?
Do you have any ideas?"

There may be times when you can avoid the conflict by choosing to not engage in it, even if it means not pushing the activity that is appropriate or necessary. Though this is often seen as
giving in, with proper planning and in the right context, such a
move could otherwise be the beginning of an interactive pattern
in which conflict is minimal or absent.

- **Determine whether the conflict can be resolved**
  Conflict resolution is often determined by each party's motivation to resolve the conflict, as well as beliefs about whether the
  conflict can be resolved and an understanding of the other's position. Your motivation to pursue resolution will be heavily influ-

enced by your perceptions of the *costs* associated with resolving the conflict measured against the *benefits* of doing so.

Some people find the stress of conflict or confrontation overwhelming or unbearable. These individuals are highly motivated to resolve conflict by making concessions because the reward of lifting the conflict burden usually (for them) far outweighs the oppressive feeling of being in conflict. In such cases, the desire for relief from pressure trumps the immediate benefit of winning.

Others have a high tolerance for conflict and disagreement. They are willing to wait things out or even live with the conflict unless it is settled on their terms. Such response can evolve from highly valued principles, temperament, stubbornness, or the ability to weather ambiguity or indecision.

A smart response to conflict is to habitually analyze and weigh the costs and benefits of continuing or resolving the conflict. It is even smarter to tally these columns on your opponent's side, too (to the extent you can conjecture). Armed with this information, you are in a better position to persuade your adversary of the benefits (to him) of settling the dispute.

Incidentally, a similar process holds true for internal conflicts as well. When you have an internal conflict, you have a divided mind. You represent both sides of your mind. In this case, you are negotiating internally, but the principles are essentially the same: assess the costs and benefits for each side, and appeal to the other side for willingness to settle based on described advantages.

- **Evaluate and highlight the benefits of resolving conflict with your opponent versus the costs of continuing it**
  Along with desire, one of the strongest motivators in human behavior is having or perceiving a vested interest in something. Often, perceived value is heightened by competition. Pride often factors into the assessment of value and the dedication to prevail. These factors can blend into a compelling desire to win, and the desire is often about *being right*. You have heard, no doubt, "It's the principle that drives me." (A canny attorney once told me, "When someone says it's the principle he's interested in, it may be the principal or the interest, but it's really about the money.") Some people are, in fact, truly motivated by principles and

integrity. However, in the practical world (which also runs under God's principles and omnipresence), the cost of being right can trounce the end reward. As the saying goes, you can win the battle, but lose the war.

As anyone who has been involved in a lawsuit can attest, prolonged conflict can become quite costly, and because of this reality, legal conflicts are often resolved through settlement. Even the most virtuous souls may find wisdom in cutting their losses.

Nature helps animals survive by showing displays of strength, size, and grandeur in order to intimidate potential predators and ward away attacks. An inflated display makes opponents evaluate the risks of engagement. People behave similarly. A show of strength or the presentation of a good case will make your opponent think twice, and it may serve to deescalate the conflict. *My muscles are bigger than your muscles* has and always will be a popular method of getting the other guy to back down, give in, or go away.

However, this strategy need not be aggressive or threatening; it can be logical, or even mathematical. Showing your opponent the costs to him of continuing the conflict—even to the point of his victory—is a powerfully persuasive tactic.

This tactic is equally true and useful when applied to your own internal battles. Deciding upon a course of action that will end a conflict may be smart and economical. To recognize and highlight this value is tremendously enlightening and strengthening. It is a source of personal empowerment to pull up stakes when you figure out that continuing the conflict will result in a lose-lose situation. Your opponent may or may not appreciate this revelation. Anyone who has contested a divorce understands this.

Knowing that you can sustain conflict, yet choosing not to because it makes more sense to end it is a stride toward true independence and living more intact.

- ## Acknowledgment of cause-and-effect
  The principles of cause-and-effect operate on every level of human endeavor. Ideally, we teach these principles to our children, and their assimilation of the doctrines can profoundly affect whether or not they are able to live intact lives. In addition to the reality-

based concepts of consequences as they relate to survival, there are additional levels that relate to ethics and morality. God wants us to recognize that goodness produces predictable effects. So, too, does evil. Following your principles will sometimes result in conflict because of the opposition of good and evil and because people can and do have antagonistic interests and principles.

Standing up for what is right may make you unpopular. You may have experienced this in grade school, where a report of cheating or bullying results in unpopularity or retribution. Politicians or community leaders may sacrifice reelection because they championed a principled cause.

- **Unforeseen effect to attributed cause**
  Sometimes unanticipated consequences happen, even to those who think strategically and make it a practice to deliberately consider cause-and-effect before they act. For example, you may pursue an investment or business dealing, only to be surprised at undisclosed costs, unforeseen complications, or unexpected duplicitous actions on the part of others. In such situations, conflicts you never saw coming are thrust upon you. The decision to resolve, contest, or live with the new developments require that you make choices.

- **Consequences and righteous conflict**
  Though unanticipated developments may invoke unforeseen conflict, there are times when you may decide to act, knowing full well that your position will result in conflict. Standing up to neighborhood drug dealers, embarking on a dangerous war mission, even challenging your child's objections to rules or sanction will often result in opposition, negative consequences, or hardship for you. Taking a stand will propel you into the storm on the wings of your principles, beliefs, and the unwavering commitment to your character.

- **Character**
  Remember that choice is the continuing act of being you. Your choices are the mechanism by which you develop and establish your character, the set of qualities that identify and distinguish

you. Choosing to distinguish your desires, beliefs, motivations, and commitments will necessarily create some conflict because you are differentiating yourself from whatever would chip away at or obliterate your character.

Conflict can result when your character is challenged. Free will allows for opposition and the challenging of boundaries. You get to choose what constitutes your boundaries and the composition of your character.

- **Self-Interest**
  Even those with outstanding character will encounter a certain amount of conflict. In the natural order, there is competition for survival at every level. Self-interest helps us survive and thrive, but it also forms the foundation for conflict. Even in a nonadversarial context, self-interest presents continual conflicts. The merchant who wants to sell you products is not responsible for how you budget your purchases. The temptations of calories and ways to spend our time and money can conflict with responsible limitations and choices.

THE ROLE OF CONFLICT

Conflict occurs in the material and the spiritual realms. It is a testing ground for the ability to handle challenges and for the development of character. Conflict is essential in helping us to establish boundaries, define who we are, and seek truth and justice. Conflict is also an opportunity to think critically and strategically, exercise compassion and self-control, and to develop a more practical and godly manner of living intact. As an integral part of God's design, conflict is, in the final analysis, part and parcel of being human. How you handle life's conflicts is a key measure of your capacity to live within God's design and to live intact.

CHAPTER 15
ANGER AND HURT

Living intact entails your being able to handle vulnerability and bro-kenness. This book has already provided you with powerful tools for doing so, but there remain critically important elements that must be addressed.

God has woven into the fabric of the human condition a range of behaviors and emotions that are linked to physical survival, protection against threat, connectedness with others, and making sense of our life experiences.

Anger and hurt are integral parts of this cloth. Understanding the dynamics of the interrelationship of these two components and develop-ing our capacity to manage, integrate, and eliminate the associated pain significantly enhances the likelihood of our being able to live a more intact life.

WHAT IS ANGER?

Anger is a reactive feeling of displeasure, hostility, or indignation that results from a real or imagined threat, insult, frustration, or injustice that are directed at you or at others who are important to you. This neurologi-cal and emotional response correlates with a powerful stimulation of the nervous system and specifically with an overarousal of the cingulate gyrus and amygdala.[35]

---

35. The cingulate gyrus and the amygdala are brain structures located deep within the brain. The cingulate gyrus is associated with focus, hyperfocus, and obsessive thinking. The amygdala is thought by many scientists to be the seat of emotional response.

Although anger is a natural biological response, this emotion can be triggered inappropriately and can become a habitual reaction that is both maladaptive and counterproductive. This chronic anger must clearly be addressed because it can erect formidable roadblocks to living harmoniously.

TYPES OF ANGER

There are essentially four types of anger. These four types—each oriented toward a different goal and serving a different purpose—are as follows:

1. **Threat to survival anger**—The function of this instinctual physiological or mental response to danger or perceived threats is to protect against death, injury, or harm (including psychological harm and insult). The stimuli that elicit threat to survival anger may be either *actual or imagined*.
2. **Hurt anger**—The function of this physical or psychological response is to express upset, offer protection, and mask vulnerabilities.
3. **Manipulative anger**—The function of this habitual psychological response is to get one's way, control another for selfish ends, or modify someone else's behavior through fear and intimidation.
4. **Righteous injustice anger**—The function of this response typically involves less physiological arousal than the other types of anger. The response reflects a mix of cognitive and emotional displeasure regarding specific events or conditions perceived as unfair or oppressive, according to a set of values. It is usually a more controlled anger, and its objective is to seek justice and righteousness.

RELATIONSHIP BETWEEN ANGER AND HURT

Recognizing that anger is a primal response that arises when danger is sensed and understanding that anger establishes distance and serves to keep danger at bay allows us to get a better handle on this all-too-common reaction. As previously stated, anger is a natural and sometimes useful mechanism that is subconsciously designed to hide weakness and camouflage vulnerability. Responding aggressively and with hostility can disguise a wide spectrum of wounds and pain. Becoming angry is tantamount to saying, "I'm hurt, ashamed, threatened, exposed, or vulnerable, and I don't want to expose my weaknesses and helplessness."

Unfortunately, the camouflage can also be self-deceiving and so effective that many people fail to realize how entwined their own anger is with the hurt or vulnerability they are experiencing. Anger serves as a defense that shields the outside world from seeing that you are emotionally at risk. It is also serves to protect and insulate you from having to confront your susceptibility, injury, insecurity, and/or fears.

ANGER AS AN ALARM SYSTEM

When you become angry, your nervous system enters fight-or-flight mode. You become highly aroused, defensive, and reactive to whatever you perceive is a threat to you. Your heart rate increases and you are stressed. Because anger focuses the mind on danger, frustration, or pain, your mental flexibility and rational problem-solving abilities are imperiled. Blood pressure may increase, activity in the front of the brain tends to activate, and heightened aggressive responses may occur.

As these physiological changes occur, the narrative tries to interpret what is happening, both to clarify the situation and to send signals sustaining the physiological response as an aid to coping and surviving. Essentially, an alarm system within the body signals that your security is compromised and alerts you that danger could be imminent.

This alarm system is clearly useful in the face of actual threat or attack; it helps to activate and mobilize resources to resist or avoid the threat. However, the anger can persist long after the threat has vanished or has been explained and/or neutralized. This "state of alarm" taxes the body's resources and depletes energy and attention needed for other tasks. It also establishes an imbalance in self-regulation that, if maintained for extended periods, tricks the body and mind into accepting this heightened arousal as the default mode. Protracted anger is, thus, disruptive and unhealthy.

ANGER AS A HABIT

When anger is provoked and sustained as a frequent response to frustrating or threatening situations, it can become a habit. Though it may arise as a function of instinct and adrenal response, the surges and continuation of anger are maintained under operant conditions and schedules of reinforcement (see chapters 5 and 6). The person who is habitually angry typically does not *like* to be angry; he or she just becomes angry "automatically" with seemingly little or no provocation. Such people are often described as having a "temper" or a "short fuse." People who have to deal with such individuals can feel as though they are "walking on eggshells" in trying not to upset or incite them. It is an uncomfortable way to live and it is antithetical to living intact.

Habitual anger and protracted hostility often derive from nervous system and brain irritability; in most cases, the brain is overaroused and highly sensitized. This pattern of anger responds very well to training with EEG neurofeedback (see chapter 9). Neurofeedback calms the brain and emotions, so people no longer feel so easily offended or provoked.

Parents often bring their children to me and describe them as angry. Typically, these children are sullen, oppositional, moody, and can be aggressive or explosive over little things when they don't want to do something or they don't get their way. Parents implore me to "find out what's making my child so angry." More often than not, I find that there is no traumatic incident, no grudge, no abuse or mistreatment. Rather, I usually conclude that the child has nervous system issues that can be successfully and rapidly treated by training the brain with EEG neurofeedback. Undoubtedly, there could be significant incidents in the child's history or a set of circumstances that are the source of grudges and resentments producing an angry disposition. And certainly, poor diet or lack of sleep can contribute to being cranky and out of sorts, as can side effects of drugs and withdrawal. The suspected deep, subconscious, perhaps mysterious psychological reason for the anger often turns out to be a manifestation of and justification for an overreactive brain. *The solution is to deal with the brain in the present context and not as the residual byproduct of past experiences.*

As a culture, we have been indoctrinated by the pervasive influence of Sigmund Freud, Carl Jung, and others to believe in the power of the subconscious and the role of early experiences as determinants of behavior and disposition.[36] People tend to think that intractable anger has deep-seated psychological roots that can only (or best) be sorted out through verbal or physical catharsis (e.g., extended talk therapy, punching pillows, role-playing drama, etc.). I have found that these methods do not work well—in fact, they tend to reinforce anger, rather than do away with it.

A secondary reinforcing issue in the case of habitual anger is the effectiveness of the narrative in justifying anger. The physiology of anger and its cognitive correlates are intertwined. This entwinement is also endemic to many emotions and attitudes. The anger response, however, is fueled by adrenaline, which launches the nervous system into fight-or-flight mode. The brain receives status signals that shout, "High alert—Danger!" These signals need some interpretation and explanation, particularly when there is no immediate discernible danger. So the mind *invents* explanations, usually in the form of rationalizing the anger as a "have-to" response to conditions induced by someone or something else. In effect, the habitually angry person says, "Of course I'm angry. What did you expect? I have to be angry because so-and-so..." This self-deception serves to alienate people and to keep the angry individual from recognizing that his response is physiologically programmed, mentally rationalized, spiritually destructive, pragmatically counterproductive, and severely limiting in the exercise of flexibility and choice.

Once the appropriate interventions are implemented to decelerate the habitual fight-or-flight response, behavior modification can significantly help in changing the "pay-off" values of browbeating others through anger (again, see chapters 5 and 6). As you might expect, people who have gotten their way through intimidation must learn new ways of negotiation, compromise, sacrifice, social skills, and evaluation in order to effectuate goal-oriented behaviors with sensitivity and patience.

TURNING OFF THE ALARM

The notion of anger as an alarm system deserves further attention. It is useful and often necessary to terminate anger in the moment. When it gets out of hand, anger can be very destructive, causing disruption, transgressions of social decorum and societal rules, and even injury. The

---

36. For more on this, see chapter 8: the section on Traditional Theories about Wholeness.

consequences of unbridled outbursts can have long-term effects that are likely to lead to confrontations with the criminal justice system, social alienation, and the destruction of careers, relationships, and reputations.

From our experiences in life, we recognize that it is prudent to refrain from further inflaming an angry person. This and other strategic cause-and-effect realizations comprise what is referred to as common sense. In fact, many people are taught the skills for calming others through professional or business training. Customer service representatives usually receive training in how to deal with frustrated or irate customers. Law enforcement professionals and crises negotiators also receive similar albeit more intensive training. They are taught to handle explosive interpersonal confrontations by speaking gently and patiently and without getting irritated and exasperated.

A gentle answer turns away wrath, but a harsh word stirs up anger. (Proverbs 15:1)

But what if you had a "magic bullet" that could immediately defuse anger? Indeed, there is such a remedy: Thought Field Therapy—the tapping solution. You can turn off the alarm that triggers your anger within a few minutes by employing the tapping procedures. The self-help algorithms can be especially effective (see appendix C).

There is a secret, however, that you must be aware of in order to make this resource work: you have to understand the nature of your *own* anger, and you must recognize that when you are riled up, there is a tendency to become self-righteous, prideful, self-justified, and determined to unleash your anger. You can combat this instinct by methodically intervening with tapping, all the while ignoring thoughts you may have about how silly the procedure is and rationalizing how your anger is appropriate and justifiable.

In order to succeed with turning off the alarm through tapping, you must do two things:

1. Determine that no matter how good or right it feels, the anger is not useful or appropriate, and you would definitely be better off without it
2. Discipline yourself to practice and implement the TFT algorithms as soon as you recognize that anger is overtaking you (and

be sure to tap on the side of the hand and under the nose to correct reversals, as outlined in the TFT procedures (see chapter 10 and appendix C)

The nature of anger is that it is self-righteous, can become addictive, and tends to accelerate and intensify in response to the defenses or overtures it elicits and provokes. Telling someone to calm down is at least as likely to inflame the angry person as to calm him.

When I am dealing with angry people, I ask them if they would like to not be angry and if they believe that this could be more beneficial for them and produce better results.[37] If they assent, I treat them with TFT (usually Voice Technology). As an incentive, I say that I will listen to them as long as they want to talk—*after* I treat them with tapping. Of course, the need to vent incessantly vanishes after successful treatment, paving the way for intelligent, rational, productive discussion. They discover that they can, in fact, proceed with life minus the baggage of anger.

Imagine the healing and social cooperation that could ensue if people worldwide would employ these methods to calm down. Many feuds and wars could be averted if people would disembark from the carousel of anger. How much hate and racism is triggered and perpetuated because people become provoked and then habitually seek justification for their emotions and prejudices!

Pride can be a wicked force when it tricks us (through the narrative) into believing we are right and justified and uses our vulnerability and physiology to make us resist peace and calming. We have tools to help us through this dilemma that can help us overcome our weakness. But ultimately, free will and the choice to apply these tools is pivotal in the equation.

SPIRITUAL ASPECTS OF ANGER

Thus far, we have discussed anger from a neurophysiological perspective. Of course, anger, like so many issues in life, has spiritual roots as well.

---

37. This works better when the person is not directly angry with me, and it also tends to be easier to do in my professional capacity. However, the TFT technique works, and if you can get past the pride and defensive surliness of anger, it will work for you, both on yourself and on others.

øTake Pride ɜnAnger

God becomes angry, too. He is a God of feelings, including angry feelings, so we can relate to him. After all, we are made in his image (Genesis 1:26–27; 9:6). The Bible is full of references to anger (at least 580), and it emphasizes God's jealousy, hurt, and disappointment when man puts other gods and idols before him.

But God's anger is not sin, nor is it derived from sin. Rather, God's anger is a righteous anger. It is in response to injustice, of man's inhumanity to man, and of man's disobedience to God. It is an anger that comes from love, righteousness, and disappointment with willful separation, rather than from bitterness, resentment, or entitlement. Because God is holy and has created a just universe, he is grieved when man turns away from him. Through anger, God lets man know that God is sovereign, powerful, and right and just. But even God does not stay angry. He is a forgiving deity, even though he is always right and legitimate.

In the Old Testament, the book of Hosea recounts the touching story of God's steadfast love for Israel despite Israel's unfaithfulness. The story is told through the prophet Hosea, whose wife, Gomer, was unfaithful. Through this story, God compares Israel's turning to other gods to marital infidelity, as exemplified in the case of the adultery of Hosea's wife. God threatens and indicts Israel, but then restores her.

"Rebuke your mother, rebuke her, for she is not my wife, and I am not her husband. Let her remove the adulterous look from her face and the unfaithfulness from between her breasts. Otherwise I will strip her naked and make her as bare as on the day she was born; I will make her like a desert, and turn her into a parched land, and slay her with thirst. I will not show my love to her children, because they are the children of adultery. Their mother has been unfaithful and conceived them in disgrace. She said, 'I will go after my lovers, who give me my food and my water, my wool and my linen, my oil and my drink.' Therefore I will block her path with thornbushes; I will wall her in so that she cannot find her way." (Hosea 2:2–6)

"I will betroth you to me forever; I will betroth you in righteousness and justice, in love and compassion. I will betroth you in faithfulness, and you will acknowledge the Lord. In that day I will respond," declares the Lord—"I will respond to the skies, and they will respond to the earth;

and the earth will respond to the grain, and the new wine and oil, and they will respond to Jezreel. I will plant her for myself in the land; I will show my love to the one I called 'Not my loved one.' I will say to those called 'Not my people,' 'You are my people'; and they will say, 'You are my God.'" (Hosea 2:19–23)

"How can I give you up, Ephraim? How can I hand you over, Israel? How can I treat you like Admah? How can I make you like Zebolim? My heart is changed within me; all my compassion is aroused. I will not carry out my fierce anger, nor will I turn and devastate Ephraim. For I am God, and not man—the Holy One among you. I will not come in wrath." (Hosea 11:8–9)

This passage clearly provokes readers to search within and ask themselves, "Would I be angry if my partner was repeatedly unfaithful? Could I forgive, as God did and does?"

The righteous anger that characterizes God's response is also a part of human experience. When there is injustice—a child is raped or killed, a population is oppressed, a perpetrator is exonerated on a technicality—it is natural to feel angry and affronted. But you should not take pride in this response (for this is self-righteousness), and you should not continue to let the anger fester. Listen, again, to the Lord:

"In your anger, do not sin: Do not let the sun go down while you are still angry, and do not give the devil a foothold." (Ephesians 4:26–27)

Do not repay anyone evil for evil. Be careful to do what is right in the eyes of everybody. If it is possible, as far as it depends on you, live at peace with everyone. Do not take revenge, my friends, but leave room for God's wrath, for it is written: "It is mine to avenge; I will repay," says the Lord. On the contrary: "If your enemy is hungry, feed him; if he is thirsty, give him something to drink. In doing this, you will heap burning coals on his head." Do not be overcome by evil, but overcome evil with good. (Romans 12:17–21)

We see, then, that anger—though natural—can be overextended, habitual, and destructive. Anger blocks God's blessings. Anger is detrimental to your health, and it interferes with your freedom. Anger is like a waste product: it must be discharged, lest it contaminate healthy and intact living.

GETTING RID OF ANGER

Rather than wait for the intensity of anger to subside, or to live with a seething temperament, defensiveness, and readiness to erupt at provocations or injustices (actual or perceived), it is far better to eliminate the anger. This does not mean repressing it, smothering it, pretending it's not there, or not acknowledging it. It does not mean that you shouldn't verbalize your anger. It *does* mean, however, that you don't dwell on it or nurture it.

Here are the steps for dealing with and eliminating your own anger:

1. **Recognize that in most cases, anger is a response to hurt.**

    When you come to see anger as a protection and masquerade for hurt and vulnerability, you will turn your energies toward healing and becoming more intact, rather than taking out your frustrations insensitively. This self-awareness will heighten your social keenness, empathy, and ability to come before God in reliance on him and with expectations of his help and healing.

2. **Ask if the anger is serving a useful purpose and, if so, what are the costs and side effects of using anger to achieve that purpose.**

    Though it may feel good (and justified) to be angry, when you list the drawbacks of anger, you will notice that the cost almost always outweighs the benefits. If you can objectively (and this may take some assistance) analyze how effective anger is in contributing your desired outcomes, you will be surprised to discover, time after time, that anger gets in the way, rather than facilitates attaining your objectives.

    Once you decide that anger is not useful, you are more enlightened and you can choose to confront and evaluate the possibilities for actually ridding yourself of the anger. You will have more clarity and greater incentive to do so.

3. **Review honestly what you believe to be the trigger for or object of your anger; ask yourself whether you believe and**

feel that the person who caused you this difficulty intended to hurt or malign you.

If this is how you feel and how you see things, then you need to address your anger at this person and the circumstances surrounding the perpetration. If you conclude that the action triggering your anger was unintentional, then you may want to address the hurt as the most significant culprit.

When dealing with someone who is narrowly focused on being the recipient or victim of an inconsiderate act, I always ask the questions, "Is there any *other* plausible explanation or interpretation for what happened? Is it *possible* that the person you are angry at did *not intend* what occurred to hurt or slight you?"

It's fairly unreasonable (even when riled up, but especially afterward) to deny that it is impossible for any other explanation or interpretation to exist. After all, the object of the anger would likely have a differing view. Also, just by asking the question, you are implying that you might have an alternative explanation for the intent. This strategy opens the door to objectivity, the use of reason, and a consideration of your owning the anger instead of blaming it externally.

A good example of how this works is the case of my patient, Jeff. As a middle-aged professional, Jeff was very successful in business and very involved with his family. But Jeff was obsessed with and distracted by his perfectionism and his fear of making mistakes and being rejected and humiliated. According to Jeff, he struggled for years with procrastination that he attributed to fear of failure. Though Jeff responded quickly and successfully to Voice Technology (his anger and other negative emotions disappeared completely within a few minutes), he had some residual concerns that events in his childhood were responsible for this interference in his adult life.

As I listened to Jeff, he explained that his father was a harsh and punitive man. As a result, Jeff developed an intense fear of and anger at his father. Before treating Jeff for his anger, I asked him if he thought his father meant to alienate and hurt him. Somewhat surprised by my question, Jeff reflected and assured me (and himself) that his father was actually loving, and meant the best; he was just "that way," not realizing the collateral damage his manner and actions inflicted.

Once Jeff understood that the damage caused by his father was inadvertent and not committed intentionally, he was able to address the real issue: *hurt*. A few minutes of targeted tapping (while tuning the relevant thought fields around hurt) quickly relieved Jeff of his misconstrued "anger" at his father. The results have endured.

4. **Review the obstacles to overcoming anger.**
   a) not wanting to get rid of anger
   b) rehearsing whatever happened and the justification for being angry (this is a hindrance, since it reinforces the anger)
   c) pride
   d) fear of showing weakness or vulnerability
   e) rationalization of being misunderstood
   f) belief that external circumstances or people are responsible negative advice
   g) inability to forgive

If necessary, sort through these barriers, one by one, until you run out of excuses. Consider that overcoming anger is a choice, and reflect upon the opportunities you have to make choices about how to handle anger in a way that edifies your character. It is a way of implementing secret #5: *Embrace challenge as the way to turn obstacles and frustrations into opportunities and successes.* (Refer back to chapter 8.)

5. **Administer the TFT tapping procedures.**
   Use the TFT algorithms as soon as you recognize that anger is overtaking you (and be sure to tap on the side of the hand and under the nose to correct reversals, as outlined in the TFT procedures in chapter 10 and appendix C).

   Most people are amazed at how effective TFT is for anger—even anger that has burned or simmered for years. Many cases of anger are reactions to trauma; often, getting rid of trauma or anger for good requires only a single treatment. Self-treatments are not always as effective as professionally administered treatments (since many professionals use advanced diagnostic techniques to determine precise sequences of tapping points.) But they frequently work quite well. (If you do not experience relief with the self-treatment algorithms, seek help with a professional trained in TFT.)

6. **Ask God for help in freeing you from anger and healing your hurts.**

7. **Thank God for freeing you from the shackles of anger and for providing solace and comfort.**

8. **Pray for the welfare and godliness of the person with whom you were angry.**

9. **If the anger persists over time, consider seeking treatment with EEG neurofeedback to train your brain and nervous system to stay calm in the face of provocation.**

DEALING WITH ANGER IN OTHERS

There is a saying: *Hell hath no fury like a woman scorned.* Perhaps this is sage advice. However, the truth is that you will encounter anger and fury even in the absence of doing anything to provoke it. How, then, can you effectively deal with an angry person in a godly and effective manner?

Here are some tips for dealing with anger in others:

1. **Recognize that the angry person probably feels hurt or threatened.**

    By connecting angry displays with the underlying feelings (even as you remain a target of invective, threats, or aggression), you are more likely to stay calm and not become inflammatory.

2. **Tell yourself that people who are hurting need understanding and compassion.**

    Even as you are weathering an angry assault, come from a place in your heart of acceptance and soothing. Imagine a child who gets injured and begins to wail and fight because of the fear and pain. This is what much of anger represents.

3. **Acknowledge the anger and share your sympathy.**

    It helps to "get" the angry person's vehemence without being sanctimonious or indulgent. A concise verbal acknowledgment will usually slow down the tirade. "I do understand that you are angry. I'm sure you have good reason to be angry.[38] Is there anything I can do right now to make things better?"

4. **Validate the concern and suggest that you are not the enemy.**
"I realize that you have a grievance, but I'm not in a position to make restitution. Maybe there is a better outlet to help you get relief."

5. **Accept responsibility if you are culpable. Clarify your intent.**
"You are justified to be angry with me. I didn't do (whatever the person is angry about) to hurt or cross you. Perhaps I didn't take into consideration how upset you would become, and for that I'm sorry."

6. **Set limits on insulting, aggressive or abusive behavior.**
"I do sympathize with your upset feelings. However, I will not be a punching bag. You got your point across. I would like us to be respectful of each other, and I insist upon it. Please talk to me in a lower voice, or I will end this conversation."

7. **Offer the angry person a method of releasing the anger more appropriately.**
The best way would be to do TFT tapping. However, rarely are people receptive to that idea in the heat of the moment. Make some suggestions and bargain for time. If appropriate in the situation, you might say, "Perhaps you need a few moments to yourself. If you still feel upset later, I can show you how to do some self-soothing *after which* I will listen to you again at length."

8. **Allow the distress and anger of others to evoke compassion and prayer on your part.**
Be thankful that you have learned about the deceptive and custodial nature of anger. Reflect upon how difficult it must be to live with the anger someone has shown to you, especially on a chronic basis. Praise God for your awareness and understanding, and thank him for leading you out of the darkness. Pray that God might shed light and comfort on those who are angry.

9. **Treat yourself with TFT tapping to calm your reactions to an angry person.**

---

38. The good reason is actually the intense secretion of adrenaline! Notice how you can, with a simple, almost cryptic statement, acknowledge the person's upset and provide sympathy without committing yourself to sharing his point of view.

You will be pleasantly surprised at the calmness and self-control that treating yourself will help you maintain.

Living intact requires that you learn coping mechanisms to recover from brokenness. Lashing out at others, harboring bitterness, rage, or resentment are counterproductive detours. God understands your pain, and he will provide comfort if you earnestly ask him. Frequent anger is a protective veneer that alienates you from people and from God. Capitulating to this emotion is tantamount to enslavement.

There are better ways to deal with anger than to nurture it or vent it upon others. In the following chapter, you will learn how to use the gift of forgiveness toward this end.

My dear brothers, take note of this: Everyone should be quick to listen, slow to speak, and slow to become angry, for man's anger does not bring about the righteous life that God desires. (James 1:19–20)

Refrain from anger and turn from wrath; do not fret—it leads only to evil. (Psalm 37:8)

An angry man stirs up dissension, and a hot-tempered one commits many sins. (Proverbs 29:22)

"Come to me, all you who are weary and burdened, and I will give you rest. Take my yoke upon you and learn from me, for I am gentle and humble in heart, and you will find rest for your souls. For my yoke is easy and my burden is light." (Matthew 11:28–30)

CHAPTER 16
GUILT AND FORGIVENESS

We live in a world governed by rules, procedures, and laws. In addition to the laws of nature, there are the laws of man and the laws of God. Failure to heed the laws of nature can have dire consequences.[39] Breaking the laws of man (such as civil and criminal codes of conduct) can bring sanctions and penalties. And disobedience to God's laws (as revealed by his Word, the Bible) results in sin and its attendant outcomes (guilt, separation from God, brokenness.)

Guilt without forgiveness demands payment. Sadly, most of us are more familiar with guilt than with forgiveness.

Every society and every culture has boundaries and taboos. These are established to facilitate the peaceful and productive functioning of communities, protect their inhabitants, protect property and people, and preserve traditions and the sanctity of life. Sometimes, we may seemingly "get away" with transgressions, escape external consequences, and transcend internal conflict, but, in the end, there are three judges to whom we must sooner or later answer: God (and his natural laws), society's laws, and our conscience.

All who sin apart from the law will also perish apart from the law, and all who sin under the law will be judged by the law. (Romans 2:12)

---

39. Consider the saying, "Gravity doesn't care."

The sins of some men are obvious, reaching the place of judgment ahead of them; the sins of others trail behind them. In the same way, good deeds are obvious, and even those that are nt cannot be hidden. (1 Timothy 5:24–25)

Living intact requires regulating a balance among states of mind and conditions that are based on the tangible facts that constitute reality. If we are to live responsibly in the world that *is*, rather than in an illusory world designed to conform to and perpetuate our comfort level, we must inevitably deal with boundaries, violations, and consequences. This accountability creates the context for having to pay the piper at some point and to experience guilt.

GUILT AS A DUALITY

Guilt is an actuality, and it is also a state of mind.

> *As an actuality, guilt is the fact or occurrence of doing something wrong. It is a violation or transgression of boundaries or rules.*
>
> *As a state of mind, guilt is an awareness of having done, wanting to do, or thinking about doing something wrong—that is, violation or transgression of boundaries or rules. Guilt, is typically accompanied by feelings of shame and regret.*

To be guilty is to have done something wrong, transgressed a boundary, or violated a rule or law. Guilt is contingent upon our being able to differentiate objectively right from wrong. You can be guilty of breaking the law, cheating at a game or in a relationship, and even of violating your self-imposed limits. In a world of relativity—where "you do your thing and I do mine"—there can be no guilt because guilt depends upon absolutes: clearly defined parameters of what is allowed and what is not allowed. In practice, guilt is determined by subjection to an accepted standard: a law, a rule, or a commonly accepted standard.

As a state of mind or an emotion (more aptly, a state of *heart*), guilt may or may not be aligned with a judgment of culpability that is rendered based upon the facts and evidence. You can also *feel* guilty, irrespective of the facts and evidence and irrespective of whether or not others see or agree with your perceptions of events that have transpired.[40]

We are reminded at every turn of sanctions and prohibitions, instructions, and guidelines: *obey the speed limit, do your work, pay what you owe, leash your dog, recycle, use less gas and electric, eat healthier foods,* and so forth. If we disobey the rules, we may suffer from the criticism of others and from pangs of conscience triggered by our inner narrative.

Guilt can be a double-sided blade. When we experience it, we are often distressed not only by the negative feeling, but also by the guilt associated with believing that we deserve to experience negative emotions because of our "evilness." Moreover, we can also be burdened by the guilt of having to struggle with and obsess about our own tendencies to have negative thoughts.

GUILT AS A NEGATIVE EMOTION

Guilt comprises an issue that can pose a major obstacle to living intact. It ranks high on a list of insidious negative emotions that can rob us of peace of mind and wellness.

As is the case with other negative emotions, guilt is an unpleasant state of mind, and it can be linked to arousal states influenced by perceptions, imagination, or associations with previous experiences. If these arousal states are maintained inappropriately or for extended periods, they can seriously impair our capacity to enjoy life.

That all negative emotions can have a direct impact on behavior is indisputable. The emotions of anger and fear are two of the most notable examples. Anger can cause us to lash out, and fear can make us withdraw or flee. Though feelings are by nature subjective, they are often rooted in the real world. We are supposed to be afraid when threatened by a gunman, and we will naturally feel embarrassed if we find ourselves in a position that robs us of respect or dignity. In such cases, negative emotions are helpful *temporary* motivations that provide impetus to repair or exit from a threatening or damaging situation. When the threatening stimulus disappears, the negative emotion usually does, too. (Of course, traumas and phobias are notable exceptions.)

---

40. God, of course, sees everything that goes on, including your feelings, though he may not agree with you about them.

Guilt, however, is different from other negative emotions in that it can be a *condition* as well as a *feeling*. You can be fearful or sad for good "reason," but you only *feel* that way. You can *be guilty* of a transgression by applying objective standards regardless of whether or not you actually feel guilty. To make matters more confusing, you can *feel* guilty without actually *being guilty*! Here we have a complicated interrelationship where the feeling of guilt can be related to or independent of an objective condition.

Living intact requires maintaining connections with and responding to reality, not the world of wishes and greater expectations (see chapter 11). Therefore, it is important to distinguish between *true guilt* and *false guilt* (see below).

GUILTY? IT DEPENDS

As previously stated, the concept of guilt is one that necessarily depends upon the standards of right and wrong. Guilt involves a violation or transgression of an accepted or imposed societal boundary that delineates right from wrong. When you cross that boundary, you are guilty. The frame of reference clearly matters. What or who establishes the boundary? Certainly, governmental laws that comprise standards by which guilt can be determined apply to everyone. Acknowledgment of a standard does not imply agreement with or approval of that standard—it simply serves to demarcate a boundary that separates guilt from innocence.

For example, I live near a park where I like to exercise my dogs. My dogs like to run, and so I often let them off the leash. They are well trained, and I am respectful of other people's territory and privacy, as well as the social conventions of city life. However, there is a city ordinance (clearly posted) that all dogs must be leashed in the park. I don't like this city ordinance, although I realize it also applies to me and my dogs. Usually, I "get away" with violating this ordinance, justifying to myself all the while that it is really okay to let my dogs run, as long as they are not bothering anyone. As you might expect, however, occasionally there are people in the park who object to my dogs (on or off the leash). As these objecting people run from my dogs or yell at me, I hurry to leash my dogs. My inner narrative denounces them for being unreasonable, angry, dog-phobic, etc., even as I smile or apologize. Fact is, though, I am guilty of violating the city ordinance—whether or not I am caught, called on it, or no one notices. My guilt depends upon violating the law, not upon how I feel.[41] I had no say in making this law, though I am civic enough to have a strong opinion about it.[42]

THE ROLE OF CONSCIENCE

The feeling of guilt is an awareness of having done something wrong or committed a transgression, accompanied by a feeling of shame and regret.

So, what does it mean to feel guilty?

Whether or not a guilty feeling corresponds to a transgression, a guilty feeling always relates to the emergence of *conscience*—the internal sense of right and wrong influencing thoughts, feelings, and actions, and urging you to do right rather than wrong. Your conscience is the compass that directs your narrative to make you feel guilty.

Though some believe otherwise, the Christian view is that everyone is born with a conscience, just as everyone is born with a heart. A conscience is God's voice inside you, guiding you (and your narrative) in his ways, the true ways of right instead of wrong. Unfortunately, the reminding voice of conscience can be quieted, corrupted, or even extinguished, and your moral compass can be flawed so as to give false readings until you become dangerously lost. This can happen as a result of deliberate and repeated willful rebellion or through the dulling and warping of one's thinking through substance abuse or corrupting human influences. It also can occur through developmental neglect, whereby the neurological mechanisms for self-soothing do not develop properly, leaving the brain with an impaired or limited capacity for empathy or compassion.[43]

---

41. I feel fine about letting my dogs off the leash. Interestingly, I don't *feel* guilty, even though I know I am violating a law. I feel uncomfortable, embarrassed, even self-pitying on occasion when some dog-phobic person snarls at me for running my dogs off the leash. This conundrum trouble me because my dogs do need to run somewhere, I live in a city, and I need to be considerate and respectful of other people, even the difficult ones. I do feel guilty about not feeling guilty about violating this city ordinance!

42. Before you smugly judge me, consider your own attitudes, behaviors, and inner narratives with respect to speeding, jaywalking, and other minor violations you may have committed.

43. There is a psychological disorder called Reactive Attachment Disorder in which the failure to develop the capacity for compassion and empathy is thought to arise from maternal neglect or absence during the very early stages of life. This is a common syndrome in children placed in orphanages shortly after birth. EEG neurofeedback is an effective treatment to help such individuals become more emotionally sentient.

Whatever the origin, when the conscience does not perform as God designed, a conspicuous and destructive lack of remorse encourages selfish and dangerous behavior. Extreme examples of this are found in the actions of sociopaths whose antisocial behaviors are marked by crimes with little or no feelings for their victims.

Keeping in mind the conscience as pivotal, let's differentiate between *true* and *false* guilt.

TRUE GUILT AND FALSE GUILT

True guilt is the awareness or existence of a feeling, behavior, or intent related to doing or having done something wrong; it is usually accompanied by a feeling of anxiety, shame, or regret. True guilt is identified by the *conviction* or the *acceptance* that one's actions, feelings, or intentions are *wrong* according to a doctrine of law or truth. True guilt may also be labeled *actual*.

False guilt is the awareness of a feeling, behavior, or intent accompanied by a feeling of anxiety, shame, or regret. False guilt is distinguished from true guilt by its *absence of transgression*—that is, false guilt feels like you have done or *might do* something wrong, even when no actual transgression has been committed. False guilt is not "pretend" because, unlike pretending, false guilt carries no recognition that the feeling and its circumstances are make-believe. They seem real and feel real, though they are not. False guilt may also be labeled *imagined*.

The following matrix compares and contrasts the characteristics of and interrelationships among true and false guilt and their associated feelings:

	True Guilt	False Guilt
Feel Guilty	Violation of law or rule Convicted by conscience Remorse and anxiety	No transgression or wrongdoing Powerlessness and anxiety Habitual compulsion
Do Not Feel Guilty	Violation of law or rule Unaware of transgression Lack of remorse	No transgression or wrongdoing No dissonance Non-issue
Believe You Are Guilty	Recognition of actuality Understanding of reality Guided by reason	Lack of true facts Faulty reasoning False assumptions

GUILTY FEELINGS AND FALSE GUILT

I have often treated patients who are tormented by the sense of guilt over what they have done or think they have done wrong. They review the past, brood and berate themselves, and cannot let go of self-recriminations. Guilty feelings haunt them and they feel trapped. In many cases, these people have not accurately examined the source of their guilty feelings and the foundation for true guilt: doing something wrong.

Why do people become stuck in feelings of false guilt? The phenomenon can be attributed to several factors:

1. Anxiety and the role of the narrative in justifying the feelings
2. Faulty reasoning and false assumptions about causality
3. Lack of factual examination supporting actual transgressions
4. Resignation and hopelessness

Let's examine how each of these can underpin sustained feelings and beliefs about guilt in circumstances without actual wrongdoing.

A good example of unfounded guilt occurs when someone has been molested or otherwise abused physically and/or psychologically. In such cases, the person is, in reality, a victim. However, enduring feelings of false guilt and shame often accompany beliefs about the role the victim has or may have played to elicit or deserve the perpetration.

1. **Anxiety and the role of the narrative in justifying the feelings**
    Victimization precipitates trauma. The nature of trauma is that feelings perseverate (continue in the absence of relevant stimuli) and immobilize victims in the grip of continuing negative emotions. The narrative intervenes and attempts to "explain" the presence of the trauma by linking the gripping feelings to some rationale and to the dynamic of sequential causality.

2. **Faulty reasoning and false assumptions about causality**
    Led by the narrative, the victim assumes that he or she *must* have done something to encourage or facilitate the traumatic event. Perhaps true guilt over past transgressions encroaches, overtaking and contaminating the victim with guilt by associating previous sins and the present traumatic but unrelated event. A person with a guilty conscience may fear punishment and suspect that it has come in the form of the traumatic event. (The fear of God is not equivalent to superstition, whereby irrational interpretation is attributed to unnerving events as a way of explaining them.)

    Or, perhaps the randomness of danger is so odious and overwhelming that the narrative invents explanations to shield against the peril of vulnerability and helplessness. (e.g., "I must have done something to encourage and deserve this or else it could not have possibly happened.")

3. **Lack of factual examination supporting actual transgressions**
    The victim of sexual assault or other abuse often fails to examine and evaluate objectively whether he or she committed some act of wrongdoing that precipitated the perpetration.

    Overwhelmed by the crushing burden of guilty feelings, a victim typically needs assistance to sort out the facts from the reactive feelings. Yet, the nature of guilt is that the associated shame makes people want to keep it private. Acknowledgment is perceived as admission of culpability, and so the bearer of guilty feelings proceeds with no outlet or input to separate feelings and facts from fiction and solid reasoning.

4. **Resignation and hopelessness**
   The persistence of false guilt frequently accompanies and validates other negative feelings and beliefs. When sufferers are without hope, they find explanations for the constraints, whether or not such thinking stands the test of reality.

   Guilty feelings, resignation, and hopelessness form a triad of despair that engender obsessive submission to the tyranny of behavioral compulsions: habits that repeat themselves despite the pain of guilt-ridden victims who feel powerless to break the cycle of their own self-defeating habits.

   This type of false guilt serves as the distracting preoccupation that means, simply: *you are going to do it again.*

HABIT GUILT

There is a false guilt that derives from succumbing to the repetition of undesirable behaviors or habits. This guilt, which masquerades as wrongdoing, is the feeling of inevitability that you will commit the same behavior over and over again—usually against yourself. In effect, you are rationalizing and minimizing the inevitability of negative, counterproductive behavior, as in:

"I'm going to have that dessert, even though I shouldn't."

"I hate to nag you, but..."

"This is extravagant, but I deserve it."

"I really should exercise; however, I'm tired."

"I haven't cleaned the house in weeks. I will get around to cleaning and straightening the house later."

"I should study more."

It makes sense that there can be overlap between the sense of remorse over "guilty pleasures" (e.g., dessert), avoidance, other "shoulds" and "oughts" and actual wrongdoing. The violation of one's own standards and boundaries is certainly cause for concern, as it can impair self-confidence, reliability, and integrity. However, remember that true guilt involves the breaking of an actual law or collectively understood standard. If you break your word when someone is depending on you, or if you break God's word, then indeed you are guilty, and feeling guilty would be appropriate. But if you fail to exercise or keep to your diet as you had hoped, this does not necessarily qualify as guilt (though you may feel justifiable regret).

Feeling guilty over disappointing yourself or even the expectations of others can also serve as an excuse for continuing certain behaviors. Expressing guilt about a recurrent negative self-indulgence can serve as a palliative and a justification for carrying on with habits that are difficult to break. The narrative can be quite adept at protecting you from the impact of failure by admitting to false guilt as a consolation when you fail to meet expectations.[44]

You would be far wiser to employ the tools of living intact to correct undesirable habits than to resort to excuses or minimize the effects by engaging in false habit guilt. (You might want to review chapters 5 and 6.)

GUILT AND TUNA FISH

It is not always clear or easy to determine guilt and to peer through the filters of self-delusion and worldly justification that allow escape, or at least the illusion of it. Many people live without the Word of God as a compass. Their only reference point may be their feelings. They have few valid standards against which to judge transgression. In their attempts to flee from self-recrimination and free themselves from negative emotions (including resentments), these people spend their energies refusing to accept "guilt trips" they perceive to be imposed on them by others.

The problem with this approach to "self-liberation" is that unbridled desire, self-justification, and relativistic truth can easily distort the presence of true guilt. The only one who can lay guilt upon you is God, and his conviction is not a "trip," but rather a stark reality.

In helping some of my patients appreciate the quandary of distinguishing among the types of guilt and ferreting out actual guilt, I've sometimes used the example of tuna fish.

When I was a boy, I frequently ate tuna fish. This was always in the form of canned tuna mixed with mayonnaise—the way my mother made it for me. Mostly, it was Star-Kist brand tuna with Hellman's mayonnaise

---

44. Interestingly, this type of guilt is a compensatory attempt to bridge the gap between greater expectations and lesser expectations (see chapter 11).

and Wonderbread. She called it "tuna salad." This is what I was used to eating, although I realized that other people didn't share my tuna salad enthusiasm.

You do your thing, and I'll do mine could have been my diet mantra in those days. Occasionally, I would be served a slightly different mash of tuna and mayonnaise on rye bread, and this I tolerated with stoic restraint and self-congratulations on my sense of adventure. Nothing, however, prepared me for the "tuna salad" I was served at the local Greek restaurant.

In the Bronx, where I grew up, neighborhoods had their plethora of restaurants with a variety of ethnic specialties. Most of the "American restaurants" were owned and operated by Greek Americans. I went to one of them in my neighborhood quite frequently, as it was common for me to eat lunch in a restaurant by myself. My customary meal was a cheeseburger; however, on one occasion, with the nagging voice of my mother in my head, I decided to follow her advice and order something "healthy like tuna salad." So I did.

When my lunch arrived, I was confused and miffed. Set before me was a large plate adorned with lettuce, tomatoes, a few unfamiliar relishes, and in the middle was a circular mold of something tan and smelly. This was, of course, the tuna, right out of an upended can and situated amongst greens on the plate. I was horrified. I complained to the waiter.

"There must be a mistake—I ordered tuna salad!"

"Yes, that's tuna salad, kid."

Of course it was. But it didn't look anything like the whitish-tan, mashed-with-mayonnaise stuff that my mother put between slices of white bread. My stomach was growling, my expectations were confounded, the world was not behaving agreeably, and the tuna I thought I knew was apparently a tricky chameleon.

But tuna is tuna—a fish that swims in the sea, gets caught by man, and is served and processed as food in many different ways. It doesn't always wear a can, look like a round mold, or marry mayonnaise. Nonetheless, it is indeed tuna.[45]

---

45. One of my favorite activities is to purchase fish directly from the wholesalers at the piers in San Francisco. As varieties of fish are dragged into warehouses, I get to see them, barely hours out of the water, in their natural form. I watch the fishmongers cut and filet the fish, and I take it home to braise or eat raw. This is a far cry from the tuna salad sandwiches of my youth. Then again, I recall that white bread grew in plastic bags that hung on special trees somewhere

Similarly, guilt is guilt. It is transgression and wrongdoing, no matter how disguised or dressed up. It may be how you feel or what you've done, or it may be both. True guilt occurs when you violate a rule or law, whether or not you feel guilty or believe you are guilty. Though your beliefs and feelings are more realistic when they coincide with a factual assessment of what happened, true guilt depends upon transgression. It happens when you are out of step with God.

RESOLVING GUILT

Once you understand what guilt really is, the requirements for absolving it are straightforward. It is easy and natural to hide from guilt, but doing so detracts from living intact and results in distance from God. To know God is to face guilt and human vulnerability, but it is also to know *forgiveness*. Without forgiveness, guilt would still exist, but it would be unbearable. Fortunately, the supreme Creator of the universe has put in place the gift of forgiveness. It is the grace and mercy of forgiveness that allows man to overcome sin—with God's help—and to face reality, on God's terms, with responsibility, humility, and compassion.

The first step, obviously, is to acknowledge your guilt. You must be clear that you are truly guilty of wrongdoing. This requires good reality testing as well as a desire to follow God and to understand and accept his principles. Add to these a clarification as to whether your guilt is true guilt (based upon transgression) or a chameleon of denial, habit guilt, or anxiety/trauma combined with false assumptions.

When you face the realities of your true transgressions, it is time to confess. This means coming to God and acknowledging that by his standards (which often include rules made by man) you have transgressed and are guilty of sin. Oh, how difficult it is for man to admit that he is not right! But, if you are at odds with what God says, you are nevertheless wrong, because God is *always* right.[46] Admit to God that he is right in seeing your sin, that you are sorry for what you have done, that you want his forgiveness, and that you need his help in not transgressing again.

---

outside the Bronx. I took this for granted in the days before I felt guilty about environmental sustainability.

46. Overcome pride, and life will be so much easier and more fruitful!

GUILT, REMORSE, AND REPENTANCE

When you recognize and acknowledge your own guilt, you are agreeing with God. This is a necessary first step toward being forgiven. But you must also repent. This means truly being sorry for your transgressions. You must experience and express (particularly to God) remorse for your misdeeds in thought, feeling, and action.

God wants to forgive you. He wants this because he truly loves you (not your sinful heart or behaviors). He wants to foster closeness between you and him, but because he is just and holy, sin and transgression stand in the way. Therefore, God requires repentance and remorse, and he will then forgive you if you sincerely ask.

THE BLESSING OF FORGIVENESS

Forgiveness means giving up any and all claims you may have regarding wrongs or perpetrations done to or against you. To forgive is to pardon somebody for mistakes or wrongdoing. When you forgive, the debt is forever canceled. Nothing remains owing on that wrong or transgression.

Note that forgiving does not mean forgetting. Forgiving someone doesn't give you amnesia; but neither does it mean that you continue keeping score. The nature of memory is that emotional memory is different from unemotional memory. You can recall facts or events with varying degrees of accuracy and thoroughness. However, such recollections are not *compelling* in the way that emotional memories can be. Intense emotional memories can evoke preoccupation and obsession when they are negative or traumatic.

When you harbor anger or resentment against someone, or when you feel guilty or ashamed, you could become preoccupied with the uncomfortable or painful thoughts associated with those memories. Forgiveness erases the pain and discomfort.

Many people are unable to forgive. This characteristic often has tragic implications. The inability to forgive eats away at health, happiness, and the quality of relationships and contributions. Lack of forgiveness imposes an unnecessary burden; yet so many people live as if that weren't so. It primarily reflects a spiritual problem, though there are practical anchors that tether the heart. In order to forgive, you must experience how it feels to be absolved. Not having had this experience of absolution deprives you of the correct frame of reference. Compare this to the challenge of learning how to speak when one is deaf. There is no frame of reference or model for how words sound.

Spiritual deafness (or blindness or insensitivity) occurs naturally—it is man's nature. There are circumstances and events in life that can skew development toward dysfunctional patterns with regard to the capacity to experience and model compassion and forgiveness (review chapter 4 on the first secret of living intact: developing self-control and compassion).

Even though you may have had harrowing experiences, perhaps even having suffered abuse, neglect, or trauma that have left you hurt, angry, resentful, or mistrustful, there is a path to healing through forgiveness that God provides. First, however, you *must experience* being forgiven.

BEING FORGIVEN

You cannot experience being forgiven unless you know and accept that you are guilty. Being guilty means that you have transgressed. When a person transgresses, there are usually consequences. Sometimes these are harsh, but sometimes they are minimal, such as receiving probation or not having a violation go on your record. (Since God is omniscient, everything you ever do or think goes on his record of you. Thank God he is forgiving!)

Circumstantial consequences may satisfy the payment for certain transgressions. But paying a minimal price does not necessarily relieve guilt. Getting rid of guilt in the eyes of God and the eyes of man (including your own) requires a spiritual absolution. Feeling or being guilty shackles your conscience and emotional freedom. Only God can release you from the bondage of guilt. And only when you experience this can you truly forgive others—exactly what God wants you to do.

> *For if you forgive men when they sin against you, your heavenly Father will also forgive you. But if you do not forgive men their sins, your Father will not forgive your sins.* (Matthew 6:14–15)

The bible contains at least 212 references to guilt and at least 279 references to forgiveness.[47] According to God, the business of guilt and forgiveness is quite important—so vital, in fact, that he sent his son,

---

47. Compare this, for example, to the approximate 112 references to money.

Jesus Christ, to die on the cross as a payment and atonement for *all of mankind's sins, past, present, and future!* This fact is not only the core of Christianity—it is the basis for making possible all the secrets, elements, and tools that comprise living intact.

Forgiveness is essential to spiritual and emotional cleansing and healing. Think what it's like to be really dirty: I mean totally grungy, smelly, skin crawling, bacteria and filth all over you; and imagine what it would be like to live that way for days, months, even decades! Hard to think about, isn't it? Now think about being total cleansed with soap, disinfectant, soothing water, gentle scrubbing and massage. Imagine feeling completely refreshed, skin soft as a baby's, relaxed, feeling and smelling good... This exercise is but a faint whiff of the aroma of Christ that will embrace you when you experience the forgiveness of our loving God!

> *But thanks be to God, who always leads us in triumphal procession in Christ and through us spreads everywhere the fragrance of the knowledge of him. For we are to God the aroma of Christ among those who are being saved and those who are perishing. To the one we are the smell of death; to the other, the fragrance of life.* (2Corinthians 2:14–16)

THE PEACE OF FORGIVENESS

When you see something wonderful, eat great food, or hear enjoyable music, you naturally want to share it with others—tell them about it, help them find it, and savor their enjoyment. Experiencing forgiveness and wanting to share that joy with others trumps any feeling I have ever had. Beyond the feeling, it activates miracles.

Forgiving others brings a peace that has no equal, save the comparison of being saved. When you forgive, you will feel a comfort and refreshment and lightness. You will know the freedom from the burden of grudge, anger, and resentment. You will feel closer to God and bask in his approval, because you have acted righteously. You will delight in the peace that mercy brings forth. Moreover, you will feel good about yourself because you have acted maturely and responsibly. Ironically, you will gain a better sense of control of any situation that has been controlling you because of your own lack of forgiveness. And you will observe more astutely the nature of other people and of human emotions as you wait for God to act in the life of the person you forgave.

Then Peter came to Jesus and asked, "Lord, how many times shall I forgive my brother when he sins against me? Up to seven times?" Jesus answered, "I tell you, not seven times, but seventy-seven times. Therefore, the kingdom of heaven is like a king who wanted to settle accounts with his servants. As he began the settlement, a man who owed him ten thousand talents was brought to him. Since he was not able to pay, the master ordered that he and his wife and his children and all that he had be sold to repay the debt. The servant fell on his knees before him. 'Be patient with me,' he begged, 'and I will pay back everything.' The servant's master took pity on him, canceled the debt and let him go. But when that servant went out, he found one of his fellow servants who owed him a hundred denarii. He grabbed him and began to choke him. 'Pay back what you owe me!' he demanded. His fellow servant fell to his knees and begged him, 'Be patient with me, and I will pay you back.' But he refused. Instead, he went off and had the man thrown into prison until he could pay the debt. When the other servants saw what had happened, they were greatly distressed and went and told their master everything that had happened. Then the master called the servant in. 'You wicked servant,' he said, 'I canceled all that debt of yours because you begged me to. Shouldn't you have had mercy on your fellow servant just as I had on you?' In anger his master turned him over to the jailers to be tortured, until he paid back all he owed. This is how my heavenly Father will treat each of you unless you forgive your brother from your heart." (Matthew 18:21–35)

When you forgive others, you are being obedient to God. When you do not forgive, you are living outside of God's protection and blessing. This provides a foothold for succumbing to spiritual and practical influences that are critical, detrimental, and ungodly. Failure to forgive is tantamount to causing yourself pain.

On the other hand, forgiveness is one of the most unselfish acts you can perform. Forgiveness is often not easy, but it is up to you to take the initiative in forgiving.

FORGIVING OTHERS

Let's review what forgiveness involves and then delineate steps to forgiving others.

Forgiveness is the giving up of resentment against someone and the right to get even, no matter what has been done to you. It is the surrendering of the right to hurt someone back. Forgiveness cancels the debt forever.

Lack of forgiveness is the deliberate, willful refusal to give up your resentment and asserting the right to "get even" based upon the wrongful idea that somebody needs to pay the debt. In short, lack of forgiveness demands payback. (Ironically, it is the lack of forgiveness that actually demands the payment from you.)

Many people say, "I want to forgive; I simply can't." Or, "How can I forget that terrible thing he did?"

Let's emphasize again: forgiving does not mean forgetting. It means that the memory is no longer important to your heart and emotional mind.

To overcome the obstacle of a mind and heart that are stuck, I have found TFT tapping to be invaluable (see chapter 10). I consider it to be a sacrament, actually, given by God to help us in our human frailty and stubbornness that puts resistance (and psychological reversal) in the way of forgiveness.

Therefore, I wholeheartedly recommend (and use myself) TFT procedures at the slightest hint that forgiveness is not flowing naturally and quickly.

Here are the steps:

(Review the TFT procedures in chapter 10. Review appendix C, where you will find an algorithm for forgiveness.)

1. State out loud: "I want to be over any and all stubbornness in my hear and obstacles to forgiving (name) for (whatever has been done)." Tap on the side of your hand, and repeat the preceding statement.
2. Follow the algorithm treatment for forgiveness (appendix C), making sure to tap on the side of your hand and under your nose in the prescribed sequences (to correct reversals).
3. Acknowledge that you have experienced God's forgiveness.
4. Confess your negative emotions (anger, hostility, bitterness, resentment, rage, etc.)—"This is what I've felt and done. This is my attitude. It is not the right attitude."
5. Acknowledge to God that lack of forgiveness is a violation of his Word and principles

6. Ask God for forgiveness—"Forgive me for my (anger, hostility, bitterness, resentment, rage, etc.) toward (name) for whatever he or she has done. (Be specific.)

7. Ask God for help in forgiving the specific person for the specific act.

8. Declare that the debt is forever canceled for the specific person for the specific act.

9. Thank God for freeing you from the slavery and bondage of being unable to forgive.

10. Pray for the welfare and godliness of the person you just forgave.

Forgiveness is an act of choice. It may be among the most difficult choices you will ever make—and you will need to make it over and over again. Forgiveness exemplifies the golden rule. The capacity to forgive will bring you joy and contentment throughout your life as well as incalculable golden opportunities to live a life that is both rewarding and intact.

CHAPTER 17
REJECTION AND LONELINESS

Hear, O Lord, and be merciful to me; O Lord be my help. You turned my wailing into dancing; you removed my sackcloth and clothed me with joy, that my heart may sing to you and not be silent. O Lord my God, I will give you thanks forever.

(Psalm 30:10–12)

The desire to be connected with other human beings is one of the most basic drives and needs a person has. Besides basic survival, the evolutionary function of the nervous system is principally to meet the challenges of social interaction. To be recognized, appreciated, understood, needed, wanted, and integral in the lives of others gives meaning to life. Though it may not be a conscious preoccupation, the quest to develop and maintain satisfying relationships with others strongly motivates us.

Just as sensitivity to pain teaches us to be careful, wary, and protective in order to be safe and to thrive, the vulnerabilities of rejection and loneliness can inhibit motivation and risk-taking in the arena of emotional connectedness. The experience of rejection and loneliness can traumatize, can launch us into anxiety, depression, fear, hopelessness, and despair, and can derail us from emotional well-being, fulfilling relationships, and living intact.

THE NATURE OF REJECTION

Rejection is a natural part of life. To reject is to refuse to accept, believe in, or make use of something. To reject is to exclude or turn away someone or something not deemed good enough.

Rejection is a biological, chemical, and physical process, as in the rejection of inedible foods or substances that are poisonous or incompatible. Rejection is also a social process. It is a natural outgrowth of competition and the result of the exercise of preferences. In the quest for connectedness and economic survival, those who possess attributes and skills valued by society typically have a greater chance of attaining the most coveted and rewarding jobs, attracting the most desirable mates, and reaching the highest status level.

Beyond the obvious material bases for rejection, it is also a spiritual phenomenon. When we *feel* rejected, we are wounded and hurt. Often, we feel lonely. We become fearful and anxious about our value and its inextricable ties to physical survival and psychological stability. Rejection can be an actual threat or a perceived threat. Either way, the sense of rejection mobilizes self-protective activity. Stress levels elevate along with corresponding fight-or-flight responses of the nervous system. The narrative rises to the occasion by interpreting—or misinterpreting—threats to well-being and safety. Depending upon one's temperament and experiences, responses to rejection can range from sour grapes ("Oh, I didn't want that anyway.") to possessiveness, jealousy, aggression, and even vengeance. The feeling of rejection can cut deeply into one's sense of worthiness, trust, security, and intimacy.

Because there is justice in the universe, breaking the rules may also result in rejection. If you misbehave, you can have privileges taken away. Indeed, even *you* can be taken away. The quintessential example of this was the eviction of Adam and Eve from the Garden of Eden.

God is deeply concerned with rejection. (The Bible contains at least 114 references involving rejection.) He is a jealous God, and when we reject him, he becomes hurt and angry. As humans, we are made in God's image. We react this way, too. However, God exercises prerogative in is reactions because he is sovereign. He also shows us how to "get over" hurt and anger and deal with rejection.

One of the most significant themes in the Bible is the theme of rejection. The Old Testament tells the story of Israel's repeated rejection of

God, and the New Testament reveals mankind's habit of rejecting God in the person of Jesus. The struggle between good and evil is a continuous process of choosing one and rejecting the other.

Thus, the issue of rejection is prominent among the challenges of living intact.

A TWO-WAY STREET

The feelings of isolation, withdrawal, criticism, shame, anger, or defensiveness that rejection can cause are normal responses. Ironically, we tend to be highly sensitive to rejection *by* others and somewhat oblivious to the rejection *of* others. Maturity helps to sensitize us to see the issues more clearly, and rejection is one of the seminal life experiences that allow us to develop empathy and compassion. No one likes to feel rejected. Learning to weather rejections and other disappointments is part of adjusting to life, developing a robust and healthy self-image, and finding a meaningful place in relation to others and to God.

From biological to social to spiritual, rejection is one phenomenon that profoundly shapes who we are and plays an intricate role in the development and maintenance of self-control. When you exercise good judgment, you are discriminating (as opposed to being prejudiced and prejudging), and make good choices, you are rejecting harmful influences—people, substances, and circumstances that can disrupt your self-control or damage you. Rejection in moderation is, therefore, a necessary and useful challenge that you must learn how to handle. Of course, when you are on the receiving end of repeated, callous, insensitive, or unintended rebuffs, life can indeed seem cruel and unfair.

To make choices is to reject one thing and choose another. Sometimes, it is necessary or appropriate to reject someone, even though that person will feel the pangs resulting from your choice. Though rejection is a two-way street, the rejection *you* focus on is what *you feel* when you are cast aside.[48]

UP CLOSE AND PERSONAL

Rejection comes in many forms: experiencing a devastating job loss or relationship breakup, being cut from the team, hearing a rude

---

48. Many people also feel pain, empathy, and compassion when they reject others. This can be in the realm of healthy awareness and sensitivity.

comment or criticism, having a request turned down, perceiving indifference to your opinion, comment or joke, having your credit score lowered, or just not being acknowledged. Some rejections can be traumatic and crushing; many are minor and seemingly insignificant. Cumulatively, however, rejections can eat away at confidence, self-esteem, and the motivation to persevere.

Rejection deals a blow to one's ego. It reduces the sense of importance. While this may be humbling, realistic, or even helpful, it never feels good to be reminded that you are dispensable. Rejection can seem harsher when it is unexpected, and some rejections may come unpredictably and regardless of one's efforts to monitor and adjust expectations (as in the occurrence of sudden death or loss due to injury).

Unanticipated rejection can be especially traumatic, but the mundane rejections that people experience repeatedly can interfere with the ability to focus on positive elements and practice goal-oriented, satisfying behaviors. Some people can shrug off rejection ("like water off a duck's back"), whereas others take things personally. Temperament plays a significant role in how one handles rejection. Certain people are, by temperament, highly sensitive to personal criticism, whereas others are more sensitive to criticism about their work.

Your ability to accurately perceive and interpret responses to yourself or your efforts will affect how you recognize and handle rejection and whether you correctly "get" what is really happening in a particular situation. (Refer to the section on "Acquiring Wisdom" in chapter 12 and to "World Skills" in appendix D.)

At one end of the spectrum may be the salesperson who just doesn't take no for an answer and who appears inured to rejection. At the other extreme is the highly anxious and self-conscious person who is devastated by virtually any comment or look that might be construed as criticism and rejection. In each of these cases, self-image and distorted sensitivity can lead to inappropriate or maladaptive responses to rejection. Clearly, how you interpret and respond to actual or perceived rejection reflects how and where you see yourself in relation to the world and your narrative.

A MATTER OF BOUNDARIES

In the discussion about expectations (see chapter 11), I describe expectations as an intersection where reality meets desire. Expectations form a bridge for traversing perception and reality. They are boundaries that separate the area of what you want from the area of what you get. Boundaries can be physical, psychological, or rule based. They delineate rights to property, privileges, and behavior. Boundary violations may occur from misconstrued expectations, but they invariably result in sanctions and will elicit from others a reiteration of their expectations.

When rejection occurs, it always involves boundaries. The markers for inclusion or exclusion are established, and the boundaries are determined. A rejection means you are outside the boundaries for acceptance or inclusion. Whether or not you expected the rejection, you must identify and adapt to the particular form of exclusion you experience. In order to accommodate the rejection adaptively, you need a working sense of personal boundaries that preserves your dignity, worth, and sense of general belonging.

Someone with a strong ego may react to rejection with an attitude of "Oh, well, it's *their* loss," and move ahead without apparent negative impact. An overly sensitive person will internalize the rejection with exaggerated meaning for both the specific situation and the person's core self-worth. This is where rejection can overcome normal defenses, hijack the narrative, and lead to extended forays into depression, anxiety, self-pity, loneliness, and inflexibility.

When dealing with rejection, it is vital to maintain healthy boundaries in order to choose properly among the responses for asserting yourself, accepting the inevitable, reframing the meaning and consequences of the rejection, and formulating a plan to handle the challenges, weather the rejection, and adopt reasonable alternatives.

How do you maintain healthy boundaries? By developing and knowing who you are, what you are good for and good at, and to whom you belong. Of course, this is a tall order, but when you think about it, isn't this a constant requirement of living in the world and with yourself? Fortunately, once again, God sets the prototype and gives guidance in this area of living intact that helps us to face rejection, interpret it properly, know good boundaries, and become peaceful and content, no matter what the circumstances. (Philippians 4:11–13)

BIBLICAL ALLEGORIES

Scripture abounds with themes of rejection. Adam and Eve rejected God's prohibition regarding the Tree of Knowledge, so he ejected them from the Garden of Eden. The Old Testament recounts how the Israelites repeatedly rejected God in favor of lesser gods and idols.

Over and over again, God forgave the Israelites and restored them to favor and mercy. God made known his displeasure, even his jealousy and anger over rejection by his chosen people. Yet he took them back after subjecting them to consequences. (Deuteronomy 31:15–21; Psalm 60:1; 78:59; 89:38; 94:14; 118:22; Jeremiah 15:6; Hosea 8:3; Zechariah 10:6)

In the Old Testament, the prophet Isaiah tells of the rejection of the Messiah:

> *He was despised and rejected by men, a man of sorrows, and familiar with suffering. Like one from whom men hide their faces, he was despised, and we esteemed him not. Surely he took up our infirmities and carried our sorrows, yet we considered him stricken by God, smitten by him and afflicted. But he was pierced for our transgressions, he was crushed for our iniquities, the punishment that brought peace was upon him, and by his wounds we are healed. We all, like sheep, have gone astray, each of us has turned to his own way; and the Lord has laid on him the iniquity of us all. (Isaiah 53:3–6)*

The New Testament tells of the rejection of God in the form of Jesus. (Matthew 21:42; Mark 9:12; 12:10; Luke 6:22; 10:16; 17:25; John 3:36; Acts 7:39)

What, then, can we make of biblical messages, the matter of boundaries, disillusioned expectations, the reciprocal nature of rejection, and a manner of handling rejection that contributes to living intact?

HANDLING REJECTION

When you face rejection, the tasks at hand are to salve the hurt, put it in perspective, exercise dignity, self-control, and even compassion, and respond in a way that allows you to heal and move ahead. The Lord has demonstrated that feeling hurt is natural and that it is okay to express it. In the natural order of free will and competition, one cannot and will not always get what one wants. Rejection does not mean unfairness (although that happens, too), but it does evoke opinions and attitudes about the reasons for it.

Because of the hurt and connection with vulnerability that rejection elicits, it can prompt resentment, rebellion, or a response of shutting down. Clearly, God is concerned about and opposed to this way of reacting. Becoming surly over rejection suggests that you know better than God and that you deserve to get your way. It constitutes a rejection of God's manner of doing things—not that you should sheepishly accept every turn of events as the will of God, but rather that you should evaluate your own emotional reactions for motives of wanting to substitute your will and your "rights" for God's plan.

Another common response to rejection is the embrace of self-pity and the continuation of negative feelings and preoccupation with loss or hurt. This, too, is a rejection of God in the form of rejecting his mercy, for God heals the brokenhearted, and he beckons us to roll our burdens and anxiety unto him. (Matthew 6:25–34; 11:28; 1 Peter 5:7)

God uses rejection to humble us, to draw us closer to him for comfort, and to prepare us for a provident future that we cannot entirely predict, foresee, or understand. How many times have you rued a loss, a missed opportunity, a broken or rejected relationship, a spurned overture—only to find out later that something better was in store for you?

Of course, not everything works out gloriously for every individual (especially on the individual's terms). Dreams and bones can be shattered, and painful events like rejection are difficult to accept.

God tells us to rely upon him, to seek his comfort, and that he will never leave or forsake us. (Deuteronomy 31:6; 31:8; Psalm 9:10; 37:28; 94:14; Hebrews 13:5) It is up to every individual to believe those promises and to exercise dependence upon them. Doing so in the face of rejection yields the following:

1. You will be comforted emotionally and spiritually.
2. You will respect the boundaries that God has established for your rights and entitlements.
3. God will hear your prayers and implorations, and eventually he will answer you if you are attentive to him and willing to hear his answer.

4. You will understand and accept God's declaration that his grace is sufficient (John 1:16; Romans 5:17; 2 Corinthians 12:9; Philippians 1:20), and you will experience that sufficiency so that rejection loses its sting.

5. You will grow to see rejections as part of God's plan for you, and you will eagerly await the new opportunities hidden in the future beyond present rejections.

6. You will listen for God's guidance as to what you should do after your plans, desires, or expectations have been thwarted.

7. You will moderate your tendencies to become indignant when things don't go your way or to rebound from self-pity, negative moods, or moribund aspirations.

8. You will eventually come to see some rejections as logical precursors (in retrospect) for opportunities and blessings.

9. You will put rejections in perspective, knowing that, as a child of God, you *belong*. You have eternal security and value because God promises you that if you believe and accept it.

10. You will circumvent unnecessary rejections because you will build healthy boundaries based upon God's commands and wisdom.

11. You will be sensitive and wary of rejecting God's wisdom and his will for you, and you will respect his command to love and put others ahead of you, thereby exercising caution in overlooking or rejecting others.

12. You will identify with God and the feelings of grief and compassion that he suffered, that Jesus suffered, when men rejected him. You will come to experience rejection with true connection to your emotions—not as a victim, but with human and godly sensitivity, as well as with responses of forgiveness and reconciliation.

SELF-ESTEEM AND REJECTION

Perhaps you have experienced devastating rejection, and your self-esteem has suffered. How are you to recover?

Let's acknowledge that rejection can chip away at self-confidence and ego strength. But these concepts are not the same as self-esteem.

Self-esteem is the value with which we regard the various aspects of ourselves. It is not the same as self-confidence. A teacher may be supremely confident in her ability to teach math, but may also suffer from poor self-esteem. A spelling champion is confident with words, and a bully is confident asserting dominance; yet each of these people may hold himself in low regard, despite high confidence in the context of a particular level of functioning.

Self-*esteem* can be differentiated from self-*concept*. The ideas we have about ourselves comprise our self-concept, and the values we place on these ideas constitute self-esteem. Each of us has ideas and beliefs that structure our identity, character, and essential qualities, and distinguish us as distinct and separate from all others. Self-esteem reflects the honor with which we regard our reputations and ideas about ourselves. It is the product of our needs for *significance* and *security*.

Self-esteem contains two essential components:

1. What am I good *at*?
2. What am I good *for*?

What am I good *at?*

Learning to survive independently requires a host of functional and integrated skills. Growing up involves the labor of practicing skills, applying them to satisfy needs and wants, and carving out areas of specialty in which we can perform well. Discovering what we are good *at* shapes and fortifies our ideas about who we are, thus molding our sense of significance by establishing niches of competence and contribution. Security is reinforced by the confidence that what we do is valuable— therefore, we are valued, needed, and desired.

The exercise of mastery and competence at producing and performing is inseparable from our images of ourselves. We depend upon others for feedback about how well we accomplish tasks, demonstrate our capabilities, and compensate for weaknesses. Through recognizing and honing skills that exhibit achievement, adaptation, accommodation, and adjustment of expectations, we determine what we are good at.

What am I good *for?*

Our society allows adults to freely ask each other the question, "What do you do for a living?" This social convention permits us to describe what we are good at. The more sensitive and private question, "What are you good *for?*" is usually encountered in the cloistered environs of a therapeutic milieu, spiritual/religious discussion, or philosophic inquiry.

We enter the world completely dependent on others to care for us and about us. This requires unconditional love—an acceptance, inclusion, and caring that is unfettered by expectations of performance or reciprocity. Eventually, we learn about conditional love, approval, and rewards, which are contingent upon performance and other criteria. We never lose that profound need for unconditional validation of our worthiness—to be loved, accepted, treasured as individuals, irrespective of skills, performance, personality, limitations, or burdens.

When we are loved unconditionally, we are secure. Where we are wanted, valued, cared for, we feel we belong. A self that is honored and regarded so highly by others is surely significant.

Rejection has the potential for denigrating your beliefs about what you are good at and what you are good for. When these core beliefs take traumatic or repeated hits, your self-esteem can erode. Therefore, you need to rebound with evidence and conviction of your worth. This will allow you to parry the impact of rejection and focus instead on what you are good at and what you are good for.

When you are turned down for a job or a date, declined for credit, or scorned in your attempts to show prowess, it is embarrassing and frustrating. It is tempting to want to complain or crawl into a hole. In these situations, remember that just because you did not meet some requirements, it does not mean you are unworthy or that your abilities are any lower than they were before you made your bid.

To help yourself, you can do the following:

1. Identify the negative emotions that accompany the rejection. Use TFT to tap away these negative intrusions (see chapter 10).
2. Remind yourself that God is in control and that he is looking out for you. Ask him to guide you in your interpretation of and response to the rejection.
3. Review in your mind your motivations for whatever application or overture was rejected, and list the attributes and abilities that prompted your desire to try.

4. Take charge of your narrative by telling yourself that this rejection is not the end of the world; better still, it will be accommodated and put into the background with the next successful opportunity. Appeal to your narrative to research such opportunities.

5. Assess the consequences of the rejection, and determine whether your chances of success were overestimated. Figure out whether you should discount this rejection ("They didn't realize my value...") or whether you should factor it into future bids or attempts ("How qualified was I compared to other applicants?" "Perhaps I need to practice more before trying out for that team.").

6. Reflect upon the people who appreciate you and what you do. Remember your successes, including the ones that took multiple attempts.

7. Reinforce yourself for taking initiative, even though you were rebuffed.

8. Think about people who hold you in high regard. Imagine them consoling and encouraging you.

9. Visualize future attempts and imagine being welcomed and included. Tell your narrative to rehearse these scenes.

10. Know that Jesus was rejected, though he offered truth, compassion, and salvation. Jesus didn't like being rejected, but he didn't take it personally. (Matthew 21:42–43; Mark 9:12–13) Tell the truth about the situation and model after Jesus. Hold people accountable, show discernment, restraint, and compassion—and move on. (Isaiah 52:2; Matthew 10:14; Mark 6:11; Luke 9:5)

11. Consider that God will never forsake you or abandon you (Hebrews 13:5), that you are precious to him (Psalm 72:14; Isaiah 43:4; 1 Peter 2:4), and that he has vested you with gifts and talents that he will show you how to use. (Romans 11:29; 12:6; 1 Corinthians 12:1; 12:4; 12:9; 12:28; 12:31; 14:12; 2 Corinthians 9:9; Ephesians 4:8; Hebrews 2:4)

LIFE'S LONELINESS

No man is an island. We are connected and interdependent, and yet we are separate. Being alone is not the same as being lonely. You can be alone in the sense of solitude, dedication, work, or a journey. Jesus often sought to be alone (Matthew 14:23), and he found spiritual sustenance in using alone time with God, the Father.

You can be alone and still have satisfying relationships with people. Sometimes, circumstances require us to sustain periods away from those in whom we take comfort and delight. But company is not always a measure of the absence of loneliness. Many people feel alienated and lonely when, by outward appearances, they are engaged, related, and seemingly conducting normal activities and interactions. Many a revered celebrity has suffered intractable loneliness.

Because we are individuals—separated by bodies, interests, and destinies—and because there is competition, sin, and death, loneliness is part of the human condition. It is triggered by circumstances, but it is actually a state of mind. By now, you realize that living intact is about changing states of mind as well as actual circumstances. And certainly, you have tools to change your state of mind.

Perhaps you experience loneliness more than fleetingly. Maybe you have lost a partner or dear companion. It is not uncommon to feel protracted loneliness when someone you love (or even a cherished pet) dies, when a friend moves away, or when people you felt close to move on to the next phase of their lives and focus their attention and energy on a new baby, a new relationship, or an expanded family.

Maybe you feel lonely because, instead of experiencing a loss, you have yet to meet your soul mate. Or perhaps you find yourself in a milieu where people don't share your ideas or values. These situations can understandably give rise to feelings of separation, alienation, and loneliness. What can you do? How can you change this state of mind?

Loneliness is a feeling that can be triggered by separation and/or rejection. You can feel lonely because someone abandoned you or because the people and opportunities available to you are not appealing. (In the latter case, it is you who are rejecting.) You can make choices about settling for less than is ideal in order to relieve loneliness. This involves deliberate actions as well as adjustment of expectations.

You can also address loneliness as the state of mind that it is.

When Jesus accepted his plight and purpose on Earth, he was lonely. He took on this loneliness as a sacrifice and atonement for man's sins, and it temporarily separated him from God—the ultimate loneliness!

When you are separated from God, you are vulnerable to loneliness. The distractions and pleasures of the world may temporarily occupy and entertain you, but ultimately, true fulfillment comes from a right relationship with the Almighty.

What if you do have a close and faithful relationship with God, yet you are still lonely? These are the times to appeal to God, to plead his promises of meeting your needs and never abandoning you, and to identify with Jesus who willingly experienced the devastating loneliness and separation from God to pay for all that man has done wrong. Identifying with Jesus will salve your loneliness because it will enable you to cast your anguish upon the Lord (Psalm 68:19; Matthew 6:25–34; 11:28; Psalm 94:19; Philippians 4:6–7; 1 Peter 5:7) and to experience hope and faith that God understands your plight and will bring you relief.

There are times when each of us is lonely and afflicted. Waiting patiently upon the Lord is necessary to see us through. We are not immune to sensitive feelings or emotional trauma. None of us can predict when life may pummel or rob us. However, if you experience protracted or recurrent loneliness, there are also practical steps you can take to help ward off this existential angst:

1. If you are feeling lonely within a relationship, find the courage to discuss your feelings with your related partner. Take care to do this without blaming. Ask permission to discuss some private feelings and secure an agreement from your partner to let you finish without commenting or interrupting. Make sure to use "I" messages, as in, "I don't know why I'm feeling this way, but I…"; "I feel especially lonely when…"

2. Solicit the feelings of others, especially those with whom you have (or are supposed to have) close relationships. If you confide your loneliness without complaint or self-pity, it may surprise you that others also confide in you that they are lonely, too. This would not be a case of "Misery loves company" but, rather, a basis for drawing closer because of shared intimate feelings.

3. Review your expectations about how you believe others should express closeness. You may be internalizing things far differently than they are intended. Other people may be busy or self-pro-

tective, and this could lead you to believe they don't care, don't understand, or are shunning you.

4. Along the lines of expectations and values, consider that relationships are precious, and the serendipity of drawing close to someone is a gift from God. Cherish it when it happens, and consider it a blessing when like-minded souls unite. Strive to feel complete within yourself, not depending upon another human being to relieve your anxiety or provide your sense of sufficiency or groundedness.

5. Get involved in the lives of others. Meeting the needs of others almost always surpasses feelings of loneliness. Volunteer, let people and organizations know you are available and willing.

6. Develop healthy relationships, even if they do not offer all that you are seeking. You may not find a soul mate, but can still find satisfaction in developing and maintaining two-way flows in relationships that are sparing of the intimacy you crave. Small friendships can pay big dividends.

7. Look for people to mentor. Teaching a child, doing a favor, filling in when needed, lending your expertise—all can work wonders in edifying your sense of what you are good at and good for.

8. For the sake of company and to feel a part of someone and something, consider participating in activities that may not excite you. For example, you may not particularly enjoy gardening, group meetings, bowling, or playing games, but these are ways to meet and relate to people. If you want closeness and relief from loneliness, don't be too fussy about the activities that secure this.

9. I've often found that "shallow" relationships deriving from routine daily activities provide me with a great sense of satisfaction and belongingness. They supplement and, at times, become a substitute for the deeper relationships that fulfill me. The merchants where I shop recognize me and, over time, imbue a welcome and warm recognition that make me feel valued and a part of the community. It's not just about spending dollars; it's being out there and conversing and exchanging on a routine basis that gratifies me. You'd be surprised how asking about the lives of those who serve you can open up doors to new relationships and/ or feelings of connectedness. Offer to buy a cup of coffee for your

grocer; tell a joke to your dry cleaner. By doing so, you are letting down your guard and practicing openness to disclosure by and acceptance from others.

Rejection and loneliness will sometimes affect even the sturdiest and most popular among us. Remember that these states will pass if you use the tools of altering your mind state productively, challenge your narrative, take practical steps to connect and unite with others, and rely upon God for sustenance.

And we know that in all things God works for the good of those who love him, who have been called according to his purpose. For those God foreknew he also predestined to be conformed to the likeness of his Son, that he might be the firstborn among many brothers. And those he predestined, he also called; those he called, he also justified; those he justified, he also glorified. What, then shall we say in response to this? If God is for us, who can be against us? (Romans 8:28–31)

For I am convinced that neither death nor life, neither angels nor demons, neither the present nor the future, nor any powers, neither height nor depth, nor anything else in all creation, will be able to separate us from the love of God that is in Christ Jesus our Lord. (Romans 8:38–39)

But we have this treasure in jars of clay to show that this all-surpassing power is from God and not from us. We are hard-pressed on every side, but not crushed; perplexed, but not in despair; persecuted, but not abandoned; struck down, but not destroyed. We always carry around in our body the death of Jesus, so that the life of Jesus may also be revealed in our body. (2 Corinthians 4:7–10)

Therefore we do not lose heart. Though outwardly we are wasting away, yet inwardly we are being renewed day by day. For our light and momentary troubles are achieving for us an eternal glory that far outweighs them all. So we fix our eyes not on what is seen, but on what is unseen. For what is seen is temporary, but what is unseen is eternal. (2 Corinthians 4:16–18)

CHAPTER 18
ENTITLEMENT AND HUMILITY

Intertwined with the myriad of choices you make throughout life are repeated themes and patterns that shape your outlook and character. As you face challenges, opportunities, disappointments, and unexpected turns, the decisions you make will relate not only to actions and consequences, but to your fundamental understanding about who you are and your relationship to God and the world around you. When confronted by things that don't go the way you wanted, your reactions both reflect and contribute to core attitudes that you hold about the ways life works.

Living intact is based upon the premise that discrepancies routinely arise between desire and actuality and that we must effectively use the challenge process to resolve these inherent breakdowns, dissatisfactions, and discrepancies that result from our desires for what life should be and our actual experiences living life. Your response patterns to discrepancies, frustrations, and brokenness reflect both conscious and subconscious beliefs and attitudes about what you are entitled to and what should happen when you don't get it.

ENTITLEMENT AND EXTREMES

We have all encountered overly selfish people. When we have to deal with such people routinely, patience wears thin, and our abilities to serve and sacrifice in the face of limited appreciation and often unrealistic and excessive demands can be sorely tested. The self-centered person interprets things in terms of his own needs and desires. Such a person tends to be short on empathy and compassion, especially in situations where these responses are needed and expected by those who depend on him. An extreme form of this behavior is called narcissism. In clinical psychiatric and psychological terms, narcissism involves excessive self-admiration or self-centeredness and an overestimation of one's personal abilities, characteristics, and worth. Narcissism is considered a personality disorder, and those individuals who display prominent narcissistic strains typically face substantial difficulties in social and occupational adjustment. Ironically, one advantage of narcissism is a strong ego and often the ability to withstand adversity and rejection, but there are invariably great costs. Narcissists have great difficulty sustaining satisfying relationships and maintaining their reputation, integrity, and reality orientation. They are also subject to God's disapproval and suffer a loss of his favor and rewards.

Narcissism and selfishness revolve around the core attribute of *entitlement*—the sense of privilege, inalienable prerogatives, and the immutable "right" to do or receive anything that they desire. When these characteristics are predominant, we recoil in amazement at the unabashed egotism that the person's behavior, attitudes, and false sense of entitlement convey. We think, "*What makes him think he deserves this? What gives him the right to...? How dare she think she is entitled...?*" We typically respond by marveling incredulously at the person's brazen insensitivity reflected in his displays of entitlement, and we shake our heads at how this overly selfish individual somehow has failed to recognize how others react to his distorted sense of privilege. Paradoxically, most of us fail to notice our own less obvious sense of entitlement and the ways that this insidious form of pride and greed can pervade our outlook and interfere with living intact.

SELFISHNESS, OTHERS, AND THE MIRROR

My mother used to say, "There, but for the grace of God, go I." She often intoned this short homily when she encountered someone who was experiencing obvious misfortune. Her list of hardships included people with gross physical anomalies, victims of tragedy, and even people displaying socially inept or unacceptable behavior. I admired my mother's ability to temper her tendencies to judge with her penchant for displaying compassion for others. I highly esteemed her capacity to identify with another's misfortunes and to have empathy for even those who were remote and so dissimilar to her.

As I grew more mature, I began to recognize that people who display gross and even abhorrent behaviors and characteristics are potentially what I—and every human being—might also manifest, were it not for God's grace. I am not suggesting that I am (or you are) guilty of overt abhorrent transgressions. I am, however, confessing that I have within me an active narrative that continually seeks to self-justify, excuse, or minimize my selfishness, rationalize why things should go my way, and why the world (and God) is unfair when things don't unfold according to my plans and desires. I am eerily similar, spiritually speaking, to a former patient who confided to me blithely that she was "a legend in my own mirror."

Put bluntly, I have reached an awareness that I also struggle with a sense of entitlement. This is one of the greatest challenges to living intact. To feel and act entitled is not simply a personal flaw, but it is endemic to the human condition. It emanates from the exigencies of survival and development and extends, in some people, to a blind and self-deceptive prison where the attitude that one is being victimized and that the world owes us favors chips away at satisfaction and productive living.

The sense of entitlement is at odds with God's intent for us, and it is the antithesis of humility. *"There, but for the grace of God, go I"* is a functional insight that helps govern the narcissistic tendency to go one's own way, whatever the consequences. The insight allows us to choose humility over entitlement. It is easy and tempting to point the finger at prominent examples of entitlement (e.g., Tiger Woods, Lindsay Lohan, etc.). Ironically, whether or not we engage in recriminations of the behavior of the rich and famous, as previously indicated, it is common for us to overlook and underestimate our *own* entitlements. *Every time we make an excuse or feel sorry for ourselves, we are exhibiting a type of entitlement.* Excuses and self-pity are the narrative's way of declaring that we deserve better results or more consideration.

REASONS FOR ENTITLEMENT

On a psychological level, entitlement serves to gratify the ego, protect against the fear of abandonment or insignificance, and reinforce the fragile and often dissipating sense of importance and belonging. On a spiritual level, entitlement asserts one's sovereign privilege and right to leave God out of matters or to usurp his supremacy. To claim rights or privileges or to assume outcomes favorable to oneself or one's desires that are not biblically based is to challenge God's authority and sovereignty.

The self-protective aspect of the natural self leads into this deceptive folly. Let's examine the underpinnings of entitlement:

Need for attention

The need for attention is obvious and ubiquitous. There is little else that competes or compares with attention and recognition. Attention is a powerful reinforcer: it mollifies doubts, soothes anxieties, testifies to our existence and importance, and imbues a sense of power and control. Moreover, one can even command attention without the conscious assent of others (refer to chapter 6).

It is no wonder, then, that this need for attention becomes exacerbated and serves as a powerful manipulative tool in the repertoire of those who require it and feel that they deserve it.

Sense of being wronged (injustice and victimization)

It is natural and human to feel hurt when injury or rejection occurs or when circumstances offend one's sense of fairness. After all, people do take advantage, injustices seem to abound, and the "right" thing to do often succumbs to greed, pride, and other failings.

However, some people seem career bound as victims. They project a fragile and extensive vulnerability to all manner of pings, intrusions, and slights that occur routinely in life. Moreover, they collect these grievances and injustices[49] and wear them as armor to shield against an ever-suspect environment that does not respect or cater to them. The persisting sense of being wronged finds social validation in a society where selfishness and "me" culture is exalted and reinforced. The attitude of "look what they've done to me" can become an insidious part of a person's narrative. When this happens, external events assume a conspiratorial cast, and the "victim" continuously looks for confirmation of perceived injustice.

Privilege as a statement of importance

By definition, privilege means entitlement—to an advantage, right, or benefit that is not available to everyone. Belonging to a select club,

---

49. *Collecting injustices* is the satisfying, though pungent, process of reviewing, refining, and extending the list of resentments, grievances, and notations of those who have failed to recognize one's special status. I have jokingly referred to this pattern as an indicator of the diagnosis of *Righteous Indignation*.

moving to the head of the line, getting the best seat or parking space,[50] even being allowed to speak first all convey a sense of importance, indicating that one is "special" and more significant.

Going "first-class" is about more than comfort and taste: it reveals a need for reinforcement that one truly matters. What better way to demonstrate this than by buying or demanding "the best"?

Inflated sense of self-worth

One of my friends has a saying: "I'd like to buy you for what you're *really* worth and sell you for what you *think* you're worth."

In the quest for importance, recognition, and acknowledgment, and as a defense against feelings of inadequacy, many people aggrandize themselves and their abilities. The tendency to romanticize the past can also play into these fantasies. *The older I get, the better I was* captures the illusory memories of past grandeur.

An inflated sense of self-worth is the bedrock that justifies entitlement. The subconscious reasoning says, "Since I am worth a whole lot, then this should be obvious, and others should defer to my higher position in life's pecking order." Unfortunately, this way of thinking (even subconsciously) undermines a right relationship with God and, thereby, satisfying and appropriate relationships with people.

True self-worth comes from basking in the love, recognition, and security offered by the Almighty. What other people think and see is far less important. When you follow God's principles, his light shines through, and others do see him in your actions and attitudes (Matthew 5:14–16). Ironically, caring less about what people think, but caring very much *for* them and what God thinks about them, leads to increasing your esteem in the eyes of others.

ENTITLEMENT DISGUISES

Entitlement is especially offensive when it manifests brazenly and conveys a sense of superiority. Displays of egotism or the demand for preferential treatment turn off most people, and such behavior can elicit a

---

50. Embarrassingly, I remember that after my minor knee surgery many years ago, I became annoyed with my orthopedic surgeon when he would not extend my handicapped parking privileges. Though I was able to walk just fine, my desire for comfort and advantage blinded me to his discernment and my own sense of entitlement.

backlash of resentment and desire to remove the self-entitled person from his vainglorious pedestal.

More frequent than the overt and excessive narcissistic displays are the more subtle ways that entitlement creeps into attitudes and patterns of behavior. Some manifestations are:

Self-pity

Feeling sorry for oneself is a good way of masking entitlement. When you feel sorry for yourself or rue your misfortunes, you are taking the position that you deserve better. You are thereby at odds with the universe and specifically with God's way of running things. To reiterate: excuses and self-pity are the narrative's way of declaring that you deserve better results or more consideration.

Resistance to change

It may seem a stretch to see that resistance to change is a form of entitlement. Some people like the status quo and are reluctant to "fix things that aren't broken." However, no one is entitled to a fixed universe. Things do change, and we need to adapt, not only for survival, but in order to better serve others.

A startling example of how resisting change favors entitlement is the continuing human tendency toward racism and ethnocentric attitudes of superiority. Besides intolerance, resistance to change can assume subtle disguises that partially hide the sense of entitlement under the cloak of affection. Life is full of loss; though losing a loved one, a friend, or a pet may cause anguish, we are not "entitled" to keep them. No one "owns" anyone else. Friendship, love, family, possessions—these are all gifts from God, and he is sovereign in his will to bestow them for a while and then to take them away. This applies to our very lives as well as the events, people, and acquisitions we so easily take for granted.

Self-sufficiency (pride)

To assert privilege over others implies that one is more worthy and deserving. The hierarchy of privilege assumes that one has *done* something (even by association) to merit preferential treatment. A degree of pride in one's work and accomplishment is laudable. To support oneself and stand on one's own feet financially and emotionally is indeed commendable and admirable. However, no one survives alone, nor does anyone meet and rise above life's challenges and obstacles without repeated support from other people and from God. Some people, in their hubris or arrogance, refuse to acknowledge this truth.

An excess of pride or self-sufficiency can turn virtue into entitlement. When self-reliance becomes a preoccupation, it lends itself to idolatry of one's own abilities and verve. Success is much sweeter and more realistic when it includes the credit due and needs of others.

Rejection of God

I know so many people who don't figure God into their lives. I am torn about this, because I care for them. Admittedly—with embarrassment—I care for some more than others—the ones who are "good people"—moral, generous, sensitive, caring, attractive, and admirable for their traits and achievements. These folks inspire my respect. Regardless of their virtues and deeds, however, their failure to include, credit, and fear God speaks loudly of their sense of entitlement. This is because God's absence in their lives leaves only their own determination and self-absorption to account for their results.

To disown God, to dismiss him from the equations in one's life is an entitlement to the worship of selfhood. Rejecting God is tantamount to taking full credit for one's role in the universe. It is a smug and naïve oversight that leaves a person vulnerable to the forces of evil. The rejection represents a pernicious disguise of entitlement.

ENTITLEMENT AND EXPECTATIONS

Endemic to entitlement is the expectation of favor or preferential treatment. People who feel entitled *expect* certain treatment from others. As you may recall from chapter 11, expectations form the bridge between reality and desire. Persistent discrepancies between greater and lesser expectations lead to dissonance between one's model of what the world should be and one's experience living in it.

For those with a hefty sense of entitlement, such discrepancies are often not tolerable. In response to reality and in order to assert and reinstate privilege, people who feel entitled often strive to establish and retrieve what they believe is their due. As you can imagine, the collateral damage is substantial.

The entwinement of expectations and entitlement is also represented in everyday life of "normal" people. The current economic downturn has set many back on their heels. While it seems reasonable for people to expect employment suitable with respect to their training and experience, it is commonplace for young people to expect that careers will be handed to them. Many college students assume that, upon graduation, they will find well-paying jobs in their chosen field. When their expectations are not fulfilled, they are prone to become resentful and sometimes to remain in denial about the economic realities.

Whereas entitlement has a fitting place in our lives and our expectations,[51] it can take over like a cancer and destroy your ability to live intact.

HUMILITY

There is a solution to the problem of inappropriate entitlement. It is divinely ordained and meant to help you assume right and healthy relationships with God and others in the world around you. It is the practice of humility.

Humility is the quality of being modest or respectful. To be humble is to be deferent and without pretensions. However, do not mistake temperamental modesty or false humility for real humility, which is an attitude of the heart. A person can be shy or unassuming, yet still harbor resentment and a grudge that the world has wronged him (i.e., that he has things coming to him). Humility carries a truly unassuming and sacrificing attitude, a willingness to put others ahead, and modesty about one's own importance. Humility is the opposite of pride, arrogance, and self-centeredness. Actually, humility counters the Self in that it requires something to which to defer.

God teaches, expects, and rewards humility. Jesus Christ taught and practiced it. The Bible contains at least ninety-one references to humility. It is the mechanism by which man can assume a proper perspective on life and in relation to the Almighty. God humbles us to remind us who is really in charge and to prepare us for his blessings (Deuteronomy 8:10–18). He reminds us to refrain from prideful illusions:

---

51. For example, a warrantee entitles you to repairs on certain products. Marriage entitles people to legal and personal privileges. Children are entitled to be protected and nurtured.

But remember the Lord your God, for it is he who gives you the ability to produce wealth, and so confirms his covenant, which he swore to your forefathers, as it is today. (Deuteronomy 8:18)

God tells us to be like Jesus, who demonstrated the ultimate in humility by emptying himself as a sacrifice for all human sin:

Your attitude should be the same as that of Christ Jesus: Who, being in very nature God, did not consider equality with God something to be grasped, but made himself nothing, taking the very nature of a servant, being made in human likeness. And being found in appearance as a man, he humbled himself and became obedient to death—even death on a cross! (Philippians 2:6–8)

The Bible further exhorts us to live with a humble demeanor:

But he gives us more grace. That is why Scripture says: "God opposes the proud but gives grace to the humble." (James 4:6)

Humble yourselves before the Lord, and he will lift you up. (James 4:10)

Young men, in the same way be submissive to those who are older. All of you, clothe yourselves with humility toward one another because, God opposes the proud but gives grace to the humble. Humble yourselves, therefore, under God's mighty hand, that he may lift you up in due time. (1 Peter 5:5–6)

Be completely humble and gentle; be patient, bearing with one another in love. (Ephesians 4:2)

BECOMING HUMBLE

Like many human flaws, those of pride, arrogance, and entitlement are easy to see in others, yet hard to spot or admit in ourselves. Is it because of ego, the narrative, or a spiritual blindness and defiance that prevents us from submitting to God and his will? This is the crux of the matter when it comes to living in the world as it is, rather than as we might wish. To superimpose one's will over God's will is foolish and doomed. Needless to say, it works at cross-purposes with living intact.

Turning from entitlement to an attitude and lifestyle of humility is a gradual and difficult course, yet its rewards are unsurpassed.

The steps toward humility are both sequential and nonlinear, both methodical and spiritual. Maturation and the impact of life experiences and lessons learned over time are requisites for becoming humble. Yet they are not sufficient, for many people mature and live through tempering experiences without becoming humble. There is a spiritual dimension that allows some people to "get" the paradox of their smallness in the scheme of things along with the glorious revelation of how much God loves them and the rest of us.

Although age and experience matter, some individuals show humility early in life. One shouldn't mistake shyness, anxiety, or deference for humility. One can have a quiet temperament and behave unobtrusively, yet harbor rebellion and resentment in the heart. True humility arises from the profound experience that God is omnipotent and loving, that he has made provision for our sins and weaknesses, and that his mercy and grace abound. Even children can experience this in great measure (Matthew 19:14).

MY TRANSFORMATION

At the beginning of this chapter, I acknowledged my own tendencies toward entitlement. In this book, I have described some of my struggles along with the tools and principles that have helped me overcome them. The purpose of *Living Intact* is to assist you in understanding and using these tools and principles for your benefit and to grow in grace, wisdom, and yearning to become closer to God. Perhaps some of my struggles will resonate with you.

Long before I knew about the tools and principles described in this book, I struggled rather ineffectively with life, with myself, and with the world on its own and God's terms. I was a mixture of love and sensitivity, arrogance and pride, ambition and hopelessness, keenness and blindness, self-awareness and oblivion, and other attractive, obnoxious, and contradictory qualities. Being imperfect, I continually strive to improve myself. I'm a work in progress, as are you. Though life is far better for me now,

I still remember the pivotal moments and periods that turned things toward a better direction.

I suffered from depression and anxiety for many years, but there were two periods that stand out as nadirs in my despair. The first was during my late adolescence, and the second was around the time I turned thirty. I recount this because each of these periods, while contributing to my overall development, produced different outcomes in my choices, beliefs, intactness, and ultimately in my life's direction and contribution.

My first period of despair led to recovery through self-sufficiency and entitlement. My second led to God's salvation and the revelation of humility.

I had a stormy adolescence that included arguing and fighting with my parents, running away from home, and periods of both illicit and prescription drug use. When I was sixteen, I had a physical fight with my father, whereupon I left home. I returned home under the auspices of psychiatric therapy, which included episodes of hospitalization and intermittent medication with the older psychotropic drugs. I graduated high school with excellent grades (though I had quit the varsity basketball team) and headed off to college. This was in the 1960s, and I used the era as an excuse for partying and rebellion. Eventually, I dropped classes, became more excessive in my habits, escalated into a nervous breakdown, and sank into a deep depression. I was arrested and jailed for drug possession and forced into rehabilitation. This only made me angrier and more resistant. After a binge of living on the streets in several U.S cities, I returned to New York, reenrolled in college, and began to rebuild my life. At that time, I longed for what I remembered as my former glory—being a respected athlete and student and being on a fast track toward achievement. I had been popular and socially comfortable, though not in the circles in which I sought to be admired. I was cocky but insecure, ambitious yet pessimistic.

After about a year of recovery, I returned to my former university and got on track toward a bachelor's degree and a more normal lifestyle. I quit drugs, plunged into physical training and health, worked full-time, and developed rewarding and socially validating relationships. I became "well-adjusted" and productive. I was delighted to be functioning and feeling well. I reveled in the tenuous approval of my parents and respected elders. I achieved. Moving in a swift undercurrent, I soon was swept up in the rapids of entitlement. I became consumed by striving for self-gratification, obsessive goal orientation, and the belief that success—on my terms—was my right and that I had it coming to me after a painful and lengthy detour. My narrative said that I was misunderstood, underestimated, maligned, and deprived of rewards and triumph.

My newfound adjustment and achievement was laudable, but it was marred by my sense of entitlement. I never felt recognized or appreciated enough. I was unfulfilled and unhappy. Unknowingly, I projected these sentiments on the circumstances, attributes, and actions of others for my own inner restlessness and lack of fulfillment. Unwittingly, I chose to believe my narrative and to feel undervalued and entitled.

I earned my three university degrees, met my first wife, and began my career. After two years in Los Angeles, we moved to San Francisco. Unbeknownst to me at the time, God had set things in motion, and my life was about to descend to one of its lowest points. God wanted my attention.

Within months after moving to San Francisco, I lost my beloved dog to illness. He had been my best friend for over a decade, and I became deeply depressed. My wife was cantankerous and distant, and my job was not going well. I was broke and in debt. I was gaining more weight. The walls of my life were moving inward, and I saw no way out. Everything looked bleak. I was worthless, and life was bitterly disappointing. It wasn't supposed to turn out this way. It was unfair. I was neglected and deprived.

During bouts of tears and hours alone, I cried out in anger and desperation. I railed and pleaded with a God who was supposed to be there, but whom I couldn't see or connect with. I yelled at the universe, for no one else was listening. I had come to the end of myself.

And then, something happened.

One evening, my friend Gary came over to our house to visit. While his wife talked with my wife in another room, Gary listened to my woes sympathetically. I knew that Gary was a Christian, though he had grown up Jewish. I liked him very much, and I admired his composure and positive attitude. Gary had talked to me about Jesus before, but now I listened more openly since I had reached bottom with regard to confidence, self-respect, and belief that my own abilities and resources could sustain me.

Gary invited me to pray with him. He prayed that Jesus would come into my heart, provide for and take care of me, relieve my anguish, and make me a part of his kingdom for eternity. I felt strange and awkward, and I had that familiar and uncomfortable feeling that someone was trying to sell me something I didn't want. After a few minutes, that uncomfortable feeling disappeared, and I became flooded with a profound sense of relief and calmness. It felt a bit like finishing a road running race, except nothing hurt. Gary sat with me and hugged me; then, he talked about what it is like to walk with God. I heard him in the background; my immediate sense of relief and serenity overcame me. I had surrendered without failing. My life had changed forever![52]

That was about thirty years ago. Over the ensuing decades, I have matured and grown in grace with God's guidance and blessings. Many people in my life thought this Christian-Jesus thing was another fad, but this endeavor has been different—rewarding, transforming, and enduring. The remarkable thing about Jesus is that the more I get to know him, the sweeter he is!

It has taken time, of course, to refine the many rough edges in me. I committed my life to God long before I discovered the tools and secrets in *Living Intact*. Had I not made that pivotal decision, I probably would have still benefited from the powerful technologies that help people, but I doubt that I would have the quality of life and happiness that comes through humility and submission to God.

It is fascinating how choice and challenge work together to help us grow and to influence perception, receptivity, and the flow of life-changing decisions. Previously described techniques such as EEG neurofeedback, Thought Field Therapy, and behavior modification can be used to shape and mold character, develop self-control, and get rid of troubling symptoms. These techniques and protocols circumvent the need for willpower in meeting challenges. They make us *capable* of greater humility, as they improve our brain function, sensitivity, awareness, and emotional equanimity. Yet the fundamental choice to surrender, submit, and defer to God's higher authority is an act of individual will and intention of the heart (Proverbs 4:4; 4:21–23). That the choice to surrender one's will is the ultimate determinant of free will is an astounding and divine paradox.

TRANSFORMING YOURSELF

If you are a follower of Jesus, then you already know what I'm talking about. If you are not yet committed, but considering the possibility of

---

52. Thank you, Gary!

walking with God, as he desires, then I invite you to sink to your knees—both of them—and pray:

> *"Dear God, please hear me and accept me with all of my troubles and flaws. Forgive me for my sins, including my pride and selfishness. Wash me clean and allow me to enter into your rest forever. Let Jesus and your Holy Spirit be my guide and teach me your ways. Help me to be humble and to love others, as you love me. In Jesus' name, I pray. Amen."*

As you allow the transformation of humility to occur, you will increasingly recognize your own tendencies to put yourself first, assert your privileges and rights, and justify your entitlements. With God's help, it will gradually become easier for you to set aside your beliefs and feelings about what you are owed. You will more keenly discern how others harbor and display these entitlement tendencies, and you will see how it blinds them.

You will become less frustrated when life doesn't deliver what you want in the manner and time you desire. You will handle conflict better, as you become less invested in "winning" and more focused on surrender, sacrifice, and peace. You will savor and appreciate what you have and feel more comfortable about releasing what is withheld, required, or taken away. You will grow toward greater understanding that *everything* in your life is a gift from God.

You will become less demanding, more patient and understanding. You will cherish the blessing of sympathy and empathy and look for opportunities to practice and exercise them. Others will feel more at ease with you, and you will notice a decrease in the frequency and intensity of threat.

The wonder and mysteries of nature will capture your fancy with renewed excitement and awe. You will find the energy to serve others, even when you are depleted. You will continually experience the astonishing revelation that you are at once and forever small and insignificant in the scheme of things and yet unique, precious, loved, and very important to God. You will want to share this blessing with others because you know how much it means to you.

As you grow more familiar with humility, you will love more deeply and find it easier to relinquish your old habits.

Love is patient, love is kind. It does not envy, it does not boast, it is not proud. It is not rude, it is not self-seeking, it is not easily angered, it keeps no record of wrongs. Love does not delight in evil, but rejoices with the truth. It always protects, always trusts, always hopes, always perseveres. Love never fails. But where there are prophecies, they will cease; where there are tongues, they will be stilled; where there is knowledge, it will pass away. For we know in part and we prophesy in part, but when perfection comes, the imperfect disappears. When I was a child, I talked like a child, I thought like a child, I reasoned like a child. When I became a man, I put childish ways behind me. Now we see but a poor reflection as in a mirror; then we shall see face to face. Now I know in part; then I shall know fully, even as I am fully known. And now these three remain: faith, hope and love. But the greatest of these is love. (1 Corinthians 13:4–13)

It will be much easier for you to connect with and depend on other people without feeling inadequate or incomplete. Instead of feeling entitled, you will relinquish demands and neediness and accept instead the reality that you do need other people, but not to confirm your worthiness or identity. You will combine pride and satisfaction in your work and abilities with a humble recognition that it is God who dictates what succeeds and what does not bear fruit and that you need to depend upon him, even as you strive in your own work and sacrifice.

I am the true vine, and my Father is the gardener. He cuts off every branch in me that bears no fruit, while every branch that does bear fruit he prunes so that it will be even more fruitful. You are already clean because of the word I have spoken to you. Remain in me, and I will remain in you. No branch can bear fruit by itself; it must remain in the vine. Neither can you bear fruit unless you remain in me. I am the vine; you are the branches. If a man remains in me and I in him, he will bear much fruit; apart from me you can do nothing. If anyone does not remain in me, he is like a branch that is thrown away and withers; such branches are picked up, thrown into the fire and burned. If you remain in me and my words remain in you, ask whatever you wish, and it will be given you. This is to my Father's glory, that you bear much fruit, showing yourselves to be my disciples. (John 15:1–8)

Most of all, when you replace entitlement with humility, you will experience deepening and continuing gratefulness for what you have and the opportunities and second chances afforded you. Forgiveness will become first nature for you; when others crowd or bear down upon you with their pressing needs and entitlement, you will understand, forgive, and pray for them.

For this reason, since the day we heard about you, we have not stopped praying for you and asking God to fill you with the knowledge of his will through all spiritual wisdom and understanding. And we pray this in order that you may live a life worthy of the Lord and may please him in every way: bearing fruit in every good work, growing in the knowledge of God, being strengthened with all power according to his glorious might so that you may have great endurance and patience, and joyfully giving thanks to the Father, who has qualified you to share in the inheritance of the saints in the kingdom of light. For he has rescued us from the dominion of darkness and brought us into the kingdom of the Son he loves, in whom we have redemption, the forgiveness of sins. (Colossians 1:9–14)

DEALING WITH ENTITLEMENT IN OTHERS

There is an old saying that goes: *we are all the same in kind, but different in degree.* As you grow and mature and become more understanding and accepting of the world and others as they are, you will recognize how the sense of entitlement generates selfish, insensitive, and difficult behaviors in those around you. This unfolding awareness, along with the tools and secrets of living intact that you have learned in this book, will help you deal more lovingly and effectively with people when they are difficult.

We have to manage and set limits for others even when they don't play by the rules we take for granted. The store clerk or your co-worker may feel burdened or stressed and think nothing of being insolent or demanding. Your spouse may brood over what he or she does not have and blame you for not providing it. Your child may complain about his limited privileges and restrictions you impose on his computer use and electronic access, or he may act as though he expects *you* to do his homework.

How can you deal with unreasonable behavior from others—especially the ones you really care about—when they cannot see or refuse to acknowledge and modify their own sense of entitlement? How can you be humble and still not let others walk all over you?

As usual, let's use God's Word as a starting point. What does the Bible say about this? What does God say about how to respond when people treat you poorly? Listen to Jesus:

> *You have heard that it was said, Eye for eye, and tooth for tooth. But I tell you, Do not resist an evil person. If someone strikes you on the right cheek, turn to him the other also. And if someone wants to sue you and take your tunic, let him have your cloak as well. If someone forces you to go one mile, go with him two miles. Give to the one who asks you and do not turn away from the one who wants to borrow from you. You have heard that it was said, 'Love your neighbor and hate your enemy.' But I tell you: Love your enemies and pray for those who persecute you, that you may be sons of your Father in heaven. He causes his sun to rise on the evil and the good, and sends rain on the righteous and the unrighteous.* (Matthew 5:38–45)

Throughout the decades when I have read these words, I have wrestled—and still do—to understand and apply them. Does this mean to give in and let everyone have his way? I don't think that's what Jesus is saying. Clearly, Jesus speaks unpopular truths, stands up to people, and sets limits through his ministry and his teachings. He is not a doormat. When Jesus tells us not to resist and evil person, to go the extra mile with him and not turn away, he is expressing the humility of not reacting with entitlement or the expectation of favor. Jesus exhorts us to love our enemies and to pray for those who persecute us. He is not telling us to find evil or antagonistic behavior *acceptable*. He is telling us to *expect* it and to receive it without retaliating in kind. *God causes his sun to rise on the evil and the good, and sends rain on the righteous and the unrighteous* (Matthew 5:45).

God's wisdom translates into practical measures you can take when the entitlement that others display becomes inappropriate or offensive. If you refrain from responding to entitlement with indignation, anger, or self-righteousness, you will be much more flexible in your options to set limits and to control both yourself and the future responses of the person who acts entitled. "Turning the other cheek" means restraint from lashing out in retaliation. It does not mean "Hit me again." When you refrain—turn the other cheek—you are saying to the offender, "Look at what you've done. Yet I still love you and pray for you, that you will see the error of your ways." Going the extra mile and not turning away from the one who wants to borrow from you does not imply giving money or possessions you cannot afford to anyone who asks. Rather, it means not resisting an offender by trying to overpower him with force or will. Instead, honor the other person by submission and with sacrifice and service. Recognize and honor his needs and his feelings without necessarily reacting or agreeing. Allow him to see your humility and lack of privilege. This manner of responding preserves the integrity of both parties and paves the way for self-entitled person to recognize his offense and the overstepping of boundaries.

Let's examine how to put this into practice. Suppose your spouse feels entitled to have dinner prepared and to be waited on, even though you have had a long, hard day and don't feel well. He may be demanding and sarcastic, expecting you to perform and criticizing you for what he sees as lacking. The natural temptation is to snap back, put him in his place, and bemoan your set of burdens and injustices. Of course, you can anticipate where that will lead—into further resentment, stubbornness, and degradation of the feelings and respect. Instead, try the following:

1. **Acknowledge the need and the feelings**
   "I know you're hungry and you probably don't understand why dinner is not ready. It looks to you like I've had hours to prepare while you've been working, and you might feel that I don't appreciate you since I don't have dinner ready."

2. **Validate the expectations and ask if there are other possibilities**
   "It probably seems to you that I should have dinner ready instead of keeping you waiting while you're hungry. I can see how you would feel entitled to this. I wonder if there might be any other way possible to look at the situation—any mitigating circumstances or other points of view..."

3. **Set limits and ask for reality testing**
   "Your expectation that I prepare dinner every night according to your specifications is unrealistic. Sorry to disappoint you, but I

work all day, too. If you think I'm being rebellious or unreasonable, why don't we ask some of our friends how they work these things out? I'm even willing to bring this before your parents or our minister or counselor. Perhaps I can talk with one of your friends or co-workers about how he deals with his spouse."

4. **Negotiate an agreement or compromise**

    "I understand your frustration, and I do apologize for not meeting your needs. Perhaps we could come up with a more satisfying and workable arrangement. How about if I make dinner three nights a week and you make dinner two nights a week? We can bring in prepared food two nights—you pick it up one night, and I'll pick it up the other."

5. **Request commitment**

    "I need to hear from you that you're willing to try a new arrangement. I promise to call you a half-hour before dinner time and let you know how I'm progressing and what you can expect. I'd like you to ask me how my day went and to be respectful when you talk to me because my feelings are sensitive. Do I have your agreement on that?"

Let's replay this with a homework scenario:

1. **Acknowledge the need and the feelings**

    "I hear your complaints about getting too much homework, needing help with it, and not having enough time. I know what it feels like to have too much to do."

2. **Validate the expectations and ask if there are other possibilities**

    "You seem to think that I *have* to help you with homework and that you don't have to do it unless I sit there with you. I've also heard you say that you have no homework on several occasions, and I subsequently found out that you did have more work to do than you said. Perhaps we should sit down with your teacher and hear from her exactly what is expected, how well you are doing it, and how much I should help."

3. **Set limits and ask for reality testing**

    "The truth is that it's *your* homework and *your responsibility* to finish it. I have already graduated (fifth, sixth, etc.) grade. Any help

I give you is a gift. You are not entitled to have me do homework with you, and you certainly are mistaken if you expect me to do it for you."

4. **Negotiate an agreement or compromise**
"I am willing to help you under certain conditions. One is that you sit down at the assigned time with all of your materials and a complete list of your assignments—what is due and when it is due. Two is that you have a good attitude—no whining, complaining, blaming, or raising your voice. Three is that you begin by doing what you can and you make a list of questions for me at the end. Four is that you thank me each time I assist you."

5. **Request commitment**
"I will only help you with your homework if you agree to what I asked. I do want you to be successful, and I am willing to help. I need your agreement and cooperation. Do I have your word on this?"

It is common for children to complain that something is "not fair" when they are under duress or they don't want to do something. This "not fair" argument is a disguise for entitlement. When people (especially children) complain that something is not fair, it often means that they are not getting their way. Of course, the self-centered sense of entitlement recruits the narrative to make a compelling case for victimization and unfairness.

Here is a helpful way to pierce such self-absorbed fantasies: tell the person that "fairness" always depends on a set of rules. In order for something to be unfair, some rule must be broken or violated. *Ask what rule was broken that resulted in the situation being unfair.* Then, gently suggest that what seems unfair to him may actually be his resentment that he didn't get what he wanted, rather than a rule being broken that resulted in unfairness.[53]

I often use sports analogies to make this point. Many people understand and follow sports, they accept the rules, and they can follow a logical

---

53. Of course, there are many instances of unfairness where people might complain they are victims, and this is justified and true. If you are robbed, scammed, or the victim of a perpetration, then clearly someone has broken a rule resulting in unfairness to you. In such cases, you are not acting with entitlement, although the perpetrator may be doing so (as though the rules don't apply to him).

argument when they are not absorbed in the heat of their own emotions. I might explain that in baseball a foul ball is when the ball lands outside the foul lines and a fair ball is when it lands in between those lines. Nobody who understands baseball disputes that rule, although they may become angry and blame the umpire.

When teams compete, any given play or call makes one team less happy than the other. However, fairness is based upon rules, not how someone feels about the ruling. Of course, not getting one's way doesn't necessarily result from a competition with people, but the idea gets across that we can deceive ourselves into believing that an outcome unfavorable to us is actual foul play or injustice.

In dealing with others' sense of entitlement, you will find it useful to invoke the secrets of living intact. Maintaining your composure and self-control, eliminating negative emotions, manipulating outcome probabilities by properly using reinforcement, and partnering with the challenge process (see chapter 8), helping others become more flexible, and seeing more adaptive possibilities all work toward creating better harmony and functionality.

It is startling to see how hubris and self-aggrandizement can blind people to their own shortcomings and render them impervious to reason. It is humbling to realize how loved we are and how many gifts we receive, even in the absence of getting every outcome we desire.

MODESTY AND CONFIDENCE

Since humility carries qualities of being modest, respectful, deferent, and unpretentious, how can you be humble and still be confident? Isn't it vital to have self-respect and confidence and to take pride in your abilities and performance, even as you practice and display the attitude and demeanor of humility? The answer is yes—you can have and display both.

Being confident is not the same as being boastful, and being humble does not exclude letting your talents, efforts, and intentions shine.

Confidence is the habit of expecting favor from life's ordinary opportunities and of practicing greatness in the face of seeming insignificance. Again, we see the inspiring and humbling paradox of ordinariness and greatness and of insignificance and importance. When you are confident, you expect favor (that things will go your way), and this is based on past experience. When you are modest and confident, you work quietly to manifest the narrowing discrepancy between your greater expectations and lesser expectations. You can state your abilities and achievements, but you don't need to trumpet them. You are secure in that they are evident.

Humility will bear fruit in modesty. When you turn to God, he is on your side. Even when the chips are down and you are unsure of yourself, God is backing you up, and he is in control. There is no better confidence.

> *Keep your lives free from the love of money and be content with what you have, because God has said, "Never will I leave you; never will I forsake you." So we say with confidence, "The Lord is my helper; I will not be afraid. What can man do to me?"* (Hebrews 13:5–6)

PRODUCING GLOBAL CHANGE

Think about how much selfishness and conflict there is in the world. How many traumatizing atrocities are perpetrated that reflect the assumptions of what people believe that they are entitled to? How much insidious damage caused by indifference to the environment, the people who cohabit our planet, and the natural laws that govern it!

It is easy to criticize politicians and leaders for wars, shambling policies, and social and economic neglect. It is more difficult to look inward to one's heart and outward to one's own habits that are contributing to the desolation and marching to the silent beat of entitlement.

If I can pay my bills, am I entitled to ignore the plight of those without sufficient basic resources or opportunities? If I have enough, can I justifiably deny contribution to God's causes? What should I do about my carbon footprint—the ways I use petroleum, my recycling habits? How should I eat, not only for my own health, but for the health of the planet?

At the material level, I take plenty for granted. I feel entitled to running water, waste disposal, electricity, and even wireless service. How miffed I can become when there is a power outage or when a cell phone call is dropped! Yet these are smaller matters when compared with the patterns of letting one's nervous system accelerate into habitual aggression and the ensuing entitlement that the narrative concocts in self-justification. Perpetrations abound, both intentional and incidental, when entitlement slips into control.

Given the proper awareness and the tools to self-regulate and exercise compassion and self-control, growth in humility becomes a more available and appealing choice. The subjugation of entitlement and the development of humility go a long way toward reducing human suffering.

VI

AN ULTIMATE QUESTION

CHAPTER 19
MUST YOU SUFFER?

I am the cause of my experience and the effect of God's will.
—Mark Steinberg

If you ask about the ultimate goal in life, many people would answer that their aim and desire is to be happy. However construed by each individual, happiness is held and offered as the supreme value and the overriding desire by the majority. Virtually every parent I have queried (including my own) expressed with earnest pleading the hope that his child would attain and experience happiness. Though rarely defined and poorly circumscribed, happiness is, nonetheless, so often enshrined as paramount.

All I want is for him to be happy in life!

Is it any wonder, then, that our culture views suffering as the enemy, a foe to be cast out, eschewed, numbed, diminished, and even denied? If happiness—or well-being—is the objective, then suffering would seem to embody all that is to be avoided. To the extent that happiness, contentment, and well-being are defined as the absence of suffering, the two states are diametrically opposed and mutually exclusive.

In an age of medical marvels, technology, affluence, heightened communication, awareness, and global movements toward enlightenment, suffering is widely held to be *needless*—a vestige of dark age ignorance, corrupt politics, greed, and institutional dogma. This modern view protests the inevitability of suffering, seeking instead to alleviate, reduce, or eliminate the harsh realities facing the poor, bereft, oppressed, and needy. It is a view that rebels against the oppression of authoritarian or monopolistic governments and social orders. The belief that suffering is the result of man's inhumanity to man is buttressed by the tenet that humane treatment will greatly reduce suffering, and that this endeavor—the relief of pain and suffering—is among the noblest of virtues. It is a foundation for the creed of modern medicine. The belief that suffering can and should be reduced abuts the somewhat dissonant philosophy of acceptance and transcendence of life circumstances. Contrasting attitudes would appear at odds:

- striving to control the misfortune of suffering versus accepting life on its own terms
- holding man responsible for inflicting and ignoring suffering or for relieving suffering and building utopia versus the relegation to a God-controlled universe

These apparent paradoxes beg for explanation and resolution. In actuality, they are neither contradictory nor exclusionary. Their seeming opposition arises from a misunderstanding of suffering and from a worldview that is relativistic rather than absolute.[54] From a relativistic perspective, truth and reality vary, depending upon the originating point of view. Thus, there can be multiple truths and realities according to who is the central observer (and of course, in accord with that observer's needs and self-interests).

---

54. In Christian doctrine regarding truth, relativism is the belief that truth (including right and wrong) is determined by its value to and proof by the observer. It is the belief that concepts such as right and wrong, goodness and badness, or truth and falsehood are not absolute, but change from culture to culture and situation to situation. Thus, the philosophy of "live and let live" or "you do your thing and I'll do mine" are acceptable variants of relativistic thinking, which necessarily revolves around the human self as a source of truth and point of reference. Absolutism, by contrast, is the belief that values such as truth and morality are absolute and not conditional upon human perception. Absolutism is fundamental to Christian thinking in that it acknowledges God as the creator and source of all that is truthful and the maker and determinant of right and wrong. This view holds that such truth is knowable by man through God's Word, the Bible, though it is not necessarily convenient to man's purposes.

A metaphor of nature may serve to illustrate: relatively speaking, the view and the reality look different to the eagle than they do to the rodent. From the broader perspective of absolutism, the eagle preys upon the rodent, not vice versa, and the two animals are intertwined in the greater scheme of things.

Similarly, suffering appears different to one who suffers than it does to one observing (or ignoring or avoiding) the suffering. From the relativistic perspective, suffering can seem unfair, oppressive, pointless, manipulative, and so on, depending upon your beliefs and what you have and are experiencing. From an absolute perspective, however, suffering is a universal experience. It is woven into the fabric of life, survival, death, and, yes, rebirth. This inevitability does not dictate a passive, blind acceptance, a victim mentality, or a rationale for domination, cruelty, or selfish manipulation. Rather, it begins to explain that suffering has a purpose, and it points to a path for using suffering as a steppingstone toward living intact.

From a godless perspective, suffering is an unfortunate, harmful, and often needless byproduct of man's selfishness and callous behavior. Certainly, the state of the world would supply evidence to support such a conclusion. But that is only part of the picture. In a God-filled view, suffering plays a large and important role in man's growth and enlightenment.

WHAT IS SUFFERING?

Suffering is the experience of undergoing great discomfort, distress, or pain in body or mind. Suffering can be physical, psychological (mental or emotional), or spiritual. To suffer is to endure or put up with something painful or unpleasant. For example, you can suffer an injustice or an indignity from an offense that is perpetrated upon you. You can suffer a loss. You can suffer from a disease or affliction. You can even suffer someone's boorish manners or bad company.

Suffering connotes vulnerability and the state of being at a disadvantage. When you suffer, you are made to confront your limitations, regardless of your beliefs about the cause of the suffering. The experience has humbling effects. Though suffering implies some continuation of discomfort or adversity, its duration and intensity vary. So also do the results vary, depending upon the situation, the person, and the perception and interpretation of the sufferer. Indeed, we all suffer, for that is a profound part of being human.

Suffering is not the same as pain. Though the two are closely allied, each bears distinct attributes that teach in different ways. Pain is primarily an experience of sensation. Traditionally traced to neural pathways, pain is the nervous system's mechanism for survival, a major defense against activity that can be harmful. Unfortunately, pain often persists after the "lesson" is well learned. Pain is also psychological/emotional. The stigma attached to this type of pain—that it is not real, but only in one's head—often makes it worse for the victim, adding shame and isolation that intensifies the pain.

* Pain may hurt, but not always humble, its victims.*Whereas pain is often equated with vulnerability, suffering is often equated with powerlessness. Wounds and injuries may cause pain and may leave lasting brokenness. Brokenness may cause suffering and/or pain.*Suffering invariably causes brokenness. However,*suffering also carries with it the power for healing.*To be broken is to experience vulnerability and that one is dependent upon something more and other than oneself for rebuilding to become intact.*Brokenness and suffering induce and intensify humility. Reaching the limit of oneself and depending upon God for rescue and healing imbues a spiritual sustenance and power.

For example, many athletes suffer pain from training or injuries. Pain may disable them temporarily with grave discomfort. However, their suffering may be minimal or absent in the sense that their ego remains intact, and they weather the pain in anticipation of resuming their activities. On the other hand, a person could lose his job and, thus, his sense of identity, productivity, and belonging. This might be a case without physical "pain" but with much suffering.

No one likes pain or suffering. When you hurt, you want to make it go away. There are postmodern medical names for this, such as "pain control" or "pain management." Have you ever heard of "suffering control" or "suffering management"?

People have different thresholds for tolerance of pain. In some circles, high pain tolerance is unabashedly considered a mark of character. The ability to endure pain, but not let it stop you, is even embedded in the cultural adoration of sports and hero worship.*But *suffering* is an intensely private and personal experience in which no one exults—except those who recognize the potential for suffering to reconstitute what is broken, bereft, vulnerable, and imperfect.

Surely, I am not advocating stoicism or repression of feelings in the face of suffering. Like you, I too experience pain, hurt, and suffering. When I do, I want to relieve it, and I often cower from or flee its oppression. But I have also experienced the cleansing effects of suffering, and though I do not seek it, I have learned that it is a powerful way to live intact and to become closer to God.*Suffering is an important pathway to building character and to fulfilling what you are meant to be and to accomplish.

PARENTAL SUFFERING

My mother and father taught me important lessons about suffering. When I experienced adversity, setbacks, and disappointments, insult, or injury—and it seemed to happen frequently—I would complain and vent my hurt, anger, and frustration. My mother sought to protect and console me as much as she could (too much, by many accounts). For many years, I selfishly blamed her for contributing to my sense of inadequacy and lack of independence because she was always *there*. I suspected that she engineered my insufficiency so she could rescue me and underscore how much I needed her. (I gained support for this fantasy from the many books I read and therapists I saw.) However, my mother ultimately reinforced an important lesson that I've found most helpful over the years. When I was despondent, hurt, or at odds with the world, she would often say, "Into every life some rain must fall." For me, this softened the harsh reality of suffering, and it modeled for me, metaphorically, that hardship and suffering are a part of life, experienced by everybody, and that I had better accept it. Moreover, my mother, a fierce and prideful protector and competitor, taught me to bow in the face of overwhelming circumstances. By telling me about the rain in life, my mom let me experience the suffering she could not relieve, and she imbued me with the knowledge that I would survive it with dignity until the sunshine appeared once again.

My father reacted to my troubles and my suffering in a different manner. Given to defensiveness, suspicion, and fear, my dad would routinely blame me overtly for my suffering, citing the particulars of my behavior that he thought were to blame. He often subsumed his capacity for compassion beneath a strangulating view that the world was a threatening and hostile place and that I deserved what I got for venturing out into it. According to my father, the world was out to get you, and if it got you, it was your own fault. Though he had great intellect and sensitivity, my father felt weak and stupid, and he projected these outward. In the abstract, he had pity and compassion upon the less fortunate. Day-to-day, he viewed suffering as the result of a hostile world preying upon weakness and stupidity.

In my childish hubris, I studied my father and apparently concluded that what I should model from him was the highly polished family trait of feeling sorry for myself. I progressed assiduously along this path until I reached a Rubicon that changed me forever. Ironically, it was my father's leadership in suffering (and a prelude to my own development in the ability to weather and grow from it). The event took place when I was nineteen and my father's father was dying. Grandpa was taken to the hospital by ambulance, and my father knew the end was near. At the time, my dad and I were not getting along, as usual. During the stretch of months leading up to grandpa's demise, my dad and I had barely talked. My anger toward him seethed, yet I was torn between my prideful indignation and a gnawing sense of compassionate urgency, as my dad was losing his father, his best friend.

After grandpa's admission to the hospital, we had a period of waiting while the doctors attended to him. The traumatic day had diverted our attention away from food, but hunger was catching up with us. My father turned to me and said, "Well, if we're going to suffer, we might as well do it properly. Let's get something to eat, son."

✳ *If we're going to suffer, we might as well do it properly.* What an amazing attitude! It took me by surprise, this posture of submission and resolve. My father had yielded to the inevitability of suffering in this moment, and he accepted it and prepared to endure it with dignity.

Thus, I gleaned from my parents the attitude that suffering was, to some extent, inevitable and that one should accept and endure it with dignity. Though my parents were ambivalent models—complaining, blaming, ranting, self-pitying, like so many people do—they ultimately faced their circumstances, imperfections, and adversities with a humble acceptance and the resilient persistence that so often accompanies faith-based suffering.

But we have this treasure in jars of clay to show that this all-surpassing power is from God and not from us. We are hard pressed on every side, but not crushed; perplexed, but not in despair; persecuted but not abandoned; struck down, but not destroyed. (2 Corinthians 4:7–9)

Were I to tell you that I learned the lessons of suffering well from my parents, I would thereby oversimplify and gild my own gradual, arduous development, and I might also inadvertently impede your own spiritual growth. The seeds my parents planted took years to flower through the soil of my life. As God led me through agonizing adversity and a maze of illogical and barely interpretable events, I habitually resisted. My mantra was that circumstances were unfair and that I was entitled to better treatment and improved outcomes.

WHEN LIFE IS NOT FAIR

In a world where things don't go your way, where life hurts and your own hurts pall in the pathos of watching the horrors of genocide, cruelty, and even natural disasters, the conclusion that life is unfair seems justifiable. This was my outlook and also my rationalization for the inner reactions and outward behaviors I chose over many years. My attitudes and choices seemed logical and right (to me) because life was so capricious and random. Not that I was overtly cruel or wantonly destructive or even that much more selfish than the next person. Rather, my reactions to adversity, to the circumstances and events that knocked me off my high horse or kept me demoralized were responses aimed at venting grievances and/or correcting what I felt were glaring inequities placing me at disadvantage. My main methods were to complain or to escape. This style led to great dissatisfaction in the face of my unavoidable suffering.

Eventually, I grew to understand that my own issues with entitlement were subtle and intellectual enough to veil my indignation that life would vex and deprive me, that people wouldn't treat me right or recognize my efforts, and that providence would withhold its treasures and subject me instead to depression, weight problems, desperate financial straits, physical pain, and interpersonal despair. Vacillating between muted self-pity and righteous indignation, I tried to wheedle or power my way into a better deal with God. Though he showed me mercy, as I could never have deserved or even imagined, he also let me suffer.

My God, My God, why have you forsaken me? Why are you so far from saving me, so far from the words of my groaning? O my God, I cry out by day, but you do not answer, by night, and am not silent. (Psalm 22:1–2)

O Lord, do not rebuke me in your anger or discipline me in your wrath. Be merciful to me, Lord, for I am faint; O lord, heal me, for my bones are in agony. My soul is in anguish. How long, O Lord, how long? (Psalm 6:1–3)

Because my nature tends to be logical and analytical, I sought to understand and to sequence the occurrence and purpose of my suffering. Alas, that did little to palliate me or to relieve my distress. Once again, I was bargaining with God, explaining my worthiness and need for him to reveal his mysteries to me.

I have seen the burden God has laid on men. He has made everything beautiful in its time. He has also set eternity in the hearts of men; yet they cannot fathom what God has done from beginning to end. (Ecclesiastes 3:10–11)

Consider what God has done: Who can straighten what he has made crooked? When times are good, be happy; but when times are bad, consider: God has made the one as well as the other. Therefore, a man cannot discover anything about his future. (Ecclesiastes 7:13–14)

WHEN LIFE ISN'T FAIR

- God tells us we will have troubles—it is universal, though not divided equally.
- The Bible talks about inequities, injustices, and suffering.
- Unfairness and suffering may be consequences of individual behavior, collective wrongdoing, or God's inscrutable designs.
- Inequities, injustices, and suffering are burdens that can humble us and test our attitudes toward God.
- Inequities, injustices, and suffering affirm our belief in laws and rules, yet also transcend these statutes in the expression of their insufficiency to cope with life.

- Unfairness and suffering are challenges to develop wisdom in order to better cope with, understand, and appreciate the nature of life.
- Unfairness and suffering are challenges to our notions of personal sovereignty and control.
- Unfairness and suffering allow us to examine and affirm the nature of rules, laws, justice, and righteousness from God's perspective.
- God gives Jesus as a reason and sacrifice (payment) for unfairness, sin, and suffering.
- God gives Jesus as a model for reactions to suffering.
- God gives Jesus as a partner in suffering for a higher calling when life isn't fair.
- Unfairness and suffering are opportunities to confront our limitations and self-centeredness about how things should be.
- Unfairness and suffering are opportunities to overcome challenges, especially with regard to our self-sufficiency, faith, and dependence upon God.
- Unfairness and suffering are challenges to use God's tools, experience his grace, and to grow in character.
- Life's unfairness and suffering give our responsive choices more meaning, value, and contribution.
- Unfairness and suffering are opportunities to draw closer to God, to cherish his ways and his gifts, and to experience compassion and connection with others.

So what could I do when the best of my will, craft, wiles, and determination fell far short of insulating me from suffering or salving its infliction?

Into every life some rain must fall. (Pearl Steinberg)
If we're going to suffer, we might as well do it properly. (Daniel Steinberg)

I hated pain, and I cringed from the fatigue that makes cowards of us all. I needed a better solution. I felt tired, defeated, and alone. Bereft of other remedies—and accepting what God had placed in my way and upon my heart—I began to tolerate my suffering with gradual acceptance and occasional embrace. This process, and eventual transformation, was made possible through the surpassing power of God's Word in scripture. Each time I read the Bible, God spoke to my heart in more meaningful ways about my suffering, my experience, and what he had in store for me.

THE SECRETS OF SUFFERING

Though God retains his mysteries about why some things happen (even those that seem disastrous, cruel, or unfair), he gives some explanation and clear direction about the reasons for suffering and the proper reactions to it.

The apostle Peter offers a splendid and comforting summary of the issues surrounding suffering in the epistle of 1 Peter. This message was written to assuage the sufferings that first-century Christians experienced as they tried to live faithfully in a pagan and hostile society and in the face of ostracism and persecution. Though modern times are different, the parallels of adversity are strikingly similar, and we can find recapitulations of Peter's context in today's social ills, individual dysfunctions, and spiritual challenges.

Despite its opportunities and material abundance, our society is fraught with hostility, closed doors, intolerance, exclusion, aggression, and symbolic idol worship (self, glamour, ambition, money, etc.). Undercurrents of repression, racism, and political factions temper religious and social freedoms. Self-indulgence and intolerance vie for prominence, yielding the predictable surfeit of suffering. As we live longer and develop and exploit our planet, medical and technological advances have only scratched the surface of relieving suffering. Ironically, we have incurred sufferings unknown in previous times, even as we eliminate the agonies of more primitive eras. At an individual level, the personal suffering attributable to character flaws, bad habits, genetic influences, and personal misfortune continues at a rate that seems inestimable. And then, there are natural disasters and catastrophes deemed "acts of God."

The suffering about which Peter wrote applies broadband. Whether you experience a broken leg, a broken heart, a broken promise, or a broken carburetor, your efforts to live and remain intact will collide with adversity that more often than not includes suffering. Being a good person and living a righteous and moral life will not insulate you from the rain that falls into every life.

The words of Peter—God's words—speak clearly and cogently to all suffering. For God's universe is one of recapitulation in which what comes to pass recapitulates with the same essence and wisdom that is God's nature. For some, the replay includes harsh circumstances, poverty, persecution, or oppression. For others, it may be physical or mental handicaps, or perhaps great loss. Your suffering is appointed and joined by God, planned and permitted by him in a divine effort to make you aware of him and his grace, mercy, and invitation.

SECURITY IN SUFFERING

As nature girds its inhabitants to guard against potential threat and future challenges, so man gravitates toward security. To "suffer properly" involves, paradoxically, an embrace of suffering that offers the security of withstanding threat, surviving brokenness, and accepting the divine grace that carries you through the adversity. Living intact does not mean you will escape suffering. It means that you will use the assaults, threats, and challenges that impinge upon you to attain and preserve the peace and soundness of being that is the security God promises. Here is the foundation of that security:

> *Praise be to the God and Father of our Lord, Jesus Christ! In his great mercy, he has given us new birth into a living hope through the resurrection of Jesus Christ from the dead and into an inheritance that can never perish, spoil, or fade—kept in heaven for you, who through faith are shielded by God's power until the coming of the salvation that is ready to be revealed in the last time. In this you greatly rejoice, though now for a little while you may have had to suffer grief in all kinds of trials. These have come so that your faith—of greater worth than gold, which perishes even though refined by fire—may be proved genuine and may result in praise, glory and honor when Jesus Christ is revealed. Though you have not seen him, you love him, and are filled with an inexpressible and glorious joy, for you are receiving the goal of your faith, the salvation of your souls.* (1 Peter 1:3–9)

The security that prevails despite suffering is that which God provides through Jesus Christ. Note that it is past, present, and future. The past is the factual history of Jesus's earthly suffering, his death, and his resurrection. God has interrupted his recapitulation of nature with a singular departure in the person of Jesus, who brings a new covenant, a better replacement for the covenant God made with Moses. There has never been anything like it. Jesus came and went twice, and we are awaiting the third and final time. It is a recapitulation like none other. When Jesus was on earth, he served as a model for suffering. He not only suffered oppression, persecution, temptation, and rejection, but he suffered physical torture to the point of death. The present is the manner in which you can model after Jesus to live a more intact life in your own skin. The present also includes the Holy Spirit, that ineffable presence of God that indwells and give peace and power to believers. The future is the millennial kingdom where suffering will be gone.

Though Jesus was perfect, he suffered. Though he could have summoned his divine powers to avert suffering, he deferred to the will of God the Father. Why? Because Jesus's suffering was the atonement of mankind's sins—all sins and ever since!

REASONS FOR SUFFERING

If Jesus suffered to atone for everybody's sins, why then must you suffer? For one thing, it is an opportunity to emulate Jesus.

You may say, "No thank you. I accept Jesus, I revere and worship him, but what kind of 'Godfellow' would require me to suffer while claiming to be sacrificing and merciful?"

The apostle Peter puts it this way:

Who is going to harm you if you are eager to do good? But even if you suffer for what is right, you are blessed "Do not fear what they fear; do not be frightened." But in your hearts set apart Christ as Lord. Always be prepared to give an answer to everyone who asks you to give the reason for the hope that you have. But do this with gentleness and respect, keeping a clear conscience, so that those who speak maliciously against your good behavior in Christ may be ashamed of their slander. It is better, if it is God's will, to suffer for doing good than for doing evil. (1 Peter 1:13–17)

If you wear an attitude of hope despite suffering, others will notice and will be inspired and comforted by you. God places suffering in your life for reasons other than punishment, just as he did with his son, Jesus. The suffering of Jesus was a demonstration and a model. Jesus's life and suffering are models for how to live *in* the world (material reality) without being *of* the world (becoming attached to the pleasures and pains of the senses and flesh). The model of suffering that God wants you to emulate is not one of resignation or dissociation, but one of making God's sufficiency a priority. When you experience suffering in this manner, you will experience joy and relief as well as hardship. The discomfort, angst, and pain lie in the realm of your human vulnerability; the peace and ability to tolerate and put suffering in perspective reside in the spiritual dimension. Suffering "properly" involves the capacity to be hurt and broken without coming apart or sacrificing your integrity. Only through God can you do this, and thank God for that! Otherwise, you and I would put our hope in that which perishes, the things that moth and rust destroy and where thieves break in and steal (Matthew 6:19–21). This includes pride and dependence upon things, circumstances, and even our physical attributes and bodies.

All that you have is temporary—all, that is, except your word and God's Word. Christ's suffering frees you to let go[55] of your desperate and doomed attachment to that which is perishing. Suffering is a method for doing so.

> *Therefore, since Christ suffered in his body, arm yourselves with the same attitude, because he who has suffered in his body is done with sin. As a result, he does not live the rest of his earthly life for evil human desires, but rather for the will of God.* (1 Peter 4:1–2)

God steers you away from self-pity and from using circumstances and suffering as excuses to behave in ungodly ways:

> *For you have spent enough time in the past doing what pagans choose to do—living in debauchery, lust, drunkenness, orgies, carousing and detestable idolatry. They think it strange that you do not plunge with them into the same flood of dissipation, and they heap abuse on you. But they will have to give account to him who is ready to judge the living and the dead.*

---

55. *Letting go* is a spiritual process and an exercise of practiced skills. The Self skill of *permeability* discussed in chapters 3 and 13 is both a method and a result of letting go. Suffering teaches you how to let go. The connecting bridge is one of letting go in order to experience the spiritual blessings of suffering.

For this is the reason the gospel was preached even to those who are now dead, so that they might be judged according to men in regard to the body, but live according to God in regard to the spirit. (1 Peter 4:1–6)

Though Peter wrote in the context of persecution of Christians in the first century, his message carries deeper and broader meaning for the kind of suffering you may experience. The differentiation between body and spirit with regard to both suffering and judgment is important. It is a key to unlock your ability to "suffer properly." Jesus suffered in his earthly body so that God's spirit could absolve your sin and all the sins of humanity. Jesus experienced his body (including the hurting), but he was not "attached" to it in that he experienced a higher purpose in his suffering. Peter advises to *"arm yourself with the same attitude"* in order to *"not live the rest of earthly life for evil human desires, but rather for the will of God"* (1 Peter 4:1–2). This experiential shift is radical because it exhorts a reason for suffering that is productive and worthy, rather than pointless and painful.

Furthermore, Peter continues to remind that people will *"be judged according to men in regard to the body, but live according to God in regard to the spirit"* (1 Peter 4:6). This reveals that you will be judged at different levels and by different standards—those of men and those of God. You can choose which standards take priority for your inner experience and attention. Similarly, you can choose to become absorbed in suffering at the biological level of sensory discomfort and pain and at the psychological level of self-pity, self-preoccupation, and resentment, or you can depend upon God to make worthy the portion of your suffering that falls outside of his mercy.

REACTIONS IN SUFFERING

Just as the natural world and the cycles of life and human development follow principles of recapitulation, so do the themes of spiritual growth and character development. In your efforts to live intact, you have many opportunities to recapitulate Christ, and modeling your suffering after him is a significant one of them.

Jesus's suffering and his willingness to bear it benefited others. You, however, don't have to be persecuted or martyred in order to make a difference (Hebrews 12:4). Your own allotment of personal struggles and suffering are enough challenge for you to transform hardship into blessing for yourself and for others.

People notice how you bear with adversity. Are you quick to cry out and complain? Do you yell, "Foul!" and wave the banner of unfairness? If so, you have lots of company. Your feelings are understandable, and in the context of man's judgment and sensory, fleshly pursuits, your complaints may be justifiable. Suffering, however, is much too stressful, and its occurrence is far too significant to squander it *solely* on experiencing discomfort and seeking relief. (Of course, you should seek relief when possible, though sometimes, you will face suffering that finds no corporal relief.)

How, then, should you react to suffering? Scripture provides clear direction:

> *The end of all things is near. Therefore be clear minded and self-controlled so that you can pray. Above all, love each other deeply, because love covers a multitude of sins. Offer hospitality to one another without grumbling. Each one should use whatever gift he has received to serve others, faithfully administering God's grace in its various forms. If anyone speaks, he should do it with the strength that God provides, so that in all things, God may be praised through Jesus Christ. To him be the glory and power forever and ever. Amen (1 Peter 4:7–11)*

HOW TO PROPERLY COPE WITH SUFFERING

1. **Do not be surprised or take offense when you are beset by trials and suffering.**
   Your years of living should serve as evidence that the trials, trouble, adversity, and "the rain that must fall" in your life come as no surprise. You can expect these without being morose or negative or "waiting for the other shoe to drop" with suspicion or an ominous attitude. Such expectation is part of maturity and wisdom. Anticipating hard times and even some suffering is not pessimistic; it is realistic when you have the right mental and spiritual framework. As in other areas of life, preparation is key. Heed the words of Peter:

   > *Dear friends, do not be surprised at the painful trial you are suffering, as though something strange were happening to you. But rejoice that you participate in the sufferings of Christ, so that you may be overjoyed when his glory is revealed. If you are insulted because of the*

name of Christ, you are blessed, for the Spirit of glory and of God rests on you. If you suffer, it should not be as a murderer or thief or any other kind of criminal or even as a meddler. If you suffer as a Christian, do not be ashamed, but praise God that you bear that name. For it is time for judgment to begin with the family of God; and if it begins with us, what will the outcome be for those who do not obey the gospel of God? (1 Peter 4:12–17)

And the words of Jesus:

"I have told you these things, so that in me you may have peace. In this world you will have trouble. But take heart! I have overcome the world." (John 16:33)

2. **Adjust your expectations and exercise choice and spiritual skills.**

   On the basis of scriptural direction and insight, you can adjust your expectations to anticipate and accept suffering and choose to see it in perspective. Suffering is part of a bigger picture in which things have a purpose in God's plan and the events you experience are temporary, but make lasting impressions upon your character and the good of others. The discussion of greater and lesser expectations (chapter 11) may help you to deal with your expectations and make conscious choices to exercise the spiritual dimensions (including gifts and claims upon God's promises) to help you weather difficulties.

   Now if we are children, then we are heirs—heirs of God and co-heirs with Christ, if indeed we share in his sufferings in order that we may also share in his glory. I consider that our present sufferings are not worth comparing with the glory that will be revealed in us. The creation waits in eager expectation for the sons of God to be revealed. (Romans 8:17–19)

3. **Take steps to eliminate or minimize discomfort, pain, and anguish.**

   The presence of suffering does not mean you should be passive. For the sake of yourself and others, do what you can to minimize or eliminate discomfort and the experiences of suffering that are so agonizing—acute pain, fear, feelings of loneliness and abandonment. Remember that relieving suffering is a calling, and you just might find yourself fit for it. Do what you can to provide relief. But be smart and use the (material and spiritual) tools of God wisely. Assert yourself, resist Satan, and hold man accountable. After you have done all that you can, stand firm, and leave the rest to God (Ephesians 6:10–18).

4. **Be clear minded and self-controlled.**
When you are down and at the effect of adversity, you are more prone to temptation. Evil is always lurking, and Satan competes with God to turn circumstances to his advantage. Determine that your weakness will lead you to rely upon God's strength. That is courageous, and it is what God wants. Be on your guard, lest suffering tempt you into bad attitudes or behaviors in pursuit of relief.

Knowing God leads to self-control. Self-control leads to patient endurance, and patient endurance leads to godliness. (2 Peter 1:6)

A person without self-control is as defenseless as a city with broken-down walls. (Proverbs 25:28)

Be self-controlled and alert. Your enemy the devil prowls around like a roaring lion looking for someone to devour. Resist him, standing firm in the faith, because you know that your brothers throughout the world are undergoing the same kind of sufferings. And the God of grace, who called you to his eternal glory in Christ, after you have suffered a little while, will himself restore you and make you strong, firm and steadfast. (1 Peter 5:8–10)

5. **Pray and love others.**
It is an old truism that helping others diverts you from wallowing in your own problems. When you are suffering, remember to turn to God and to others. Ask and give. Such activity is amazingly healing, and you should make its practice automatic in your repertoire.

There is a satiric Zen twist on the Western self-reliant temperament that goes like this:
Instead of: "Don't just stand there. Do something!"
Substitute: "Don't just do something. Stand there."
We might say: "Don't just do something, don't just stand there. Pray!"

The end of all things is near. Therefore be clear minded and self-controlled so that you can pray. Above all, love each other deeply, because love covers a multitude of sins. (1 Peter 4:7–8)

O Lord, hear my prayer, listen to my cry for mercy; in your faithfulness and righteousness come to my relief. (Psalm 143:1)

"I cried like a swift or thrush, I moaned like a morning dove. My eyes grew weak as I looked to the heavens. I am troubled; O Lord, come to my aid!" (Isaiah 38:14)

Comfort, comfort my people, says your God. (Isaiah 40:1)

Praise be to the God and Father of our Lord Jesus Christ, the father of compassion and the God of all comfort, who comforts us in all our troubles, so that we can comfort those in any trouble with the comfort we ourselves have received from God. For just as the sufferings of Christ flow over into our lives, so also through Christ our comfort overflows. If we are distressed, it is for your comfort and salvation; if we are comforted, it is for your comfort, which produces in you patient endurance of the same sufferings we suffer. And our hope for you is firm, because we know that just as you share in our sufferings, so also you share in our comfort. (2 Corinthians 1:3–7)

6. **Use your gifts.**
    Just as God has saddled you with afflictions and with qualities you wish you didn't have, he has also created you with gifts. To doubt that is to deny what God says. Search for those gifts, and hone and use them to benefit others. What a powerful weapon to combat suffering!

We have different gifts, according to the grace given us. If a man's gift is prophesying, let him use it in proportion to his faith. If it is serving, let him serve; if it is teaching, let him teach; if it is encouraging, let him encourage; if it is contributing to the needs of others, let him give generously; if it is leadership, let him govern diligently; if it is showing mercy, let him do it cheerfully. (Romans 12:6–8)

Each one should use whatever gift he has received to serve others, faithfully administering God's grace in its various forms. If anyone speaks, he should do it with the strength that God provides, so that in all things, God may be praised through Jesus Christ. To him be the glory and power forever and ever. Amen (1 Peter 4:10–11)

7. **Practice reality testing to test and know the will of God.**
   You have learned about the importance of reality testing to equip you in dealing with the practical world and relating to and meeting the needs of others. This skill is vital in determining for yourself what role suffering plays in your life. Beware of the two extremes that may lead you astray and nullify the value and purpose of suffering:

   • The belief that seeking relief would run counter to God's purpose in teaching you a lesson
   • The numbing of sensitivity to or avoidance of awareness of the fulfillment and growth God intends through your suffering

Learning is not always easy. Practicing reality testing in the midst of suffering is a valuable and effective way to learn discernment. It is a building block of wisdom.

Blessed is the man you discipline, O Lord, the man you teach from your law; you grant him relief from days of trouble, till a pit is dug for the wicked. (Psalm 94:13)

Test everything. Hold on to the good. (1 Thessalonians 5:1)

8. **Reflect upon the model of Jesus and how your imitation of and identification with him in suffering breaks the dominion of sin in your life.**

    Suffering leads you to be mindful of the will of God. Out of powerlessness and dependence it teaches acceptance. Christ is your model for suffering. He suffered even though he was blameless. He didn't like it. He experienced pain, distress, desperation, alienation, abandonment—yet he accepted suffering in the will of God. Jesus's suffering was, and is, a miraculous living example of the conquest of sin and death. The Bible says, *"He who suffers in his body is done with sin. As a result, he does not live the rest of his earthly life for evil human desires, but rather for the will of God"* (1 Peter 4:1–2). Meditate on the meaning and implications of this: by taking the same view of suffering as Christ took, which is to accept it in the will of God, you break the dominion of sin in practical experience. That is, you break the power of pain and suffering (as vivid examples of the fleshly, sensory nature) to rule you. By refusing to run from or fear suffering, you remove comfort from the mantle of idolatry. "Putting to death the flesh" means that experiences of the body and natural world are deferred in favor of the spirit, which is eternal life that aligns us with God. This doesn't mean a masochistic attraction to pain, and it doesn't imply a fatalistic predilection for negativity or disappointment. It does mean that suffering is part of a larger picture in which every experience is held up to God's standards and ordination.

    Therefore, since Christ suffered in his body, arm yourselves with the same attitude, because he who has suffered in his body is done with sin. As a result, he does not live the rest of his earthly life for evil human desires, but rather for the will of God. (1 Peter 4:1–2)

    Paradoxically, in "putting to death the flesh," you can make yourself less sensitive to sensory anguish and more sensitive to the spiritual life that surpasses fleshly distress. The "death" that the apostle Paul talks about in Romans 8 is a lack of identification with and receptiveness to the hurts of the body;

the "life" he proclaims is the new ability to tolerate fleshly chains, discomforts, and distractions because the spirit of God can live in you through Christ.

But if Christ is in you, your body is dead because of sin, yet your spirit is alive because of righteousness. And if the spirit of him who raised Jesus from the dead is living in you, he who raised Christ from the dead will also give life to your mortal bodies through his spirit, who lives in you. (Romans 8:10–11)

9. **Ask God for guidance and blessing in your character as you strengthen your faith and hope.**
    As difficult as it is, suffering builds the character necessary to maintain the attitude of hope that sustains you in a disappointing and injurious world. Hope and faith enable you to keep focused on God's presence and provision. Character, your evolving identity and reflection of divinity, is built partly through suffering.

    And we rejoice in the hope of the glory of God. Not only so, but we also rejoice in our sufferings, because we know that suffering produces perseverance; perseverance, character; and character, hope. And hope does not disappoint us, because God has poured out his love into our hearts by the Holy Spirit, whom he has given us. (Romans 5:2–5)

    Therefore we do not lose heart. Though outwardly we are wasting away, yet inwardly we are being renewed day by day. For our light and momentary troubles are achieving for us an eternal glory that far outweighs them all. (2 Corinthians 4:16–17)

10. **Resolve to do good and commit your exercise of choice to the things of God.**
    Even in suffering, you always have choice. You can choose to be bitter, to resent and complain, or you can be humble and look to God for what he has in mind. Suffering is an opportunity to test your resolve, build your character, and manifest the presence and care and grace of God in your life.

So then, those who suffer according to God's will should commit themselves to their faithful Creator and continue to do good. (1 Peter 4:19)

Commit to the Lord whatever you do, and your plans will succeed. (Proverbs 16:3)

All of you, clothe yourselves with humility toward one another, because "God opposes the proud, but gives grace to the humble." Humble yourselves, therefore, under God's mighty hand, that he may lift you up in due time. Cast all your anxieties on him, because he cares for you. (1 Peter 5:5–6)

As water reflects a face, so a man's heart reflects the man. (Proverbs 27:19)

When times are good, be happy; but when times are bad, consider: God has made the one as well as the other. Therefore, a man cannot discover anything about his future. (Ecclesiastes 7:14)

SUFFERING INTACT

You approach the conclusion of a book that purports to lead you to a better life, an endurance with more reward and less pain, a path away from strife and suffering. Yet in this chapter, as I address the realities of suffering, the message is partly that some suffering is unavoidable, that it is part of natural life, and that God has placed it in your life as a teaching device, a model for you to imitate Christ, and a blessing to develop your character and expectations of grace and glory. God wants to inspire your humility, allegiance, appreciation and worship, and dependence upon him. What better way to do this than to bring you to your knees?

However, God is sensitive to your anguish and fragility, and he has created paths and palliatives for the relief of suffering. Otherwise, this book could not exist, nor could the legions of healing methods and healers who precede and follow me. God desires your comfort, though perhaps not in the self-indulgent, hedonistic ways of the fleshly nature. God has created remedies and principles for restoration, healing, and growth. He also allows suffering to recapitulate his new covenant through Jesus and to bestow the brokenness that is necessary to become intact, appreciate restoration and reconciliation, and to live under his protection and in his Spirit.

You were made to dislike and avoid pain and suffering. This nature will always characterize you as long as you live in your body, and it is meant for your survival. Therefore, do not embrace pain as if its relief would deprive you of the lessons God wants to teach you. Seek relief in sensible and healthy ways. Know also, however, that suffering is a state of mind and of spirit, and it is one of God's ways to shape you. Unpleasant as it may be, suffering is embraceable as a challenge that will assist you in living intact.

WHAT YOUR PARENTS DIDN'T TELL YOU

You may have had a wonderful upbringing—loving parents, nurturing home, good education, wholesome friends, and moral training. Or perhaps you were not so fortunate. Maybe you grew up in circumstances of severe wanting, where you had little opportunity to develop the skills and protective mechanisms to gird you against life's misfortunes. Perhaps you are handicapped or facing discrimination or ostracism. Maybe you are battling some grievous affliction that restricts you or causes pain. Possibly you are among the victimized and have experienced a great loss or injury. If so, my heart goes out to you. I admire your fortitude and courage, and I sympathize with your pain and loneliness in these struggles. I pray for your persistence in the face of what can seem like overwhelming odds against you. Together, we wonder at the mysteries of why some people are slated for worldly riches and recognition while others are less fortunate.

Your situation notwithstanding, I have some great news for you. Insofar as suffering is concerned, your situation and your past matter very little. This is also true regarding whatever your parents did for (or to) you.

As parents, we try to protect our children. We teach and guide them and prepare them as best we can for independent living. Our children regard us (at least for a while) as all-powerful and knowing, and we foster this respect. We try to hide our failings, hoping that our young ones will not see or copy our foibles. We also hope that they will not ask the hard questions about our behaviors and our past, and we cringe from the notion that they will disrespect or disregard us. No matter how good or bad your parents were, this dynamic also occurred between them and you, too.

In preparing you for life, your parents emphasized what they thought was important: skills, beliefs, attitudes, values, etc. Perhaps they told you about your family history, including the accomplishments of family members, genetic traits, special abilities and vulnerabilities, and the rest of it. You may have been adopted; if so, your parents likely struggled with the issue of how to talk with you about your having more than one or two parents. If you grew up in a Christian home, you probably heard about being "born again"—the process of transformation that occurs when you accept Jesus Christ as your Lord and Savior.

It is unlikely, however, that your parents taught you about the need for you to *be adopted*. This refers to the adoption of believers in Christ into the family of God.

In love he predestined us to be adopted as sons through Jesus Christ, in accordance with his pleasure and will. (Ephesians 1:5)

We know that the whole creation has been groaning as in the pains of child-birth right up to the present time. Not only so, but we ourselves, who have the firstfruits of the spirit, groan inwardly as we wait eagerly for our adoption of sons, the redemption of our bodies. (Romans 8:22–23)

How do you get adopted, and what has this to do with suffering?

When you become a Christian, you accept Christ as the bridge between sinful man (including you) and a holy God. All of your sins and transgresions are forgiven. This is no excuse to continue misbehaving;[56] it is a payment of a debt you could never pay yourself. Christ is the ultimate insurance policy: fully paid for life (eternally) and *complete coverage for everything*! Your being born again entitles you to other privileges, such as being adopted into the family of God. This means that your identity (upon request) is shifted to incorporate inclusion (similar to a married woman adopting her husband's name). This shift has potentially miraculous implications for the ways you react to situations—including disappointments, insults, ingrained habits, and your responses to pain and suffering.

---

56. See Romans, chapter 6, for Paul's brilliant discussion on the relationship between grace, law, and the continuation of sin.

By including yourself in the family of God, you lay the foundation for freeing yourself from old behavior patterns. Forget about struggling in therapy for years and years in order to overcome destructive family patterns. In my decades of clinical practice, the single best predictor I have observed for improving adaptive responses to adversity is the patient's identification with the family of God. This doesn't mean that you will automatically break free from bad habits[57] simply by grace. It does mean that identifying with the blessings of salvation, forgiveness, compassion, and godly virtues allows you the freedom and capacity to "suffer properly" and to differentiate between the godly acceptance of that burden and the self-pitying complaint and avoidance that typically characterizes most family dysfunction.

You see, what your parents didn't tell you is that the process of raising you and requiring respect, allegiance, apprenticeship, and modeling (and even conscious or subconscious worship) of their ways of surviving carry with it a certain amount of dysfunction. All families are like that, even the best ones. Your genetic endowments and vulnerabilities, along with years of family and environmental programming predispose and condition you to respond in certain ways. The surest way to liberate yourself from those adverse effects is by becoming a new being in Christ (Romans 12:1–2; Ephesians 4:23–24). As a member of the family of God, you are free to *choose* your responses to adversity, including how you will handle suffering. There is no magic or fantasy involved. There is a spiritual transformation, a new habit of contentment and peacefulness in circumstances (Philippians 4:11–13). It is a miracle of sorts that God can cause this any time and anywhere within the human heart.

A FINAL RECAPITULATION

The known universe recapitulates itself in many ways. Nature repeats its cycles and recapitulates biological variants and manifestations of environment and ecology. Scientific and mathematical principles congregate around the systems of rules and logic that testify to God's genius and reliable wisdom. There are repetitions in history and in the character of man through the ages. Children look and act like their families and, more or less, remind the world of their ancestors.

---

57. Changing habits requires commitment, work, and appropriate tools, as described in detail in earlier chapters in this book.

From a developmental perspective, children grow through stages and practice skills that help them achieve the milestones of independence. As they advance through higher levels of reasoning and physical and neurological maturity, new experiences become selectively sorted to confirm or reject that which will help them survive. These include conceptual reasoning and the ability to abstract and generalize to include and act upon new situations that are similar in essential organizing principles, but which may contain slight variations that must be recognized and processed according to a more familiar and higher-order schema. Continually, these routine and necessary functions are accomplished vicariously through watching others, learning from their consequences, and saving oneself time and possible harm. This is true in situations ranging from scholastic exam analogies to avoiding bad food.

By the time you become "self-sufficient," you have inadvertently accumulated a profile of defenses and belief systems to support your efforts, validate your efficacy, and justify your outlook and attitudes. Much of this comes apart when hard times overwhelm and you become beset by financial difficulties. At that point, you wait it out, reorganize your approach, or reach out for help. Concurrently, you will probably rethink some of your positions on certain aspects of reality.

This process occurs in the spiritual realm, too. Though some people may continue for long stretches in an arrested state of development, we are designed to improve through recapitulations of situations that challenge our beliefs and operating principles. Developing spiritually is a step-by-step, stage dependent process, similar in nature to the milestone-laden path of physical and mental development. In using Christ as a model for how to live and grow and respond to adversity and a world that seems increasingly foreign even as it becomes more familiar to us, the principles of biological development also apply. Modeling oneself after Christ at successive levels of growth and maturity may be described as the foundation of developmental Christianity. Paradoxically, blossoming Christlikeness enables us to live *in* the world (appropriately) without becoming *of* the world (despairingly). To do so requires successive recapitulations in the process of accepting what is handed to you and donating what you no longer need.

It is ironic that the family that raises you in the discipline and hope that will spawn your independence also saddles you with generational baggage. However, there are welcoming committees in heaven and here on earth (probably nearby in your own community) that will join you in attaining the freedom to be your own person, ideally a person who appreciates and fears God and who wants to become more like him.

True independence and autonomy requires giving up dependence on childish entitlements and becoming dependent instead on the strength of God. Your word and God's Word are all you really have in this life. Thankfully, they are enough. Make your word count and be unshakeable, like God's Word. Develop a character that is increasingly Christlike and God pleasing. Surely, as you go along, some rain will fall into your life, and there will be sprinkles—perhaps sometimes torrents—of suffering. They will be temporary, and you have the tools to parry some adversity and the strength and grace to weather the unavoidable—as Christ did, because he did, and because he is the same and he helps you yesterday, today, and forever (Hebrews 13:8).

> *"Never will I leave you; never will I forsake you." So we say with confidence, "The Lord is my helper; I will not be afraid. What can man do to me?"* (Hebrews 13:5–6)

In perspective, your suffering will seem a passing shadow in the complete and encompassing glory of eventual light. In the meantime and on the way, allow life to get more of the right things out of you, and seek more of the rewards that God has in store for you by practicing the tools and techniques he has made available and the blessings he offers for living intact.

APPENDIX A
SCHEDULES OF REINFORCEMENT

In reinforcement and learning theory, different schedules exert differing effects on the occurrence, strength, and longevity of behaviors. A schedule is a pattern of reinforcement, whether it occurs naturally or by planned intent. Some schedules, such as *continuous* reinforcement schedules, are useful for building or shaping new behaviors, but are less effective for maintaining them over time. Other schedules, such as *intermittent* reinforcement schedules, are more effective for keeping behaviors intact once they are shaped. A continuous reinforcement schedule is a pattern of reinforcing a behavior every time it occurs. Examples include the following: getting a product out of a vending machine every time you put money in the slot, launching a software program and seeing the appropriate icons appear on the screen, playing a CD and hearing music, or calling a familiar telephone number and hearing the phone ring. An intermittent reinforcement schedule produces a pattern of reinforcing responses sometimes, but not always. Examples are these: sales pitches that result in sales, asking someone for a date, going fishing, or gambling.

Each of these reinforcement schedules has specific properties that predict the probabilities of behaviors under certain conditions. Continuous reinforcement schedules produce high rates of response early in the conditioning. The behaviors they reinforce remain consistent at high levels as long as the reinforcement is continuous—namely, the behavior is reinforced each and every time it occurs. Once the reinforcement stops, behaviors conditioned by such a schedule will drop off quickly and dramatically. For example, if you put money into a soda machine and did not get a soda, how many times would you repeat the process with that particular machine? If you interacted unsuccessfully with something or someone where you expected a familiar response, it wouldn't take many disappointments to dissuade you from continuing. An apparent contrast to this cause-and-effect principle involves gambling, which is insidiously addicting for some people, even for those who lose repeatedly. This seeming anomaly is explained by the fact that gambling behavior is maintained on a variable intermittent ratio reinforcement schedule, in which the occasional win trumps many disappointing losses.

You would only try to operate a familiar, but uncooperative, machine a very few times before concluding that it doesn't work and another course of action is needed. You would probably not return to a restaurant where your first encounter was unpleasant. Continuous reinforcement schedules are helpful in establishing connections and associations between particular behaviors and expected outcomes where the two were previously not connected. Therefore, this schedule is useful in raising the probability of new or unstable behaviors. However, since they depend upon high rates of reinforcement, they are costly and inefficient for maintaining behaviors over the long term.

Intermittent reinforcement schedules, by their very nature, only reinforce *sometimes*. Because of this, they are not very good for building new behaviors because the association between response and reinforcement needs consistency to take root. However, once a behavior is established, intermittent reinforcement schedules are highly effective for keeping behavior levels stable over long periods of time, *even in the absence of a great deal of reinforcement*. This is because the behavior pattern has adjusted to long periods of drought or nonreinforcement. With intermittent reinforcement schedules, such absences are built into the schedule.

In addition to reinforcement schedules that are continuous or intermittent, reinforcements may occur by *ratio* or by *interval*. A ratio schedule is one where reinforcement occurs after a certain number of responses. This may be one response, such as ordering a meal, or a multiple of responses, such as making numerous sales calls. Also, ratio schedules may be *fixed* or *variable*. In a fixed schedule, the amount or number of responses necessary to gain reinforcement is set (such as the response from putting money into a vending machine to get a bottle of soda or a pitcher throwing three strikes to strike out a baseball batter). An interval schedule is one in which reinforcement is delivered at time intervals (either fixed or variable). Some examples include plane schedules, paychecks (for those on salary), or musical chairs. On interval schedules, the reinforcement does not depend on the amount of the response, but rather on a time schedule that is either established (e.g., receiving your paycheck) or changeable (e.g., playing musical chairs).

Again, each of these schedules has particular characteristics that predict response patterns. Ratio schedules tend to produce high levels of response. People learn that the payoff depends upon what they do. Interval schedules, by contrast, produce spike-type response patterns in which there are very low response levels and prolonged periods between responses in accord with the expected interval. Think of the gate activity at an airline terminal. Picture the activity two hours before the flight takes off, twenty-five minutes before takeoff, and then fifteen minutes after takeoff. The specified interval of reinforcement (in this case, the plane leaving for its destination) controls the rate of passenger response according to a set and predictable timetable.

The properties of these schedules and their influences on rates of responding have multiple and profound uses in controlling behavior and manipulating habits. Ratio and intermittent schedules are better suited to independence, self-reliance, and the gradual "stacking" of behavior chains (the "inch-by-inch" approach), whereas interval and continuous schedules are better suited to environmentally dependent behaviors, such as teamwork and stage or game performances.

APPENDIX B
BEHAVIOR REDUCTION AND PROBABILITIES

When you want to reduce or eliminate behaviors, it is important to think in terms of probabilities. You are no doubt familiar with the saying that the glass that is filled halfway may be described as half full or half empty. This is usually quoted to describe attitudes as optimistic or pessimistic, but we can also use the metaphor to introduce probabilities. We can describe such a glass as having a 50 percent probability of becoming full and a 50 percent probability of becoming empty. If the container is large or heavy, however, it is going to be easier to fill it gradually with liquid than to dump out an amount on the chance that we will leave the container half full. To expand this example even further, think of filling a bathtub with the right amount of water at the right temperature for your comfort. Which is easier: monitoring the tub's filling and adjusting the temperature, or draining (and perhaps refilling) a full tub that is too cold or too hot?

How does this apply to behaviors? Assume that a bad habit or unwanted behavior is like a container filled nearly to the top. We could infer that the history (and probability) of activity vis-à-vis this container has resulted in its becoming more full. Why? Because it is more full than empty. The container's fullness has been reinforced. Said differently, the container is more likely to be noticed for its fullness than its partial emptiness. Now, substitute for the container a behavior called nagging and for the volume of liquid a heightened tendency to nag. That is to say, the container that offers nagging behavior is pretty full. The fuller it is, the more difficult it is and the more work it takes over time to modify it. And unless we have a drain to reduce the fullness of an unwanted behavior (don't we wish!), we are likely to make a mess in trying to empty it. Thus, it is much easier and more controllable to take a different container and fill it carefully the way we want. Let's call this container something that is rather opposite of nagging—say, complimenting and praising—and gradually modify it. Every time we notice the level of liquid in the complimenting and praising container, we add a few drops to it. This is called reinforcement. It gradually makes the behavior rise. After a while, the volume rises to a level that builds a character of "fullness" such that the nature of the behavior level of complimenting and praising is noticeably (and reliably) more full than empty. At that point, evaporation is barely noticeable, especially when we are paying regular attention to the fullness of complimenting and praising.

What about the nagging container? Two things: first, as we devote attention to the complimenting and praising container, we pay less and less attention to the nagging because the complimenting and praising is much more satisfying and the return on investment so much more "rewarding." Second, the less attention we pay to nagging, the more it evaporates and slowly drains over time, even as we don't notice. This is ignoring in its most natural and most workable incarnation. This type of benign neglect in the service of a goal-directed outcome is a worthy and productive strategy.

APPENDIX C
THOUGHT FIELD THERAPY (TFT)
ALGORITHMS FOR SELF-HEALING

The tapping sequences listed in this appendix are *algorithms*—that is, they are recipes that are based on the distillation of many successful treatments that have eliminated negative emotions in others.

Read and familiarize yourself with the material in chapter 10 before administering the tapping sequences.

Refer to the diagrams to locate the appropriate tapping points.

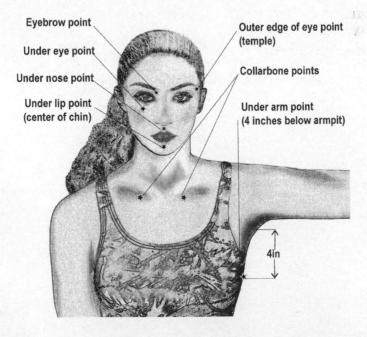

Eyebrow point

Under eye point

Under nose point

Under lip point
(center of chin)

Outer edge of eye point
(temple)

Collarbone points

Under arm point
(4 inches below armpit)

4in

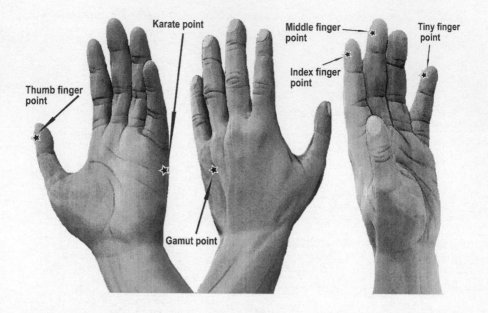

Please note that when you read the following instructions, you may initially feel tentative and/or intimidated by the described procedures. In fact, these procedures are actually very easy to apply. It just takes a bit of practice to get the hang of them. Put any apprehensions you may have on hold and simply follow step-by-step, easy-to understand and easy-to-use procedures. Mastering these methods can be life-altering.

Before you begin each treatment, rate your discomfort or negative feeling about the particular issue you want to treat on a scale of 1 through 10, with 1 meaning that you have none of the symptom whatsoever at present and 10 meaning that the symptom is as bad as it can be for you.

GENERAL GUIDELINES

1. You can use either hand to tap, as well as either side of your body.
2. You can tap with slight pressure—firmly, lightly, and quickly.
3. For the major holon sequences (a holon sequence is a series of meridian tapping points—see below), tap ten times on each point.
4. When tapping on the karate point (side of the hand) or under the nose, tap twelve times.

5. When the gamut point (see diagram) is used as a tapping point in a major holon sequence, it will be designated as "G50"—this means you tap it fifty times.
6. When you do the nine-gamut sequence, you will tap persistently in the gamut point as you do the eye movements and humming and counting.
7. While doing the nine-gamut sequence, breathe naturally and deeply, and keep your head still (move only your eyes).

ADMINISTERING THE TFT ALGORITHMS

Administering the TFT algorithms involves:

1. Making the appropriate statements out loud (see below)
2. Tapping a major holon sequence (the specific order of tapping points listed)
3. Then, doing the nine-gamut sequence
4. Then tapping again the major holon sequence. **Essentially, you sandwich a nine-gamut sequence in between repetitions of the major holon sequence for each statement:**

"I want to be over... (the specific symptom or negative emotion)."
"I want to be *completely* over... (the specific symptom or negative emotion)."
"I *will be completely* over... (the specific symptom or negative emotion)."

APPLYING THE NINE-GAMUT TREATMENT SEQUENCE

The nine-gamut treatment will result in your distress or negative emotion being reduced even further. Continue to think of your distress or negative emotion and tap solidly (with two fingers) the gamut point on the back of your hand (see diagram). It is located behind and between the little finger knuckle and the ring finger knuckle on the back of your hand. It doesn't matter which hand you use, but many prefer to tap with the dominant hand on the back of the nondominant hand. Keep your head straight with your nose pointed ahead while you do the nine-gamut treatment. Tap about five times for each one of the nine gamut positions while you continue to think of your distress or negative emotion throughout the whole series:

While tapping gamut point on back of hand, do the following:

a) Close your eyes

b) Open your eyes

c) Point your eyes way down and way over to the right

d) Point your eyes way down and way over to the left

e) Whirl your eyes around in a circle

f) Whirl your eyes around in the opposite direction

g) Rest your eyes, and hum any tune—more than just one note (for about five seconds)

h) Count aloud to five

i) Hum again (it is important to repeat this)

The steps are listed in order below. Refer to the headings below for specific negative emotions to select the appropriate major holon sequences. The nine-gamut sequence is the same for all algorithms.

SUMMARIZING THE STEPS

1. Say out loud, "I want to be over... (the specific symptom or negative emotion)."

2. Tap twelve times on the karate point (side of the hand). Then, tap twelve times under your nose (between the nose and the upper lip).

3. Repeat out loud, "I want to be over... (the specific symptom or negative emotion)."

4. Tap the first *major holon* sequence (the tapping points in the order listed).

5. Do the nine-gamut sequence.

6. Again, tap the first *major holon* sequence (the tapping points in the order listed).

7. Tap any additional major holon sequence listed; then, do the nine-gamut sequence; then, again tap the additional major

holon sequence. If there is only one major holon sequence, go on to the next step.

8. Say out loud, "I want to be *completely* over... (the specific symptom or negative emotion)."

9. Tap twelve times on the karate point (side of the hand). Then, tap twelve times under your nose (between the nose and the upper lip).

10. Repeat out loud, "I want to be *completely* over... (the specific symptom or negative emotion)."

11. Repeat tapping the first *major holon* sequence (the tapping points in the order listed).

12. Repeat the nine-gamut sequence.

13. Repeat tapping the first *major holon* sequence (the tapping points in the order listed).

14. Repeat tapping any additional major holon sequence listed; then, do the nine-gamut sequence; then, again tap the additional major holon sequence. If there is only one major holon sequence, go on to the next step.

15. Say out loud, "I *will be completely* over... (the specific symptom or negative emotion)."

16. Tap twelve times on the karate point (side of the hand). Then, tap twelve times under your nose (between the nose and the upper lip).

17. Repeat tapping the first *major holon* sequence (the tapping points in the order listed).

18. Repeat the nine-gamut sequence.

19. Repeat tapping the first *major holon* sequence (the tapping points in the order listed).

20. Repeat tapping any additional major holon sequence listed; then, do the nine-gamut sequence; then, again tap the additional major holon sequence.

HOLON MAJOR SEQUENCES

Refer to the steps listed above. Remember to make the appropriate statements, tap on the karate point and under the nose, and sandwich the nine-gamut treatment in between repetition of the major holon sequences. The nine-gamut sequence is abbreviated as 9GSQ, which means: do the nine gamut, then repeat the major holon sequence you did right before the nine-gamut.

ANXIETY (SIMPLE)
- Eye, arm, collar, 9GSQ

ANXIETY (COMPLEX)
- Eye, eyebrow, eye, eyebrow, arm, collar, 9GSQ
- Arm, eye, arm, collar, eyebrow, collar, eye, eyebrow, arm, collar, 9GSQ

CRAVINGS
- Eye, collar, arm, collar, 9GSQ

FEAR (GENERAL)
- Eye, eyebrow, eye, collar, arm, collar, eye, 9GSQ

FEAR (PHOBIC)
- Eye, arm, middle finger, eye, collar, under nose, eyebrow, eye, middle finger, eyebrow, index finger, eye, arm, middle finger, collar, middle finger, arm, collar, eye, collar, 9GSQ
- Eye, collar, eyebrow, tiny finger, eye, middle finger, collar, tiny finger, collar, middle finger, eyebrow, collar, index finger, collar, 9GSQ

DEPRESSION
- G50, collar, eyebrow, tiny finger, eye, arm, temple, eye, arm, collar, 9GSQ
- G50, EYE, EYEBROW, EYE, TINY FINGER, EYE, COLLAR, INDEX FINGER, EYE, TINY FINGER, ARM, COLLAR, 9GSQ
- Eyebrow, middle finger, tiny finger, eye, temple, arm, collar, G50, eye, 9GSQ

TRAUMA (SIMPLE)

- Eyebrow, eye, eyebrow, temple, collar, eyebrow, eye, tiny finger, eye, temple, arm, collar, G50, eyebrow, 9GSQ

TRAUMA (COMPLEX, WITH ABUSE AND SELF-CRITICISM)

- Eye, arm, under nose, G50, eyebrow, eye, tiny finger, temple, arm, collar, eye, eyebrow, eye, G50, 9GSQ
- Eye, G50, middle finger, tiny finger, eyebrow, 9GSQ
- Index finger, collar, arm, index finger, eyebrow, eye, under nose, middle finger, tiny finger, eye, collar, 9GSQ
- G50, eyebrow, middle finger, tiny finger, temple, arm, collar, eye, eyebrow, index finger, temple, tiny finger, eye, eyebrow, 9GSQ
- G50, eye, eyebrow, index finger, middle finger, collar, eye, temple, eye, index finger, eye, eyebrow, tiny finger, 9GSQ (nine-gamut, then repeat major sequence)
- Eye, G50, index finger, middle finger, arm, eye, index finger, collar, eyebrow, G50, tiny finger, collar, index finger, eyebrow, eye, collar, 9GSQ
- Eye, temple, arm, middle finger, temple, index finger, G50, eye, tiny finger, collar, arm, collar, eye, 9GSQ
- Temple, eyebrow, G50, index finger, tiny finger, collar, arm, index finger, under nose, middle finger, G50, eyebrow, under nose, temple, arm, eye, index finger, middle finger, tiny finger, under nose, G50, eyebrow, 9GSQ
- Index finger, eye, eyebrow, G50, middle finger, central vessel, eye, G50, 9GSQ

ANGER

- Eyebrow, tiny finger, eye, arm, temple, eye, arm, collar, tiny finger, collar, 9GSQ

HURT

- Eyebrow, G50, eyebrow, collar, eye, arm, collar, tiny finger, eye, arm, collar, G50, collar, 9GSQ

FEELING OVERWHELMED

- Eye, arm, eyebrow, eye, eyebrow, arm, eyebrow, tiny finger, middle finger, collar, 9GSQ

GUILT

- Eye, arm, under nose, G50, eyebrow, eye, tiny finger, temple, arm, collar, eye, eyebrow, eye, G50, 9GSQ

FORGIVENESS

- EYE, ARM, TINY FINGER, TEMPLE, EYEBROW, EYE, EYEBROW, UNDER NOSE, TINY FINGER, G50, TEMPLE, ARM, COLLAR, EYE, EYEBROW, COLLAR, 9GSQ

EMBARRASSMENT

- Eye, arm, eyebrow, eye, eyebrow, eye, arm, collar, 9GSQ

WORRYING

- Eye, eyebrow, eye, collar, arm, collar, eye, collar, arm, collar, 9GSQ
- Eye, arm, collar, eye, 9GSQ

IRRITATION AND IMPATIENCE

- Eye, eyebrow, middle finger, tiny finger, eye, collar, arm, eye, 9GSQ
- Eye, G50, index finger, eye, G50, eyebrow, tiny finger, eyebrow, 9GSQ
- Eye, G50, eyebrow, middle finger, temple, index finger, middle finger, 9GSQ

STRESS

- Eye, eyebrow, arm, collar, 9GSQ
- Arm, eye, arm, collar, eyebrow, collar, eye, eyebrow, arm, collar, 9GSQ

GRIEF

- Eye, arm, under nose, G50, eyebrow, eye, tiny finger, temple, arm, collar, eye, eyebrow, eye, G50, 9GSQ
- G50, eyebrow, middle finger, tiny finger, temple, arm, collar, eye, eyebrow, index finger, temple, tiny finger, eye, eyebrow, 9GSQ
- Eye, G50, middle finger, tiny finger, eyebrow, 9GSQ
- G50, eye, eyebrow, index finger, middle finger, collar, eye, temple, eye, index finger, eye, eyebrow, tiny finger, 9GSQ (nine-gamut, then repeat major sequence)
- Eye, G50, index finger, middle finger, arm, eye, index finger, collar, eyebrow, G50, tiny finger, collar, index finger, eyebrow, eye, collar, 9GSQ

LOVE PAIN AND REJECTION

- Eyebrow, G50, eyebrow, collar, eye, arm, collar, tiny finger, eye, arm, collar, G50, collar, 9GSQ
- G50, eye, eyebrow, eye, tiny finger, eye, collar, index finger, eye, tiny finger, arm, collar, 9GSQ
- Eyebrow, eye, eyebrow, temple, collar, eyebrow, eye, tiny finger, eye, temple, arm, collar, G50, eyebrow, 9GSQ
- Eye, arm, under nose, G50, eyebrow, eye, tiny finger, temple, arm, collar, eye, eyebrow, eye, G50, 9GSQ

PROCRASTINATION

- Eye, arm, eye, collar, eyebrow, eye, middle finger, eyebrow, index finger, eye, arm, middle finger, tiny finger, collar, middle finger, arm, collar, 9GSQ
- Eye, collar, eyebrow, tiny finger, eye, middle finger, collar, tiny finger, collar, middle finger, eyebrow, collar, index finger, collar, 9GSQ

APPENDIX D
SELF HABITS, WORLD HABITS, AND INTEGRAL HABITS

Being able to handle challenges is a requisite to living intact. It calls for specific skills and habits that can enable us to effectively manage ourselves and our interactions with others and the world around us.

These habits—summarized and described in three categories—are acquired and developed through natural growth and maturation, learning and experience, and deliberate dedication and practice.

Self habits—the ways in which you maintain and run your body and mind.

World habits—the practical skills that help you operate effectively within an environment. These habits include how you deal with other people and how you get what you want and need.

Integral habits—the crossover between your personal inner world and the world you share with others. These habits are your resources for adapting to, accepting, interpreting, harmonizing, accommodating, and integrating with *what is* and *what happens* during the course of your life.

Self habits, world habits, and *integral habits* comprise the tools you use to manage the business of living and to make sense out of your experiences. These habits include many routine and automatic skills, such as regulation of body functions, ways to calm yourself, and applied reasoning skills that you develop naturally, as well as those other skills you may require to become more productive and fulfilled.

Self habits are those capabilities that enable each of us to function and maintain ourselves as separate independent beings. This does not mean biological or social functions per se (such as the ability to feed, dress, transport oneself or to carry out responsibilities), but rather involves the regulatory capacities that enable us to adjust to changing conditions and events both within and beyond our initiation or control. It is relatively easy to think of the biological necessity of maintaining body temperature and respiration, yet it is a bit more of a stretch to conceptualize self habits as including the maintenance of *emotional* temperature, the self-control to not falter or become unglued whenever life surprises, confronts, scares, or disappoints, and the perceptual organization to observe objectively the effects of how we act and to make adjustments as needed.

Self-regulation

Self-regulation refers to the body/mind's ability to regulate itself and its level of arousal (e.g., mood, attention, perception, sleep/wakefulness, stress), rebound from exertion, recover from adverse environmental or internal events; maintain cortical and hemispheric efficiency, and initiate internal "housekeeping." To develop, exercise, and maintain self-regulation, EEG neurofeedback is recommended.

Self-soothing

Like self-regulation, self-soothing involves your ability to control your arousal system and respond effectively to its internal and external triggers and provocations. Self-soothing entails the *de-activation* of the mechanisms involved in overarousal. Also, it requires a conscious effort or action to take charge of the overarousal and to decelerate it. Thus, self-soothing engages the body/mind's capacity to calm itself and lower or eliminate adverse states of excitation. This applies particularly to anxieties, fears, and traumas.

Soothing another person involves the process of diminishing that person's pain or discomfort. To soothe someone is to make that person less angry, anxious, upset, or "worked up."

Self-soothing is initiated when you make a deliberate choice to calm yourself down. It is an invaluable tool for dealing with a world (and also with your own particular reactions to stimuli and your own particular personality traits and proclivities) that can be annoying, frustrating, and agitating.

There are, course, many ways to soothe yourself. One of the best ways is to apply TFT tapping.

Self-control

Self-control involves components of self-observations, adjustments, and appraisal of the effects and interactions between oneself and the environment. Specific skills include self-monitoring, self-reinforcement, self-evaluation. We need these to appraise our effectiveness upon the environment and to understand how we affect our environment and others in it.

Frustration tolerance

Developing frustration tolerance requires that you accept and internalize a basic truth, namely, that issues may sometimes prove to be more complex than you thought and may demand more deliberate reasoning and patience. To attain your goal, you may have to deliberately activate a series of steps. These steps necessitate that you be able to learn from your past positive and negative experiences, assess your mistakes until you find the solutions to the challenges you are facing, and remain focused and on-track until you succeed in achieving your objectives. Frustration tolerance can be improved by intentionally exercising self-regulation, applying self-soothing techniques, acquiring the necessary mental flexibility that allows you to envision the larger picture, and recognizing the strategic cause-and-effect connections embedded in the small steps that are requisite to attaining your long-term goals.

Permeability

Permeability requires flexibility, the capacity to identify with others, and empathy. It is a manifestation of the ability to attach and detach, to see events and circumstances from different points of view; it is the ability to become involved and, alternatively, to disengage and let go of an issue so that it can filter through you rather than get stuck in your mind.

World habits are the skills that help us operate effectively within and upon the environment. They are the pool of resources upon which we draw to get things done, meet our needs, and productively utilize behaviors and resources in dealing with the world around us. Living intact involves exercising judgment, utilizing reasoning skills, acquiring insight, making accurate predictions, developing efficient strategies and tactics, and applying effective goal-directed behaviors.

Reasoning

Reasoning skills are predicated on your ability to perceive essential similarities and differences, analyze information, organize and apply cause-and-effect principles, and learn from both positive and negative life experiences. To reason accurately requires that you be able to distill significant events and recognize the essential unifying principles and that govern life (see chapter 9).

Reality testing

The ability to see and understand things as they are (rather than according to one's needs, prejudices, internal narrative, and wishes) is critical. To a great extent, reality testing depends upon natural consequences and consensual agreement—that is, the process of validating and confirming how others around you perceive reality and, when appropriate, accepting and accommodating these realities.

Behavior exchange

In order to get along in the world, you must make agreements and compromises with others. Essentially, these are behavior exchanges. These comprise skill sets with offering something of value to others and establishing a fair medium of exchange. Behavior exchanges are exemplified by commercial transactions and also by agreements in friendships and intimate relationships. Implementing satisfying behavior exchanges involve having something that others want, being able to present and "sell" these desirable elements, and being able to negotiate and compromise on what is fair value.

Communication of experience

These abilities include knowing how to ask for help, clearly state your needs, convey your boundaries, opinions, feelings, and values so that others receive what you communicate in the way that you intend, and be experientially and emotionally accessible to others.

Commitment

Commitment requires that you be able to give and keep your word. It is one of the foundations of purposeful behavior, and it is a cornerstone of decision-making and goal-orientation. Commitment is also the adhesive connection to social interdependency.

Integral **habits** form the domain of crossover between one's personal and inner world and the world of consensual reality — that is, the world shared communally with those around us. Integral habits represent the interface from which we construct life's meaning and satisfaction, as well as our own contributions and purposes. They help us align more harmoniously with a universe that often operates against our wishes. They allow us to grow and make the most of our experiences so that we may live more fully intact.

Spiritual perspective

Having spiritual perspective means living with an acknowledgment and belief in aspects of reality beyond present and tangible experience. This includes the capacity to incorporate supernatural phenomena with rational thinking and sensory experience. A spiritual perspective is necessary to exercise hope, faith, and love, and live in relationship with God.

Integrity

Integrity refers to the state of being sound and undamaged, complete or unconflicted in relationship to one's word. It also implies adhering to high moral principles and standards. Having integrity means being reliable and keeping one's word.

Connecting with others emotionally

People are predisposed by their basic nature to establish connections and to bond with others through interactions involving mutual physical and emotional experiences. This union entails reaching out, risking, acknowledging, and accepting the differences and similarities between our emotional experiences and those of other people.

Humility

To be humble is to make less of yourself and your own importance and needs. Humility is having respect for others, abandoning pride and pretension, and putting others first. Humility is the opposite of entitlement.

Developing purpose beyond oneself

Living intact is not done in isolation. It requires the capacity to transcend one's own immediate needs and identity. It entails sacrificing for others, having compassion and empathy, adapting yourself and one's perspective to include other people. Developing this purpose requires embracing and fitting into a world that does not revolve around oneself.

MORE ON SELF HABITS, WORLD HABITS, AND INTEGRAL HABITS

The descriptions in this appendix are intended to provide a framework for constructing healthy and productive habits and skills for living intact. They form the underpinning for the Living Intact Assessments and can provide baselines for measuring your current LIQ (Living Intact Quotient) and guidelines for growth and improvement.

For more information about the Living Intact Assessments and to find out about publications, events, and growth opportunities for living intact, visit www.livingintact.com or www.marksteinberg.com.

REFERENCES

Bates, W.H. (1977). Better Eyesight Without Glasses. New York: Jove

Callahan, R. (2002). Tapping the Healer Within. New York: McGraw-Hill

Callahan, R. (1981). A rapid treatment for phobias. Collected Papers of International College of Applied Kinesiology (ICAK)

Callahan, R. (1981). Psychological Reversal. Collected Papers ICAK

Callahan, Roger J. (1985). Five Minute Phobia Cure. Wilmington, DE, Enterprise, (out of print).

Callahan, R. (1993). The Five-Minute Phobia Cure Video. Indian Wells, CA

Callahan, R. (1993). The Love Pain and Post Traumatic Stress Video. Indian Wells, CA

Ellis, A. (1962). Reason and Emotion in Psychotherapy, New York: Lyle Stuart

Gazzaniga, M. (1985). *The Social Brain*, New York: Basic Books

Koestler, A. (1967) Ghost in the Machine, New York: Penguin

Othmer, S. and Steinberg, M. (2010) EEG neurofeedback therapy, in *Clinical Addiction Psychiatry*, New York: Cambridge University Press, edited by David Brizer, M.D. and Ricardo Castaneda, M.D.

Pignotti, M. and Steinberg, M. (2001). Heart rate variability as an outcome measure for Thought Field Therapy in clinical practice. *Journal of Clinical Psychology* 57, 1193-1206.

Steinberg, M. and Othmer, S. (2004) *ADD: The 20-Hour Solution,* Bandon, OR: Robert J. Reed Publishers.

Warren, R., (2003) *Purpose Driven Life*, Zondervan Publishing

ACKNOWLEDGMENTS

For decades, so many people have contributed to my growth, knowledge, and contributions. These include my patients and friends, as well as my mentors. Among the people I especially thank with great praise and gratitude for making this book possible are the following:

Lawrence Greene, my friend and colleague, whose perspicacious editing and advice helped to form *Living Intact* into accessible language. Larry challenged my ideas and clarity, as well as my linguistic conventions. His encouragement through the years is inestimable.

Dr. Siegfried Othmer, who introduced me to the world of EEG neurofeedback and who remains my colleague and mentor on this revolutionary journey of transforming the world, one brain at a time.

Dr. Roger Callahan, my colleague, mentor, and pioneer in changing lives through Thought Field Therapy. Roger's courage and brilliance in discovering and developing TFT served as a model for my pursuit of truth and excellence in healing, regardless of skepticism and criticism.

Dr. Peter Wilkes, my dear friend and pastor of the church I attended while raising my family. Peter taught me how to be a Christian father and how to emulate and worship our heavenly father.

Dr. Von Capell, the late psychologist and mentor who taught me much of what I know about therapy and clinical practice. Most of all, Von taught me how to be a winner.

Dr. Ron Gentile, my academic advisor and lead professor in graduate school. Ron was one of the best teachers I ever had, and he inspired and led me to acquire the psychological and educational knowledge I use everyday in my personal and professional life. Ron made education fun and relevant.

Gary Gubitz, my friend who was there and willing the night God chose to lead me to Christ. Gary stayed and prayed with me as I made the most important choice of my life.

Dr. Grayce Stratton and Meg White, who provided feedback in the early stages of this book and who provided validation and encouragement.

Dr. Milton Huang and Robert Lungaro, whose scholarship, sensitivity, and hard work enrich the lives of others by improving their brains and hearts.

Richard Rosenbaum, literary agent and Christian brother, who believed that the messages in Living Intact would reach many people and who helped to spread the Word.

ABOUT THE AUTHOR

Dr. Mark Steinberg is a licensed psychologist with expertise in clinical, educational, and neuropsychology. He appears regularly on television to offer his psychological expertise on topics pertaining to health, behavior, and living a more satisfying and productive life. He treats children, adolescents, and adults, offering a range of services dealing with attention and mood disorders, behavior problems, family and communication issues, developmental disabilities, educational and learning problems, parenting challenges, habit change, addictions, and neurological disorders (including headaches, seizures, and sleep disorders).

Over the course of his practice, Dr. Steinberg has administered over 50,000 evaluation and treatment procedures.

By blending the latest technological advances with traditional and scientific methods, Dr. Steinberg improves functioning and eliminates problems that have persisted for years. He is well-known for his pioneering work with EEG neurofeedback and Voice Technology, the treatment that eliminates negative emotions in minutes.

Dr. Steinberg has made many appearances on local and national television. Widely consulted as a medical expert, he has won local and statewide awards. He is the co-author of the popular book, *ADD: The 20-Hour Solution*. He offers seminars as well as individual psychotherapeutic services.

His clinic, Mark Steinberg, Ph.D. & Associates, is located in Los Gatos, California. For information, call (408) 356-1002 or visit www.marksteinberg.com.

Made in the USA
Charleston, SC
26 June 2015